What is Italian America?

Selected Essays
from
The Italian American Studies Association

Edited by

George Guida, Stanislao Pugliese, Alan Gravano,
Peter Vellon, and Jennifer Kightlinger

ITALIAN AMERICAN STUDIES ASSOCIATION

Library of Congress Control Number: Available upon request

© 2015 by Italian American Studies Association & Authors

All rights reserved. Parts of this book may be reprinted only by written permission from the author, and may not be reproduced for publication in book, magazine, or electronic media of any kind, except for purposes of literary reviews by critics.

Printed in the United States.

Published by
ITALIAN AMERICAN STUDIES ASSOCIATION
(formerly, American Italian Historical Association)
John D. Calandra Italian American Institute
25 West 43rd Street, 17th Floor
New York, NY 10036

ISBN 978-0-934675-64-2

Table of Contents

Where Is/Was Italian America?

Being "Italian" in Buffalo: Francis E. Di Bartolo on Provincialism, Fascism and the Battle for Italian-American Identity during the Interwar Years—*Matthew R. Giorgio* (3)

Italians in Dade County, 1910-1930: An Introduction to an Untold Story—*Antonietta Di Pietro* (30)

For God And Country: St. Lucy's Italian American Parish Responds—*Salvatore J. LaGumina* (59)

The Impact of World War II on San Francisco's Italian-American Community: Continuity and Change—*Tommaso Caiazza* (81)

Italian Americans: The Move to Suburbia—*William Egelman* (98)

Household Shrines in Italian America: The Restaurant as Domestic *Ex Voto* in a South Florida Italian Family—*Jonathan O'Neill* (112)

Who Are Italian Americans?

The Assimilationists: Sarah Wool Moore and The Society For The Protection Of Italian Immigrants—*Teresa Fava Thomas* (133)

Early Deaths in the Italian Enclaves at the Turn of the 20th Century: A Great Granddaughter's Perspective—*Alexandra de Luise* (148)

Italianità Americana: A Study of Ethnic Identity Among Second-, Third-, and Third-Plus-Generation Italian Americans—*Angelyn Balodimas-Bartolomei* (156)

A Knowledge Management System (KMS) for the Italian Historical Emigration—*Fabio Capocaccia and Carlo Stiaccini* (185)

What Is Italian American Politics?

The Heyday of Italian-American Congressional Politics in East Harlem: La Guardia, Lanzetta, and Marcantonio in the Races for the U.S. House of Representatives—*Stefano Luconi* (203)

Italy's Postwar Migration and the Campaign for the Reform of the U. S. National-Origins Quota System, 1950-53—*Stefano Luconi* (222)

Italian-American Political Leadership in the Tea Party Era: Conservative, Progressive, Reactionary?—*Laurie Buonanno and Michael Buonnano* (245)

WHAT ARE THE ITALIAN AMERICAN ARTS?

"The performance of it all": Lady Gaga and a Legacy of Female Italian American Pop Icons—*Roseanne Giannini Quinn* (267)

Is Tony Manero Gay?: Masculinity, Sexuality, and Ethnicity in *Saturday Night Fever*—*Stelios Christodoulou* (286)

A History of the "Palooka"—*Courtney J. Ruffner Grieneisen* (312)

The Italian Tarantella—*Vera Lynn Lentini* (327)

A Counter-Reading of Women's Stasis in the Family Sagas of Barolini and Mazzucco—*Dennis Barone* (333)

Women at a Crossroads: Rites of Passage in Italian America—*Camilla Dubini* (343)

The Italian Influences of Fellini and Pirandello on Don DeLillo—*Rebecca Rey* (357)

New York City as Place in Don DeLillo's Fiction—*Alan J. Gravano* (378)

CONTRIBUTORS

ANGELYN BALODIMAS-BARTOLOMEI is Associate Professor of education at North Park University in Chicago and Coordinator of the ESL Teachers Endorsement Program and MALLC (Masters of Literacy, Language & Culture) Program. Her areas of research include Comparative International Education, Greek / Italian / Jewish ethnic identity, the Greek Romaniote Jews, the Griki of Southern Italy, and Holocaust Education in addition to being the author of "Footsteps through Athina."

DENNIS BARONE is the author of America Trattabili (a study of Italian American narrative, Bordighera Press, 2011), editor of New Hungers for Old: One-Hundred Years of Italian-American Poetry (Star Cloud Press, 2011), and co-editor with Peter Covino of Essays on Italian American Literature and Culture (Bordighera Press, 2012). He is currently completing a study of Italian American Protestants.

LAURIE BUONNANO is Professor and Director of Public Administration at Buffalo State University. She is the co-author (with Michael Buonnano) of the forthcoming book, *A Singular History: Shaping Italian-American Identity* (University of Florida Press) and co-editor of the collection *The New Transatlanticism: Politics and Policy Perspectives* (Routledge, 2015).

MICHAEL BUONNANO is Professor of English and Anthropology at the State University of Florida, Manatee/Sarasota. He is the co-author (with Laurie Buonnano) of the forthcoming book, *A Singular History: Shaping Italian-American Identity* (University of Florida Press) and author of *Sicilian Epic and the Marionette Theater* (McFarland Press, 2014).

TOMMASO CAIAZZA is a PhD student in Social History at the University Ca' Foscari, Venice. He studies the Italian immigration experience in San Francisco in the first half of the 20th century, with particular regard to the phenomenon of the ethnic leadership and the social construction of ethnicity and race. His interest in Italian-American studies dates back to his course of studies at the University of Rome "La Sapienza," where, in 2011, he obtained the Master's degree, defending a thesis on the impact of World War II on San Francisco's Italian-American community.

In 2004, while at the Port of Genoa, FABIO CAPOCACCIA founded CISEI, the International Center for Studies on Italian Emigration, to capitalize on the cultural heritage of historical emigrants leaving their country through the Port of Genoa. President of CISEI ever since, he helped set up the first National Archive on Italian Emigration, now listing 3 million names. In 2008 he was, by the Italian Minister of Foreign Affairs, appointed Member of the Scientific Committee of MEI, the National Emigration Museum at Vittoriano in Rome. Mr. Capocaccia is also a Professor, now retired, of Electronic Technologies at the University of Genoa, and has published over a hundred technical papers.

STELIOS CHRISTODOULOU has written extensively on Italian American masculinity in film. He is a graduate of the University of Kent.

ALEXANDRA DE LUISE is an Associate Professor at Queens College, City University of New York, Flushing, in the library department. She has delivered papers at the IASA conferences since 2010. Her essay on the reading interests of early Italian immigrants was published in the Winter 2012 issue of *Italian Americana*. She is currently serving on the board of the Italian American Studies Association, as Curator.

ANTONIETTA DI PIETRO is Instructor for Italian at Florida International University. She is co-author of *Italian All-in-One for Dummies*.

CAMILLA DUBINI is currently a PhD Candidate at University College of London. Her research interests include the cultural relationship between Italy and America and the work of Cesare Pavese. Her PhD research concerns the cultural production of third- and fourth-generation Italian Americans. It focuses on the idea of community that emerges from the disintegration of Little Italies, in works of literature and movies from the 1990s.

WILLIAM EGELMAN is Chair of the Sociology Department at Iona University. He has written books on Social Problems, Family, and Race and Ethnic Relations, and has authored a number of articles on various ethnic groups in the United States. His current research interests are in the area of recent immigration patterns to the United States, and the impact of assimilation through the generations.

MATTHEW GIORGIO earned his Bachelor of Science in Social Studies Education from the State University of New York, College at Buffalo and has spent the last decade teaching Humanities in diverse school settings across the United States. While completing his M.A. in American Studies from the University of Massachusetts, Boston, Mr. Giorgio focused his studies on the areas of ethnic identity formation and whiteness. He is presently a history teacher at Greenhill School in Addison, Texas where he continues to research and write on a variety of topics including ethnic studies, white privilege, and pop-culture.

ALAN J. GRAVANO has an MFA in Poetry and an MA and PhD in English from the University of Miami, Florida. He is co-editor of this volume, has published two essays on Don DeLillo, most recently "New York in Don DeLillo's Novels." He has also served as editor of the academic journal *Italian Americana*.

COURTNEY J. RUFFNER GRIENEISEN is Professor of Language and Literature at the State College of Florida, Manatee/Sarasota. She has published work as contributing editor for the Edgar Allan Poe book in Harold Bloom's *BioCritiques* series, and has published an article for the MLA in *Teaching Italian American Literature, Film, and Popular Culture*. In addition to publishing, Courtney is a founding editor of the literary journal *Florida English*. In her spare time, she can be found researching Ezra Pound, reading articles on organized crime in Italy or perusing historical details on the Borgia family. She lives in Bradenton, Florida with her husband, Jeff, who is a poet, a scholar.

SALVATORE J. LAGUMINA is professor emeritus and Director of the Center for Italian American Studies at Nassau Community College, the author of nineteen books, and numerous articles on the Italian American experience. His works include: *WOP! A Documentary History of Anti-Italian Discrimination in the United States*, 1973; *The Italian American Experience: An Encyclopedia*, 2000; *The Humble and The Heroic: Wartime Italian Americans*, 2006; *Hollywood's Italians: From Periphery to Prominenti*, 2012. A recognized authority on Italian American history he has received many educational and literary awards, including, among others, The Society of Catholic Social Science, The Association of Italian American Educators Award, The Pietro Di Donato/John Fante Literary Award. He has served as guest lecturer and visiting professor at Wesleyan and

Adelphi Universities. He is a founding member of the American Italian Historical Association (AIHA), served as its national president and founder/president of the Long Island Chapter of the AIHA. He has been a board member of the Commission for Social Justice OSIA since its inception.

VERA LYNN LENTINI is pursuing a Master's Degree in English with a focus on Teaching Writing, at Montclair State University in addition to working full-time at a private company. A proud Italian-American, Vera has traveled to Italy six times and completed ethnographic cultural research in the South as well as in the archives at NYU. In 2010 she published a study of songs and dance in *A Sud dell'Europa–Dalla Carta di Barcellona all'Unione per il Mediterraneo*, and a collection of poems in Plangere's "Writing Identities" at Rutgers. A Phi Beta Kappa scholar and former Rutgers College Presidential Scholar, Vera plans to finish her Master's Degree and teach. She is excited to share Italian culture with others and happy to be included in this IASA volume.

STEFANO LUCONI teaches U.S. history at the University of Padua in Italy and specializes in Italian immigration in the United States. His books include *From* Paesani *to White Ethnics: The Italian Experience in Philadelphia* (2001); *Little Italies e New Deal* (2002); *The Italian-American Vote in Providence, Rhode Island, 1916-1948* (2004); *Dalle piantagioni allo studio ovale: L'inserimento degli afro-americani nella politica statunitense* (2013). He also edited, with Dennis Barone, *Small Towns, Big Cities: The Urban Experience of Italian Americans* (2010).

JONATHAN O'NEILL is an Instructor and PhD candidate at Florida Atlantic University.

ROSEANNE GIANNINI QUINN teaches English, Women's Studies, and Intercultural Studies at De Anza College in the San Francisco Bay Area. For the past twenty years, she has researched and published in Italian American literature and culture and feminist theory. She is very much interested in the writing of the San Francisco Beat poets and their contemporary legacy. She has an essay on Carole Maso in the collection *Essays on Italian American Literature and Culture: A Decade and Beyond of Insights*. Currently, she is writing a monograph entitled *When the Evening Shadows Fall: Italian American Women Narrate the Popular and the Avant-Garde*.

REBECCA REY is a Tutor at the University of Western Australia. She has written and published extensively on the work of Don DeLillo.

CARLO STIACCINI is a member of the Department of History and Philosophy of the University of Genoa, where he also teaches Contemporary History at Scuola di Scienze Umanistiche. Since 2007 he has worked at CISEI–International Center for Studies on Italian Emigration, as scientific and research coordinator for the Archives Project and for the implementation of the Knowledge Management System. He is a member of the board of Archivio Ligure of Popular History (ALSP), and a member of the scientific international board of *Mnemosyne*, a review published by the University of Louvain, Belgium. From 2009 he has served as Scientific Referent for the Museo dell'Emigrazione in Rome and for MuMA–Istituzione Musei del Mare e delle Migrazioni in Genoa. He has written a number of essays for books on war and migration.

TERESA FAVA THOMAS holds an MA and a PhD in history from Clark University. She is a professor of history at Fitchburg State University, where she teaches Italian American History: Immigration and Identity, as well as Modern Italian History, and World Civilizations, and serves on the advisory board and archives committee of FSU's Il Centro per la Cultura Italiana. She has recently published articles in *Altreitalie* and *News on the Rialto*, and is completing a manuscript on immigration from the Veneto to central Massachusetts.

Where is/was Italian America?

Being "Italian" in Buffalo
Francis E. Di Bartolo on Provincialism, Fascism and the Battle for Italian-American Identity during the Interwar Years

Matthew R. Giorgio

Being "Italian" in Buffalo throughout the Interwar years was not a fixed identity. Rather, to be Italian was a label and a misnomer; a performance; a negotiation; and a renegotiation. Like projecting the various regions of southern Italy onto Buffalo's west side, instead of one singular and cohesive Little Italy, there existed what could be described as several "Littler Italies." This stratification allowed Old World social separations to play out in the United States.[1] The curtain appears to have closed on these productions, however, and reopened on new performances of a shared Italian identity at various *festi* across Buffalo following the boot steps of Mussolini's March on Rome. What happened next in Italy, in the years leading up to World War II, had a direct and calculated effect on the national identities of the city's Italian population. For as the American press refocused its attention away from Mussolini's resurrection of Rome to the ever-growing threat of War Fascism, the national identity many Italians had adopted was now called into question.

One resident of Buffalo's Little Italy, Francis E. Di Bartolo, played a key role both in recording this transition and in facilitating the renegotiation of the community's collective identity as ethnic Americans. By focusing on Italians' voices within both the Ital-

---

[1] Stefano Luconi, "Becoming Italian American in the US: Through the Lens of Life Narratives" *MELUS Literary Studies* Vol. 29, No. 3/4, (Autumn - Winter, 2004) 152. For more on *il campanilismo*, Luconi finds that in southern Italy "separate villages often meant separate worlds."

ian-language newspaper of Buffalo, New York and the city's mainstream press, especially as collected by Di Bartolo, this paper argues that Italian provincialism, Benito Mussolini's rise to power, the dissemination of fascism within the United States and the second Italo-Ethiopian War each contributed to a debate over what it meant to be Italian in the City of Light. Building upon scholarship within the field of Italian-American Studies, which has explored the dual processes of becoming Italian and Italian-American in the United States, Di Bartolo's personal papers exemplify the research of Conzen et al., which hold that ethnic groups are "constantly recreating themselves and ethnicity is continuously being reinvented in response to changing realities both within the group and the host society."[2] As Di Bartolo's life shall also reveal, the process of ethnicization is a negotiation—one that involves a dialogue between mainstream and sidestream cultures as well as a dialogue within the community itself.

Newspaper articles translated by and about Francis Di Bartolo throughout the interwar years also expose debates over fascism as an ideological dimension of the battle over how best to create a public stance as Italian-Americans. Both sides of the debate, fascist and anti-fascist, however, stressed Italian compatibility with "American principles and ideals," which, if followed, would have worked to affirm the move from provincialism to new identifications as Italian-Americans.[3] Francis Di Bartolo's translations from Buffalo's Italian-language newspaper, *Il Corriere Italiano*, and his personal letters continue to "speak" today, as a modern reading and interpretation of these reveal the interwar years to be influential upon

---

[2] Kathleen Neils Conzen, David A. Gerber, Ewa Morawska, George E. Pozzetta and Rudolph J. Vecoli; "The Invention of Ethnicity" *Journal of American Ethnic History*, Vol. 12, No. 1 (Fall, 1992) 5.

[3] Conzen et al., 6.

the creation of both a pan-provincial Italian identity and a hyphenated-American identity.[4]

At the time of Francis Di Bartolo's immigration in 1904, Buffalo, New York had become one of the nation's leading immigrant destinations, with 75% of its population a strong mix of Germans, Poles, Irish, Canadians, Russian Jews, and southern Italians.[5] Resulting from Italy's belated unification in 1861, however, *campanilismo*—nationalism on a village-size scale— continued to divide southern Italians along lines of regional identities. This provincialism was preserved in Buffalo by southern Italians' reliance upon *paesani* and *compari*. Italian towns were reconstructed block-by-block across Buffalo's west side, as immigrants from sixteen villages and over a hundred provinces took residence alongside their *paesani*.[6] Unlike many of his contemporaries, however, Di Bartolo appears to have arrived in Buffalo with a pan-provincial understanding of what it was to be "Italian."

Di Bartolo's inclusive definition of Italianness likely developed as a result of his upbringing and personal experiences. Unlike other Italians in Buffalo, Di Bartolo left his birthplace of Siracusa, Sicily, to study at the University of Rome prior to his emigration. In doing so, he may have also traversed the barriers of *campanilismo* in the process; for there within the capital he was sure to have encountered, perhaps even embraced, Italian nationalism in all its various cultural and political forms.[7] A familiarity with pan-Italian

---

[4] The personal papers, articles, correspondences, photographs, and scrapbook of Francis Di Bartolo were donated to the Buffalo and Erie County Historical Society in 1962.

[5] For information on Buffalo's growing immigrant population see Virginia Yans-McLaughlin, *Family and Community: Italian Immigrants in Buffalo, 1880-1930*. (Urbana: University of Illinois Press, 1982) 36. The figures for Italians in Buffalo come from Michael La Sorte, *La Merica: Images of Italian Greenhorn Experience*, (Philadelphia: Temple University Press, 1985) 119.

[6] Yans-McLaughlin, 58, 62-64, reveals how chain migration reinforced and recreated provincialism in Buffalo.

[7] Spencer M. Di Scala, *Italy: From Revolution to Republic – 1700 to the Present*. (Boulder: Westview Press, 1995) p. 184-190.

unity, however, would not have been a foreign idea for Di Bartolo, on account of his father's role within the Waldensian Church. While other Italians sojourned in Western New York to labor along Buffalo's docks and rails, Reverend Antonino Di Bartolo had come as a missionary, to assist all Italian immigrants, regardless of province or region, with their transition to life in the United States.[8] We can see these values at play in the younger Di Bartolo's own life as president of the Joseph Garibaldi Society. In an announcement of the society's formation, *The Cortland Standard* reported that Di Bartolo was interested in improving "the character, the quality and the general standing and condition of the Italian Immigrants." Di Bartolo was so invested in the cause that he had even announced plans to travel to Italy, to meet with the king, with whom he would discuss improving the "character of Italian diplomats" to the U.S.[9]

Di Bartolo did travel to Italy and served there in the Italian army for two years before returning to Buffalo. Back in the U.S., his service in WWI on the American side and his success as a lawyer had cast him as "a leader in Italian affairs" by 1919.[10] Di Bartolo, now a naturalized citizen and a permanent resident of Buffalo, like many of Little Italy's residents, continued to follow Italian news and politics. Therefore, the lawyer was certain to have heard that back in Italy the former Marxist Socialist follower, Benito Mussolini, had just founded his own political party turned personal army—*Gli Fasciti Italiani di Combattimento*. Furthermore, he must have read with awe, and it seems a hint of suspicion, on October 26, 1922, that Mussolini, with the support of his *Fasciti*, had com-

---

[8] William Form, "Italian Protestants: Religion, Ethnicity, and Assimilation," *Journal for the Scientific Study of Religion* 39: 3 (Sep. 2000): 309-311.
[9] "Joseph Garibaldi Society." *Cortland Standard*. 15 June 1911: 5. Print.
[10] "Italians Here Are Urged to Disavow Duce." *Buffalo Courier-Express* 14 June 1940: 1. Print. For more biographical on Di Bartolo see Henry Wayland Hill, LL.D. ed. *Municipality of Buffalo, New York: A History 1720 – 1923, Vol. III*, (New York: Lewis Hist. Pub. Co. Inc., 1923) 216.

pleted his symbolic "March on Rome" to reclaim and resurrect the "immortal spirit of Rome."[11]

It was while on a trip to Rome in 1924 that Francis Di Bartolo, in his own words, first "became convinced of the horrors of Fascism."[12] As an American citizen, the Johnson-Reed Act did not affect Di Bartolo's ability to enter in and out of the U.S. the way it must have many of his contemporaries in Buffalo.[13] During his stay, Giacomo Mateotti, a deputy in the Italian Parliament and outspoken critic of Mussolini's policies, was murdered. "That murder was traced to Mussolini," Di Bartolo told the *Courier-Express* in an interview years later. "Then I knew what the Fascist regime really was."[14] As Di Bartolo and other key figures in Italian-American communities and the U.S. government as well came to these realizations Mussolini ordered his consular officials to increase dissemination of fascist propaganda in the U.S., to block Italians' assimilation into U.S. culture—all in an effort to create a pro-Fascist voting bloc in the United States.[15] As Stefano Luconi points out, in that regard, Mussolini is thought to have "spurred the naturalization of the Italian immigrants so that they would become eligible for the franchise, and fascism could exploit their

---

[11] Francis Ludwig Carsten, *The Rise of Fascism*, (Berkeley: University of California Press, 1982) 62.

[12] "Italians Here Are Urged to Disavow Duce." *Buffalo Courier-Express* 14 June 1940: 1. Print.

[13] Mark Goldman, *High Hopes: The Rise and Decline of Buffalo, New York*. (New York: State University of New York Press, 1983) 212. For more on immigrant reactions to the Johnson-Reed Act in Buffalo.

[14] "Italians Here Are Urged to Disavow Duce." *Buffalo Courier-Express* 14 June 1940: 1. Print.

[15] Alan Cassels, "Fascism for Export: Italy and the United States in the Twenties," *The American Historical Review*, Vol. 69, No. 3 (Apr. 1964), 707-8, for more on Mussolini's orders to his consular officials; Cannistraro, Philip V., "Fascism and Italian-Americans in Detroit, 1933-1935" *International Migration Review*, Vol. 9, No. 1 (Spring, 1975) 33, documents this same event.

votes to lobby Congress and the White House to the benefit of Italy."[17]

Up until 1927, Di Bartolo appears to have been a peripheral player in the anti-fascist movement, having had continued correspondence with and having worked on behalf of anti-fascist leaders, Gaetano Salvemini and Alberto Giannini. By 1930, Di Bartolo had taken a more public and active role in the anti-fascist movement. Through their letters, Salvemini and Di Bartolo had developed a close relationship, eventually speaking together and planning behind the scenes.[18] The two were even listed by *The Erie County Independent* as having been barred from Italy by Mussolini. The paper detailed that Di Bartolo's "anti-Fascist activities have been signally recognized by the Black Shirts in the posting of his picture at the frontiers and ports of entry."[19] It could be said that Di Bartolo's local efforts laid the groundwork for a public and private battle between fascist and anti-fascist camps over the definition of what it meant to be Italian in Buffalo. For by the end of 1928, Francis Di Bartolo and certain members of Buffalo's Italian community had received evidence of Mussolini's plan to dissemi-

---

[17] Stefano Luconi, "The Italian-Language Press, Italian American Voters, and the Political Intermediation in Pennsylvania in the Interwar Years," *International Migration Review* (Winter, 1999) Vol. 33, No. 4, 1037.

[18] Di Bartolo Papers, Folder 3, Letter dated 10 May 1928 from Alberto Giannini, director of *Il Becco Giallo*, translated from Italian by the author. Alberto Giannini and Gaetano Salvemini are regarded as the founders of the anti-fascist movement and the Anti-Fascist Alliance of North America (AFANA) is thought to have been born out of their writing and lectures. In April of 1927, Di Bartolo had been in contact with both men and in the first of numerous correspondences with Salvemini, Di Bartolo requests that Salvemini come to Buffalo to lecture on the topic of fascism on April 10, 1927. In May of 1928, Di Bartolo had also received a letter from Alberto Giannini in which the publisher personally thanked Di Bartolo for his "contribution" to the movement. The correspondence also relays that, upon Salvemini's request, Di Bartolo was to distribute copies of *Il Becco Giallo* throughout Buffalo.

[19] "Di Bartolo to Address Women's Club on Subject of 'Mussolini.'" *Erie County Independent.* 9 January 1930. Print.; "Di Bartolo Lectures Before Village Forum Next Thursday Night." *Erie County Independent.* 12 March 1931. Print.

nate fascist propaganda throughout the region. In a joint "Resolution against Fascist Propaganda in the United States" between the Perseverance Social Benefit Association and the Italian-American Civil Liberties Club, the organizations declared that they had "become aware of a concerted action by the Fascist Government of Italy to spread its propaganda in the United States of America by the coordinated efforts of its consular officers…and subsidized press bureaus."[20] Both Italian institutions cited an official banquet held "in honor of the Fascist Consul General" in which "a local fascist organization was formally inaugurated" on December 1, 1928, as further evidence that fascist preparations were already underway in Buffalo. The resolution continued by stating that through the "lavish distribution of medals" consular officers were attempting to entice the city's Italians toward fascist sympathies. Lastly, the document claimed that where efforts such as these failed, intimidation and force would be used against those "hostile to the doctrines of Fascismo." [21] As Di Bartolo would later attest himself, not only was fascist propaganda now being circulated throughout Buffalo, but an attempt to silence the anti-fascist opposition was also in the works.

Perhaps motivated by this latest fascist affront, many of Di Bartolo's anti-fascist energies from 1929 until the mid 1930s focused on exposing the role of Buffalo's Italian Vice-Consul, Dr.

---

[20] Di Bartolo Papers, Folder 3, Correspondence circa 21 December 1928 titled "Resolutions Against Fascist Propaganda in the United States Unanimously Adopted by the Perseverance Social Benefit Association…and Unanimously Endorsed Italian-American Civil Liberties Club of Buffalo, N.Y." Guglielmo, Thomas. *White on Arrival.* (New York: Oxford University Press, 2003) p. 114. Guglielmo also found "Italian consular offices and agents" to be "steadily growing in importance" in Chicago as well throughout the twenties and thirties. Referring to the consulate as "ubiquitous," Italian consular agents, playing the part of rooks within Mussolini's political maneuvering, were strategically dispatched throughout U.S. cities that contained high quantities of Italian emigrants.

[21] Di Bartolo Papers, Folder 3, Correspondence circa 21 December 1928 titled "Resolutions Against…"

Rocco Spano, in promoting support for fascism.[22] Throughout this period Di Bartolo tracked Spano's presence at various Italian community events, by translating articles from *Il Corriere Italiano* in which the vice-consul was featured.[23] As Conzen et al. have argued, these events, such as banquets, parades, and nationalist celebrations, were an important means "for the formulation of…a self-concept" among a given group.[24] Yet, Spano's brand of Italianness was not the self-concept Di Bartolo wished to promote. On numerous occasions throughout this time period, Di Bartolo staged his own speeches and meetings, to speak out against fascism. Yet, his lectures, promoted and recounted by the mainstream press, spoke to a different audience than those who attended Spano's banquets. While Di Bartolo mingled with mainstream America at formal dinners and lecture halls, working-class Italians flocked to hear Vice-Consul Spano and to raise a glass to Italy.[25]

---

[22] Di Bartolo Papers, Folder 3, Letter dated 5 June 1929 from the American Civil Liberties Union to Di Bartolo, translated from Italian by the author; "Italians Here Are Urged to Disavow Duce." *Buffalo Courier-Express*. 14 June 1940: 1. Print. By June of 1929, Di Bartolo had filed a formal complaint with the American Civil Liberties Union as the lawyer had apparently become the target of intimidation and threats by those associated with the fascist movement in Buffalo. Given the potentially dangerous circumstances around claiming a public stance against fascism Di Bartolo appears to have initially taken a behind the scenes role within the movement. In an interview Di Bartolo declared that he was frequently a target of intimidation and threats and provides evidence in the form of a threatening letter dated September 1935 which read in part: "Degenerate—You don't realize the evil you bring to your fellow countrymen with your absurd and cowardly assertions. If the Americans had any intelligence they would inflict on you the punishment that was endured by the slaves."

[23] The presence of post script "Translator's Notes" (later denoted by the abbreviation "TN") suggest that Di Bartolo was translating the articles from Italian to English for unknown parties, public or private.

[24] Conzen et. al, 5.

[25] "Di Bartolo Tells Chamber of Italy Under Mussolini." *Erie County Independent*. 6 March 1930. Print.; "Di Bartolo Lectures Before Village Forum Next Thursday Night." *Erie County Independent*. 12 March 1931. Print.

Through this act of "toasting" Buffalo's new Vice-Consul, Spano made efforts to redefine Italianness among the city's Italians by first seeking to redefine Italy itself. One of the first articles among Di Bartolo's collection recounts a banquet held in honor of the city's new vice-consul in the spring of 1930. According to Di Bartolo's translation, Spano delivered a "masterpiece of Fascist history on the progress of the motherland...and exalted the person of Benito Mussolini as the savior of Italy."[26] Spano, through this toast, appears to have sought to associate a revitalized Italy with fascist "progress." Furthermore, the vice-consul credits not only Benito Mussolini as the person responsible for this progress, but to accentuate his point bestowed upon *Il Duce* the title of "savior." This may be seen as the first of many attempts by Vice-Consul Spano to redefine Italianness as synonymous with Mussolini and fascism. Whether the Vice-Consul was attempting to fulfill Mussolini's goal of creating loyal fascists who held first allegiance to Rome (as Di Bartolo would later claim), or simply consolidating a group of Italian-sympathizing expatriates, toasts such as these appear to have been concern enough to Di Bartolo's to have prompted the lawyer to more actively join the debate over what it meant to be Italian in Buffalo.[27]

---

[26] Di Bartolo Papers, Folder 4, *IC*. "Lawyer Joseph J. Lunghino Exalts the Fascist Regime." 1 May 1930.

[27] Di Bartolo Papers, Folder 1; Letter dated 13 November 1930; Di Bartolo Papers, Folder 3, Letter dated 18 June 1930 from the Office of Naturalization. By June, Di Bartolo had used his connections with District Director of Naturalization, Leroy N. Kileuau to secure passage for Salvemini to his summer home in Ontario, Canada. Throughout 1930, Di Bartolo continued to turn to Salvemini for guidance and information regarding the fascist presence in Buffalo. By November, Di Bartolo had written Salvemini to inform the professor that he had "accepted an invitation extended by the Foreign Policy Association to debate on Fascism" in Rochester and asked Salvemini for advice and any "valuable suggestions." The letter is revealing in demonstrating Di Bartolo's decision to take a public stance as an anti-fascist despite the threats he had received from fascist forces in Buffalo. Throughout the rest of the decade, Di Bartolo would continue

Throughout 1931, as Spano moved to promote a public pride in being Italian, local and national forces prompted him to protect his definition of Italianness from any and all opposition. For in January of that year, the anti-fascist cause Di Bartolo had embarked upon received a local jolt when the *Buffalo Courier Express* published criticism of Mussolini. In response, Spano condemned the article and wrote a letter to the editor in defense of Mussolini, stating that *Il Duce* "is a man of peace."[28] Di Bartolo's translations for February reveal that the *Buffalo Times*' coverage of statements critical of Mussolini made by U.S. General Smedley D. Butler had created "a protest against the publication."[29] By March the "Butler-Mussolini Incident," as it had come known to be known, appears to have dissipated, for by summer Spano was now toasting to his largest reported crowd to date. According to one article's translation, "thousands of Italians" had gathered together to attend what appears to be the city's first "Italian Day" celebration. Spano, once more the "toastmaster" of the event, concluded his toast by urging "his listeners to maintain high their pride and love for the Italy that must never be forgotten by her emigrated sons."[30] Thus, while the vice-consul worked throughout 1931 to defend and clarify his definition of Italianness he also appears to have made an effort to cultivate an Italian pride among the city's once provincial Italians, a pride all Italians might credit to Mussolini and Fascism.

Throughout the early thirties, the vice-consul spoke of a new Italy—one that was Roman, glorious, and one in which all Italians should take pride. Spano's speeches at local community events like

---

to write to Salvemini to keep him updated on fascist activities in western New York.

[28] Di Bartolo Papers, Folder 4, *IC*. untitled translation. 8 January 193.

[29] Di Bartolo Papers, Folder 4, *IC*. "Letter of Protest to Buffalo Times." 26 February 1931; for more on the "Butler Mussolini Affair" see Ellery C. Stowell, "The General Smedley D. Butler Incident," *The American Journal of International Law*, Vol. 25, No. 2 (Apr., 1931) 321.

[30] Di Bartolo Papers, Folder 4, *IC*. "Italian Day at Midway Park on Lake Chautauqua." 16 July 1931

those mentioned above suggest that the process Thomas Guglielmo describes as existing elsewhere in the US, where "both the fascist state and powerful Italian American community organizations worked tirelessly throughout these years to build a more unified Italy and Italian diaspora," was also taking place in Buffalo. This process may have also led some Italians in Buffalo to move toward a more united affiliation as Italian nationals.[31] These men and women have come to be known as philofascists—Italian immigrants who adopted a public stance as fascist-sympathizers in order to claim Italian pride from the glories Spano proclaimed Italy now conferred upon them.[32] Perhaps the most devout of the philofascists in Buffalo were the Ex-Combattenti.

Believing it "advisable for the harmony of the Italian community," Spano urged the National Association of Ex-Combattenti Section Luigi Cadorna, to send delegates to the Federation of Italian Societies so that the Ex-Combattenti might "live in fraternal friendship with the other Italian societies."[33] According to Di Bartolo's translator's notes, the lawyer had grown suspicious of the Ex-Combattenti as well as *Il Corriere Italiano*, believing the paper to be "at the disposal of the Ex-Combattenti whenever there is cause to exalt or praise their activities." Di Bartolo appears to have been right, for not only was Spano's recommendation approved, but by the following year the Vice-Consul, in a toast, praised the "Italian communities [who] have on every occasion demonstrated and affirmed their spirit of devotion to the motherland."[34] Although the extent to which Spano's statement accurately characterized Buffalo Italians cannot be supported by Di Bartolo's translations alone, the

---

[31] Guglielmo, Thomas. *White on Arrival*, 125.
[32] Di Scala, *Italy*, 256.
[33] Di Bartolo Papers, Folder 4, *IC*. "Welcome Visit (to Buffalo) of Grand Officer Gianni." 6 April 1933. Not only was Spano's motion approved but the Ex-Combattenti, without definitive proof may be the fascist organization the Perseverance Club wrote of, for Spano appears to be their leader and they are featured in numerous articles.
[34] Di Bartolo Papers, Folder 4, *IC*. untitled article. 15 February 1934.

Vice-Consul's statement does suggest, at the very least, that some members of certain Italian institutions had absorbed his fascist propaganda of pride and unity in being Italian.

By 1934, some within the American press had grown concerned with Mussolini's militaristic bravura, now commonly referred to as "War Fascism." In response, the Vice-Consul attempted to mobilize his philofascist followers in defense of Italy's name.[35] According to European reports made late in the summer of 1934, the military had committed acts of aggression near Welwel, Ethiopia. By August, Spano claimed that the city's mainstream press once more "misrepresented the truth, [and] tried to place Italy in a bad light." Spano then encouraged the Italian community to "fight against anti-fascist activities" and to "unite in pushing the programs which the Duce has formulated for the future destinies of the great Italian nation."[36] Once more in November, this time at a celebration to commemorate the March on Rome, the vice-consul "alluded to the great efforts that the duce and *fascismo* are making and give to Italy today a place in the sun worthy of our people, great and strong." Spano concluded his speech by, perhaps referencing the League of Nations' growing concern over Mussolini's military buildup outside Ethiopia, attempting to rally Buffalo Italians with a call to engage "against international envy and pettiness."[37]

Like the League of Nations, Francis Di Bartolo had also grown concerned over Italy's militaristic aggression in Ethiopia. In a public speech made in September 1935 and reprinted in the *Courier-Express*, Di Bartolo made clear his beliefs that, contrary to Mussolini's assertions, annexation of the African nation would neither solve Italy's population problem, increase its natural resources nor,

---

[35] Di Bartolo Papers, Folder 4, *IC*. untitled article. 15 February 1934.
[36] Di Bartolo Papers, Folder 4, *IC*. "Grand Success of the Second Annual Picnic of Ex-Combattenti Section of Buffalo." 8 August 1934.
[37] Di Bartolo Papers, Folder 4, *IC*, "Solemn Commemoration of November 4th." 7 November 1934.

most important, add to Italy's international prestige.[38] Beyond the human sacrifice and the financial cost of funding Mussolini's imperial conquest of Ethiopia, Di Bartolo appears to have been primarily concerned with what the consequences of such a war might do to the image of Italy and the reputation of Italians all over. Di Bartolo explained that while "[Italians] had been exploited sometimes and had endured social and economic inferiority, their condition had improved." The anti-fascist appears to have been asking why some Buffalo Italians had adopted a philofascist public stance while simultaneously reminding the Italian community that it was opportunity in America that improved their quality of life. After all, although Italian "whiteness" was generally accepted, it was still common practice for Italians to be "othered" by the mainstream community. Di Bartolo himself appears to have straddled the line between life within mainstream society and the sidestream culture, but his words may have served as a warning to those in Little Italy to reconsider how they performed their Italianness.

Seeking, if nothing more, than to protect the Italian name, as he saw it, from the potential damage Italian militaristic aggression may inflict, Di Bartolo sought to challenge the public's perception of Mussolini, Italian and mainstream alike. He called upon Italian leaders to maintain peaceful relationships everywhere, for the benefit of the homeland and for those Italians living abroad. As Di Bartolo questioned "the authority of *Il Duce* to speak and to act for the 40 millions of Italians who are, after all, frightfully interested in the issue," he may have been calling upon everyone else to do the same. Foreshadowing events to come, Di Bartolo added, "If his policies truly reflect the wishes of a majority of the people, why does he continue to enforce an absolute censorship that totally robs them of the benefits of world opinion? Why is it mortally dangerous for anyone in Italy to raise his voice in opposition?"[39]

---

[38] "Taking Ethiopia Would Not Help Italy, Di Bartolo Says." *Buffalo Times*, 12 September 1935: 1. Print.
[39] "Taking Ethiopia…"

As Di Bartolo asked these questions, however, he opened himself up to criticism and attacks from the city's philofascist community. Diggins explains that "pro-fascists assumed that any criticism of Mussolini and his regime bespoke a slander on Italy itself."[40] In Buffalo, such criticism may have also been viewed as a threat to Italy's name. Thus, just two weeks after Di Bartolo's speech, headlines in the *Courier-Express* reported: "Society Expels Di Bartolo for Recent Speech." According to the article, the Societa di Racalmutese had held a special meeting "for the purpose of discussing the speech made by Mr. Di Bartolo." At that meeting the Societa di Racalmutese unanimously decided "to condemn said speech as inopportune, incorrect and anti-Italian, and therefore profoundly offensive to all Italians and Italo-Americans residing here, because their love and loyalty to America cannot detach the natural sentiments of devotion and respect for the country of their origin." Having worked to redefine Italianness as synonymous with the glories and achievements of Mussolini and fascism for the past six years, Vice-Consul Spano's propaganda may have been responsible for the mutual-aid-society's decision. The article concluded by quoting society president Angelo Taibi as stating the society's purpose, "To affirm solemnly their undying faith in the holy rights of the destiny of Fascist Italy and the attainment of all final political and economic ideas pursued by *Il Duce* for the betterment of the Italians and the grandeur of Italy."[41] Therefore, in publicly admonishing Di Bartolo's definition of Italianness and displaying a definition that more closely resembled Spano's, this once-provincially organized society appears to have developed a pan-provincial stance as Italians, to profit from the glories of fascist Italy.[42] Furthermore, it seems that while Di Bartolo worked to protect the Italian name and the Italian people of Buffalo through his own

---

[40] Diggins, *Mussolini and Fascism*, 108.
[41] "Society Expels Di Bartolo for Recent Speech." *Buffalo Courier-Express* 24 September 1935: 7. Print.
[42] "Taking Ethiopia…"

definition of Italianness, the Societa di Racalmutese had also offered a way in which to safely defend Italianness as both American and Italian.

The Second Italo-Ethiopian War brought about yet another opportunity for Buffalo Italians to conceive of themselves as one group, united in support of Italy as fascist forces called upon them once more to take a pro-fascist public stance. Following the Italian invasion of Ethiopia in October 1935, Italian consular agents were ordered to step up their propaganda campaign and by February of 1936, *Il Corriere Italiano* had also sent out its own "Message to the Community."[43] According to Di Bartolo's translation, the paper had encouraged its readership to "come with the flags and standards of your societies that your soul vibrates in unison with the soul of fascist Italy." The article appears once again to play up Buffalo Italians' emotional attachment to Italy while also inviting the audience to think of themselves as one group united in support of fascist Italy.[44] In fact *Il Corriere* claimed that "The Entire Italian Community" had already "United in the Campaign Pro (Italian) Red Cross" back in November. For despite the depression years of 1935 and 1936, Buffalo's Italian community had donated over twenty-seven thousand dollars to Italy.[45] It was also reported that numerous couples had even contributed their gold wedding bands

---

[43] Diggins, *Mussolini and Fascism*, 290. Italian Commendatore Bernardo Bergamaschi of the Fascist Ministry of Propaganda ordered consular agents to reeducate the public through motion pictures and daily meetings of Italian cultural societies.

[44] Di Bartolo Papers, Folder 4, "Message to the Italian Community – Fellow Countrymen!" 6 February 1936.

[45] Di Bartolo Papers, Folder 4, *IC* – "The Entire Italian Community United in the Campaign Pro (Italian) Red Cross" 14 November 1935. The articles suggest that Buffalo Italians may have been donating to the Ethiopian Campaign under the guise of the pro-Italian Red Cross. Their decision to give financially to Italy may imply that Buffalo Italians were more interested not in fascism but for the future success of Italy as the articles from 1935 have stated.

as part of Mussolini's new holiday, "Il Giornata delle Fede," in an effort to see Italy victorious.[46]

The Second Italo-Ethiopian War may have also worked to alter the way in which mainstream Buffalonians viewed Italians as well. Both Fascist propaganda from Italy and the U.S. press independently marketed the Italo-Ethiopian War in terms of a race war between "blacks" and "whites." Even Di Bartolo, who publicly sympathized with Ethiopia, likened the situation to American slavery, calling it a "social injustice."[47] Up until the Depression years, however, "'swarthy' Italians," writes Sociologist Stanely Lieberson, had "represented a greater threat to the citizens of Buffalo"; for it was not until the final years of the Great Migration that a significant African-American population had settled in the city.[48] As a result, both African-Americans and Buffalo Italians began competing for mainstream America's empathy throughout the conflict, prompting renowned Civil Rights activist W.E.B. Du Bois to stop in Buffalo to address the Ethiopian Conflict.[49] Although Italian-Americans rarely regarded the Ethiopian Conflict in racial terms, Luconi has found that Italian-Americans may have benefitted from the juxtaposition of the two groups by the U.S. media and from African-American race pride.[50] Furthermore, with the conquest of Ethiopia complete and Mussolini now declaring Italy an empire in May of 1936, Spano began leading Italian cele-

---

[46] Di Bartolo Papers, Folder 4, *IC*, "Solemn Manifestation of Italianity." 13 February 1936.
[47] "Buffalo Attorney at Olcott Dinner Scores Dictators." *Lockport Union-Sun and Journal.* 15 March 1935. Print.
[48] Yans-McLaughlin, 116.
[49] Lillian Serece Williams, *Strangers in the Land of Paradise: Creation of an African American Community in Buffalo, New York, 1900-1940.* (Bloomington: Indiana University Press, 1999) 120.
[50] Luconi, "Becoming Italian…" 157. From his analysis of the Ethiopian Conflict, Luconi found that "antagonism with blacks was key to Italian Americans' accommodation within US society;" Conzen et. al., 16. suggest that the "proximity or absence of 'others' in the immediate environment" could also affect one's invention of ethnicity.

bration festivities which may have created spaces where Buffalo Italians could publicly and collectively celebrate their Italianness.[51]

Following numerous Italian victory celebrations, Western New Yorkers once more grew concerned over War Fascism and were now directing those suspicions at Vice-Consul Spano. Beginning in May of 1936, Lockport officials refused to grant the Vice-Consul a permit for an Italian Parade.[52] According to Di Bartolo's translation, "various Lockport citizens are opposed to the Victory Celebration." The editorial ended by asking that area Italians make good use of their rights as American citizens, to protect their names as Italians, stating "we trust that the Italian voters of Lockport will know how to avenge themselves for this affront at the future election of the present officials."[53] When festivities were finally scheduled the Lockport Board of Education had only "permitted the use of the auditorium of one of the city schools on the condition that Dr. Spano should not speak."[54] In order to keep his message alive, Spano was forced to adapt and to negotiate. That July the Vice-Consul added an important change to his definition of Italianness: a love and respect for the land of adoption, the United States.

Spano, therefore, attempted to ease American fears, by stressing Italian compatibility with American ideals. The following month, he advised his audience to "educate your children to love this nation, to earn their bread with honesty and work. Teach them to love America, but do not forget to engrave in their hearts the sacrosanct love for the faraway fatherland, Italy."[55] Spano, as

---

[51] For more on festivals see Conzen et. al, 28.
[52] Di Bartolo Papers, Folder 4, *IC*. "Great Celebration of May 24th." 21 May 1936.
[53] Di Bartolo Papers, Folder 4, *IC*. "Great Celebration of May 24th." 21 May 1936.
[54] Di Bartolo Papers, Folder 4, *IC*. "The Celebration of the 'Day of Faith' in Lockport, N.Y." 28 May 1936.
[55] Di Bartolo Papers, Folder 4, *IC*. "Solemn Feast of Faith at Lockport, N.Y." 16 July 1936.

his later speeches make clear, appears to have been attempting to encourage Buffalo Italians to become citizens, so that their rights as Italian-Americans might serve to assist Mussolini and his future imperial goals. In fact, a May article from *Il Corriere* reveals that Spano may have sought to cast criticism of himself onto men like Di Bartolo. The translation states that there existed "the current belief that Italian-American professional men do not know how to be good American citizens and at the same time cultivate affection for the land of origin."[56] Perhaps it was an attempt to legitimize dual loyalties while discrediting the speeches and anti-fascist work of "professional men" such as Di Bartolo; either way, by stressing Italian compatibility with Americanism, Spano's definition of Italianness, minus the allegiance to fascism and Mussolini, seems to have evolved to resemble the definition Di Bartolo sought to promote.[57] For by the end of 1937 and into 1938, Spano's boilerplate toast now continued to marry Italianness with American principles and ideals as he continually "advised all present to be good American citizens and to retain always in their hearts the sentiments of love from the beautiful fatherland, Italy, the new *Fascismo* and Mussolini."[58] But toasts and speeches like those above could not alone undo the damage Mussolini had done to the American image and definition of Italianness.

War Fascism had manifested itself in numerous ways following the Ethiopian Conflict, each time creating fear and anxiety within Americans across the nation. To begin, rumors of a military alliance between Mussolini and Hitler were confirmed when American media reported on the "Rome-Berlin Axis" late in 1936. Then the following year Mussolini voluntarily deployed his Black Shirts

---

[56] Di Bartolo Papers, Folder 4, *IC*. "The Celebration of the 'Day of Faith' in Lockport, N.Y." 28 May 1936.
[57] Di Bartolo Papers, Folder 4, *IC*. "Solemn feast of Faith at Lockport, N.Y." 16 July 1936.
[58] Di Bartolo Papers, Folder 4, *IC*. "Success of the 'Montemaggiorese Club' Ball" 4 November 1937.

to aid Francisco Franco in the Spanish Civil War.[59] An American public scared and angry with Italy may have had a direct impact upon Buffalo Italians, causing the ethnic community to reevaluate their stance as philofascists. For by March of 1938, as Italian planes killed about a thousand civilians during the Bombing of Barcelona, even Buffalo Italians were starting to turn away from Spano's definition of Italianness and toward Di Bartolo's. In a letter to Di Bartolo, Pasquale Di Fabio and Andrew Zavarella, President and Recording Secretary of the Italian-American Workers' Club, stated that their organization had discussed Di Bartolo's anti-fascist work. The two wrote that "The Italian American Workers Club inc. had a vote upon endorsing your unselfish and unrestrained work on enlightening the part of the country of the horror of fascism and dictatorship which is imposed upon our mother country." The vote appears to have been in Di Bartolo's favor, as the letter concluded with the hope that Di Bartolo would continue his "noble work."[60]

As public support for Di Bartolo's work grew, so too did Spano's message to work against anti-fascist forces. Before an audience gathered to commemorate the anniversary of the founding of the "Italian Empire" in May 1938, Spano took a moment out of his toast to address the anti-fascist opposition. Perhaps referring to *Il Becco Giallo*, the most outspoken anti-fascist publication, Spano spoke out against the "yellow press that tries continually to blacken Italy." Spano then "urged the Italians to unite in a fraternal embrace under the idea of fighting together for the glory of imperial Italy; and he ended by urging all present to love the country of their adoption but to keep always intact in their hearts the passion for the fatherland of their origin."[61] While this was a public affair,

---

[59] Diggins, 322.
[60] Di Bartolo Papers, Folder 3, Letter dated 9 March1938 from the Italian-American Workers' Club.
[61] Di Bartolo Papers, Folder 4, *IC*. "The Grand Commemoration of the Second Anniversary of the Foundation of the Roman Empire." 19 May 1938.

Spano may have also been less conspicuously at work disseminating fascist propaganda.

One way in which to also unite the ethnic community as Italians was through Italian language classes. In Di Bartolo's view, however, these classes were also a site in which to further mobilize area Italians to take a public stance in defense of fascist Italy. At a picnic celebration in Jamestown, New York, in July 1938, Spano presented medals to students who had mastered the art of the Italian language. To further cultivate affection for the fatherland, the students then recited a branch of Italian history. Di Bartolo's translations reveal that "Dr. Spano made plain the necessity of studying the Italian language in addition to the English, because only in that way the Italian shall be able to demonstrate that they are intelligent people who know the history of the country of their parents, and will therefore be able to defend it."[62] Di Bartolo continued to view these courses with suspicion and believed the textbooks in use to promote fascist propaganda. "It is interesting to note," Di Bartolo remarked in a translator's note following the article, "that the same Fascist propaganda school books were used in the Jamestown classes that were used in the classes held in Buffalo."[63]

As Di Bartolo discovered what he considered to be proof of the dissemenation of fascist propaganda, Spano continued to stress Italianness as compatible with Americanism. At the anniversary celebration of an Italian organization that same month Spano "urged them to be always good citizens because it is the wish of the Duce that all the Italians in these communities should become citizens, essential members of this republic and continue always to maintain intact the love towards their fatherland and to the Catholic religion; especially in these moments of education and of trou-

---

[62] Di Bartolo Papers, Folder 4, *IC*. "From Jamestown, New York: The Grand Picnic of the Churches of Saint James of Jamestown." 28 July 1938.

[63] Di Bartolo Papers, Folder 4, *IC*. "From Jamestown, New York: The Grand Picnic of the Churches of Saint James of Jamestown." 28 July 1938.

bled prejudices in the international life, maneuvered by obscure forces and irreconcilably hostile to the life of our great fatherland, Italy."[64] Perhaps referring to not just local but national dismay over Mussolini's official anti-Semitic campaign two weeks prior, the vice-consul appears to have been encouraging the Italian community to naturalize as American citizens. In this way, Mussolini would amass a large voting bloc should he need to call upon American Italians to protect Italy from potential U.S. sanctions through their power of the ballot as he had during the Ethiopian conflict.[65]

But as Mussolini's Rome-Berlin Axis dragged the Italian nation into World War II following the German invasion of Poland in September of 1939, the tide in the debate over what it meant to be Italian in Buffalo began to permanently shift in Di Bartolo's favor. Spano made several last ditch efforts to continue to encourage area Italians to display a pro-fascist stance as loyal Italian-Americans. At an "Italian Business Men's Association" banquet the Vice-Consul praised "the Americans of Italian race, who, obtaining credit in our community and who show their remarkable progress in the offices that they conquer in politics, maintain the spirit of the Italians of which Italy today is proud." He advised all Italians that "it is our duty to rid ourselves of the feeling of inferiority. We must value ourselves and show that we are children of a great nation."[66] While Di Bartolo would not have disagreed with this last statement he would begin to renegotiate how best to publicly perform this Italianness.

---

[64] Di Bartolo Papers, Folder 4, *IC*. "The Ceremony of Installation of the Cultural Dopolavoro Club." 9 February 1939.

[65] Diggins, 304-6 points out that during the Ethiopian Conflict, Italy was already facing an embargo by the League of Nations and as the United States threatened to cut off oil supplies. Through the pen strokes of a letter writing campaign in 1936 Italians across the U.S. showed their frustration with Roosevelt by not voting for the Democratic ticket.

[66] Di Bartolo Papers, Folder 4, *IC*. "The Twenty First Annual Installation of the Italian Business Men's Association of The Fourth Ward." 22 February 1940.

According to headlines within the *Buffalo Courier Express* of June 14, 1940, "Di Bartolo spared no words in condemning his homeland's participation in the European conflict." In an interview published just four days after Mussolini's declaration of war against Great Britain and France, Di Bartolo stated that "this latest act by Mussolini...has set Italy back several generations;" adding that Mussolini's alliance with Hitler has "hurt the people of Italy in and out of the peninsula." It was this idea that concerned Di Bartolo the most perhaps. Believing that Italian Americans had, in his words, "fallen prey to" fascism Di Bartolo sought to do damage control in order to protect the Italian name. To Di Bartolo, "Fascism simply is a disease from which Italy now is suffering." In his opinion Italy meant "3,000 years of civilization. Mussolini halted that civilization by taking the country by force of arms." Therefore, the statements made above may have served as Di Bartolo's own attempt to counter Spano's propaganda and challenge the definition of Italianness that the Vice-Consul sought to promote.

As the interview continued, Di Bartolo presented his perspective on how best to create a public stance as Italian-Americans. The first step in the process would be to disassociate Mussolini altogether from displays of Italianness. Di Bartolo claimed that "the least we former Italians of Buffalo can do is demonstrate in the conduct of our daily lives the fact that Mussolini is not the true interpreter of the Italian people." Perhaps seeking to simultaneously excuse and remedy Buffalo Italians' affection toward modern Italy, Di Bartolo stated a "Fascist nucleus, operating by remote control, proceeded to catechize the multitudes with the new gospel and to proclaim that all Italians wherever located owe first allegiance to the government of Rome." Seeking to renegotiate an alternatively protective public stance as hyphenated Americans, Di Bartolo added, "Italian-Americans, many of whom have unwittingly fallen prey to this indoctrination, owe first allegiance to the government of Washington." Unwilling to give an exact figure to how many of the 60,000 Italian living in Buffalo were followers of fascist Italy, Di Bartolo did state that those who were philofascists had "been fooled by the confusion between the present Italian government and the real Italy as they knew it, and as their forefathers knew it." By this time, Di Bartolo was well aware of the potential consequences for taking and promoting such a public stance.

In the interview, Di Bartolo "declared that he frequently had been the target of intimidation by local devotees of Mussolini." Local fascist followers, Di Bartolo continued, had consistently accused him of being a communist "simply because I am not a Fascist." Yet, Di Bartolo moved to make clear just how important a public anti-fascist stance was to defining one's self as American when he said, "the Fascists...reject the idea that one who disagrees with them can possibly be devoted to the democratic ideal of Americanism."[67]

The Italian invasion of France just days prior had created a new wave of fear and concern among the American public; and with fascist Italy's entrance into WWII on the opposite side of American sympathies, Di Bartolo also "expressed fear that many Italian-American right here in Buffalo may suffer from the activities of the Mussolini-directed agents."[68] Di Bartolo further "pointed out that many Italian-Americans, wholly loyal to the principles of Americanism, may become suspects simply because of these Black Shirt infiltrations." Just as Spano had urged Buffalo Italians to overcome their feelings of inferiority Di Bartolo seems to have urged this point as well, as a means of excusing Buffalo Italians' philofascist sentiments. "Sullen individuals," he reported "suffering inferiority complexes, experience a sort of animalistic satisfaction in the bullying methods practiced by the Fascists." In Di Bartolo's opinion, these individuals had not adopted a pro-Italian/pro-fascist public stance because they agreed with fascism's political ideologies, but rather for the potential social, economic, and psychological benefits such a stance may have afforded them. Di Bartolo concluded by

---

[67] "Italians Here Are Urged to Disavow Duce." *Buffalo Courier-Express* 14 June 1940: 1. Print.
[68] Di Scala, 265.

asking Buffalo Italians to take a positive stance as Italian-Americans against fascist Italy. He told Buffalo Italians to "have the courage to come out and say what I believe they feel – that they will have no part of Fascism and are willing to bear arms for the United States and against fascist forces, should that step be unavoidable." Di Bartolo concluded by countering claims that an antifascist stance was equivalent to being undemocratic, as fascist propaganda would have Buffalo Italians believe, saying instead that those Italians who are unwilling to denounce Mussolini "are necessarily dangerous, for their reticence denotes a lack of complete devotion to democratic government." [69] The lawyer's words seem to have finally resonated among area Italians, for by the summer of 1940 Italian-Americans began declaring their undying allegiance to the United States of America.[70]

From Fascist Italy's entrance into WWII until the United States' declaration of war against Italy on December 10, 1940, Italian-Americans remained in a state of limbo; teetering between hope and fear. On the one side they waited, hoping that their adopted country would remain neutral in war; on the other side they watched, fearful they might soon be asked to raise arms against their *famiglia* in the fatherland should war be unavoidable.[71] But, the final translations among Di Bartolo's papers reveals that fear won out; this was however, a fear of losing the privileges and status that had come with Mussolini's initial rise to power. By May, *Il Corriere Italiano*, the former mouthpiece of Mussolini in Buffalo, was reporting that presidents of Italian societies and clubs had come under fire for refusing to raise funds for Italy. The paper made clear that these individuals should not be labeled "anti-Italian," because due to "existing conditions in this nation against

---

[69] "Italians Here Are Urged to Disavow Duce." *Buffalo Courier-Express* 14 June 1940: 1. Print. In Di Bartolo's words, Buffalo Italians "remained spectators as a rule."
[70] Diggins, 349.
[71] Diggins, 351.

everything which is Italian... and considering the positions of all Italians in the city who earn their bread in America, we have determined that it is the first duty of every Italian to love the nation that provides the well-being of their families." The article went on to advise Buffalo Italians, just as both Vice-Consul Spano and Di Bartolo had, to instead show their love and support for the Fatherland "by being excellent Italo-American citizens."[72] An article in early June reveals that Buffalo Italians had further scaled back Italian events "considering the strenuous differences between Italy and this nation."[73] Di Bartolo's final translation, coming one month before the Japanese attack on Pearl Harbor, recorded an unostentatious celebration to mark the armistice ending WWI. Among the present guests was "Dr. Rocco Spano," who was not quoted as having made a speech. The article did, however, stress that at the present time Italy and the U.S. shared friendship and concluded by encouraging "everyone to continue their devotion toward this adopted nation, without, however, forgetting the country of their birth," just as Di Bartolo had argued months before when he sought to protect the Italian name from Mussolini and War Fascism.[74]

Why, over the course of 12 years, do Francis Di Bartolo's translations stop here? One of the final articles concluded with a translator's note which read that, in Di Bartolo's opinion, "the attitude seems to be that conditions are such now that, by reason of the American war effort and the uncertainty of the international situation, it is better for philofascists and Italian organizations in general to lay low and make the best of it and wait for return to

---

[72] Di Bartolo Papers, Folder 4, *IC*. "For the Works of Assistance in Italy." 21 February 1941.
[73] Di Bartolo Papers, Folder 4, *IC*. "The Ex-Combattenti Honor the Grave of the Grenadier Pannucci." 5 June 1941.
[74] Di Bartolo Papers, Folder 4, *IC*. "The Ex-Combattenti Commemorate the Armistice." 6 November 1941.

conditions which prevailed before the present war."[75] Perhaps with the definition of Italianness he had sought to promote now accepted by the once fascist-sympathizing *Il Corriere Italiano* and Buffalo's Italian organizations, Di Bartolo may have felt satisfied that his anti-fascist work had come to fruition. Perhaps with Italian Vice-Consul activities across the U.S. suspended as of June 1941 (the reason Rocco Spano was no longer was listed as "Vice-Consul Spano" but rather simply Dr. Spano) the debate had been officially ended by the American Government. Declaring loyalty to Italy over the United States had become too dangerous.[76] The reason may also lie in the fact that by this time Francis Di Bartolo had been tapped by the government of the United States' Office of Strategic Service (OSS) to once more fight in defense of his adopted country. A precursor to the CIA, the OSS recruited numerous Italian-Americans to serve both the U.S. and aid the Italian Resistance.[77] Thus, it seems that with the American entry into WWII, Di Bartolo had broadened the anti-fascist fight and defense of the Italian name, moving them from a local to an international stage.

Recent scholarship within the fields of Italian-American Studies and Ethnic Studies have examined the multiple ways in which Italian immigrants have become ethnic Americans. The debate between fascism and anti-fascism in Western New York, as well as the interwar years as a whole, presented Buffalo Italians with many opportunities to not only unite as a singular Little Italy but also with the opportunity lay claim to and publicly demonstrate their rights as ethnic Americans. The events of this time period also forced Buffalo Italians to dialogue intra-ethnically and with main-

---

[75] Di Bartolo Papers, Folder 4, *IC*. "For the Works of Assistance in Italy." 22 February 1941.

[76] Lawrence Di Stasi, *Una Storia Segreta, The Secret History of Italian American Evacuation and Internment during World War II* (Berkeley: Heyday Books, 2001) 137.

[77] "Di Bartolo Dies; Cited in OSS Case." *Buffalo Courier-Express*. 25 July 1966: 11. Print.

stream America over questions of what being Italian meant and how best to perform that identity. Although Di Bartolo's translations do not account for the numbers, demographics or audience responses of those in Buffalo that were drawn to the banquets, picnics, and various *festi* at which Dr. Spano delivered his toasts and speeches, it seems possible that Di Bartolo's and Spano's collective message of living in accordance with the principles of Americanism created a public stance that may have worked to affirm the move from Italian provincialism to new identifications as Italian-Americans.[78]

---

[78] Conzen et. al., 6.

Italians in Dade County, 1910-1930
An Introduction to an Untold Story

Antonietta Di Pietro

The 1910 U. S. census tallied a mere eighteen Italians in Dade County. This figure increased to 128 in 1920 and 271 in 1930, but the number of Italians or Americans of Italian descent living in South Florida was still negligible compared to the sizable communities then existing in the Northeast or Midwest of the United States. The 1912 *Bollettino dell'Emigrazione* reports that among the over two million Italians who lived in North America at the time, some 500,000 resided in New York, 100,000 in Chicago, 80,000 in Philadelphia, and 50, 000 in Boston (Cordasco and Vaughn Cordasco 117).[1] The number of Italians residing in South Florida would still be insignificant if it included the many young men who filled the shacks of Dade County building sites or the out-of-the-way camps floating among the Florida Keys, who remained uncounted.[2] Overlooked by both the Italian and American governments, these Italian migrants have left faint traces in the historical record. This paper attempts to reconstruct and contextualize the signs left by Italian immigrants in Miami and its surroundings in the period 1910 to 1930, by using two large-scale construction projects as case studies: the extension from Miami to Key West of

---

[1] Cordasco Francesco and Vaughn Cordasco Michael, *The Italian Emigration to the United States, 1880–1930: A Bibliographical Register of Italian Views Including Selected Numbers from the Italian Commissariat of Emigration, Bollettino Dell'Emigrazione* (Fairview, N. J.: Junius-Vaughn Press, Inc. 1990) 117.

[2] 1910 Manuscript Census, Miami Dade County, microfilm, Miami-Dade Main Library; 1920 Manuscript Census, Miami Dade County, microfilm, Miami-Dade Main Library; 1930 Manuscript Census, Miami Dade County, microfilm, Miami-Dade Main Library.

the Florida East Coast Railway (1905-1912), and the erection of James Deering's Villa Vizcaya. Both ventures offer a glimpse into the involvement of Italians in the life of South Florida.

DISCOVERING ITALIAN MIGRANTS

By the 1880s, migrants had become a topic to address and a problem to solve for both the American and Italian governments. Following the 1885 United States Alien Contract Labor Law, which prohibited the importation and migration of foreigners and aliens under contract or agreement to perform labor in the United States, its territories, and the District of Columbia, the Italian government passed the first Italian law on emigration to regulate private agents' recruitment activities and to prevent abuses of emigrants (1888). This legislation represented an effort to crush the "padrone system."[3] Nevertheless, only in 1901 did the Italian government constitute a Commissariat of Emigration, to organize an ordered exodus of its people.[4] The Commissariat provided health inspection and other controls at ports of embarkation (Palermo, Naples, and Genoa), organized assistance to immigrants at their arrival in the countries of destination, and regulated their remittances (which made up a considerable amount of the Italian national product).[5] But on both sides of the Atlantic, the subject of Italian migration was not widely researched from an academic standpoint until years later. According to Rudolph J. Vecoli the

---

[3] For Gabaccia, padroni were middlemen who sometimes financed trips of labor migrants across the seas, they were "[…] labor agents who exacted a commission from their clients. They sold jobs to men eager to migrate. […]". Donna Gabaccia, *Italy's Many Diasporas* (Seattle: University of Washington Press, 2000) 64-5.
[4] "National Capital Topics. The Foreign Contract Labor Bill Passed," *The New York Times*, 19 Feb. 1885: 3.
[5] Elizabeth Cometti, "Trends in Italian Emigration," *The Western Political Quarterly* 11, no. 4 (1958): 820–34. For Italian remittances: Dino Cinel, *The National Integration of Italian Return Migration: 1870–1929* (New York: Cambridge University Press, 1991) 141-3.

"rediscovery of ethnicity" in the 1960s set in motion research and discussion among American immigration historians. They became interested in the theme of "the making of Americans" and debated whether immigrants to the US remained distinct ethnic groups or if they were assimilated into an American "melting pot" (Vecoli 404-12).[6] In the years of the civil rights movement, the ethnic dimension of American life rose to a new level. From this period on, the bibliography on Italian immigration in the United States soared, with an abundance of titles that explored the phenomenon from multiple perspectives: European (Italian) migration 1) as the result of the transformation of European society in the nineteenth century; 2) as the recreation of "fragments" of immigrants' mother country in host societies; 3) as a social process that points at the sameness of immigrants and colonists throughout the history of the U.S.; 4) as a disruptive factor on native societies, when emigration became repatriation; and 5) as significant marker of American nationality.[7] Emigration became the focus of extensive research in

---

[6] Rudolph J. Vecoli, "European Americans: From Immigrants to Ethnics," *International Migration Review* 6, no. 4 (1972): 404-12.

[7] as the result of the transformation of European society in the nineteenth century see: Frank Thistlethwaite, "Migration from Europe Overseas in the Nineteenth and Twentieth Centuries," in *Rapports, V: Histoire Contemporaine, Population movements in modern European history*, ed. Herbert Moller (New York: Mcmillan,
1960) 73–92; Philip Taylor, *An Unsettled People: Social Order and Disorder in American History* (New York: Harper & Row, 1971); as the recreation of "fragments" of immigrants' mother country in host societies, see: Louis Hartz, *The Founding of New Societies: Studies in the History of the United States, Latin America, South Africa, Canada, and Australia* (New York: Barcourt, Brace & World, 1964); as a social process that points at the sameness of immigrants and colonists throughout the history of the U.S. see: Maldwyn Allen Jones, *American Immigration* The Chicago History of American Civilization (Chicago: University of Chicago Press, 1960); Rowland Berthoff, *An Unsettled People: Social Order and Disorder in American History* (New York: Harper & Row, 1971); as a disruptive factor on native societies, when emigration became repatriation see: George R. Gilkey, "The United States and Italy: Migration and Repatriation," *Journal of Developing Areas* 2 (1967): 23–36; as significant marker

Italy in this same period.[8] Before the 1960s, Italian intellectuals had concentrated their attention on issues of political unification and of construction of an Italian national identity—thus mirroring the Italian government's views on emigration.[9] Defining Italian national identity had been an unresolved question since Italy's unification in 1861; hence, in the late nineteenth and early twentieth centuries, the Italian political leaders focused their nationalistic anxiety on the examination of those aspects of emigration that dealt with emigrants' representation abroad, and on the juxtaposition of regional versus national identities. The scholarship of this period explores the ways in which expatriates remained or became "Italians," but after the 1960s it opened to further interpretations and analysis.[10] This more recent scholarship has used resources in

---

of the American nationality see: Philip Gleason, "The Melting Pot: Symbol of Fusion or Confusion?" *American Quarterly* 16, no. Spring (1964): 20–46.

[8] Rudolph J. Vecoli, "European Americans: From Immigrants to Ethnics," *International Migration Review* 6, no. 4 (1972): 426.

[9] Antonio Rosmini, *La Costituzione secondo la Giustizia Sociale: con un'Appendice sull'Unita` d'Italia ed una Lettera sull'Elezione dei Vescovi a Clero e Popolo* (Firenze: Pietro Ducci, 1848); Antonio Balbiani, *Giuseppe Mazzini, ovvero Quarant'anni d'apostolato e di Cospirazione per l'Unita` d'Italia* (Milano: Francesco Pagnoni, 1872); Massimo d'Azeglio and Marco Tabarrini, *Scritti Politici e Letterari di Massimo d'Azeglio* (1872); Gian Pietro Vieusseux, *Archivio Storico Italiano, Deputazione Toscana di Storia Patria* (1909); Italo Raulich, *Storia del RisorgimentoPolitico d'Italia* (1927); Cesare Spellanzon and Ennio Di Nolfo, *Storia del Risorgimento e dell'Unita` d'Italia*, Vol. 2 (1933); Luigi Einaudi, *Un principe mercante: studio sulla espansione coloniale italiana* (Torino: Fratelli Bocca, 1900).

[10] Mark I. Choate, *Emigrant Nation: the Making of Italy Abroad* (Cambridge: Harvard University Press, 2008).
Giorgio Candeloro, *Storia sell'Italia moderna, Vol.10* (Milano: Giangiacomo Feltrinelli Editore, 1984); Franco Bonelli, *La Crisi del 1907. Una tappa nello sviluppo industriale in Italia* (Torino: Fondazione Einaudi, 1971); Alberto Aquarone, *Le Costituzioni Italiane* (Milano: Edizioni di Comunita`, 1958); Giampiero Carocci, *Giolitti e l'Eta` Giolittiana* (Torino: G. Einaudi, 1961); Emilio Franzina, *La grande emigrazione. L'esodo dei rurali dal Veneto durante il secolo XIX* (Venezia: Marsilio, 1976); Ercole Sori, *Le Marche fuori dalle Marche. Migrazioni interne ed emigrazione all'estero tra il XVIII e il XX Secolo*, Quaderni di "Proposte e Ricerche" (Ostra Vetere, 1998).

federal, national, and private archives to document the extensive Italian presence in the world, the many temporary or permanent diasporas of peoples "with identities and loyalties poorly summed up by the national term 'Italian'," as Donna Gabaccia describes the flow of migrants that have left Italy from time "immemorial." In eighty years, from 1790 to 1870, 2,000,000 Italians emigrated, while 14,000,000 did so between 1876 and 1914. In the years 1916-1945 the number of departures dropped to 4,000,000, but 7,000,000 people left from 1945 to 1975. Italians represented 10% of the world migrants from 1815 to 1915, and the United States received the largest number of them (Gabaccia 1-6).[11]

ITALIAN EMIGRANTS IN ATLANTIC ARCHIVES: MIAMI AND ITS ADJOINING NEIGHBORHOODS

Public and private archives on the two sides of the Atlantic contain a wealth of data on Italian emigration. Based on these records, recent studies in Italian mobility examine various aspects of the formation and operation of *Little Italies* established in North America. With the exception of a few specific references in Roselli's *The Italians in Colonial Florida: a Repertory of Italian Families Settled in Florida under the Spanish and British Regimes* (1940), and in Pozzetta and Mormino's *The Immigrant World of Ybor City: Italians and Their Latin neighbors in Tampa, 1885-1985*, Italians living in the Miami area have not received much attention. The number of Italians in southeastern Florida was never very large, but what makes this enclave interesting is its direct participation in the establishment of Miami, which engendered different dynamics of acculturation requiring close analysis. Before this research can proceed, however, the vicissitudes and experiences of Italian immigrants in Miami, which are not well known, must be brought to light. People moved en masse to the newly formed city of Miami in the early 1900s. In 1896, the year of Miami's incorporation, 368

---

[11] Donna R. Gabaccia, *Italy's Many Diasporas* (Seattle: University of Washington Press, 2000) 1-6.

registered voters lived in the area, which comprised the two small communities of Lemon City and Coconut Grove.[12] Mostly homesteaders and black laborers, they lived in "Colored Town," in the northwest section of Miami (today's Overtown), separated from Julia Tuttle's and William and Mary Brickell's residences lying along the north side of the Miami River.[13] They all bustled along Avenue D (today's Miami Avenue), the retail and political district and the nucleus of the community. With Miami's incorporation, and thanks to Julia Tuttle's and the Brickells' entrepreneurial efforts, the number of people residing in Miami grew to 1,681 in 1900, to 5,471 in 1910, to 29,549 in 1920, and to 110,637 in 1930.[14] The ever-expanding community of Miami included Italians. The 1910 census counted eighteen people of Italian descent: 3 in Lemon City; 3 in Fulford; 1 in Allapattah; 6 in Miami proper; 3 in Hallandale; and 2 in North Miami.[15] Comparing the number

---

[12] George, Paul. *Miami: One Hundred Years of History: The Seminole Wars.* Historical Museum of Southern Florida. Lemon City was a small community in the early 1900s. It got its name from the numerous lemon trees that grew in the area. Apart from a 'railway warehouse' along the Florida East Coast Railroad, the community had nothing that resembled a city. In 1925, Miami grew to incorporate Lemon City, Little River to the North, and Buena Vista to the south. For Coconut Grove, see: Livingston, Grant. "The Annexation of the City of Coconut Grove." *Tequesta, the Journal of the Historical Association of Southern Florida* LX (2000): 32-55.

[13] For Julia Tuttle (1849-1898), the business woman who moved to South Florida in 1891, see Wright E. Lynne, *More Than Petticoats: Remarkable Florida Women* (Guilford: TwoDot, 2001); in 1871, the entrepreneur William Brickell (1817-1908) and his family moved to Miami from Cleveland, Ohio.

[14] United States Federal Census, 1900; 1910; 1920; 1930.

[15] United States Federal Census, 1910.
Captain William H. Fulford gave his name to the community existing in present day North Miami Beach in 1926. In 1927 Fulford was incorporated, but in 1931 became part of Miami with the name of North Miami Beach. Allapattah, "alligator" in the Seminole language, bordered the northwestern part of Miami. The Seminole Indians occasionally lived in Hallandale Beach, where they gathered roots and hunted. Hallandale is named after Luther Halland, who built a trading post in the area, and eventually became its first postmaster. It was

of Italians residing in Miami and its adjoining centers in the 1910 census with that of the Italians listed in the 1904-1911 Miami city directories leads to the conclusion that many of the Italians living in the region were unregistered in official records.[16] In fact, the number of Italians in the city directories is nearly seven times greater than the number indicated in the census (122 to 18). Considering that data from the 1906, 1909, and 1910 Miami city directories are not available, this disparity is likely an underestimation. Besides, of the eighteen Italians in the census, only two are also listed in the city directories: John Musumeci and Johnnie Varallo. The 1908 city directory indicates a Musumeci post card store located at 222 12th in Miami, and that a John Varalle had a fruit store at 721 Av. D. In the cases of both individuals, it is important to underline the inconsistencies in the record of their presence in the censuses and city directories: while Italians were clearly active in Miami in this period, their appearance in the pertinent documents is spotty at best.[17] The economic boom anticipated by Julia Tuttle and William and Mary Brickell became reality in the first two decades of the 1900s. Henry Flagler, who had built the Royal Palm Hotel in 1896, extended his railway, the East Coast Railway, to Miami, and from there to Key West, 120 miles further south. In the ensuing years, he continued to contribute actively to Miami's expansion by financing projects for the construction of water channels. Tourists, entrepreneurs, and workers flocked to Miami, which, by 1920, had incorporated Hallandale and Allapattah,

---

incorporated in 1927. See: Helen Muir, *Miami, U.S.A.* (Gainesville: University Press of Florida, 1953).

[16] The Miami city directories included data from Miami proper and Fulford, Lemon City, Hallandale, Allapattah, and North Miami.

[17] Allan Reid Parrish, *Official Directory of the City of Miami, Florida, Including General Information Concerning Churches, Lodges, Societies* (Miami: City of Miami, c. 1904; 1905; 1907;1908; 1911). United States Federal Census, 1910; 1920; 1930.

while new neighborhoods oscillated in its orbit.[18] In 1920 the Italian community in the city of Miami grew to 85 individuals, while others lived in Lemon City (7), Redland (8), Ojus (10), Miami Beach (1), Homestead (16), and Silver Palm (1).[19] After Miami, Homestead and Redland had the highest density of Italian residents in 1920; Florida (future Florida City) followed in 1930, with 11 individuals. Homestead and Redland were both located between Miami and Key Largo, and both benefitted from the construction of the Florida East Coast Railway extension from Miami to Key West (1905-12). Hordes of people, "homesteaders," reached the territory adjacent Flagler's railway, where they joined the workers camped along the line. A 1901 letter from V. Palumbo, an Italian labor agent in New York, to the general superintendent of the Florida East Coast Railway, hints of the possibility of purchasing land in Miami:

> I would start advertising in the Italian Papers for men, stating the conditions, copy of which I sent you at once. In the advertisement, I stated that he who desired to go to Florida was to purchase an acre of land, costing from $25 to $ 30 per acres, paying five dollars in cash before leaving, and the balance in monthly rates of $ 2.00 each, to be paid into the hands of the company until fully paid. In answer to this ad, I received over 300 letters: and 23 men were ready to leave on January 24th 1902.[20]

---

[18] Ojus bordered Fulford, present day North Miami Beach. As Fulford, Lemon City, and Silver Palm (present day Gould), this community was founded in 1897 and flourished as a depot during the construction of Flagler's railway extension to Miami 1896).
[19] United States Federal Census, 1920.
[20] In English in the text. Quoted in George Pozzetta, "A Padrone Looks at Florida: Labor Recruiting and the Florida East Coast Railway," *Florida Historical Quarterly* 54 (1975): 81. See also Jean Taylor, *The Villages of South Dade* (St. Petersburg: Byron Kennedy and Company, 1986) 157.
Homestead's own name originates from the Homestead Act, the 1862 federal law that gave applicants full property of acres of undeveloped land. The Italians

Redland also seems to have developed with the construction of the extension of the Florida East Coast Railway, as did Florida [City], which attracted homesteaders and was born with the railway. The peculiar origin of these centers suggests that Italians participated in the construction of Flagler's railway extension and/or were homesteaders; however, those of them who lived in Homestead and Redland in 1920 relocated, because the 1930 census shows that in that year Homestead and Redland had fewer Italian occupants than a decade earlier, and that their names did not correspond to the ones in the 1920. In 1925, the real estate market roared; Miami and its metro area swelled with speculators, developers, architects, designers, and people offering manual labor—as well bootleggers and outlaws. Lemon City, Coconut Grove and other neighborhoods became part of the city, while Coral Gables and Miami Shores were established in these years. Even if the 1926 hurricane hit locals and their properties heavily, the 1930 census shows that Miami had continued to lure an assorted public. In fact, its population grew, as did the number of Italians. They resided in Miami (184), Miami Beach (33), Coral Gables (9), Hialeah (8), Homestead (7), and Florida (11), and scattered individuals in other precincts.[21] From the pattern observed in the previous two censuses, the circulation of Italians in the late 1920s and early 1930s within Miami's neighborhoods hints at a relation between the presence of Italian workers and the projects active in the city in this period. The concentration of Italian households in Miami Beach and Coral Gables in 1930, for example, was likely correlated with the activities promoted by three

---

residing in Florida [City] were first recorded in 1930, with a peak of eleven individuals.

[21] United States Federal Census, 1930. For Hialeah: in the Twenties Hialeah was a community sizzling with artistic and mundane activities: the Spanish sport of jai-alai, greyhound racing and the realization of silent movies entertained the people who lived or visited this place, whose name means "high prairie" in Indian language. It was incorporated in 1925

pioneers since the 1910s: Carl Fisher (1874-1939), John Collins (1837-1928), and George Edgar Merrick (1886-1942). Fisher and Collins, two northern entrepreneurs funded the construction of a bridge connecting Miami to an island between Biscayne Bay and the Atlantic Ocean, which would become Miami Beach. The construction in 1913 of the longest wooden bridge of the world made the fortune of Miami, bringing, since its inception, tourism and business. Another northerner, George Edgar Merrick, developed Coral Gables and promoted improvements and innovations in Miami's urban planning at the same time. He began the construction of U.S. 1, the Tamiami Trail, another bridge to Miami Beach, Old Cutler Road, and the Miami Canal Highway. In 1925 Merrick donated the land and the funds necessary to build the University of Miami.[22] As the construction of Miami Beach's wooden bridge was beginning, the Chicagoan magnate James Deering (1859-1925) purchased from Mary Brickell 130 acres of land on Brickell Point in Coconut Grove, overlooking Biscayne Bay, to build a "palatial country retreat in fanciful emulation of the European past' (Olin and Rybczynski 5).[23] James Deering, an exemplar of the powerful and wealthy industrialists of the last quarter of the nineteenth century, "appropriated many of the trappings and social customs of the Old World: horseback riding and foxhunting, shooting, yachting, art collecting, entertaining on a grand scale," to mask his "parvenu status in comparison to titled Europeans" (5). [24] The wealthy new American patrons opened their mansions to artists and to specialized workmanship. In Deering's case, they were sculptors and stonecutters who contributed to the realization of his Miamian villa, Vizcaya. Sevillian in its name and decorated with Italian features in a

---

[22] David Nolan, *Fifty Feet in Paradise: The Booming of Florida* (San Diego: Harcourt Brace Jovanovich, 1984).
[23] Witold Rybczynski and Laurie Olin, *Vizcaya: An American Villa* (Philadelphia: University of Pennsylvania Press, 2007), 5.
[24] *ibid.*: 5.

tropical setting, Vizcaya was not intended as a simple reiteration of old palatial models, but as "the serendipitous product of several imaginations, a true meeting of artistic minds" (Olin and Rybczynski 9).[25] The Italians Ettore Pellegatta (1881-1940) and Edoardo Camilli (1881-) dedicated their art, and unknown workers, many also of Italian origins, committed their labor to concretize the ideas of Vizcaya's architects. While it is possible to sketch anecdotes of Pellegatta's and Camilli's lives in Miami and in Italy between 1910 and 1925, and to glimpse the activity of a few expert laborers such as De Salvo, Sam Bucci, Frank de Carlo, Joe La Morte, Victor Quardri, and Mencinni, a number of unskilled workers remain unnamed on Vizcaya's daily time sheets and pay roll. [26] Indeed, Ettore Pellegatta's status within Vizcaya's artistic community is ambiguous. His biographical blurb on the 1968 Encyclopedia of American Biography informs that he was born at Viggiu, near Milan, Italy, on February 6th, 1881. Son of a sculptor, Pellegatta studied at the Milan Academy of Art and, after serving two years of military service, came to the United States in 1901 (Dodge 217-8).[27] Pellegatta worked on several sculptural projects in New York and Washington, and in 1915 he moved to Miami, to execute sculptures for Deering's Vizcaya Villa. [28] In spite of Pellegatta's noteworthy curriculum, in October 1917, Paist, Vizcaya's project architect, proposed to fire him because he was a "good carver but had slowed up considerably, so did not compare

---

[25] *ibid.*: 9.
[26] John Cruikshank, from Freeport, New Jersey, was the contractor responsible for the stonework at Vizcaya.
[27] Edwar Dodge, N., *Encyclopedia of American Biography, New Series*, vol. XXXVIII (New York and West Palm Beach: The American Historical Company, Inc., 1968), 217–8.
[28] In New York, Pellegatta sculpted the lions placed at the main entrance to the New York City Public Library and the capitals in the main nave of the Cathedral of St. John the Divine. Here, he also sculpted the front pediment of Grand Central Terminal and did some work at the Columbia University Building. In Washington, Pellegatta worked on the two sphinxes for the Masonic Temple and on the Cathedral of the Immaculate Conception.

with the two men kept, either in ability or speed."²⁹ In a flawed Italian, Pellegatta, by then 36 years old, wrote a letter to Paul Chalfin, Deering's artistic supervisor, pleading to let him, and his family, "la mia Signora e baby," spend at least the winter before going back to New York.³⁰ In this letter, Pellegatta lamented that without Cruikschank, the contractor in charge of the execution of the stonework at Vizcaya, he was pessimistic about the results.³¹ He was a protégé of Cruikschank's, one of the many contractors employed in the construction of Deering's villa; however, he seemed to be considered rather a worker than an artist with a reputable portfolio, Cruikschank's support notwithstanding.³² Obviously, Pellegatta's plea was successful: he and his family remained in Miami, where the 1920 and 1930 censuses prove that they ("Hector Peligata and wife Gina/Lina") lived until the 1930s. After all, even if "slow," good stone carvers were very much sought after at Vizcaya. The July 17, 1916 Minutes of the Committee of the Vizcaya Project register Paul Chalfin's statement that the stone carvers' contractor, Cruikschank, "had infinite troubles in getting men, and it is apparently the prosperity of the country which is making it difficult to get stone carvers."³³ At the same meeting, Ingalls, one of the architects, made references to 6,017 stone carvers working on site. This conversation gives a clear idea of the magnitude of the project, of the volume of the investments

---

²⁹ Paist to Chalfin, 7 November, 1917, Vizcaya Gardens and Museum Archive (VGMA).
³⁰ "Dear Sir, Mi prendo la libertà di scriverle in italiano per spiegarmi più bene nelle cose che vorrei esprimermi [...]". Pellegatta to Chalfin, October 30, 1917, VGMA.
³¹ "[...] senza Cruikschank, non vedo piu` una buona riuscita [...]".
³² Pellegatta's favorable appraisal of Cruikshank was isolated. Other testimonies painted the contractor in a less favorable light. Consider, for instance, that of Telfer—or Zelfer—(presumably a stone cutter) who wrote to Chalfin in 1917: "[...] Mr. Cruikschank made it so miserable for me there [at Vizcaya] that I was forced to quit about six months ago." Telfer (or Zelfer, the hand-written, signed name has an unclear spelling) to Chalfin, -1917, VGMA.
³³ Minutes of the Committee, July 19, 1916, VGMA.

involved, of the administrative structure necessary to run such an enterprise, and of the problems arising in recruiting labor work. Payroll and record and account books of the general contractors Sykes, Ley, McGinnis and Triggs, along with correspondence between Chalfin and Deering, trace the transactions that combined art and business. Chalfin and Deering discussed hourly pay, union tariffs, personnel restlessness, and arranged to get what, or who, they wanted: De Salvo, decorator, to work on a bookcase; Sam Bucci, tile setter, to work on the Farm House; Joseph Santini, boat captain, for piloting Deering's houseboat *Nephente*. For Frank de Carlo, on March 26, 1918, they wrote a recommendation letter to the Board of Labor Employment in Brooklyn. Given the enormous scale of the project, one of the questions regarding the construction of Vizcaya centers on the provenance of the workforce. The proximity of the conclusion of the East Coast Railway extension project (1912) to the dates of the opening of the construction sites at Vizcaya's (1913) and in Miami-Miami Beach for the wooden bridge connection (1913) is conspicuous. No doubt there were many workers floating around Miami at the close of Flagler's venture available to work on Fisher and Collins' or Deering's construction projects. By looking at the extension of the East Coast Railway to Key West, we can trace the movements of these laborers in South Florida since 1901, and discover that many were Italians (Pozzetta 82).[34]

ITALIANS IN SOUTHEAST FLORIDA: WORKERS, SLAVES, OR *PEONES*?

George Pozzetta argued that Miami's booming activities, and in particular the railroad construction in South Florida, induced agents, and in some cases the same railroad employers, to tour the urban centers of the northeastern U.S. in search of laborers among the recently-arrived immigrants, who in this period were mostly

---

[34] George Pozzetta, "A Padrone Looks at Florida: Labor Recruiting and the Florida East Coast Railway," *Florida Historical Quarterly* 54 (1975): 82.

Italians and Greeks. The East Coast Railroad "hired" many of them, as the announcements in the Miami Metropolis confirm: "A car load of Italians from the north is expected here daily for works on the keys on the railroad extension"; "A large number of Greeks arrived here yesterday and proceeded to Homestead where they will work on the extension"; and " It is the intention of the F.E.C. Railway Company to secure and work as many of these men as possible and other and larger numbers of them will arrive in a few days" (Wilkinson). [35] The recruitment practices were unorthodox, and eventually led to peonage. The Italian government ordered the Commissariat of Emigration to conduct an investigation on peonage when word reached Rome that Italian emigrants were among its victims. In 1910, the Commissariat of Emigration's functionary, Count Gerolamo Moroni, submitted a report to the Italian government titled "*Peonage* in the southern states of the United States" (Cordasco and Vaughn Cordasco 96-114).[36] Moroni presented an account of what he named "crime" [peonage], providing a definition of the term, case studies involving Italians, causes of peonage in some southern states of the United States, and a list of US federal and state laws dealing with this offense. Moroni explained that "Il reato di peonage consiste nell'obbligare una persona ad un servizio a favore di un'altra, col

---

[35] Jerry Wilkinson, compiler. Krome Collection. Building the Overseas Railroad: Newspaper Clippings October 1905 to December 1906, preserved by William J. Krome and the Krome Family. Tavernier: Jerry Wilkinson, 1995. Volume 1905-06. See July 16, 1906. pg. 105; August 11, 1906. pg. 115; and August 15, 1906. pg. 118. Quoted in Joe Knetsch, "The Peonage Controversy and the Florida East Coast Railway," in *Tequesta* (Miami: Historical Association of Southern Florida, University of Miami, 1997) 9. Joe Knetsch writes that one of the main sources for his article is Wilkinson's compilation of newspapers clippings (probably all from *Miami Metropolis*) from October 1905 to December 1906, the Krome Collection.

[36] Cordasco Francesco and Vaughn Cordasco Michael, *The Italian Emigration to the United States, 1880–1930: A Bibliographical Register of Italian Views Including Selected Numbers from the Italian Commissariat of Emigration, Bollettino Dell'Emigrazione* (Fairview, N. J.: Junius-Vaughn Press, Inc., 1990) 96-114.

pretesto nel piu` dei casi, ch'essa debba estinguere, in tutto o in parte, un suo debito, preteso o reale." Peonage existed in at least six former slave-holding southern states to the 1865 abolition of slavery, but the 1867 federal Peonage Abolition Act declared peonage unlawful. Florida, Georgia, Mississippi, Alabama, New Mexico, and Louisiana challenged the Act with local statutes, which federal judges addressed case by case and declared them illegitimate. In his report, Moroni wrote that also in the case of Florida, the federal Judge James W. Locke had declared that forcibly inducing men to involuntary work under the threat of arrest or legal proceeding was also considered peonage (97).[37] But federal law collided with local habits: corrupt sheriffs and local judges often sided with entrepreneurs, to enact a practice that resembled slavery. Moroni's 1910 testimony on peonage practices against Italians working for Flagler is particularly striking:

> Peonage in Florida – In December 1906, a legal action was taken against the East Coast Florida R.R. Co., owned by the millionaire Flagler of New York. The East Coast Florida Railway Co. hired laborers to construct the Key West extension of its railway. The railway tract under construction is 153 miles long, 50 of which on land and the remaining on palafittes; it crosses the Keys Islands, united by bridges, some of which up to 5 miles long. The rocky and sandy islands have sparse tropical foliage; water is not potable; their land is covered by swamps infested by mosquitoes. Flagler's East Coast Florida R. R. is directed by Mr. Meredith, an engineer residing in Miami; its inspector is Mr. Krome, who also supervises building sites and work fields (campi di lavoro). These camps are scattered right and left of the railroad under construction, and each camp has its own engineer, "foremen," and "bosses" [in English in Moroni's text]. When bridges had not yet been constructed, the company provided a "steam-boats" service to connect the work fields.

---

[37] *ibid.*: 97 trans.: 'The crime of peonage is to oblige a person to a service in order to repay an alleged or real debt in whole or in part.'

Before October 1907, many Italians were employed in the construction of the railroad, but when I visited the camps, there were no more Italians to be found. Between 1905 and 1907, the Agency Frank Sabbia of New York and Mr. Triai, an agent of Jacksonville, Florida, recruited and sent hundreds of Italians to work for Flagler in the Florida Keys. They enticed the laborers, with the promise of an earthily heaven rich with fruit, tropical lush, and ideal climate, to a harsh work in swamps infested by mosquitoes, under tropical heat and with scarcity of water. Before the legal suit in New York, our people were subject to inhuman treatment, exploited on the job and embezzled of their miserable compensation, because food provisioning was provided exclusively by the East Coast Railroad at very high prices. Since labor camps were located on small keys (isolotti) with no connection to land, our people were not able to leave and were consequently forced to remain in involuntary servitude. Some were able to escape, to reach Miami and from there to travel north; but most of those who escaped were captured in Miami and, following the East Coast Florida Co.'s orders, arrested and condemned for vagrancy and led back to work in the Keys. A federal investigation has led to the prosecution of Meredith and Krome, accused of 'peonage' as per Section 5526 of the Revised Status, while Frank Sabbia and his agent in Jacksonville have been prosecuted based on Section 5525 of the same law. As of now, I believe that the process has not yet concluded. (99)[38]

By analyzing numerous newspapers' clippings from the Krome collection, Knetsch has been able to shed light on the recruitment system that Sabbia and Triai used to staff Flagler's project in the Keys. One of these clippings, from the Brooklyn Eagle Report in January, 1906, records an interview with E. J. Triay's (Moroni's "Mr. Triai"), in which he outlines the terms of the contract that laborers signed before leaving the principal centers of recruitment in the Northeast:

---

[38] *ibid.:* 99. My translation.

> Due Florida East Coast Railroad $12 for value received, And I hereby authorize said railway company, should said railway company at any time to become indebted to me at any time before payment hereof to apply hereon any amount or amounts for part or parts thereof so due me as same may become due and payable. The said Railway company to pay $1.25 per day without board.

Triay explained that the company furnished free transportation from Jacksonville to Miami, but that the $12 fare from New York to Jacksonville had to be paid by the men and that "this is not only implied by the contract, which is short and plainly printed, but it is also explained in a circular printed in English on one side and Italian on the other." The agent continued, "[T]he men are housed free by the company in comfortable quarters; they buy their own food, sold at the commissary department at reasonable prices, and can live well on $ 2.50 per week." (Wilkinson). [39] With a pay of $1.25 per day and an expense of $2.50 per week, laborers believed that the $ 12 transportation charge could be reimbursed in about three months; the prospect of a decent profit convinced them to sign the contract and to leave for Miami. Instead, given the inflated prices of food, which Moroni also registered, the men's debts were not easily repaid, and in fact were likely to increase. As the Brooklyn Eagle article reports, "[W]ithout a personal mode of transportation to the mainland, a worker was at the mercy of the

---

[39] Jerry Wilkinson, compiler. Building the Overseas Railroad: Newspaper Clippings October 1905 to December 1906, Preserved by William J. Krome and the Krome Family. Tavernier: Jerry Wilkinson, 1995. Article entitled: *Condition on the Keys Told by Mr. Triay*. Quoted in Joe Knetsch, "The Peonage Controversy and the Florida East Coast Railway," in *Tequesta* (Miami: Historical Association of Southern Florida, University of Miami, 1997) 7. Knetsch explains that the Triay article was sent to J. P. Beckwith, of the FEC, who passed it on to Mr. Flagler. The article was dated January 5, 1906, and is attached to some of the Brooklyn Daily Eagle stationary, and can be seen at the St. Augustine Historical Society, "Florida East Coast Railroad" files, Me 13, Box 1, Folder 20, St. Augustine, Florida.

company and its supervisors." (Knetsch 6-7).⁴⁰ This observation confirms Moroni's testimony on the conditions of peonage into which Italians were forced. Few laborers escaped East Coast Railway Co.'s *lunga mano* and managed to return to New York, where some denounced their experiences to John N. Bogart, Commissioner of Licenses for the city of New York (Carper 85-99).⁴¹ The laborers were young and in pitiable conditions. Bogart believed these men's accounts and began an investigation. He discovered what Moroni would also expose in 1910, that the Florida East Coast Railway enslaved workers through debts, by anticipating transportation charges to Miami, which men contracted to work in reimbursement. Bogart unmasked the viciousness of a system that severely debilitated individuals, often rendering them physically unable to work. They had no alternative: leaving the East Coast Railway Company's camps involved a high degree of risk, because workmen were subject to arrest under Florida's laws regulating debt. Sheriffs either convicted fugitive men to serve time in a convict-lease system, or returned them to the foremen and bosses in the construction camps to clear their debts. According to Carper, so cruel were the working conditions in Flagler's construction sites that many preferred to serve time in the convict-lease system (91).⁴² Bogart's investigation uncovered the recruitment mechanism, later described by the Italian Commissariat of Emigration to his government. Slavery charges were imputed to the railroad's officers (and Henry Flagler) indirectly. The trial against Flagler's agents—David E. Harley, Francesco Sabbia, Edward J.Triay, and Frank A. Huff—took place in November 1908, but the Judge, Charles M. Hough of the United States Circuit Court, handed down a verdict of not guilty.

---

⁴⁰ Joe Knetsch, "The Peonage Controversy and the Florida East Coast Railway," in *Tequesta* (Miami: Historical Association of Southern Florida, University of Miami, 1997) 6-7.
⁴¹ Gordon N. Carper, "Peonage in the South," *Phylon* 37, no. 1 (1976): 85–99.
⁴² *ibid.:* 91.

Mr. Hough argued that peonage was not the same as slavery, and since the prosecutors had charged Flagler's agents with slavery, they had to be released. The use of a more pertinent word would have possibly changed the verdict; peonage could not be proved because slavery was charged in the indictment, and Flagler's agents were acquitted (Knetsch 22).[43] Obviously, the trial had repercussions among the East Coast Railway's Italian laborers, because Moroni claimed that when he inspected the labor camps "there were no more Italians to be found" (Cordasco and Vaughn Cordasco 99).[44] It seems unlikely that the East Coast Florida Company's Italian workers had returned to north, given the huge demand of labor in a thriving Miami.

IMMIGRANTS AND MIAMI: A LOVE-HATE RELATIONSHIP?

Miami offered no excuse for idleness. Job offers varied: laborers, doctors, entrepreneurs, artists, merchants, and maids hurried within the burgeoning city. Once work on his mansion was completed, James Deering concentrated on staffing his household. For instance, he corresponded for three years with his employees on the subject of chauffeurs. Far from being mere administrative trivia, these letters supply multiple perspectives on Italian-American relations from 1917 to 1920, when World War I (1915-1918) was bloodying Europe. Tito Ferri seemed to belong to an "intelligent and self-respecting class of Florentines."[45] He became James Deering's chauffeur after a screening to ascertain his citizenship and military status. Given the period, the topic of citizenship and military service represented an issue in the relations

---

[43] Joe Knetsch, "The Peonage Controversy and the Florida East Coast Railway," in *Tequesta* (Miami: Historical Association of Southern Florida, University of Miami, 1997) 22.

[44] Cordasco Francesco and Vaughn Cordasco Michael, *The Italian Emigration to the United States, 1880–1930: A Bibliographical Register of Italian Views Including Selected Numbers from the Italian Commissariat of Emigration, Bollettino Dell'Emigrazione* (Fairview, N. J.: Junius-Vaughn Press, Inc., 1990) 99.

[45] Chalfin to Deering, October 27, 1917, VMGA.

between Italy and the United States. Ferri, Chalfin wrote to Deering, spoke "French very well, Italian, of course, perfectly, English quite well enough and with fluency, though by mo means in perfection, and Spanish also." [46] But the key requisite was, first and foremost, that he was an American citizen and exempted from Italian military service. Up to 1915, the number of Italian immigrants naturalized in America swelled because Italians and other Europeans were entitled to claim naturalization. But American and Italian concepts of naturalization clashed on the issue of Italian-Americans' duties, attachment, and military obligations (Gursel 353-5).[47] The Italian government surrendered the responsibility of supporting its subjects economically and socially and recognized the renunciation of Italian citizenship in a foreign country, but stipulated in the Civil Code that the loss of Italian citizenship did not imply an exemption from past obligations, including military service, especially at times of "general mobilization."[48] Of course, James Deering wished to hire Italians or Italian Americans who were exempt from compulsory military service and who could not be expatriated to Italy to fight in World War I. Edoardo Cammilli's case proved how realistic James Deering's apprehensions were. "Professor" Edoardo Cammilli, as Chalfin and Deering sometimes called him, was a Florentine sculptor residing and working in New York. Rybczynsky and Olin write that he had been a professor in

---

[46] Chalfin to Deering, October 27, 1917, VGMA.
[47] Bahar Gursel, "Citizenship and Military Service in Italian-American Relations, 1901–1918" *Journal of the Gilded Age and Progressive Era*, 7 (2008): 353-5.
[48] see US Secretary of State ad interim, *Foreign Relations of the United States: Diplomatic Papers, 1915*, Secretary of State ad interim to Sen. Henry Cabot Lodge (Washington, 1915) and G.E. Di Palma Castiglione, "Italian Immigration Into the United States, 1901–4," *American Journal of Sociology*, Sept. 1905 (1905) in Bahar Gursel, "Citizenship and Military Service in Italian-American Relations, 1901–1918," *Journal of the Gilded Age and Progressive Era*, 7 (2008): 358; 363.

Florence before the war and that, after a brief time in the Italian army, he left Italy for the United States, where he arrived penniless (Olin and Rybczynski 183).[49] In 1917 Chalfin found the Florentine sculptor and hired him to produce four caryatides to frame the twin grottos in the Vizcaya garden, at a low price. [50] Cammilli only produced four clay models, and never completed the commission because he returned to Italy. His premature departure justified Deering's premonitions, expressed in a letter dated September 23, 1918, to Chalfin:

> [I] will say that it is very unfortunate that we ever contemplated the employment of the Italian sculptor facing as he does the alternative of refusing the call of his country or leaving our work wherever it happened to be. I blame myself that I should have considered the proposition in the first place. Since we have gone so far, however, I suggest that you write him a proper kind of letter, saying that we expect him to do the work as soon after the war is over as conditions may be sufficiently normal to justify us in going ahead with the work.

By returning to Italy in late 1918, Cammilli had closed the door to future work relations with Deering. Cammilli expressed his willingness to honor his contract with Deering by going back to Miami to complete the caryatides at the condition that he receive additional commissions that would let him to "make a little money and cover my debts made in New York."[51] Deering's answer, through Chalfin, was abrupt: "After studying your [letter] carefully my own feeling is that I should not assure you of any other work in America except this particular piece of work. I must not make you a promise of any [other] work, and I shall therefore conclude not

---

[49] Witold Rybczynski and Laurie Olin, *Vizcaya: An American Villa* (Philadelphia: University of Pennsylvania Press, 2007) 183.
[50] Chalfin to Deering, September 23, 1918, VGMA.
[51] Cammilli to Chalfin, April 1, 1920, VGMA.

to ask you to return."⁵² Differently from Cammilli, Tito Ferri, with his exemption from military service, was the perfect candidate for the chauffer position offered by Deering, and in 1917 obtained the job. After three years, Ferri's household included a wife, three children and a relative, Joseph Ferri. Life in Miami was good to the Ferris; since the beginning of his employment, Tito received salary, lodging and "overcoat, tan pettees and two pairs of shoes from Brooks."⁵³ For the first two years, Deering and Chalfin kept him in good esteem—"My dear Tito," wrote Chalfin to Ferri on June 25th, 1919—and solicited his expertise in the selection of new personnel for the garage. With Ferri's recommendation, other Italians entered the scene: Ruffo ("serio…you may conclude that you have been a great benefactor to me," writes Chalfin to Ferri), and Roger Tinarelli, nicknamed "Il Bolognese" ("very agreeable," writes Chalfin). ⁵⁴ Apart from worries deriving from the U.S. participation in the war and from the consequences of military preparedness (universal military training and Americanization programs), the American draft troubled Deering. He wrote on October 1918 to his bookkeeper, Mr. Reilly, "As you know, I have been very much concerned about labor matters in Miami. On the one hand, I do not wish to do anything that is not in the interest of the Government nor anything that would hurt the feelings of the Miami community."⁵⁵ On this account, "should peace not go as rapidly as we wish and should sentiment exist in Miami, both Joseph and Tito can be put on our two trucks and I can find other chauffeurs as best I may."⁵⁶ He was torn by the necessity of running his princely household with the work of capable men and complying with the necessity, and obligations, of war, which imposed military conscription on Americans. Peace eventually

---

⁵² Chalfin to Cammilli, May 18, 1920, VGMA.
⁵³ Koch to Deering, November 9, 1917, VGMA.
⁵⁴ In Italian in the text.
⁵⁵ Deering to Reilly, October 31, 1918, VGMA.
⁵⁶ Deering to Reilly, October 31, 1918, VGMA.

arrived in November, 1918, and in 1919 Deering's concern with chauffeurs somehow lessened, because for one year the correspondence with or about the Ferris ceased. In June 1920 Deering wrote Chalfin one of the last notes on Ferri, from Vichy, in France: "You know how fond I am of Joseph [Ferri], the chauffeur. You know also that beyond his pleasant character and the fact that he drives pretty well, he is worthless as mechanic. I feel that I must in justice to myself replace him. Therefore, I want a thoroughly competent chauffeur. Can you kindly put on foot enquiries on this line? I doubt if I want an Italian unless he is like Ruffo. Another like Tito I could not stand, between you and me."[57] What ruined the relation between James Deering and Tito Ferri remains undisclosed, as did "the Mrs. Ferri's episode," which appears in another exchange between Deering and Chalfin in the same period: "Doubtless Mr. McGinnis has thought it best to spare me these details. I shall be glad to know that we have seen the last of the family."[58] Deering's comments in 1920 on the Ferris—and on Italians—were not isolated. In 1918, still in the midst of construction of Vizcaya's gardens, a Babylon of people and languages still populated Deering's universe of business and culture. Here, "an American experienced in large affairs among Italians, who should speak the language" was indispensable. [59] Chalfin made inquiries at the Italian Chamber of Commerce in New York on July 15, 1918 for a man consistent with these descriptions. Rasasco had the requisites: he spoke Italian, was born of Italian parents in America, hence was American, and had a university education, obtained (probably, Chalfin says) at Columbia University. However, Chalfin wrote to Deering on July, 15 1918, "I have done nothing about him, because I think you do not want anyone of the Italian race." This remark conformed to the anti-immigrant feeling present in the 1900-1920s United

---

[57] Deering to Chalfin, June 25, 1920, VGMA.
[58] Deering to Chalfin, December, 31, 1920, VGMA.
[59] Chalfin to Deering, July 15, 1918, VGMA.

States' society. The effect of immigration from southern and eastern Europe on American culture alarmed the US government. A joint House-Senate commission, the Dillingham Commission, was formed in 1907 and for four years studied this phenomenon. According to this study, immigration threatened American society and needed regulation. The most direct political consequences were the Emergency Quota Act of 1921, which restricted immigration from southern and eastern European countries, and the 1924 National Origins Formula, which imposed a yearly numeric limit to immigrants from each country and vetoed Asian immigration. The social consequence was nativism, which considered alien people a threat to American identity.[60] In this context, Deering's own nativist attitude toward Italians clashed with his admiration for the Italian culture of the past, which in large part inspired his villa in Miami. The new Italians in the United States at the beginning of the twentieth century came from a fragmented nation that could not keep pace with modernity and progress, its Renaissance buried by poverty and political and social conflicts. Italian immigrants, expatriates of a weak state, became a natural target for racism and distrust.

CONCLUSION

A constant flow of Italians, rejected by a dilapidated state incapable of supporting its people, left Italy for the United States from the late eighteenth century to the first decades of the 1900s. Most

---

[60] John Higham, *Strangers in the Land: Patterns of American Nativism 1860–1925* (New York: Atheneum) 4. See also, Chip Berlet and Matthew N. Lyons, *Right-Wing Populism in America: Too Close for Comfort* (New York: Guilford Press, 2000); David Brion Davis, ed., *The Fear of Conspiracy: Images of Un-American Subversion from the Revolution to the Present* (Ithaca, NY: Cornell University Press, 1971); Seymour Martin Lipset and Earl Raab, *The Politics of Unreason: Right-Wing Extremism in America, 1790-1970* (New York: Harper & Row, 1970); Leo P. Ribuffo, *The Old Christian Right: The Protestant Hard Right from the Great Depression to the Cold War* (Philadelphia: Temple University Press, 1983).

settled there permanently, though many returned to Italy. After a first phase of inattention, policy-makers in the United States and Italy produced legislation dealing with migration in the last decade of the 1800s, while intellectuals began to write extensively about these expatriates in the 1960s. The rich literature on the subject, however, still neglects the Italian immigrants in Miami and its neighboring communities, where they have left numerous, albeit ephemeral, traces. This paper, glancing at the busy activities of the newly born Miami in the period 1910-1930 and using two large-scale construction projects as case studies—the extension of the Florida East Coast Railway from Miami to Key West and the erection of James Deering's Villa Vizcaya—recognizes the presence and contribution of Italians to the establishment of Miami, and aims to reconstruct and contextualize the signs that they left. Both ventures offer a glimpse into their involvement and the relations that they developed in this area. Even if their number was never very large, Italians engendered dynamics of acculturation, which are worthy of study. For this reason, the still not well-known experiences and vicissitudes of Italian immigrants in Miami must be brought to light.

Works Cited

Aquarone, Alberto. *Le Costituzioni Italiane*. Milano: Edizioni di Comunità, 1958.

Berlet, Chip, and Matthew N. Lyons. *Right-Wing Populism in America: Too Close for Comfort*. New York: Guilford Press, 2000.

Berthoff, Rowland. *An Unsettled People: Social Order and Disorder in American History*. New York: Harper & Row, 1971.

Bonelli, Franco. *La Crisi del 1907. Una Tappa nello Sviluppo Industriale in Italia*. Torino: Fondazione Einaudi, 1971.

Candeloro, Giorgio. *Storia dell'Italia Moderna, Vol.10*. Milano: Giangiacomo Feltrinelli Editore, 1984.

Carocci, Giampiero. *Giolitti e l'Età Giolittiana*. Torino: G. Einaudi, 1961.

Carper, Gordon N. "Slavery Revisited: Peonage in the South." *Clark Atlanta University* 37. 1 (1976): 85-99.

Choate, Mark I. *Emigrant Nation: the Making of Italy Abroad*. Cambridge: Harvard University Press, 2008.
Cinel, Dino. *The National Integration of Italian Return Migration: 1870-1929*. New York: Cambridge University Press, 1991.
Cometti, Elizabeth. "Trends in Italian Emigration." *The Western Political Quarterly* 11. 4 (0958): 820-34.
Cordasco Francesco, and Vaughn Cordasco Michael. "The Italian Emigration to the United States, 1880- 1930: A Bibliographical Register of Italian Views Including Selected Numbers from the Italian Commissariat of Emigration, Bollettino Dell'Emigrazione." Collected papers. Fairview, N. J.: Junius-Vaughn Press, Inc., 1990.
Cordasco, Francesco, and Eugene Bucchioni. *The Italians: Social Background of an American Group*. Clifton, N.J.: Augustus M. Kelley Publishers, 1974.
Cosco, Joseph P. *Imagining Italians: The Clash of Romance and Race in American Perceptions, 1880- 1910*. New York: SUNY Press, 2003.
Davis, David Brion. *The Fear of Conspiracy: Images of un-American Subversion from the Revolution to the Present*. Ithaca: Cornell University Press, 1971.
Di Palma Castiglione, G.E. "Italian Immigration into the United States, 1901-4." *American Journal of Sociology*, Sept. 1905 (1905).
Dodge, Edwar, N. *Encyclopedia of American Biography, New Series*. Vol. 38. New York: The American Historical Company, Inc., 1968.
Einaudi, Luigi. *Un principe mercante: studio sulla espansione coloniale italiana*. Torino: Fratelli Bocca, 1900.
Fenton, Ewin. "Italian Immigrants in the Stoneworkers'union." *Labor History* 3, no. 2 (1962).
Franzina, Emilio. *La Grande Emigrazione. L'Esodo Dei Rurali dal Veneto durante il Secolo XIX*. Venezia: Marsilio, 1976.
Gabaccia, Donna R. *Italy's Many Diasporas*. Seattle: University of Washington Press, 2000.
Gilkey, George R. "The United States and Italy: Migration and Repatriation." *Journal of Developing Areas* 2 (1967): 23-36.
Glazer, Nathan, and Daniel Moynihan Patrick. *Beyond the Melting Pot: The Negroes, Puerto Ricans, Jews, Italians, and Irish of New York City*. Cambridge: The M.I.T. Press, 1970.
Gleason, Philip. "The Melting Pot: Symbol of Fusion or Confusion?" *American Quarterly* 16 (Spring 1964): 20-46.

Guglielmo, Jennifer, and Salvatore Salerno. *Are Italians White? How Race is Made in America*. New York: Routledge, 2003.

Guglielmo, Thomas A. *White on Arrival: Italians, Race, Color, and Power in Chicago, 1890-1945*. New York: Oxford University Press, 2003.

Gursel, Bahar. "Citizenship and Military Service in Italian-American Relations, 1901-1918." *Journal of the GIlded Age and Progressive Era* (2008).

Hartz, Louis. *The Founding of New Societies: Studies in the History of the United States, Latin America, South Africa, Canada, and Australia*. New York: Barcourt, Brace & World, 1964.

Harwood Chapman, Katryn. *The Lives of Vizcaya: Annals of a Great House*. Miami: Banyan Books, 1985.

Higham, John. *Strangers in the Land: Patterns of American Nativism 1860-1925*. New York: Atheneum. 2002.

Hirschman, Charles. "Immigration and the American Century." *Population Association of America* 42, no. 4 (2005): 595-620.

Hoglund, William A. *Immigrants and Their Children in the United States: A Bibliography of Doctoral Dissertations 1885-1982*. New York: Garland, 1986.

Juliani, Richard N., and Sandra P. Juliani. "New Explorations in Italian American Studies." In *New Explorations in Italian American Studies*. Staten Island, N.Y.: American Italian Historical Association, 1994.

Juliani, Richard S., and Sandra P. Juliani. *New Exploration in Italian American Studies*. Columbia, SC: Harbinger Publications, 1994.

Jones, Maldwyn Allen. *American Immigration*. The Chicago History of American Civilization. Chicago: University of Chicago Press, 1960.

Keeler Olds, Clarissa. *The Crime of Crimes or the Convict System Unmasked*. Washington, D.C.: Pentecostal Era Co., 1907.

Kessner, Thomas. *The Golden Door*. New York: Oxford University Press, 1977.

Knetsch, Joe. "The Peonage Controversy and the Florida East Coast Railway." In *Tequesta*, 5-29. Miami: Historical Association of Southern Florida, University of Miami, 1997.

LaGumina, Salvatore J. *WOP!: A Documentary History of Anti-Italian Discrimination in the United States*. New York: Straight Arrow Books, 1973.

Lipset, Seymour Martin, and Earl Raab. *The Politics of Unreason: Right-Wing Extremism in America, 1790-1970*. New York: Harper & Row, 1970.

Livingston, Grant. "The Annexation of the City of Coconut Grove." *Tequesta, the Journal of the Historical Association of Southern Florida* LX (2000): 32-55.

Lynne, Wright E. *More than Petticoats: Remarkable Florida Women.* Guilford: TwoDot, 2001.

Martinelli, Phylis Cancilla. "Incorporating New Perspectives into an Immigration Course." *Journal of American Ethnic History* 28. 2 (2009).

Mormino, Gary R. *Land of Sunshine, State of Dreams: A Social History of Modern Florida.* 2005: University Press of Florida, 2005.

Mormino, Gary R., and George E. Pozzetta. *The Immigrant World at Ybor City: Italians and Their Latin Neighbors in Tampa, 1885-1925.* Urbana and Chicago: University of Illinois Press, 1987.

Moroni, Giambattista. *L'Emigrazione Italiana in Florida.* rept. Bollettino Dell'emigrazione, 1915.

Muir, Helen. *Miami, U.S.A.* Gainesville: University Press of Florida, 1953.

Nelli. Humbert S. *Italians in Chicago, 1880 -1930.* Oxford: Oxford University Press, 1970.

Ngai, Mae M. "The Strange Career of the Illegal Alien: Immigration Restriction and Deportation Policy in the United States, 1921-1965." *Law and History Review* 21, no. 1 (2003).

Nolan, David. *Fifty Feet in Paradise: The Booming of Florida.* San Diego: Harcourt Brace Jovanovich, 1984.

Olson, Stuart James. *The Ethnic Dimension in American History.* New York: St. Martin's Press, 1979.

Paxton, Pamela, and Anthony Mughan. "What's to Fear from Immigrants? Creating an Assimilationist Threat Scale." *Political Psychology* 27, no. 4 (2006): 549-68.

Portes, Alejandro, and Alex Stepick. *City on the Edge: The Transformation of Miami.* Berkeley: University of California, 1993.

Pozzetta, George. "A Padrone Looks at Florida: Labor Recruiting and the Florida East Coeast Railway." *Florida Historical Quarterly* 54 (1975): 74-84.

Reid Parrish, Allan. *Official Directory of the City of Miami, Florida, Including General Information Concerning Churches, Lodges, Societies.* Miami: City of Miami, c. 1907-1911.

Report of Official Court Stenographer. "United States Vs. Sabbia, Triay and Others, Accused of Peonage." Report of Official Court Stenographer. Library of Congress. Washington.

Ribuffo, Leo P. *The Protestant Hard Right from the Great Depression to the Cold War*. Philadelphia: Temple University Press, 1983.

Rybczynski, Witold, and Laurie Olin. *Vizcaya: An American Villa*. Philadelphia: University of Pennsylvania Press, 2007.

Sori, Ercole. *Le Marche Fuori Dalle Marche. Migrazioni Interne Ed Emigrazione All'estero Tra Il XVIII e Il XX Secolo*. Quaderni di "Proposte e Ricerche". Ostra Vetere, 1998.

Taylor, Jean. *The Villages of South Dade*. St. Petersburg: Byron Kennedy and Company, 1986.

Taylor, Philip. *An Unsettled People: Social Order and Disorder in American History*. New York: Harper & Row, 1971.

"The Padrone System in the United States." *The New York Times*, 1897, 23 May 1897, 22.

Thistlethwaite, Frank. "Migration from Europe Overseas in the Nineteenth and Twentieth Centuries." In *Rapports, V: Histoire Contemporaine*. Population movements in modern European history, Herbert Moller, 73-92. New York: Mcmillan, 1960.

"United States Federal Census," 1910.

"United States Federal Census," 1920.

"United States Federal Census," 1930.

U.S. Department of Justice. *Report on Peonage*, 1908.

US Secretary of State ad interim. *Foreign Relations of the United States: Diplomatic Papers, 1915*. Secretary of State ad interim to Sen. Henry Cabot Lodge. Washington, 1915.

Vecoli, Rudolph J. "European Americans: From Immigrants to Ethnics." *International Migration Review* 6, no. 4 (1972): 403-34.

"Vizcaya Garden and Museum Archives." Vizcaya Garden and Museum Archives (VGMA). Correspondence. Miami.

Weeks, David. *Ringling: The Florida Years, 1911-1936*. Gainesville: University of Florida Press, 1993.

Wilson Gibbons, Margaret. *Florida's Labor History, Symposium*. In *Florida's Labor History, a Symposium: Proceedings*. Miami: Center for Labor Research and Studies at Florida International University, 1989.

For God And Country
St. Lucy's Italian American Parish Responds

Salvatore J. LaGumina

Four days after Japan's attack on Pearl Harbor, Congress's December 11, 1941 declaration of war against Italy confronted Italian Americans with a cruel dilemma. They were faced not only with the sober realization that the land in which they were born or that of their parents' birth was a core member of the Axis powers who threatened the world's freedom, but also with the even more frightful possibility of taking up arms against close family members and relatives. Additionally it meant living in an atmosphere suffused with distrust for six million Italian Americans, especially for the 600,000 who remained un-naturalized and thus classified as "enemy aliens." A dark, dire and disconcerting period, it nevertheless also presented a challenge, a fortuitous opportunity to demonstrate that they were indeed true-blue, loyal Americans who could be counted upon—an opportunity reflected, for example, in the spectacular response of the Italian American parish of St. Lucy in Brooklyn.

During the first half of the twentieth century, Brooklyn, New York was widely known as the "borough of churches;" it contained one hundred and twenty-nine Catholic churches, over one hundred Catholic elementary schools, and forty-five religious orders of men. Brooklyn was also the home of many immigrant/ethnic parishes, most of which were Italian American and built in the spiritual image embraced by the first and second generations (McGreevy 49). It was a period when parishioners identified themselves as members of a parish rather than a neighborhood. The "ethnic parish" concept was proffered by the American Catholic episcopate as an accommodation to non-English speaking Catholic immigrants who insisted that their traditional culture, language and customs be given prominence in the formation of Catholic parishes in their neighborhoods. There were two types of national churches: "de facto" ethnic parishes, which while corresponding to traditional geographic boundaries that served all nationalities, nevertheless were closely identified with one ethnic group, and "de jure" parishes that served Catholics of a particular ethnicity beyond traditional parish geographic boundaries—St. Lucy was a singular illustration. Accordingly many Italian parishes existed in the large Brooklyn diocese which provided not only religious services in the Italian language usually, by Italian-speaking priests, but also an array of societies, feasts, and literature that reflected the ethnic background (Tomasi 8; Sharp 173-175). A keen observer and historian described the ethnic church's immediate impact on a Brooklyn neighborhood. "The church, or course, was always a restraining and guiding force. From the earliest days in Brooklyn, it bound the Italian people together. It would be impossible to overestimate its importance" (Weld 141).

Although a number of Catholic churches served the Bedford-Stuyvesant area, including Italian national parishes St. Michael the Archangel and Our Lady of Mount Carmel, a major influx of Italian immigrants in the first decade of the twentieth century suggested the need for another national Italian parish. Consequently in 1904 Fr. Francesco Castellano of the Church of Our Lady of Mount Carmel secured a former Protestant church on Kent Avenue in the Brooklyn neighborhood, which previously had seating for three hundred but with re-modeling now accommodated 500. The new Church of St. Lucy presented an unmistakable Italian ambiance, a legacy clearly reflected in the names of its pastors all of whom up to the outbreak of the Second World War were Italian-born: Reverends Castellano, Arcese, Caruana, Arcese, De Liberty. In addition, 24 of the 26 assistant priests who served the parish into the 1940s were of Italian ancestry (*Brooklyn Diocese Archives*). Thus Fr. Anthony De Liberty, pastor, Fr. Anthony DeLaura and

Fr. William Vetro served as assistant priests in St. Lucy at the time of the Pearl Harbor attack on December 7, 1941. Notwithstanding that St. Lucy was an Italian national parish, it always included a small number of parishioners not of Italian ancestry.

By 1921 the size of the parish had grown so steadily that a new church building was constructed to accommodate 600 people and in 1922 Pallottine Sisters of Charity arrived, to undertake social and charity work including operating a day nursery (The Catholic Church 416; Diocese of Immigrants 416). The stature of the Italian parish was further enhanced in 1936 when the Brooklyn Diocese named St. Lucy the site of a Eucharistic Congress for Italian parishes, an event highlighted by a march of 5,000 worshippers representing fifteen Italian parishes (*New York Times*). The continued growth of the parish was acknowledged in a 1938 report indicating it encompassed about 15,000 parishioners, seventy percent of whom were bi-lingual English and Italian (Archives, St. Lucy). Rank and file church members were overwhelmingly proletarian, typically first and second generation poor working-class immigrants who now had to endure the privations and vicissitudes of the Great Depression. The depths of economic severity apparently served to force some to move away from the neighborhood to even cheaper more affordable housing. Typical of Brooklyn's Italian neighborhoods most men were employed in factories and other labor-intensive jobs and women frequently worked in small neighborhood clothing plants while a fortunate few younger people attended college.

Although the parish did not have a Catholic school in 1931 forty-eight parishioners (almost all Italian names) formed a St. Lucy's Social Activities Bureau that legally was incorporated for the express purpose "to instill and inspire the love for American principles and ideals" (*Brooklyn Diocese Archives*). The Society constructed a building that would become a Social and Recreation Center for after-school activities that engaged a surprisingly high number of St. Lucy's young people in church events including bands marching in feast celebrations. In that era virtually every

Brooklyn Italian parish sponsored marching bands, partly to provide a wholesome activity for youngsters who might otherwise get into trouble and partly to march in saint day processions. In his recollection of that era, Joseph C. Pagnotta tells of a St. Lucy marching band led by parishioner John Celebre who also was the noted New York City Department of Sanitation band master. Pagnotta paraded in the Society of St. Angelo feast processions as well as at funerals of deceased society members—failure to do so would incur a two-dollar fine. Marchers wore three-by-six-inch badges that bore the Italian red, white and green colors on one side and black and gold on the other side (*Brooklyn Diocese Archives*). Indeed such was the interest in this activity, that St. Lucy's pastor Fr. De Liberty underwrote two marching bands comprised of approximately two dozen young people, who met on a weekly basis, usually with the pastor present for friendly chats with members until it was time for him to say good night so that he could go to listen to his favorite radio program, "Gang Boosters" [sic].

St. Lucy's dramatic club was another parish-sponsored activity in which young Italian Americans participated enthusiastically and which brought renown far beyond the immediate neighborhood. When in 1933 the club performed its first "Passion Play" it inaugurated a tradition that would last many years in annual reenactments of the drama. The onset of war impacted the production reported *The Home News* in so far as many young men who had appeared in it previously had entered the service—Frank Caruso, however, would appear as usual because as the father of six he would not be drafted. News of this production formed a major item of communication between the home front and the war front during the war years (*Diocese of Immigrants* 110).

For St. Lucy's Italian Catholic immigrants' faith was a major and indispensable element in the inevitable adjustment from customs in Italy to those developed in the new country. Uprooted from all that was familiar their attachment to their ancient faith became even stronger as they were thrust into an alien and frequently harsh environment. Their experience validated Oscar

Handlin's assertion regarding the magnitude of religion as a way of life. "A man holds dear what little is left. When much is lost, there is no risking the remainder. As his stable place in a whole universe slipped away from under him, the peasant come to America grasped convulsively at the familiar supports...The very process of adjusting immigrant ideas to the conditions of the United States made religion paramount as a way of life" (Handlin 117). Their life activities in the parish became intertwined with the immediate neighborhood, which was the vantage point from which they viewed events of the tumultuous world beyond.

December 7, 1941, that day of infamy, when Japan attacked Pearl Harbor, marked a major turning point in American history, one that would inescapably transform the lives of all Americans, especially the ethnic populations. St. Lucy's reaction to the distressing war news was remarkable—In short order its Social Service Bureau began an activity that highlighted the parish's undisputed American loyalty by publicizing an array of visible homefront deeds in support of the battlefront through the creation of a Committee For The Armed Forces. Headed by dedicated parishioner Salvatore Basile and a capable staff, the committee meticulously accumulated names and military addresses of parishioners in the armed services, and with money raised by the St. Lucy's Service Men's jamborees and contributions, among others, from the Italian Catholic Union, from the Societies of San Francesco di Paola and Sant Angelo di Lombardi, and from a local union, began systematic mailings to service men. These missives contained "Daily Protector" prayer cards, copies of *The Home News*, and a carton of Camel cigarettes as Christmas presents. The conception of a unique and distinctive missive in the form of a 8 ½ by 11' bimonthly newsletter titled *St. Lucy's Home News* constituted a noteworthy feature of St. Lucy's activities that effectively interacted with its armed forces parishioner members. Under the editorship of Carmine A. Basile and a staff of devoted laymen members, academically inclined individuals like Thomas Vincitorio, who after his time in the service earned a doctorate and became a respected faculty member in the History Department at St. John's University. Beginning with the first edition in December 1942, the newsletter, eight to twelve pages long, was crammed full of parish-sponsored events such as the presentation of the American and Papal (yellow and white) flags bequeathed by parishioners to the parish that were placed at each side of the altar during the celebration of a High Mass, which *The St. Lucy Home News* described as "a further expression of love and loyalty to God and country which our Catholic Church believes and teaches." It informed its service members of various parish activities: charity festivals of the St. Vincent De Paul Society, the first prize Catholic Youth Award tendered to St. Lucy's Dramatic Society, and the Annual Holy Name Society Communion Breakfast. *The Home News* also published articles on popular sports activities like the successful St. John's University basketball season of 1943, which was in the midst of winning its first National Invitation Tournament. Knowing of the keen interest in sports the newsletter provided on-going anecdotal information to satisfy the most rabid baseball fans with tidbits about the Yankees' pennant-winning season as well the less successful but beloved Brooklyn Dodgers, and the much less beloved New York Giants major league baseball teams. The newsletter continually reminded folks back home of their obligation to their family members and friends fighting the battle for freedom in far-off lands. For example, the August 1943 newsletter editorial stated that:

> With the summer months speedily making their exit, we find our boys are still fighting heroically in distant lands, on strange waters, and in hostile skies that encircle the far flung parts of the globe. While great progress has been achieved there still remains much undone of that regrettable job which our men in the armed forces are determined to finish. Accordingly, it continues to rest with Americans on the home front to maintain, for our fighters the world over, the high standard of loyalty, morale and perseverance as they have demonstrated in the past.

The April 1943 newsletter informed readers about the induction of two parish young women—Catherine Mandarino and Edna Caliguri, who entered the WAACS and WAVES respectively—probably the first women from St. Lucy's to join the services. Other women from St. Lucy's Parish to enter the service included Marie Imperiale, formerly an instructor in the parish's Confraternity of Christian Doctrine program, who joined the U.S. Cadet Nurse Corps, and Vivian Foppiano who served in the Women's Army Corps (WAC).

Editions of *The Home News* chronicled the unremitting induction of local parishioners entering the service, replete with accounts of farewell parties for the newly inducted that were held at Toscano's, a popular local restaurant, and the extraordinary act of loyalty on the part of 44 year-old widower Joseph Famiglietti, who followed his four serviceman sons by enlisting in the Marines. The newsletter recounted the heroism of its boys in battle like Sgt. Ernest Bioni, who directed an action that destroyed a German tank at Nettuno, Italy, a town near his mother's birthplace, which he hoped to visit. It provided an account of Pvt. Don Sudano's participation in major campaigns in North Africa and Italy, for which he received the Silver Star, and of the Air Medals awarded to Sergeants Anthony Brasacchio and Frank Viscomi, for completing 50 and 64 bomber missions respectively, as well as non-Italian St. Lucy parishioner Sergeant Thomas Ford, for his 50 bomber missions, thereby prompting the comment: "St. Lucy's can now boast of hero representation in many fields of the various branches of the armed forces." That St. Lucy's *Home News* served a builder of self-esteem cannot be doubted. It was unambiguously proclaimed in letter after letter sent back home and could well be summarized by Corporal Joseph McCarthy's succinct message that *The Home News* was a "morale booster," a sentiment that was echoed by Sergeant Joseph I. Gallardi, who wrote from the Pacific that the "paper is the best morale builder he has read." But perhaps the biggest morale constructer edition of *The Home News* was that which contained large photographs of St. Lucy's mothers of servicemen. Although it was not its original intent, St. Lucy's *Home News* had interesting unintended consequences in spreading around the name of Brooklyn once the paper was shared with other servicemen from all corners of the nations; it made them "Brooklyn conscious" (*Home News*).

Much of St. Lucy's *Home News* special appeal was its direct reference to the parish's influence on the lives of soldiers who carried with them distinctive traits nurtured in the home parish. One example was that of the Del Casino family, whose son Anthony had already achieved popularity as a bandleader and radio singer prior to his Army induction. "Sgt. Anthony Del Casino is first trombonist in the 31st A.R. Band, one of the best in the country. No wonder—Anthony received his formal training as a member of St. Lucy's famous band." Meanwhile Vincent (Finders) Del Casino stationed in Camp Breckinridge, Kentucky "is now being called "Father Vincent" by his buddies. He is really doing a great job 'converting' the boys and teaching them the way to church. Keep up the good work, Vince." Captain Louis Vetere, assigned to a tank unit in the Pacific wrote, "I have received many gifts but there are none that I have appreciated more than *The Home News* and especially my Daily Protector. Many thanks." From former St. Lucy altar boy and usher Corporal Della Vecchia stationed in Mississippi came word that he was forming a choir to celebrate properly Christmas Eve Mass. Pfc. Joseph Spagnola, formerly a faithful member of St. Lucy's Holy Name Society as well as its Catholic Action group, became the head of the First Allied Presidium of the Legion of Mary. For Private Pat C. Strangis, former musician from St. Lucy, the highlight of his army career was the day he served as organist and leader of the choir for a Mass in Rome celebrated by Archbishop Francis Spellman.

While much of the correspondence between servicemen and newsletter editors was unimaginative and commonplace, it nevertheless spoke to the hunger of young men away from home for the first time in faraway places yearning to connect with home and hearth. Finding themselves lonely and in strange, often dangerous places, young men needed reassurance that was contained in word not only from family back home but also from the church that was so much part of their upbringing. By printing constantly changing military address updates St. Lucy's *Home News* proved to be an important interfacing vehicle for local community servicemen who had lost touch with cherished neighborhood friends whom they desired to contact. In many instances this information led to reunions in far-off parts of the globe. Corporal Joseph I. Ciccimarro, for one, expressed his thanks for his ability to contact "many friends through *The Home News* and suggests that the fine work now being done be continued after the boys come home."

The extraordinary response to *The Home News*'s request for photographs from service members planned as special newsletter feature speedily that elicited hundreds of photos, which were published in a two-page spread and spilled over onto other pages, proved to be of exceptional interest both within the confines of the parish neighborhood and from service members far away. Many of St. Lucy's soldier/parishioners wrote that not only did they personally await delivery of *The Home News*, but so did soldiers from different parts of the country who were members of their company. The communication organized and administered and financed by laymen from the home parish was acknowledged as a wholesome rarity.

The notice that former Assistant Pastor Fr. Anthony DeLaura had become an Army chaplain stationed in North Africa stirred a great deal of interest as *The Home News* provided accounts of soldiers from St. Lucy's parish making attempts to connect with him overseas—in one instance Pvt. Frank Novello did reunite with Fr. De Laura, who was then in Sicily. A friendly and accessible priest, Fr. De Laura, who saw his role as being available to any soldier regardless of religion, risked his life on more than one occasion, to bring the sacrament of extreme unction to dying soldiers on the front lines. Fr. DeLaura, who had been transferred to St. Joseph Patron of the Universal Church in Bushwick, another de facto

Brooklyn Italian parish, volunteered to become an Army chaplain and responded to assignments in which he mixed with soldiers in battle on the front lines in Africa, Italy, and France. Fr. DeLaura, inspired men by his deeds, "especially his disregard for his personal safely to administer spiritual aid while under fire." He saw his ministry as succoring not only Italian Americans or Catholics, but any and all soldiers. His pluck and bravery attracted the attention not only of major New York City newspapers but also the American Army that awarded him a Bronze Star for distinguishing himself "by meritorious service in connection with military operations against the enemy..." (LaGumina 129-130; *Diocese of Immigrants* 101-102). Pictures of a kneeling Fr. De Laura administering the sacrament of extreme unction in the Sicilian battlefield were published in *The Brooklyn Tablet* and *The Daily News* in 1944. These photos conspicuously demonstrated his courage and commitment—virtues for which the Army awarded him the Bronze Star (*Diocese of Immigrants* 102). He received the Purple Heart, "won when he was wounded in a Venture into a mine field in the Ardennes where eight wounded GIs were trapped. Despite his wounds he administered to the eight and helped them out to safety." Fr. De Laura's military heroism continued to be remembered in the post-war period (*Brooklyn Eagle*). In February 1954, for example, the Brooklyn Eagle, referring to him as the "front line chaplain" because of "the heroic deeds in behalf of the wounded and the dying on the battlefields," reported that he was the featured speaker on the occasion of the fiftieth anniversary of St. Lucy Church (*Brooklyn Eagle*).

It was also in Sicily that St. Lucy parishioner Pvt. Al Farizzi, of Sicilian heritage, served as an interpreter for his commanding officer in handling problems encountered in village occupations. Amerigo Antonelli, a Navy seaman, was another St. Lucy product who utilized his knowledge of the Italian language productively in the war effort. His commanding officer deemed his linguistic services especially meritorious in facilitating interaction and cooperation between American and Italian naval officials (*Home News*).

That St. Lucy's *Home News* editions constituted a profound force for morale building cannot be denied. It was echoed repeatedly in letter after letter of thanks and gratitude sent to the committee, some of which were published. The volume of mail was enormous; by October 1943 the parish Committee of the Armed Forces had received over 1,200 letters from parish members in the military service, virtually all of which expressed their appreciation while voicing fidelity to their faith in God and to their Catholic religion. We cannot take account of all the missives; rather the most we can do is cite a few of the more incisive ones. Late in 1942 Urban Barney Intondi, who had been an active parishioner, wrote to Fr. De Liberty about the paradox of war and the thrill he experienced knowing that the pastor was bringing

> news concretely to the hearts and minds of the people of St. Lucy's Parish the truths of Our faith as expressed in their own lives in these times of fear and stress and despair....Now that this war is a "fait accompli" Our Churches are filled with capacity with mothers praying for their young boys in far-off lands; young women praying for their sweethearts and loved ones who are fighting and dying violent deaths. For what! Will it be a peace with Peace and Justice tempered by Christian Charity? Or will it be Pock-marked with hate, greediness, selfishness and injustice to our enemies? Whether it is a just war on our part, God is the only true Judge. The fact remains that we are fighting against an aggressor who threatens our very homes and who promises to purge our religion of love and mercy and pity and humanity. I hope God is on our side. He will if we keep on praying and praying.
>
> Please remember me in your daily Mass and never cease praying for the American Soldier.

Grateful Corporal John Marra stationed at an un-identified location where he described witnessing northern lights that danced across the heavens, wrote about the solace he received from his religion. He informed Fr. De Liberty that he partook of Mass and

Holy Communion at every opportunity and expressed the soldiers' universal feeling at receiving mail from home. "Mail call is a soldier's greatest joy. People at home don't seem to realize how happy they can make their friends and relatives with a few lines of chatter."

For Pvt. Anthony Giammarino stationed in Virginia, receipt of the prayer cards, rosary beads and *Home News* brought true joy. "It gives one new courage in the things he has so much faith in. It is the same feeling that one has after he has confessed his sins and receives the Holy Sacrament. You have the feeling of security knowing that many people are praying to Our Lord for the safe return of all the men in the service." In his letter to St. Lucy's Pastor Fr. De Liberty, Sergeant Anthony A. Anzalone undoubtedly articulated the sentiments of all local servicemen when he wholeheartedly expressed the depth of meaning experienced upon receiving news from back home.

> Thanks to the St. Lucy Home News I have been able to know the whereabouts, promotions and deeds of valor of my fellow parishioners. Being away from the community for such a very long time, it is a feeling that can't be described by the mere grouping of words. The people on the home front can never understand the thrill and joy, the trembling fingers that the little Church Paper causes each and every one of us. It isn't the thought that the people back home are doing something fine and just. It is the feeling that you know where your former friends are, The fellows and girls you went to school with, you went to church wit. The lads and lassies you received communion with, received confirmation with. A lump reaches your throat every time you read of one of your buddies, what he has been doing and the work he has done. Some of us are in places where we can't maintain a correspondence that we would like to. To those that are in that category the St. Lucy Homes News is like a second front. Your paper manages us to keep together until the day when we shall be able to take up where we left off and continue our lives where we left off. As I say Father, words can't express my feelings for

the paper, a mixture of Paine, Kipling and Douglas could never say the things that are in our hearts for this deed, but all we can say is Thank you Father, for making this war as easy as possible under the circumstances.

Because statistics regarding Italian American participation in the armed services during the Second World War are rather elusive, great care must be exercised; figures frequently and categorically stated are in fact largely unsubstantiated. In the case of parishioner participation from St. Lucy's Parish, however, there is basis for substantiation because of the work of the parish's Armed Services Committee. Accordingly the December 1942 issue referred to 800 parishioners as members of the armed services, an impressive number in itself that would soon be dwarfed by a December 1943 reference to 1,600 participants—a truly astonishing number that undoubtedly understates the true total figure when one considers that enlistments and drafting of eligible parish men continued into 1944 and for part of 1945. Emphasizing and highlighting parishioner participation in the armed services was an important feature of other Italian parishes. A respected study of Manhattan's popular Our Lady of Mount Carmel, for example, while not specifying actual numbers, described intense devotion to the Blessed Mother on the part of anxious mothers who prayed for their soldier sons. These fears and prayers were expressed directly to the Madonna in letters written to her by the women of Italian Harlem and published in the parish journal" (Orsi 67).

The Home News edition of February 1944 reported that 80% of parish men—presumably those of draft age—were in the service. It was with great pride following Mass on December 12, 1944 when the parish of St. Lucy unveiled a huge scroll commemorating the 1600 members already in military service, while also leaving space for additional names should it be needed. The celebration of Mass marking the event was of such great moment that parishioners who flocked to the church filled it to overflowing and likewise squeezed together for picture-taking in front of the scroll. While there is no documentation regarding the number of casualties sustained, comparison with similar parishes would indicate they constituted a rather large number. For instance, Brooklyn's Italian parish of Our Lady of Loretto Church reported that 60 of her young men had been killed. Anecdotal reading of *The Home News* attests to the fact that wounded and Purple Heart recipients formed more than a few casualties. Still other casualties were those servicemen who were captured and became prisoners of war.

The story of Joseph Curcio offers an enthralling account of a St. Lucy parishioner whose life was saved by an astounding, if not near miraculous, circumstance. When nineteen-year old Joseph left home for the Army his mother had given him a prayer book asking him to keep it over his heart. After covering the book with a thin metal shield this is exactly what Joseph did and where the prayer book rested until a week after D Day in June 1944, when he landed in Normandy, France as part of the 30th Infantry Division, which became engaged in deadly, mortal combat at Mortain, near Barthelmy. "First, we came in and took over the town. Then the Germans counterattacked with infantry and tanks. Then we took it over again. My battalion bore the brunt of the battle. The town was in shambles. There was not a building left standing." Shortly afterwards he was captured by German forces and assigned to carry German wounded away from the front when he was hit by shrapnel from American lines. While being trucked to Paris a British Spitfire plane attacked the convoy in which he was riding. A bullet hit him in the chest pocket near the heart that held his prayer book, the very spot that held the "metal-covered prayer book that my mother had given me and which I carried over my heart. My mother said 'Carry this with you always Joe, and the Lord will protest you.' " He was hit in the leg by three other bullets and treated in a hospital by a German doctor, "who saved my infected leg by punching a drainage hole through the entire leg." After being liberated by American forces his partially paralyzed leg required long-term hospital care and on-going treatment into his eighty-seventh year. In 2012, sixty-eight years later, he continued to show the prayer book with a dent and ragged edges to fascinated onlookers (*Home News*; Schiraldi 199-203; Curcio).

Robert Guarini was another young St. Lucy man whose wartime experiences made a deep impression upon him and his relatives back home. His V Mail letters contained expressions of gratitude in receiving *The Home News* and fascinating accounts of his feelings flying over the Atlantic Ocean and his happiness in knowing they supported his efforts. "I was especially proud to hear that you side in with my folks in being proud of my present efforts" (Guarini, Letter). Entering the Army as a private in 1941, he became a bombardier with the rank of second Lieutenant and participated in numerous bombing missions over Germany. During a raid his airplane was shot down, forcing him to parachute over Germany, where he was captured and became a prisoner of war until his release in 1945. Upon his return to civilian life he became a high administrator in the New York City Department of Sanitation (Columbian Association; Basile).

One of St. Lucy's casualties whose name continues to be a rallying point into the twenty-first century was Anthony V. Manago. Born in 1921 to immigrant parents from Calabria, Italy, Manago was baptized at St. Lucy's Church, became a student in New York City public schools, and studied religion at the hands of the Pallottine Sisters. Shortly after the Japanese attack on Pearl Harbor, he joined the Marines, engaged in military action in various Pacific islands, all the time not failing to communicate with folks back home. His deep religious sense was evident in the words he wrote in one missive: "Yesterday, I received a nice medal. It's a saint I got from a girl in Brooklyn. The saint Mama gave me I lost quite some time ago, so I put this one on. You should see how nice it is!" (*Brooklyn Tablet*).

In combat Anthony Manago performed heroically in the ferocious Battle of Iwo Jima-a conflagration that lasted from February to March 1945 in which Marines sustained enormous casualties of over 26,000) including the death of Congressional Medal of Honor recipient Marine Sergeant John Basilone. (Grasso, 2010, 149-

202; Brady, 2010, 179-191) It also cost Anthony Manago his own life. For his uncommon gallantry Manago was awarded numerous citations posthumously including the Purple Heart, the Presidential Unit Citation, the "Victory Medal World War II" and the "Asiatic – Pacific Campaign Medal." His military exploits became so widely known that on April 20, 1948 New York City Mayor William O'Dwyer publicly cited Anthony as one "who so honorably gave his life that others might enjoy peace and freedom." The Brooklyn American Legion post named after him that became noted for promoting veterans' causes in the Bedford-Stuyvesant neighborhood. That was the backdrop to a June 5, 2006 resolution unanimously approved by the local Community Board requesting that a local park be renamed The Anthony V. Manago Park. A seemingly routine matter the request was frustrated by the usual municipal rigmarole. So too has ongoing red tape stymied an effort to rename a local road after him (*Brooklyn Tablet*).

The change in Italy's status following Mussolini's downfall in the fall of 1943 from a belligerent nation to that of a co-belligerent fighting on the Allied side was a significant event in Italian American neighborhoods. It presented an opportunity for countless Italian Americans to once again make contact with relatives who lived in liberated sections of Italy and who were in desperate straits. Americans of Italian descent worked assiduously to assist them with clothes and other material goods that could reach them by mail. In response to Fr. De Liberty's request for clothes *The Home News* reported that "The 'Clothes for Italy Campaign" was met with spontaneous enthusiasm by the people of the parish," as it described St. Lucy's auditorium, becoming a veritable clothes depot. The altered position of Italy also meant an opportunity for Italian prisoners of war stationed in the United States, most of whom agreed to aid the war effort by working for the United States Army. Accordingly cooperative prisoners of war were granted leave to tour New York City, visit relatives and attend functions in Italian enclaves. Like other national parishes the Church of St. Lucy participated in welcoming prisoners of war in an effort to make their prisoner status more bearable. On one occasion, June 24, 1944, five Italian war prisoners stationed in nearby Fort Hamilton were invited to a benefit bazaar and dinner sponsored by St. Lucy, where they were able to enjoy a spaghetti dinner prepared by parish women. Observers were impressed by the similarities in looks and names to St. Lucy's own lads.

St. Lucy's wartime faithful fidelity roused parishioners to a resolute determination to expend themselves in behalf of victory on both the home front and the battle field, by embracing the highly valued dispositions of patriotism and loyalty in such endeavors as raising funds and soldier morale. Those assigned to the battle front were prepared to give their greatest treasure, their lives, in fighting the enemy. The story of St. Lucy's Parish incontrovertibly mirrored that of countless Italian American enclaves whose residents humbly but heroically showed their mettle in the face of adversity. Their steadfastness was indeed a noble testimony in behalf of God and country.

The importance of *The Home News* as a crucial and essential link between the Italian Parish of St. Lucy and its parishioners away on the war front cannot be overestimated. Letter after letter testified to its vital role. The genuine gratitude for the communication link expressed in the following letter by Peter Perri well sums up the feelings of all who received *The Home News*.

> In my seventeen months out in the southwest Pacific, I have never written to thank you for your swell thoughts in sending me *The Home News*. I received about six copies and was given one by Martin De Pasquale in New Guinea last April 1944.
>
> To show some kind of appreciation I thought I'd send you some pictures of the churches, I have been photographing, as I went along....
>
> I have been in eleven landings up to date and I must say I have been in some tough ones. When I just went out to sea I received a small prayer book and beads from you, and they have been with me on every operation. If I was ever to forget them I think my good luck would never have lasted.

Many a time when I walk in different churches or hear Mass aboard ship, I can see St. Theresa in the same place as we have her in our church. She has helped me many, many times, and you will know when I'm back by receiving the largest bunch of roses anyone has ever sent her. I've waited many months tom come to St. Lucy's Church again and thank her myself for what she has done for me.

I have been very successful in my photographing since I have been in the Navy, and I'm hoping that someday I can offer my services to you.

I hope that I will be seeing you all in a few months.

God bless you,

Peter Perri, Photographer, M2/c. (*Home News*)

Notwithstanding the foregoing portrait of vibrancy, vitality and involvement that characterized the life of St. Lucy's parish life in the 1930s and 1940s, the reality was not so optimistic. In his April 1940 parish visitation report Bishop Thomas E. Molloy, while acknowledging that parishioners were "Excellent Italian people – loyal and cooperative Catholics" and that while Fr. De Liberty was "very zealous," if "untactful at times," also noted that St. Lucy was "a distinct parish cannot maintain itself except at expense of All Saints parish." The bishop observed that since unemployment was extensive and people were leaving the neighborhood, "the church should incur no new debt" (*Brooklyn Diocese Archives*).

The financial and economic picture was indeed ominous; however, with the onset of war in Europe in 1939 and even before America's entry in 1941, the weak economic picture changed dramatically, as the demand for defense workers greatly enlarged employment opportunities. As in the nation as a whole, unemployment in the neighborhood decreased significantly, thereby reversing a decline for the parish fortunes that soon seemed to be blossoming, thus postposing thoughts of demise. Considering that this was an improving atmosphere it is curious to note that the assessment rendered by official diocesan reports presented a confusing picture. On the one hand a Canonical Visitation Report of February 3, 1945 confirmed that even while the number of parishioners was decreasing and its income was increasing, the parish was in the black. Its annual income was $47,000, as opposed to ordinary annual expenses of $23,000. It possessed accounts in five Brooklyn-based banks in addition to $7,000 in war bonds. The report moreover recommended that the parish establish a school and recreation center (*Brooklyn Diocese Archives*). On the other hand a second Canonical Visitation report also dated February 3, 1945, stated annual income of $12, 000 (plus extraordinary income of $4,000) versus annual expenses of $11,000. But the most upsetting part of this second report was a hand-written recommendation that "The Parish be discontinued. New York City purchased the parish buildings August 1, 1944. Parish renting building presently. Demolition will begin after the war to make room for New York City housing project." (Brooklyn Diocese Archives). It was therefore against this mixed background that St. Lucy's congregation faced the future.

St. Lucy's relatively improved economic status sustained it for a number of years following World War II; however, its demise as an Italian parish was inevitable. Demographic changes brought about a decrease of an Italian character, as Hispanics and African Americans moved into the neighborhood and the Italian element, as in other parts of the city, began an exodus to suburbia. In 1974 St. Lucy officially was merged with nearby St. Patrick Church— thirty years after Bishop Molloy had forecast it and notwithstanding live-in protests wherein a hundred parishioners kept a vigil inside the church for two weeks in hopes of changing the diocesan decision to close the parish (*New York Daily News*). A Committee to Save St. Lucy's Church was formed and remained active for a time, sending out letters asking others to join in its mission to keep the church open, which also reminded people of the church's history. "St. Lucy's was built as a National Parish to service the needs of the immigrants and through the sacrifices of these people, flourished as and became a financial success as well as a spiritual fortress." It rejected the argument that St. Patrick's Church was more centrally located and also maintained that St. Lucy was newer and more solvent (*Brooklyn Diocese Archives*). The committee also made an appeal to the Holy Roman Rota in the Vatican, which stated it was a "formal recourse against the decision of the Most Holy Ordinary of Brooklyn to join the parish of St. Lucy with the neighboring one of St. Patrick of the Irish, and liquidating the goods of the parish" (*Brooklyn Diocese Archives*). Reference to the "Irish" parish raises the question of whether or not ethnic considerations were influential in the decision (Orsi 16; McGreevy 12-13; Morris 128-131). It is perhaps nothing more than a matter of speculation. Albeit Bishop Molloy was a product of an era in which the predominantly Irish American Catholic hierarchy looked askance at the institution of the ethnic national parish wherein immigrants attempted to reconstitute in America the forms of religious life to which they were accustomed in the old world, the extant record shows no explicit disdain of the concept traceable to the Bishop. Called a "brick and mortar bishop because of the great number of church structures built in the Brooklyn Diocese during his tenure, on at least one occasion in 1929 Bishop Molloy supported, even if grudgingly and under pressure, the creation of the Italian parish of Our Lady of Assumption Parish in Copiague, then part of the Brooklyn Diocese, with a grant of $40,000 (LaGumina, "Immigrants").

The termination of St. Lucy's Church as an active Catholic house of worship mirrored the outcome for many ethnic inner-city parishes throughout the eastern part of the United States. From the 1970s on changing demographics, the distancing of the immigrant generation from succeeding ones, the movement to suburbia, and the influx of newcomers of different traditions into their midst that perforce required major adjustments, priest shortages, among other developments, inexorably served to weaken traditional ethnic parishes. (*New York Times*; Penaluna) Of course some parishes were able to serve newer ethnic groups by learning new languages and cultural practices. When newcomers into the neighborhood were not of Catholic background the ethnic parish seemed to be less of a need. Simply put, by the 1970s the traditional ethnic national parish was in decline. In its heyday it had served a double purpose admirably, as a bridge institution which helped a generation retain language and cultural patterns while also abetting the process of Americanization. To a considerable degree this is what occurred in St. Lucy's parish. But for a great many the St. Lucy experience was their introduction to a Catholic tradition and an Italian legacy that has sustained and continues to influence them. It is an enormous source of satisfaction to reminisce about and acknowledge the many aspects of parish life that were part of this background. The World War II experience in particular stands as a ringing testimony to how deeply and energetically an Italian immigrant people and their children responded to the call from their adopted land to bear arms and to defeat a totalitarian foe that threatened their way of life and the nation's freedom.

WORKS CITED

Basile, Thomas. *Interview,* May 14, 2012.
Brady, James. *Hero of the Pacific: The Life of Marine Legend John Basilone,* Hoboken: John Wiley and Sons, 2010.
Brooklyn Diocese Archives.
Brooklyn *Eagle.*
Brooklyn *Tablet.*
The Catholic Church in the United States of America, Vol. New York: The Catholic Editing Company, 1914.
Columbian Association Department of Sanitation Twelfth Annual Dinner Dance, November 20, 1976.
Curcio, Joseph. *Interview,* June 13, 2012.
Diocese of Immigrants: The Brooklyn Catholic Experience 1853-2003. Strasbourg, France: Editions Du Signe, 2004.
Grasso, Joseph A. *Manila John: The Life and Combat Actions of Marine Gunnery Sergeant John Basilone, Hero of Guadalcanal and Iwo Jima.* Pittsburgh: Rose Dog Books, 2010.
Guarini, Robert. Letter dated October 12, 1943 to Mr. and Mrs. Carmine Basile, in possession of Thomas Basile, Massapequa Park, New York.

Handlin, Oscar. *The Uprooted*. New York: Grossett and Dunlap Publishers, 1951.

Holifield, E. Brooks. *God's Ambassadors: A History of the Christian Clergy in America*. Grand Rapids, MI: B. Eerdmans Publishing, 2007.

LaGumina, Salvatore J., *The Humble and the Heroic, World War II Italian Americans*. Youngstown, New York: Cambria Press, 2006.

_____. "Immigrants and the Church in Suburbia: The Long Island Italian-American Experience," 3-19, *Records of the American Catholic Historical Society of Philadelphia*, Vol. 98, No 1-4, March-December 1987.

McGreevy, John. *Parish Boundaries: The Catholic Encounter with Race in the Twentieth-Century Urban North*. Chicago: University of Chicago Press, 1998.

Morris, Charles R. *American Catholic: The Saints and Sinners Who Built America's Most Powerful Church*. New York: Vintage Books, 1997.

The New York Daily News.

The New York Times 28 September, 1936.

Orsi, Robert, *The Madonna of 115th Street*. New Haven: Yale University Press, 1985.

Penaluna, Regan, *Brooklyn Ink*.; on-line, June 29, 2011.

St. Lucy's Home News.

Tomasi, Silvano M. *Piety and Power*. New York: Center for Migration Studies, 1975.

Schiraldi, Glenn, R. *World War II Survivors*. Columbia, MD: Chevron Publishing Corporation, 2007.

Sharp, John K. *History of the Diocese of Brooklyn 1853-1953*, Vol. I, New York: Fordham University Press, 1954.

Weld, Ralph Foster. *Brooklyn in America*, New York: AMS Press, 1967.

The Impact of World War II on San Francisco's Italian-American Community
Continuity and Change

Tommaso Caiazza

HISTORIOGRAPHY

As noted by Philip Cannistraro, in one of his ground-breaking studies on Fascism and Italian-Americans, during the 1930s Mussolini's Regime extended its influence over the entire "structure" of Italian-American communities, this meaning the *prominenti*'s leadership and the ethnic organizations.[1] More recent literature has described Fascism's attempt to transform Italian-American communities into "lobbies" or "pressure groups," mobilizing the Italian-American population so as to influence American politics on behalf of the Fascist regime's interests, using the ethnic leadership and related organizations to this end.[2] Fascism also influenced Italian-American group identity. The antifascist exile, Gaetano Salvemeni, was the first to describe how Mussolini's nationalistic rhetoric appealed to Italian-Americans, since they thought that Fascism would raise their standing in American society.[3] Italian-Americans' need for a complete recognition as "Americans" was answered by

---

[1] Philip V. Cannistraro, "Gli Italo-Americani di fronte all'ingresso dell'Italia nella Seconda Guerra Mondiale," *Storia Contemporanea*, 7, 4 (1976): 855.
[2] See particularly, Stefano Luconi, *La diplomazia parallela. Il regime fascista e la mobilitazione politica degli italo americani* (Milano: Franco Angeli, 2000); Stefano Luconi, Guido Tintori, *L'ombra lunga del fascio: canali di propaganda fascista per gli "italiani d'America"* (Milano: M&B Publishing, 2004); Matteo Pretelli, *La via fascista alla democrazia americana: cultura e propaganda nelle comunità italo-americane* (Viterbo: Sette Città, 2012).
[3] Gaetano Salvemini, *Italian Fascist Activities in the United States* (New York: Center for Migration Studies, 1977): 16.

What is Italian America? (New York: IASA, 2015)

the impression that Mussolini was raising Italy to global-power status. Consequently, in the 1930s the sense of being Italian-American was dominated by Fascist referents.[4]

Given this broad influence of Fascism, what happened to the Italian-American communities after the outbreak of World War II? Scholars agree that during the postwar period the *prominenti* remained in charge of most Italian-American communities, in spite of their past involvement with the Fascist Regime. Two reasons explain this fact: First was the *prominenti*'s quick repudiation of Fascism when the need arose at the beginning of the war. This repudiation was partly due to the wish to preserve their own economic interests and the betterment in their own social condition. Then, during and after the War, just as before, the government and political authorities needed the support of the *prominenti* to gain leverage with Italian-American voters.[5] Similar reasons explain the continuity, from the prewar into the postwar period, in the leadership of organizations previously committed to Fascism. The Order of Sons of Italy, for example, managed to remain one of the most representative Italian-American organizations because the Order was, for the American authorities, the traditional channel of contact with Italian-American population. In fact, during the war, in spite of its previous Fascist affiliation, the Order worked closely with the American government to spread the Allies' views among Italian-Americans. Even more important, after the Allied invasion

---

[4] Luciano J. Iorizzo, "Fascism," S.J. La Gumina, F.J. Cavaioli, S. Primeggia and J.A. Varacalli (eds.), *The Italian-American Experience: An Encyclopedia* (New York-London: Garland Publishing, Inc., 2000): 215-218.

[5] James E. Miller, "La politica dei 'Prominenti' italo-americani nei rapporti dell'OSS," *Italia Contemporanea*, 32, 139 (1980):51-70; Nadia Venturini, "Italian-American Leadership, 1943-1948," *Storia Nord Americana*, 2, 1 (1985): 35-62; Philip V. Cannistraro, Elena Aga Rossi, "La politica etnica e il dilemma italiano negli Stati Uniti: il caso di Generoso Pope," *Storia contemporanea*, 17, 2 (1986): 217-243; Philip V. Cannistraro, "The Duce and the Prominenti: Fascism and the Crisis of Italian American Leadership," *Altreitalie*, 31 (July-December 2005): 76-86.

of Sicily, the Order helped the American government by redirecting messages in the Italian language to Italians in Italy suffering under Nazi occupation.[6]

As regards World War II's impact on ethnicity, it has been suggested that, together with the later Cold War climate, the war significantly diminished the importance of national identities among immigrant groups by imposing a high level of "conformity" and "patriotism" to the United States. According to John Diggins, for example, World War II was "the fuel of the melting pot."[7] Postwar prosperity, according to scholars, contributed to the same trend, so helping to increase upward mobility and Italian-Americans' identification with middle class values. Therefore, the war's aftermath is often seen as marking the disappearance of Italian-American ethnicity, which was only "revived" in the 1960s and 1970s.[8]

This essay analyzes the impact of World War II on the Italian-American community of San Francisco, focusing on the three main fields outlined above: leadership, organizational structure and group identity. In the course of this analysis, I will refer to interpretations by two scholars who have contributed significantly to the study of the Italian-American experience in San Francisco.[9] According to Italian historian Patrizia Salvetti, the war produced no change in the community leadership.[10] During wartime, a large number of

---

[6] Nadia Venturini, "Prominenti at War: The Order Sons of Italy in America," *Rivista di studi anglo-americani*, 3, 4-5 (1984-85): 441-470.
[7] John P. Diggins, *Mussolini and Fascism. The View from America* (Princeton: Princeton University Press): 352
[8] Kathleen N. Conzen, David A. Gerber, Ewa Morawska, George E. Pozzetta, Rudolph J. Vecoli, "The Invention of Ethnicity: A Perspective from the U.S.A.," *Journal of American Ethnic History*, 12, 1 (1992): 25.
[9] Patrizia Salvetti, "La comunità italiana di San Francisco tra italianità e americanizzazione negli anni '30 e '40," *Studi Emigrazione*, 19, 65 (1985): 3-39; Patrizia Salvetti, "La nascita della Bank of Italy e gli italiani di San Francisco (1904-1907)," *Studi Emigrazione*, 26, 94 (1989): 150-166; Rose D. Scherini, *The Italian-American Community of San Francisco: A Descriptive Study* (New York: Arno Press, 1980).
[10] Patrizia Salvetti, "La comunità italiana di San Francisco," 37-38.

San Francisco's Italian-American leaders were interviewed twice by the State Legislature's Un-American Activities Committee, the "Tenney Committee," which was looking for Fascist "agents" within the Italian-American community.[11] As a result of these hearings, some key leaders, who had been involved in Fascist propaganda during the 1930s, were forced to leave San Francisco during the war years, the city being a part of California's militarily strategic zone. According to Salvetti, these leaders resumed their control of the community once back in Little Italy, North Beach, at the end of the war, and there was therefore no change in the community leadership. Rose Scherini disputes Salvetti's hypothesis, by emphasizing the destructive effects of the Tenney Committee hearings, in which antifascists and pro-Fascists testified against each other, the anthropologist. Scherini suggests that the wartime crisis actually initiated the "dissolution of a lively ethnic community."[12]

Salvetti's claim of "continuity" and Scherini's claim of "dissolution" are mutually exclusive; however, both of their arguments suffer from a static conceptualization of the "community," which fails to take into account the possibility of change. They use the concept of "community" in a strictly topographical sense, to identify the population (its main figures, groups and institutions) living in a specific location like Little Italy, rather than, as suggested by Craig Calhoun, focusing on "the social bonds and political mechanisms" that hold this population together and make it work as a "community."[13] This means that the analysis needs to be directed towards

---

[11] The typescripts of the hearings are held in the California State Archives in Sacramento: Before Fact Finding Committee On Un-American Activities In California, *In the Matter of: Investigation into Matters Pertaining to Un-American And Subversive Activities*, vol. V, VI, VII, VIII, XII e XIII.

[12] Rose D. Scherini, "The Fascist/Antifascist Struggle in San Francisco," Richard N. Juliani, Sandra P. Juliani (eds.), *New Explorations in Italian American Studies. Proceedings of the 25th Annual Conference of the American Italian Historical Association* (Staten Island: AIHA, 1994): 63-71.

[13] Craig J. Calhoun, "Community: Toward a Variable Conceptualization for Comparative Research," *Social History*, 5, 1 (1980): 108.

the relationships between the various social actors composing the "community," and particularly, I propose, towards the interaction between Italian-Americans of different generations. The organization of the relationships between first and second generations necessarily evolved over time, as is evident in the leadership's dynamics. WORLD WAR II simply highlighted the demographic, socio-economic and cultural transformations that were already underway in San Francisco's "Italian-America." Changes regarded not only the community as an "actualized social form," made up of relationships and institutions, but also the community as an "imagined" construction, made up of symbols, values and cultural features "providing a sense of commonality and mutual identification."[14] I intend to investigate these meanings of San Francisco's Italian-American community, by focusing its leadership and the community's organizational structure and collective identity.

LEADERSHIP AND ORGANIZATIONAL STRUCTURE

Given the proximity to the Pacific, West Coast Italian-Americans were particular targets for the hysteria generated by Pearl Harbor. As many as 10 thousand Italian-Americans were forced to leave their homes, after the U.S. military authorities designated the West Coast as a militarily strategic zone, in compliance with Executive Order 9066.[15] Many other Italian-Americans were subject to curfews and confiscation of property; for example, fishermen had their

---

[14] Vered Amit, "Reconceptualizing Community," Vered Amit (ed.), *Realizing Community. Concepts, Social Relationships and Sentiments* (London-New York: Routledge, 2002): 1-20.

[15] U.S. Department of Justice, *Report to the Congress of the United States. A Review of the Restrictions on Persons of Italian Ancestry During World War II* (Washington D.C: U.S. Department of Justice, 2001); Rose D. Scherini, "When Italians Were Enemy Aliens," Lawrence DiStasi (ed.), *Una Storia Segreta. The Secret History of Italian-American Evacuation and Interments* (Berkeley: Heyday Books, 2001) 10-31; Stephen Fox, *The Unknown Internments. An Oral History of the Relocation of Italian-Americans During World War II* (Boston: Twayne Publishers, 1990).

boats seized and their business suspended.[16] In fact, according to scholars, as many as 20 per cent of Italian-Americans hit by internments nationwide came from the San Francisco Bay area.[17] Internments inside military camps were a type of restriction stipulated for "enemy aliens", such status being applied to non-naturalized Italian-Americans as a result of Public Proclamation 2527. These restrictions applied most particularly to Italian-Americans identified by the FBI as "potentially dangerous" for the Home Front, because they were suspected of pro-Axis sympathies.[18] Because of its prominence on the West Coast, the San Francisco's Italian-American community was identified by the Tenney Committee as "the spearhead of Fascism in California". Prominent figures, like Ettore Patrizi, editor of the largest West Coast Italian newspaper, *L'Italia*; the Catholic leader and former city police commissioner Sylvester Andriano; and the lawyer Renzo Turco were accused of being the "leaders of the Fascist movement in California."[19] As a result, they were placed under the "Individual Exclusion Program," which forced them to spend the war years in "exile," outside the militarily strategic zone of California.[20] Other well-known community figures, as we will see later on, were arrested.

---

[16] Sebastian Fichera, *Italy on the Pacific. San Francisco's Italian-Americans* (New York: Palgrave and MacMillan, 2011): 144-145; William C. Richardson, "Fishermen of San Diego: The Italians," Paola A. Sensi Isolani, Phylis C. Martinelli (eds.), *Struggle and Success. An Anthology of the Italian Immigrant Experience in California* (New York: Center for Migration Studies, 1993): 90.

[17] Rose D. Scherini, "The Fascist/Antifascist Struggle in San Francisco," 66.

[18] For a general overview on this topic see particularly Guido Tintori, "Italiani *enemy aliens*. I civili residenti negli Stati Uniti d'America durante la Seconda Guerra Mondiale," *Altreitalie*, 28 (January-June 2004): 83-106.

[19] California, Legislature, Joint Fact Finding Committee in Un-American Activities in California, *Report/ Joint Fact Finding Committee on Un-American Activities in California* (Sacramento: The Senate, 1943-1945): 1426.

[20] On Sylvester Andriano's expulsion from California see: William Issel, *For Both Cross and Flag. Catholic Action, Anti-Catholicism, and National Security Politics in World War II San Francisco* (Philadelphia: Temple State Press, 2010).

Scherini's hypothesis of inexorable "decline" or "destruction" is based on her listing of all the damaging effects to the community caused by the war. Admittedly, such damage was considerable. Not only did the leadership have to face the consequences of its previous relations with the Fascist regime, but many institutions had been forced to close or to interrupt their activities over a long period. The Italian School, for example, founded in 1885, was shut down immediately after Pearl Harbor, having received since the late 1930s the attention of American authorities and public opinion due to its part in spreading Fascist propaganda among the Italian-American population.[21] The same happened to the Italian Chamber of Commerce, which only re-started its review *La Rassegna Commerciale* in the mid-1950s.[22] The Ex-Combattenti (of the First World War) was also closed and many of its members interned or arrested.[23] Italian-language radio programs, like *La Voce dell'Italia*, stopped broadcasting,[24] and the *prominenti*'s cultural circle, "Il Cenacolo," had to meet "secretly" for several years.[25] Even the Dante Italian Hospital was closed, with the Army, in 1943, taking it over and turning it into a military convalescence hospital.[26]

---

[21] Tommaso Caiazza, "Pratiche e limiti della penetrazione fascista nelle comunità italo-americane: il caso della Scuola Italiana di San Francisco," *Altreitalie*, 45 (2012) (forthcoming issue).
[22] Information regarding the closure of these organizations can be found in Sylvester Andriano's hearings in front of the Tenney Committee: Before Fact Finding Committee, *In the Matter of: Investigation into Matters Pertaining to Un-American And Subversive Activities*, vol. VI, 1905-1928 and vol. XII, 3396-3450.
[23] See hearings: Modesto Giordano, Ivi, vol. XIII, 3531-3540 and Leo Ostaggi, vol. XII, 3627-3632.
[24] "I due Radio Programmi de La Voce de L'Italia," *L'Italia e La Voce del Popolo*, 19 ottobre, 1945
[25] See: Andrew M. Canepa, *The Founders of Il Cenacolo*, San Francisco, Il Cenacolo, 2001 (address at Renzo Turco Annual Scholarship Award Presentation, April 26, 2001).
[26] Italian-American Collection, San Francisco History Center, Dante Hospital Inc. folder: Anne Frisbie O'Neill, "Notre Dame: The Story of a Building" and Cesare Crespi, "Un grido d'amore." See also articles like: "Bisogna riprendere l'Ospedale Italiano," *L'Italia e la Voce del Popolo*, 4 novembre, 1945; "Il Dante

The War did not, however, completely destroy the community. If some ethnic organizations were closed, others were actually strengthened. California's Order of Sons of Italy, for example, increased in importance. In the 1930s the Order had had stable contacts with American politics. It had participated in lobbying nationwide in favor of Fascism; in fact San Francisco's Italian Consul Giuseppe Renzetti considered the Sons of Italy "always of a great help as a sort of cushion [cuscinetto] with the Federal or State Government."[27] Many of the leaders of the California Order were interned after Pearl Harbor, as shown by the dramatic hearing of the Order's President Anthony Fiore in front of the Tenney Committee.[28] Nonetheless, during wartime, by renewing its leadership the Order managed to preserve a prominent role within the community and became an official promoter of "Americanism" among Italian-Americans. In 1943 California's Order established a new headquarters in North Beach, in the Casa Coloniale Fugazi, the most historic community building.[29] The reputation of this building had been tarnished by its having been a center for Fascist propaganda activities back in the 1930's, many community institutions, like the Italian School, having had their offices there. The Order transformed the Casa Fugazi into the center of Italian-

---

Hospital è stato venduto. L'acquisto è stato fatto dalle suore di carità per 750.000 dollari," *L'Italia e La Voce del Popolo*, 8 agosto, 1946.

[27] Archivio Storico Diplomatico, Ministero degli Affari Esteri. Direzione Generale Affari Culturali, Archivio Scuole. Versamento 1936-1945, busta 117, posizione III-1, file Stati Uniti/San Francisco, The Italian Consul in San Francisco Giuseppe Renzetti to the Italian Ministry of Foreign Affairs, *Distretto Consolare di San Francisco – California – Situazione Generale,* Telespresso n. 15418-261, 9 maggio 1936..

[28] Anthony Fiore's hearings: Before Fact Finding Committee On Un-American Activities In California, *In the Matter of: Investigation into Matters Pertaining to Un-American And Subversive Activities*, vol. XIII: 3561-3577, 3647-3655.

[29] A history of this building is found in Andrew M. Canepa's, *Seventy-Five Years of Fugazi Hall: the story of a building, a man and a community*, in *Casa Coloniale Italiana John F. Fugazi. 75th Anniversary* (San Francisco: Italian Welfare Agency, 1988): 21-29.

American initiatives conducted on behalf not of the Fascist government back in Rome, but this time on behalf of the United States Army.[30]

The Sons of Italy benefitted from being a powerful organization nationwide; as such they suffered less from the backlash against Fascism than did other community institutions previously committed to the Italian regime. The Federation of Italian Societies, for example, in 1940 abandoned the holding of the traditional Columbus Day Celebration, for fear of being viewed as disloyal to the U.S.[31] Also the Società Italiana di Mutua Beneficenza suffered the same anxieties, becoming "more American and less Italian."[32] Moreover, since the immigrant generation was diminishing in number, very old organizations, such as the Speranza Italiana Lodge, started an unavoidable decline.[33]

Changes in the community organizational structure are evident in the new role of leadership played by the Italian-American merchants' and professionals' associations. During the war, Italian-American middle class organizations—for example, the North Beach Merchants Association—assumed leadership of the Italian-American community. These organizations did not represent merely a grouping of merchants, but an entire emerging middle class, composed of small as well as big entrepreneurs, lawyers and doc-

---

[30] "Festa inaugurale della Casa Fugazi," *L'Italia e la Voce del Popolo*, 26 settembre 1943.

[31] "Editorial," *Little City News*, September 21, 1940. See also John B. Molinari, "The History of San Francisco's Columbus Day Celebration," *Columbus. The Publication of the Columbus Celebration, 1977. Historical Issue: California* (San Francisco: Alessandro Baccari Editor/publisher, 1977): 32.

[32] Philip M. and Sandra R. Montesano, "Società Italiana di Mutua Beneficenza: 150 Years Providing Services," *Società Italiana di Mutua Beneficenza, 150th Aniversary. Souvenir Booklet* (San Francisco, October 26, 2008):10.

[33] Andrew M. Canepa, "Profilo della Massoneria di lingua italiana in California (1871-1966)," *Studi Emigrazione*, 27, 97 (1990): 102.

tors, all eager to represent Italian-American interests in the city.[34] The North Beach Merchants Association worked side by side with the Columbus Civic Club, the "only city-wide Italian-American political club."[35] The Club had originally been founded in 1931 to promote the naturalization of San Francisco's Italians and to better organize the ethnic vote in the city.[36] After the War, however, the Columbus Club became even more important than before for two reasons: The first was the acceleration in the naturalization rate among Italians during and after World War II, due to the impact of the "enemy aliens status."[37] The second reason for the Columbus Club's growing importance was the under-representation of Italians as compared to, for example, the Irish in the city administration, in spite of the Irish's being fewer in number.[38] The War's aftermath, therefore, was a very busy time for the Columbus Club, who publicly declared, from 1945 onwards, the aim of reaching every registered voter of Italian extraction. That is why Columbus Club programs were strongly "revamped" and "revitalized" within the community.[39]

The Italian Catholic Church is the other great institution whose importance increased in the War's aftermath. Once back in San Francisco, the North Beach War veterans joined the "Salesian Section" of the American Legion, while their brothers or sons, fol-

---

[34] The North Beach Merchants Association was incorporated in 1934. California Department of State, *Articles of Incorporation of the North Beach Merchants Association*, Corporation Number 157494, February 23 1934.
[35] "Anderlini Heads North Beach Group," *Italian-American News*, December 23, 1948.
[36] California Department of State, *Articles of Incorporation of the Columbus Civic Club*, Corporation number 144894, May 29 1931.
[37] Dino Cinel, *From Italy to San Francisco: The Immigrant Experience* (Stanford: Stanford University Press, 1982): 196.
[38] Frederick M. Wirt, *Power in the City. Decision Making in San Francisco* (Berkeley: University of California Press, 1974): 234-239.
[39] "Columbus Civic Club Plans Busy," *Little City News*, August 2, 1945; "Columbus Civic Club Outlines Postwar Program," *Little City News*, September 6, 1945.

lowing in their footsteps, were growing up within the popular "Salesian Boys Club."[40] The Catholic circles influenced the two Italian-American newspapers appearing in the 1940's: the *Little City News* and the *Italian-American News*.[41] The year 1948 symbolized the Italian Church's postwar success. Three second-generation Italian-American leaders, and "key members" of the Church, now made their mark in the politics of the city. John Molinari was appointed to the San Francisco Municipal Court; John Figone to the Board of Permit Appeals; and Joseph Alioto, future San Francisco Mayor, to the Board of Education. To quote Alessandro Baccari, "the city wide attention focused on North Beach."[42]

Molinari, Figone and Alioto were some of the new community leaders who emerged during the War. Wartime internments and expulsions, in fact, did not destroy the community leadership; instead they created a power vacuum. This emergence of new leaders marked a generational turnover. The *prominenti* and the new leaders were indeed "generationally" distinct. In the former group the generation of Italian immigrants, like Ettore Patrizi or Sylvester Andriano, was well represented, as well as second generation Italian-Americans born in California during the1870s and early 1880s, the decades following the early Italian emigration to California;[43] the new leaders, in contrast, were all born in San Francisco be-

---

[40] "Salesian Post of the American Legion Organized," *Little City News*, March 23, 1944. For information on the Salesian Club wartime activities see: "Juvenile But Not Delinquent. Fusco Has the Answer for N.B. Boys," *Little City News*, June 8, 1944.

[41] Catholic leader Armond De Martini was the editor of both *The Little City News* and *Italian-American News*. In the war's aftermath De Martini became President of the powerful Italian Catholic Federation. "Convention to Mark 25th Anniversary," *Italian American News*, August 25, 1949.

[42] Alessandro Baccari, Vincenza Scarpaci, Gabriele Zavattaro, *Saints Peter and Paul Church. Chronicles of the Italian Cathedral of the West: 1884-1984* (San Francisco: Published by A. Baccari, 1985): 206.

[43] See for example second generation Italian-Americans like Angelo Rossi (1878-1948); Amadeo P. Giannini (1870-1949); Frank Marini (1862-1952); Victor A. Sbragia (1882-?).

tween the late nineteenth century and the First World War: they were the sons of Italian Mass Migration to the United States.[44] Most of them belonged to Italian Catholic circles. The archetype of this second generation leader was the so called "North Beacher," a person who was born and reared in the Italian-American community of North Beach, and then had participated from youth onwards in Little Italy's Catholic activities."[45]

What most distinctly characterized this new group of leaders was their involvement in the activities of the North Beach Merchants Association and the Columbus Civic Club, the presidencies of which they shared among themselves in 1940s.[46] These new leaders were lawyers, doctors and merchants, relying mainly on class-based organizations to wield their power and influence. In the war's aftermath, some of them held positions in the City Government, such as Democrat Charles Ertola, a North Beach dentist.[47] Supervisor Edward Mancuso, known as the "Friend of the Little Fellow," was another well-known second generation Italian-American involved in City politics. He exemplified the story of second generations born of a humble immigrant family, having to combine study and work, yet rising to prominence in the city's

---

[44] Biographical information on these individuals was collected mainly through newspapers and the review of San Francisco City Hall officials *City County Record*.
[45] See particularly the figures of John Molinari and John Figone: "John P. Figone, S. F. Permit Appeals Member, Achieves Distinct Success," *City County Record*, December 1951, p. 19; "Molinari's Appointment to Judgeship Meets with Universal Approval," *City County Record*, April 1948, p. 8.
[46] See for example: "Civic Organization Meets," and "Boosters Hold Directors Meeting," *Little City News*, 4 October, 1940; "Northern Council of Civic Clubs Chooses Leaders," *Little City News*, October 25, 1940; "N.B. Merchants Elect Officers For 1941," *Little City News*, January 16, 1941; "Columbus Civic Cub Nominates Officers," *Little City News*, April 24, 1941; "Merchants Nominate Officers for 1942," *Little City News*, December 4, 1941.
[47] "Dr. Charles Alfred Ertola Supervisor," *City County Record*, March 1955. 6-7.

life.[48] The community was strongly mobilized in promoting Mancuso's candidature for Judge in the City Municipal Court in 1949.[49]

ETHNICITY

As said before, Fascism had represented in the 1930s a central reference point for Italian-American ethnicity, monopolizing the image of what it was "to be Italian." World War II, with its out and out clash between Fascism and the U.S., necessarily posed the need for a change; more precisely, to use Werner Sollors's concept, the war led to a "re-invention" of Italian-American ethnicity.[50] In the case of San Francisco, the group's symbols and cultural features were reshaped according to the new historical context of the "Great Conformism."[51] The Italian-American middle class, to which the new leaders belonged, used its own social class affiliation to redefine the community identity as a whole. The "Business Biographies," a section of the bi-monthly *Italian-American News*, dedicated to celebrating Italian-American merchants, merged Italian-American ethnic identity with typical middle class qualities, such as industriousness and acumen. Italian-Americans typified the story of the "immigrants who came to America, and who, by hard work and ability, have soared the heights in the business

---

[48] "Mancuso Municipal Judge Candidate Earns Friendship," *City County Record*, November 1949, p. 16; "Edward T. Mancuso Public Defender," *City County Record*, April 1958, pp. 10-11;

[49] "Edward T. Mancuso a Giudice della Corte Municipale," *L'Italia e La Voce del Popolo*, 5 ottobre 1949; "Aumentano
le decisioni alla candidatura a Giudice di Edward T. Mancuso," *L'Italia e La Voce del Popolo*, 13 ottobre 1949; "Perché dovremmo votare per Mancuso," *L'Italia e La Voce del Popolo*, 16 ottobre 1949; "La Federazione delle Società Italiane è per Mancuso," *L'Italia e La Voce del Popolo*, 21 ottobre 1949; "Mancuso confidente in una vittoria alle urne," *L'Italia e La Voce del Popolo*, 2 novembre 1949.

[50] Werner Sollors (ed.), *The Invention of Ethnicity* (New York: Oxford University Press, 1991).

[51] Elisabetta Vezzosi, "Società e cultura. Gli anni del dopoguerra," Federico Romero, Gianpaolo Valdevit, Elisabetta Vezzosi, *Gli Stati Uniti dal 1945 a oggi: politica, economia e società* (Roma-Bari: Laterza, 1996).

world."[52] Their stories exemplified the "dramatic and typical American success story:" They all started in a "humble way," but they were "energetic," they had "surprising business ability," they had "innovative" aptitude and, most of all, they were "hard workers."[53] By exalting these qualities, the Italian-American experience in San Francisco was able to align itself more closely with the "American Dream," after the public stigma of Fascism and enemy aliens.

Still, this "re-interpretation" of ethnic characteristics more in line with American mainstream culture should not be seen as mere "Americanization." Although the *Business Biographies* suggest that Italian-Americans demanded to be fully accepted as Americans, it was still as Americans of Italian origin. References to the motherland were still a feature of many of the articles:

> The Guido Lenci Co. exemplifies the spirit of Italian American Businessmen who have contributed much to the Development of San Francisco (…) they are active in the North Beach Merchants Association, the Columbus Civic Club and the San Francisco Athletic Club. They have always lent their support to the colorful Columbus Day Celebration.[54]

And further:

> The three partners are all related one to another, and are all from Italy. They make up their lack of formal education by their pleasant manners and their acute business perceptiveness. In other

---

[52] "Santucci and Fornaciari: Peerless Team," *Italian-American News*, March 10, 1949.

[53] "Mike Geraldi and the Fishermen's Grotto," *Italian American News*, January 27, 1949; 'Teamwork Makes Galileo Salami Firm Click," *Italian-American News*, May 19, 1949; "Homestead Ravioli Co. Is West's Largest," *Italian-American News*, June 9, 1949; "Grand Re-Opening of Crown Paint Co. This Saturday," *Italian-American News*, February 24, 1949; "Marconi's Fetes 10th Anniversary," *Italian American News*, July 14, 1949.

[54] "The Story of Guido Lenci Co.," *Italian American News*, January 13, 1949.

words, they know their business (...) the Golden Gate Ravioli Factory [is] a family unit that helps make up our cosmopolitan Bay Area.[55]

The myth of the successful businessman was actually nothing new for San Francisco's Italian-Americans. In the past the community élite had prided itself on its entrepreneurial abilities;[56] however, such acclamation shifted from big businessmen, like Italian-American cannery owners or bankers, to a wider group of small shop owners. Therefore, the Business Biographies rhetoric became a modern variant within the old leitmotiv of the "Colonia Modello," as the community had described itself back in the early twentieth century.[57] The middle class archetype drawn by *Italian-American News* reflected the "unusual" speed of San Francisco's Italian-Americans' upward mobility by means of "self-employment."[58] It also reflected Italian-Americans' involvement in the U.S's expanding postwar economy.[59] Above all, this stronger emphasis on qualities compatible with American mainstream culture was a means of moving on from the historical baggage of the 1930's when Fascism had cast such a long shadow.

As already mentioned, this did not mean, however, that Italy had disappeared in San Francisco's Italian-Americans' identity discourses or in their practices. Second-generation leaders continued to identify with the motherland and mobilized the Italian-American group on behalf of the new Republic of Italy. For exam-

---

[55] "Friendly Trio at Golden Gate Ravioli," *Italian American News*, April 7, 1949.
[56] G.M. Tuoni, G. Brogelli (eds.), *Attività Italiane in California* (San Francisco: MercuryPress, 1929).
[57] See particularly Ettore Patrizi, *Gl'Italiani in California* (San Francisco: Stabilimento Tipo-litografico del giornale L'Italia, 1911): 17.
[58] Sebastian Fichera, "Entrepreneurial Behavior in an Immigrant Colony. The Economic Experience of San Francisco's Italian-Americans. 1850-1940" *Studi Emigrazione*, 32, 118 (1995): 342.
[59] Gary R. Mormino, "It's Not Personal, It's Professional. Italian-Americans and World War II," Gary R. Mormino (ed.), *The Impact of World War II on Italian-Americans. 1935—present* (New York: AIHA, 2007).

ple, they started lobbying the American government and Congress, to obtain the most favorable conditions in the Peace Treaty between the victorious Allies and Italy and to increase the low immigration quotas granted by the law to Italy.[60]

CONCLUSIONS

World War II, therefore, did not signal the "dissolution" of the Italian American community; yet neither did the community remain the same as it had been. Indeed, WORLD WAR II needs to be considered, using Claudio Pavone's words, as the "event that reveals underground but active background," unearthing transformations that were already ongoing.[61] These transformations can be best understood in terms of the generational turnover within the Italian-American community. The second and third generations were growing, while the "Old Italians [were] Dying," to paraphrase the title of Lawrence Ferlinghetti's poem. Many of those who had participated in the Fascist/anti-Fascist struggle of the 1930s died during the 1940s, like well-known community journalists Ettore Patrizi, Ottorino Ronchi and Cesare Crespi.[62] *Prominenti* such as

---

[60] Large scale mobilizations were conducted by the Italian-American group to support the return to Italy of African colonies. Supervisor Edward Mancuso, a second generation leader, for example, tried to convince the city Board of Supervisors to address an official message to the Congress and to the U.S. President: *Memorializing the President and the Congress of the United States to take Whatever Action Is Necessary to the End That the Italian Colonies May Be Returned to Italy*, File No. 4083, in San Francisco Calif., Board of Supervisors, *Journal of Proceeding*, Monday, April 18, 1949, vol. 44, 274-275. For post-war lobby actions, see also: "Perché sia resa giustizia alla nostra patria natia," *L'Italia e La Voce del Popolo*, 10 aprile 1946; "Vogliamo una giusta pace per l'Italia," *L'Italia e La Voce del Popolo*, 27 marzo 1947; "L'emigrante," *L'Italia e La Voce del Popolo*, 17 ottobre 1946; "Dateci un passaporto," *L'Italia e La Voce del Popolo*, 13 novembre 1948.

[61] Claudio Pavone, *Prima lezione di storia contemporanea* (Roma-Bari: Editori Laterza, 2007): 149.

[62] "Ottorino Ronchi," *San Francisco Chronicle*, December 23, 1944; "Nobile, buono e generoso," *L'Italia e la Voce del Popolo*, 9 giugno 1946; "Cesare Crespi," *L'Italia e La Voce del Popolo*, 1 dicembre 1948; "L'ultimo saluto degli antifascisti di San Francisco a Cesare Crespi," *Il Corriere del Popolo*, 9 dicembre 1948.

the former Mayor Angelo Rossi and the banker Amadeo P. Giannini also died in the same period.[63] The 1950 Census outlines this generational turnover clearly: While the second generation was reaching its peak, first-generation immigrants were decreasing dramatically.[64]

World War II, with the interments and expulsions of the old pro-Fascist *prominenti*, accelerated the renewal of San Francisco's Italian-American leadership, giving second generation leaders the opportunity to take the reins of the community. The new leaders represented the growing Italian-American middle class, composed of small merchants and professionals. Their class-based organizations, such as the North Beach Merchants Association and the Columbus Civic Club, sustained community life in a period in which the traditional "Italian" organizations feared being labeled "enemy sympathizers." Through various new newspapers, this leadership also re-shaped Italian-American group identity, using typical middle class symbolic references. In this way the community's compatibility with American mainstream culture was re-established, so exorcising the ghost of Fascism. Second-generation activism helped contain what Andrew Canepa called the "generalized desire to maintain a low profile and *non dare nell'occhio*," which had affected San Francisco's Italian-Americans during the war and its immediate aftermath.[65] The Italian-American community found the resources to get over the problems posed for it by the war, so adjusting its leadership, organizational structure and collective identity to the new changing historical context.

---

[63] "La morte dell'ex Sindaco A. Rossi," *L'Italia e la Voce del Popolo*, 6 aprile 1948; "I capi dello Stato e della Nazione onorano la memoria di A.P. Giannini," *L'Italia e La Voce del Popolo*, 5 giugno 1949.

[64] U.S. Bureau of the Census, *17th Census of the United States* (Washington D.C.: U.S. Gov. Print. Off.,1952).

[65] Andrew M. Canepa, "Community Organization and the Preservation of Ethnic Heritage: The Case of San Francisco," Conference on Societies in Transition: Italians and Italian Americans in the 1980s, Balch Institute for Ethnic Studies, Philadelphia, Oct. 11-12, 1985.

Italian Americans: The Move to Suburbia

William Egelman

This paper will focus on the migration of Italian Americans from urban centers to their periphery. The paper will utilize data on New York City, and three of its major suburban counties: Westchester, Nassau, and Suffolk. Migration patterns per se cannot be derived from the data that will be presented in this paper. Rather, they may be inferred from a careful analysis of the data.

This survey of demographic patterns is not solely an exercise in population analysis. As groups move out of their ethnic urban enclaves and into somewhat more diverse suburban communities, this may be seen as a measure of assimilation. This phenomenon may be especially true for Italian Americans. Oftentimes they have been viewed as the urban-centered ethnic group. They remained in urban ethnic enclaves for a longer period of time than did most other European immigrant groups. The parallel ethnic institutions such as Italian-language newspapers and local food shops filled with imported Italian delicacies remained in place over the generations. If we begin to see evidence of their emigration from these ethnic enclaves, it may be surmised that assimilation processes may be in process.

The Data

Table 1 presents data on overall Italian American population change. Table 1A indicates the percentage change in the Italian American population for the areas under study. The urban center, in this case New York City, lost more than one quarter of its Italian American population in a twenty-year period. This reflects a dramatic decline of the ethnic community in a relatively short period of time. While the data do not indicate the reasons for this decline, they do suggest that there are two processes in play. First, there is an aging-out process. Table 2 shows us that one out of five Italian Americans in New York City is 65 years and older. This proportion is substantially higher in New York City than it is for all Italian Americans in the United States, where the proportion is approximately one out of nine. The older, closer-in suburbs also have higher percentages of the older-age cohort. On the other hand, Suffolk County, further from the city, has both a lower percentage of the older cohort and a higher percentage of the younger cohort.

The second process that may explain the urban decline in population is that of out-migration from the urban center to the suburban fringe. Suffolk County became a popular area for relocation for two reasons. First, the older close-in suburbs became saturated with population, so that little area for development remained. Second, the cost of housing in these suburbs became expensive. Suffolk County had plenty of space available at a relatively low cost. The data in these tables are again suggestive of outmigration patterns.

Table 3 indicates the proportion of Italian Americans who live in the city and suburban communities. Suffolk County has a higher representation of Italian Americans than do the other communities. Most recently, one out of thirteen New York City inhabitants is of Italian ancestry. For Westchester and Nassau, the proportion is one out of about five. For Suffolk County, it is between one out of three and one out of four inhabitants. These data suggest some degree of migration flow from central city to the suburban fringe.

The data in Table 4 presents the foreign-born population. The data indicate that Italian Americans make up an "older" immigrant group. All of the areas have foreign-born who arrived prior to 1990. Interestingly, in New York City one out of nine foreign-born came in the year 2000 or later. This is a much higher figure than what appears for the suburban communities. While this group of recent arrivals is a focal point of this paper, it is possible that more recent arrivals to New York City very well might be younger and better educated. New York City appears to be an area of destination for many young people regardless of their areas of origin. Recent Italian immigrants may be no different.

Table 5 presents data on marital status. While traditionally Italian Americans were seen as a family-centered population, these data do not reflect a distinctive family pattern among them. Nationwide, Italian Americans have the same percentage of currently married, and show very little difference in never married. Some differences in these percentages exist between New York City and its suburbs. Not surprisingly, suburban communities have higher percentages of now married and lower percentages of never married. These data may reflect selective migration patterns.

Both cities and suburbs have diverse populations; however, change in marital status often leads to changes in location. Single people form a higher percentage of urban populations than suburban populations. The substantially higher rate of never married in New York City also may be due to variations in age distribution of the populations.

Traditional family values are explored in Table 6. For all the areas indicated in the table, Italian Americans have much lower rates of births to unmarried women. Interestingly, Italian Americans show a greater disparity between births to married and to unmarried women than does the total population. For example, there is no difference in the percentage of unmarried women with a birth last year for the United States and New York City for the total population. Italian Americans have substantial differences based on location. Nationwide, one out of four births are to unmarried women. In New York City it is one out of seven. In the suburban communities it is even a smaller fraction, with Nassau having the lowest percentage with one out of approximately fourteen births to unmarried mothers. These interesting variations are in need of further exploration and research, but are beyond the scope of this paper.

Educational achievement data are presented in Table 7. Italian Americans appear to have higher levels of educational attainment than the overall population nationwide, and in all the geographic areas noted. New York City Italian Americans have lower rates of college degree and more when compared to Westchester and Nassau counties, but a slighter higher percentage than Suffolk County. Also, New York City has a higher percentage of less than a high school diploma, which, in all likelihood, reflects an older-age profile. Older Italian Americans are less likely to have attained high levels of educational attainment than younger Italian Americans.

Table 8 examines differences in levels of educational attainment based on gender. Historically, Italian American men had higher levels of educational attainment than did Italian American women. The data shown here indicate a significant change in that pattern. For all the areas shown there are no significant differences in levels of educational attainment between men and women. The older suburbs (Westchester and Nassau) have somewhat higher levels than the city for both males and females. Suffolk County has somewhat lower levels than the city. To some degree this is reflective of and a consequence of social class differences. As tables 9 and 10 will indicate, more Suffolk County Italian Americans are in blue-collar trades as compared to the residents of other areas.

Tables 9 and 10 present data on occupation and industry, which reflect those on education. As educational levels of achievement rise, there will be shifts in the occupational profile of a group. Historically, large numbers of Italian Americans, both men and women, tended to be clustered in blue-collar occupations. In Table 9 these would be represented in the bottom two rows. The most current data indicate that Italian Americans are somewhat below the national averages in these categories. The lowest percentage in these categories is in Westchester County; however, even there almost one out of eight Italian Americans are still in the blue-collar categories. In New York City, and Suffolk County the figure is closer to one out of six. These data support the idea that the blue collar tradition has not disappeared from the Italian American experience. This traditional legacy is further reflected in Table 10, if one focuses specifically on the construction category. Between six and eight percent of Italian Americans are still in construction, and this holds true for all geographic areas. Again, it is worth repeating that Suffolk County is the area with the largest concentration of blue-collar workers.

Generally, one may argue that this legacy only represents a small percentage of all Italian American workers. As the data in both tables indicate, there are very sizeable proportions of the population in higher-level white-collar occupations. Between thirty-nine percent and forty-seven percent are located in the highest-level category, "Management, business, science and arts" as cited in Table 9. The lowest figure is in Suffolk County, but even there it is almost two out of five workers are in this category.

This white collar pattern is more pronounced if one examines the data in Table 10. The categories: Finance and insurance, et al; Professional, scientific, et al; and, Educational services et al may be seen as representing higher-level white-collar occupations. Except in Suffolk County where the combination of these categories represents forty-five percent of the workforce, in all other locations these categories account for half the total workforce for Italian Americans. This percentage exceeds is the almost forty percent for all American workers.

The relatively higher levels of educational attainment, along with increased representation in white collar professional occupations, will impact income levels. As indicated in Table 11, Italian Americans have an almost 27 percent higher level of family income as compared to the total U.S. population. For per capita income, Italian Americans earn almost 20 percent more, on average, than the total population. The income levels for New York City and its suburban communities are even higher. In part, this may be explained by the higher levels of education and changes in occupational categories along with the higher cost of living for these areas in the northeast.

A last variable included for study is intermarriage. One way to ascertain the level of intermarriage is to examine the data on single and multiple ancestry Italian Americans as shown in Table 12. The multiple ancestry category means that individuals, when asked about their ancestry, will note that they have Italian ancestry and some other ancestry. These data do not indicate if the parents of the respondent are an intermarried couple. It does indicate that some ancestor was non-Italian. These concerns aside, the data do indicate some interesting patterns with respect to the ancestry of Italian Americans. Nationwide, six out of ten Italian Americans state they have multiple ancestry. Of the areas noted in the table, New York City has the lowest multiple ancestry figure; but, even here four out of ten Italian Americans have multiple ancestry. The other areas have higher percentages either approaching or exceeding one-half of the total Italian American population.

This pattern of mixed ancestry may be related to the educational and occupational variables. Increases in attainment in these areas may be related to wider social networks and a greater opportunity to meet a wider variety of peoples. While one should tread cautiously here, it is generally safe to assume that increasing levels in the mixed ancestry category indicates a move toward an assimilationist model.

CONCLUSIONS

The assimilation process is influenced by both external and internal factors (See Egelman). External factors are those events or processes that occur in the larger society outside of the specific ethnic group. An example of an external event is the perception of the group by the dominant group in the society, which includes perceptions of the group in question by other ethnic groups. Internal factors are events or processes that occur within the group. They include shifts in attitudes, educational levels, occupational patterns and spatial distribution. These two elements are interactive. Changes in societal attitudes toward a group will impact that group's opportunities. As these opportunities emerge, levels of achievement may rise with in the group, thus impacting the larger society's views of the group.

With respect to external influences, it would be fair to say that the negative perceptions of Italian immigrants that existed amongst many, but not all, Americans have undergone substantial change. The "I-don't-want-them-living-in-my-neighborhood" attitude has, in all likelihood, disappeared. Italian Americans have for the most part become part of the "white" mainstream American society. How and why this has occurred is beyond the scope of this paper. It is enough to say that there is relatively little discrimination, as compared to the past, with respect to where Italian Americans live and work and whom they date.

Gordon presented a broad analysis of the assimilation process. His overall work included two basic elements in assimilation: cultural assimilation and structural assimilation. Cultural assimilation is the process of absorbing the cultural components of the new society-eating American foods, going to baseball games, speaking English, and so on. Structural assimilation focuses on one's private and personal life. Who does one socialize with, whom does one marry, and where does one live.

Spatial assimilation may be seen as a sub-process of Gordon's structural assimilation. The theoretical starting point for the concept of spatial assimilation was Burgess's "concentric zone theory" of urban growth. Burgess argued that cities grow out from a central core that eventually would lead to a five zone model. As immigrants assimilated they would move out from the central core or the area immediately surrounding the central core-what Burgess termed Zone I and Zone II. Over time, the immigrants, or more precisely the children and grandchildren of immigrants would move to the outer fringes of the urban area or the suburbs.

Massey; Alba, Logan and Crowder; and Alba, et al, among others, have expanded upon Burgess's original ideas. Egelman, Gratzer, Nickerson, and D'Angelo have argued that this suburbanization process has even influenced the process of political assimilation. Additional research by this author, alone and with others, has analyzed some of the factors that may account for the movement out of urban ethnic enclaves and to suburban communities (see, for example. Egelman and Salvo; and Egelman)

This paper has offered evidence that assimilation is occurring in the Italian American population, and that spatial assimilation is a part of that process. Several general conclusions may be drawn from the data:

- There have been migration shifts from the central city to suburban communities and perhaps beyond
- Marital patterns, while showing some differences, appear to mimic national marital patterns
- Educational levels of achievement are significantly higher than national averages
- Italian Americans have a significant presence in the higher-level occupational categories
- Income levels, regardless of the measure used, are substantially higher for Italian Americans as compared to the national averages
- Some degree of marital assimilation has occurred with over one-half of all those identifying themselves as Italian American having mixed ancestry

Taken as a whole, these patterns appear to be reflective of larger assimilation processes. The shift to the suburbs is symptomatic of larger changes occurring in the Italian American community.

Works Cited

Alba, Richard, John Logan, and Kyle Crowder. "White Ethnic Neighborhoods and Assimilation: The Greater New York Region, 1980-1990." *Social Forces* 75 (1997):883-912.

Alba, Richard et al. "Immigrant Groups in the Suburbs: A Reexamination of Suburbanization and Spatial Assimilation." *American Sociological Review* 64 (1999):446-460.

Burgess, Ernest. "The Growth of the City: An Introduction to a Research Project." Pp. 47-62 in *The City*, edited by Robert E. Park, Ernest Burgess, and R. McKenzie. Chicago: University of Chicago Press, 1925.

Egelman, William. "Immigrant Groups Toward the Year 2000: A Conceptual Framework For the Immigrant Experience." Pp. 63-72 in *Sociology Toward The Year 2000: in The Sociological Galaxy*, edited by Charles E. Babbitt. Edinboro: Pennsylvania Sociological Society, 1983.

Egelman, William and Joseph Salvo. "Italian Americans in New York City, 1990: A Demographic Overview." Pp. 114-126 in *Italian Americans in a Multicultural Society*, edited by Jerome Krase and Judith N. DeSena. Stony Brook NY: Forum Italicum, 1994.

Egelman, William. "Italian Americans in New York City: 1980-2000. A Demographic Summary." *Italian American Review* 9 (2002):1-19.

Egelman, William, William Gratzer, Brian Nickerson, and Michael D'Angelo, 2005. "Italian American Voting Preferences." in *Greece and Italy: Ancient Roots & New Beginnings*, eds. Mario Aste, Sheryl Lynn Postman, and Michael Pierson. New York: American Italian Historical Association, 2005: 94-102.

Gordon, Milton. *Assimilation in American Life*. New York: Oxford University Press, 1964.

Massey, Douglas. "Ethnic Residential Segregation: A Theoretical Synthesis and Empirical Review." *Sociology and Social Research* 69(1985): 315-350.

Willliam Egelman • "Italian Americans: The Move to Suburbia"

APPENDIX

Table 1: Population Change, 1990-2008-2010

	U.S.	NY City	Westchester	Nassau	Suffolk
2008-2010	17,486,056	618,186	182,744	300,390	423,350
2000	15,638,348	692,733	192,205	319,602	408,568
1990	14,664,189	838,780	212,996	313,289	382,394

Source: U.S. Census Bureau, 2008-2010 American Community Survey, and earlier censuses

Table 1A: Percent Change of Total Italian Americans and for Selected Areas, 1990-2008-2010

	United States	New York City	Westchester	Nassau	Suffolk
1990-2008-2010	19.2	-26.3	-14.2	-4.1	10.7

Source: U.S. Census Bureau, 2008-2010 American Community Survey, and earlier censuses

Table 2: Age Distribution 2008-2010

	U.S.	NY City	Westchester	Nassau	Suffolk
Total population	17,486,056	618,186	182,740	300,390	423,350
Under 18 years	25.5	16.3	21.4	24.1	27.2
65 years and over	11.7	19.2	18.9	16.1	12.0
Median age	35.7	41.9	44.4	41.1	38.1

Source: U.S. Census Bureau, 2008-2010 American Community Survey, and earlier censuses

Table 3 Percent Italian population 2008-2010

	U.S.	NY City	Westchester	Nassau	Suffolk
Total population	306,738,433	8,175,133	949,113	1,339,532	1,493,350
Italian	17,486,056	618,186	182,740	300,390	423,350
Percent Italian	5.7	7.6	19.3	22.4	28.3

Source: U.S. Census Bureau, 2010 Census and 2008-2010 American Community Survey

Table 4 Italian Population Born Outside the United States

	U.S.	NY City	Westchester	Nassau	Suffolk
Total foreign born	545,254	61,587	12,862	16,496	9,631
Entered 2000 or later	16.6	11.9	3.6	4.6	2.9
Entered 1990 to 1999	11.2	7.5	6.4	5.5	7.0
Entered before 1990	72.2	80.6	90.0	89.9	90.0

Source: U.S. Census Bureau, 2008-2010 American Community Survey

Table 5 Marital Status 2008-2010

	Total U.S.	U.S. (Italian)	NY City	Westchester	Nassau	Suffolk
Pop. 15 years and over	245,645,469	13,834,655	535,127	151,288	242,082	329,550
Now married, except separated	49.6	49.3	43.8	52.5	54.9	55.4
Widowed	6.1	5.3	8.5	8.3	7.6	5.7
Divorced	10.7	10.1	7.5	7.2	6.5	7.6
Separated	2.2	1.5	1.5	1.3	1.1	1.6
Never married	31.6	33.8	38.7	30.6	29.9	29.7

Source: U.S. Census Bureau, 2008-2010 American Community Survey

Table 6 Fertility, unmarried women 15-50 years who had a birth in the past 12 months 2008-2010

	U.S.	NY City	Westchester	Nassau	Suffolk
Total population	35.0	35.2	26.0	16.8	23.5
Italian	25.6	14.9	12.7	6.8	11.2

Source: U.S. Census Bureau, 2008-2010 American Community Survey

Table 7 Educational attainment 2008-2010

	U.S. (total pop.)	U.S.	NY City	Westchester	Nassau	Suffolk
Population, 25 years and over	202,053,193	11,172,492	464,340	129,338	202,319	272,617
Less than high school diploma	14.7	7.9	13.2	9.6	8.7	7.4
High school graduate (includes equivalency	28.4	28.1	31.4	27.9	30.8	32.9
Some college or associate's degree	28.9	30.0	20.5	22.0	25.1	28.7
Bachelor's degree	17.6	21.4	20.8	21.8	20.1	17.1
Graduate or professional degree	10.4	12.6	14.1	18.6	15.3	14.0

Source: U.S. Census Bureau, 2008-2010 American Community Survey

Table 8 Educational attainment by sex 2008-2010

	U.S. (total pop.)	U.S.	NY City	Westchester	Nassau	Suffolk
Male, bachelor's degree or higher	28.5	35.0	35.7	41.4	35.7	31.3
Female, bachelor's degree or higher	27.5	33.1	34.2	39.6	35.2	30.9

Source: U.S. Census Bureau, 2008-2010 American Community Survey

Table 9 Occupation, 2008-2010

	United States (total pop.)	United States	New York City	Westchester	Nassau	Suffolk
Civilian employed population, 16 years and over	141,848,097	8,556,784	297,522	88,144	145,654	207,313
Management, business, science and arts	35.6	41.2	46.2	46.7	43.2	39.4
Service	17.6	15.7	12.8	12.6	13.3	14.4
Sales and office	25.2	27.4	28.0	28.5	29.7	29.5
Natural resources, construction and maintenance	9.5	7.6	6.7	7.7	7.3	9.8
Production, transportation, and material moving	12.1	8.0	6.3	4.6	6.4	6.8

Source: U.S. Census Bureau, 2008-2010 American Community Survey

Table 10 Industry 2008-2010 Civilian employed population

	U.S. (total pop.)	U.S.	NY City	Westchester	Nassau	Suffolk
Civilian employed population, 16 years and over	141,848,097	8,556,784	297,522	88,144	145,654	207,313
Agriculture, forestry, fishing and hunting, and mining	1.9	0.7	0.1	0.2	0.1	0.2
Construction	6.8	6.4	5.8	7.8	6.7	8.6
Manufacturing	10.7	8.4	3.3	3.9	3.6	6.2
Wholesale trade	2.9	3.1	2.9	3.4	3.2	3.4
Retail trade	11.6	12.0	8.8	9.5	10.4	12.2
Transportation and warehousing, and utilities	5.0	4.4	5.7	3.7	5.6	5.6
Information	2.3	2.7	5.2	4.1	3.5	3.2
Finance and insurance, and real estate and rental and leasing	6.8	8.4	12.8	11.6	10.4	8.2
Professional, scientific, and management, and administrative waste management systems	10.5	11.4	14.8	13.2	12.2	10.6
Educational services, and health care and social assistance	22.6	23.3	23.7	25.7	27.7	25.7
Arts, entertainment, and recreation, and accommodation and food services	9.1	9.6	7.9	6.8	6.3	6.1
Other services (except public administration	4.9	4.6	3.8	4.7	4.3	4.2
Public administration	4.9	5.0	5.2	5.3	5.9	5.8

Source: U.S. Census Bureau, 2008-2010 American Community Survey

Table 11 Income in past 12 months (in 2010 Inflation-Adjusted Dollars) 2008-2010

	U.S. (total pop.)	U.S.	NY City	Westchester	Nassau	Suffolk
Households	114,596,927	6,634,684	271,353	72,243	102,470	139,168
Median household income (dollars)	51,222	63,460	65,537	84,640	95,214	90,591
Families	76,262,975	4,284,160	149,520	47,375	78,314	106,866
Median family income (dollars)	62,112	78,753	81,176	110,261	109,616	101,805
Per capita income (dollars)	26,942	32,285	41,184	46,533	40,217	36,185
Poverty rate (all families	10.5	5.9	5.5	2.0	2.2	2.2
Poverty rate (all people)	14.4	8.6	8.0	3.9	3.0	3.8

Source: U.S. Census Bureau, 2008-2010 American Community Survey

Table 12 Single and Multiple Ancestry of Italian Americans by Area: 2011

Area	Total Population	Single Ancestry		Multiple Ancestry	
		No.	Percent	No.	Percent
U.S.A.	17,460,857	6,822,773	39.1	10,638,083	60.9
Nassau County	294,743	152,806	51.8	141,937	48.2
Suffolk County	414,294	184,467	44.5	229,827	55.5
Westchester County	177,747	96,730	54.4	81,017	45.6
New York City	589,751	348,570	59.1	241,081	40.9

Source: U.S. Census Bureau, 2011 American Community Survey

HOUSEHOLD SHRINES IN ITALIAN AMERICA
THE RESTAURANT AS DOMESTIC *EX VOTO* IN A SOUTH FLORIDA ITALIAN FAMILY

Jonathan O'Neill

INTRODUCTION

In almost two centuries of immigration to this country, Italian Americans have found a myriad of ways to honor their forebears, to express a recognition of—and an appreciation for—the ancestors who sacrificed so much in leaving a life they knew for an unknown destiny in an unfamiliar—and many times hostile—new homeland. Novels, poetry, art and, in more recent times, films have all been produced to document the hardships experienced by these intrepid souls, these quiet heroes, to render tribute to their unyielding courage in the face of abject poverty, backbreaking and often dangerous labor, and, in many instances, discrimination. An artistic medium less frequently used or recognized for this kind of tribute—but receiving more attention in recent years thanks to proponents like the artist B. Amore—are "domestic shrines," a kind of *ex voto* or votive offered in recognition of a miracle performed for the supplicant (in the case of a saint) or of a sacrifice suffered for the betterment of future generations (in the case of these "household saints," to borrow the title of Nancy Savoca's poignant film).

These domestic shrines can come in a variety of forms, from scrapbooks to family albums to collections of family artifacts (as B. Amore has assembled) and anything in between. Moreover, there is no limit as to the size or the type of votive offered. Consequently, a room, an entire house or even a restaurant can become a kind of museum dedicated to the memory of those progenitors to whom so much is owed. In the case of the Di Salvo family of South Florida, an Italian restaurant takes the form of a shrine erected to honor the parents who sacrificed so much for their children—both of whom dreamt of one day opening a restaurant in this country.

Di Salvo's Trattoria in West Palm Beach is a cornucopia for the senses. Upon entry, one is greeted by walls of family photographs and images celebrating other successful Italians, television screens streaming films with Italian or Italian American themes, a menu outlining the family's history and a plethora of dishes based on family recipes and, in many cases, bearing the names of family members or of places from the family's native Bagheria in Sicily. Using a number of literary and scholarly sources, as well as original research conducted through interviews with members of the Di Salvo family and visits to the family restaurant, this article will show how the Di Salvos have beautifully paid homage to their family's immigration experience, to the hard work that eventually allowed them to realize the American dream, and to Paolo and Rosa Di Salvo, the patriarch and matriarch of an Italian American family.

THE DI SALVO FAMILY: AN AMERICAN DREAM DEFERRED

Before considering Di Salvo's Trattoria as a tribute to the family's ancestors or the use of spaces as a form of *ex voto* offered in gratitude to the memory of those heroic figures who braved the unknown for their children and grandchildren, it is necessary to first tell the story of how the Di Salvos arrived at this point—a closely-knit family with a number of successful enterprises—in short, the story of a family that has achieved the American dream. The history of the Di Salvo family's immigration to this country is proudly displayed at the restaurant, on the back of the extensive menus. A careful observer will notice that the menu describes "[a] dream come true after 48 years" which "happened on June 15 to Mr. and Mrs. Francesco DiSalvo of 92 Overlook Place, Newburgh," Pasquale's and Tommaso's paternal grandparents (Di Salvo's Trattoria Menu). It was on that date in 1954 that "Mr. and Mrs. Paul DiSalvo and their three children arrived in New York City from Bagheria province, Palermo, Sicily," and "[w]ith their arrival, the DiSalvo family realized the dream of once again being together" (Di Salvo's).

"Francesco DiSalvo left Italy in 1907 and settled in Port Henry, NY," and two years later "[i]n 1909 Miss Gelsomina Botillo arrived from Italy" (Di Salvo's). One year later, Tommaso's and Pasquale's grandparents were married. Not long thereafter, the young couple was blessed with three children, all born in New York (menu). Interestingly, the factory in which Francesco Di Salvo worked was closed down, and while he waited, Francesco decided to take his family for a visit back home to Sicily. The year was 1914. Upon their arrival, war broke out in Europe, and Francesco was conscripted into the Italian army. The Di Salvo family's American dream had, for the moment, been deferred.

Pasquale's and Tommaso's paternal grandparents were not the only ones to have a *partial* immigration experience. Their maternal grandparents, Giacomo and Rosa, also came to this country a number of times. In fact, Giacomo—whose father was the curator of an estate in Italy and who had a close affinity with Tommaso—came to the United States on three different occasions but always returned to Italy because Rosa did not like America. The experience of emigration to America and then repatriation to Italy was not uncommon in the history of Italian immigration to this country, and many instances of partial immigrations or temporary returns to the Old Country are cited in the literary works of a number of Italian and American writers, as well as in immigration histories. One of the foremost examples of this is Anguilla, Cesare Pavese's main character in the novel *la Luna e i Falò*. After having made his fortune in America, Anguilla is dissatisfied with its transience and anonymity and thinks about leaving, "But where to go? I had arrived at the top of the world, and I had enough. So I began to think that I could pass back over the mountains" (all translations mine) (Pavese 18). Anguilla eventually returns to his town in Piedmont. Another literary return is that of Serafino Longobardi in Helen Barolini's *Umbertina*. Serafino, who had fought in Garibaldi's army, left for America when it became evident that Garibaldi's Italy would not treat the peasantry any more fairly than the previous political arrangement had, and the old nobles and their almost-feudal system of extracting from the peasant what he produced had merely been replaced by an institutionalized kind of feudalism, from a central government which was as alien to the peasantry as America. Later in the novel, Serafino "come[s] back from America to marry a woman of his village and to start a family," and then, later, when the same situation which had forced him to leave for America in the first place persists, "[r]eluctantly he agree[s] to leave" (Barolini 47).

The DiSalvo family added seven children while in Italy, among them Paolo Di Salvo, Pasquale's and Tommaso's father. Over the years, Francesco's and Gelsomina's children returned (or travelled for the first time) to America. "Finally, on June 15, Mr. and Mrs. Paul DiSalvo and children Frank, Jack and Pasquale arrived in New York to complete the long awaited reunion," and thus completing the family's immigration (Di Salvo's Trattoria menu).

It would still take many years, however, for the Di Salvo family's American dream to be fully realized. Upon arrival, Pasquale's and Tommaso's father had to work as a gas station attendant, a job that frustrated him. As Tommaso described to me in a phone interview (April 29, 2011), Paolo Di Salvo in Sicily was always his own boss, a *piccolo imprenditore* (little entrepreneur)—a trait which would later be inherited by his son, Pasquale. In America, however, lacking a familiarity with the country and its language, he was not as free as in Italy to work for himself. But Paolo never lost the desire to go into business for himself and fully realize the American dream. In fact—as Tommaso told me—he always dreamt of having his own restaurant. A few years later, Paolo was able to get a job in a restaurant (in part to learn the trade). He would go in early in the mornings to peel potatoes, prepare sauces and the like, for the day ahead. Tommaso noted that many a childhood summer was spent with his brothers, accompanying his father those early mornings to help.

Paolo Di Salvo, having worked at a restaurant for such a long time, had a concrete dream of opening his own. Since his English was limited, he had hoped his son, Tommaso, would help him with aspects of the job. At this point, however, a priest from the order of the Fathers of St. Charles Borromeo had recruited Tommaso, taking him away from what Paolo Di Salvo had hoped would be a family business. In this way, Paolo Di Salvo's dream was also deferred, only to be realized decades later through Di Salvo's Trattoria. This idea of a "dream deferred"—as Tommaso poetically described it—is ever-present in the Italian American experience. As Robert Viscusi notes, the trope of a dream deferred reappears frequently in the work of Italian American authors and "[i]n the tradition of writing that concerns Italian America, the enterprise of the patriarch...cannot overcome the break in its line of generation" (2006, 62). Two key examples of this narrative in Italian American literature are John Fante's *The Brotherhood of the Grape* and Pietro Di Donato's *Christ in Concrete*. Viscusi cites Fante's narrator, Henry Molise, who describes his father, saying "[h]e had wanted apprentice bricklayers and stonemasons" as children, and instead, "[h]e got a writer, a bank teller, a married daughter, and a railroad brakeman," (62). It is, thus, common for the Italian American patriarch to envision his realization of the American dream but for his children to pursue their own dreams.

Another example of the patriarchal dream deferred—albeit in a much more tragic way than in Fante's novel—is Di Donato's *Christ in Concrete*, in which, Viscusi notes, "[a]fter twenty years of striving, the immigrant Geremio finally succeeds one Holy Thursday in making the down payment on a house," but, unfortunately, "[t]he next day, Good Friday, he literally becomes the house that he too, at the last moment, has failed to establish" (63). He succeeds in achieving a partial dream, as it is described that "[t]hat night was a crowning point in the life of Geremio," for "[h]e bought a house" after the "[t]wenty years he had helped to mold the New World," but this dream (like so many others in the Italian American experience) is stunted before it can be realized (Di Donato 6). The idea of the generational dream, present also in Fante and in the Di Salvo family story, is alluded to in Di Donato when Geremio is on the job and his fellow workmen are teasing him about all of the children he has. "'Laugh, laugh all of you,' returned Geremio, 'but I tell you that all my kids...will be big American builders. And then I'll help them to put the gold away in the basements'" (4). This is another clear example of the ubiquity of the paternal desire for a generational line.

The difference between these tragic stories and that of the Di Salvo family, however, is that, happily, in the latter case the dream was neither broken nor was the dreamer jarred from his slumber. In Tommaso's words, their dream was simply deferred. The Di Salvo family's realization of the American dream begins with brother Pasquale's entrepreneurial endeavors. These begin with the building of a plaza in West Palm Beach, specifically intended for the opening of a Tire Kingdom. Over time, Pasquale began to build a small commercial empire in the very same plaza. There was an accounting firm in which Pasquale's children work, and recently brother Tommaso's gallery and the family restaurant were added to the shopping plaza.

This mark of the achievement of the American dream, in which a family dynasty is built from the ground up, is also a common thread running throughout Italian American literature. As Robert Viscusi notes in his literary study of the Italian American house as villa, "[s]tories of the *famiglia* which builds itself a house and then becomes a *casa* abound in Italian America," and "[w]hen written, this narrative shows up most prominently in the promotional literature of the California wineries and on the back pages of menus in prosperous suburban *ristoranti*" (2006, 62). Not to belabor the obvious parallels between the last statement and the menus at Di Salvo's, one could certainly look at the successful businesses the Di Salvo family has built up over the years—from Pasquale's construction firm, which built the shopping plaza as part of a series of strip-malls, to the accounting firm to the restaurant—as an example of an Italian American house becoming a dynasty, or a *house* in the medieval sense of the term. The Di Salvo house has certainly become the *House of Di Salvo.*

The clearest example of immigrant success and the creation of a small commercial empire in Italian American literature, however, is the family in *Umbertina*. In it, the matriarch of the Longobardi family—and the novel's title character—is able to begin a small business in which she prepared meals for her husband's fellow workmen, which then became a small grocery store, and then a large wholesale warehouse. The first business began when Umbertina's lunches began to gain popularity among the workmen and numerous orders began to pour in, leading her "to see that profits would be even greater if she had her own store of provisions instead of going out to buy them," which led to the opening of "a *spaccio*—a space, as it was known in the old country—in a little storefront on Third Street, near Scalise's bar" (Barolini 95). This *spaccio* eventually expanded, becoming "[i]n two summers [...] the Longobardi *groceria*, a grocery store" (96). Reminiscent of Pasquale's children, Jill and Scott, Umbertina's family was all involved in the family business as well, as "[Jake] took a job on the streetcar by day to add to the family earnings, which all went back into the store" (100). Jake's brother Ben did the same thing and both worked in the store itself.

Both Umbertina's family and the Di Salvo family expanded their family business to become a comprehensive commercial empire. Barolini notes that "S. Longobardi & Sons became and importing business, and Jake and Ben spent all day at the business, which was expanding into a private neighborhood bank and steamship-ticket agency as well" (103). Later on, Barolini notes that "Umbertina threw herself into work at the new place on Catherine Street with extra vehemence. The enterprises were divided: Ben managed the bank and steamship agency, while Jake ran the wholesale-produce business. Umbertina took charge of the grocery store, and the older girls ran the house and filled in at the store" (119). This is perhaps the closest literary parallel to the family empire the Di Salvo family has constructed.

Secular *Ex Voto*

Before an analysis of the restaurant as *ex voto*—a patently religious concept—a consideration of what I propose as a secular or domestic *ex voto* must be undertaken. *Ex Voto* or shrines are typically thought of as expressions of devotion or gratitude directed towards a saint or other figure endowed with the power to concede blessings or favors in many world religions (not only Christianity). As Antonella Pampalone notes, "The votive offering, as a sign of homage and testimony of faith in exchange for a grace received, has ancient origins" (83). This idea can be extended, however, to other devotional subjects, such as family members, an idea not unfamiliar to either ancient western or eastern religious doctrine. For the Japanese, to cite one example, "commemorating ancestral spirits" is considered "one of the country's most enduring social and religious traditions" (Nelson 305). The ancient Romans, particularly, erected cults and shrines to their ancestors and prayed for their help, as "ancestor worship was a vital part of Roman life" (Steadman 68). It is well-recognized that the Romans were obliged by their religion to "the dutiful discharge of cult obligations to the divine 'members of the kin group,'" an idea which—It is not far-fetched to imagine—could have worked its way into the Roman Catholic practice of building shrines for and praying to saints (Fortes 178).

As can be seen from the examples above, the idea of building shrines to family members is a common and ancient tradition. In modernity, of course, any religious connotation of tributes offered to family members has been removed; however, it is possible to speak of a *secular* shrine or homage to the family in the modern western context. In the Italian American context, this notion is particularly strong. Robert Viscusi notes that the "house"—which he describes "in the medieval sense where *house* means *family* and *family* means *house*"—can become a shrine (59). Understood in this light, the family itself can become the subject of a shrine. As Viscusi goes on to note that "anything that bears the mark of Italy can become a household god in Italian America," from the general, public representations of Italian culture—"the statue of Santa Rosalia or the panorama of the Golfo di Napoli"—to the particular aspects of Italy for each *casa*, such as family photographs, histories and even the "all-enveloping atmosphere of cookery," in the form of family recipes (60).

All of these elements can serve to make up the contents of a domestic shrine or *ex voto*. As Enzo Spera notes, "The materials which appear in what is vaguely defined as an *ex voto*...can be manifold and varied, in constitution and provenance, with the addition, sometimes heavy, of objects and documents of everyday use, ceremonial, or of an official or bureaucratic type" (91). This notion of objects serving as a link to a family's past and to Italy—thus making them apt objects for these domestic shrines—is clearly visible in a number of literary works produced by Italian American authors. For instance, in Barolini's *Umbertina*, a number of objects which tell the family history are preserved. The tin heart that the title character's first love made for her in Calabria eventually makes its way into the hands of Umbertina's great granddaughter Tina and creates a connection to her ancestor, the bedcover made for Umbertina's wedding is also preserved in the storyline—though not by the family—and serves to weave together the different generations of the Longobardi-Morosini family, and the idea of certain flora from the Old Country (specifically oleander and rosemary) are ever-present in the novel. This last point is particularly poignant when one stops to consider the *gelsomino* plant Tommaso Di Salvo's mother brought with her to this country and which her son preserved and continued to grow. It is also quite pertinent to consider Tommaso's garden in general, in which he grows beautiful tomatoes and other produce which he regularly contributes to his brother Pasquale's restaurant to be used in a number of dishes.

In *Umbertina*, this penchant for preserving a family's history through everyday objects that were important to its members is even evident in the very American family into which Tina eventually marries, the Jowers clan. As Viscusi notes, "[e]very such house is an *embassy*; that is, it refers freely to its own history" (67). To illustrate this, Viscusi uses the passage in *Umbertina* in which Tina is discovering Jason's family history by just observing the objects in the Jowers household. Barolini writes of Tina's room in the Jowers home that it contained a maple bed "[a]t the foot of [which] stood an old sea-chest used by a Jowers sea-captain on some trip to the ends of the earth. There were hooked and braided rugs on the floor and a child's Chippendale chair by the fireplace" (421). After going through a litany of family artifacts in the Jowers home, Barolini then likens it to the home/shrine of her much older Venetian father's side of the family, noting that "[t]he room was prepared in a reproduction of an early style. Everything was right. It was the equivalent of the fine Italian hand among the old families of the Veneto. Both were seafaring families; *both had accumulated wealth and possessions and pride*" (italics added) (421). Even a cursory reading of this passage indicates the importance attached to family objects as representative of history, achievements and (in the Italian American experience, particularly) hardships.

Barolini even continues this trope of the family object through the young Jowers-Morosini family, which begins to amass a collection of family artifacts of its own when Jason gives Tina an antique carved comb, a family heirloom his ancestor had brought back to his wife, in lieu of an engagement ring. Upon hearing the story behind the comb and observing its detail, that of "the undulating figure of a unicorn, whose graceful body ended in a mermaid's curled tail," Tina excitedly notes that "'[n]ow we have two powerful totems for our family-to-be,'…wrapping her arms around him in a tight hug—'this and my Calabrian tin heart'" (418). The imagery here is powerful, as it is an overt admission of the importance of objects in witnessing and then passing along, to future generations, a family's history. As Viscusi poignantly notes, "*La casa italoamericana* must do more than offer shelf space to old Caruso records or a place in the garden to wrap the fig tree in winter;…it must turn its face outward, as the embassy does, and must surely keep its inward gaze, recalling the strenuous doubling of the mind that makes immigrant Italians into Italian Americans" (68). This last part, that of the inward gaze, is particularly important in the creation of Italian American household shrines (like Di Salvo's trattoria) because it recognizes the importance of the *casa* (or family) looking inward and recognizing the sacrifices of those who came before the observer of such objects.

This example of everyday objects that create links to the past being used in these domestic *ex voto* is carried further when one considers the "memory boxes" created by Italian American artist B. Amore, who "integrate[s] materials from museum archives of oral histories with artifacts, sculpture, family writings," among other objects, to recreate "her families' (D'Amore and De Iorio from Avellino) immigrant experience" (Scarpaci 307). Amore's memory boxes, which assume the form of triptychs (yet another religious allusion), consist of a number of artifacts. For instance, in her *Family Stories* Triptych, she includes artifacts as diverse as a prayer book, a work lantern, a ravioli cutter, a Neapolitan coffee pot and a shaving brush (Amore). In addition to all of these, the triptych is set against the backdrop of many family photographs and its doors are lined with handwritten family stories.

The importance of photographs is undeniable in this medium as "the photographically reproduced image begins to gain a presence in votive compositions and *assemblages*, especially starting with the years straddling the First World War, becoming in recent decades a definable form of devotional objectification" (Spera 91). Photographs and images are particularly important to the Di Salvo family shrine, as they are present throughout the restaurant, from the moment one walks in to the moment one is handed the menu, which also features a collage of photos of Pasquale's family interspersed with images of the family's ancestors. Particularly interesting and dripping with history is the dining room in the back of the restaurant which the family affectionately refers to as the "wedding room," an allusion to the great number of wedding portraits displayed therein. I had the opportunity to tour the wedding room with Pasquale's brother, Tommaso, who explained the subject of many of the pictures and used each story to weave the history of the Di Salvo family together.

One portrait which stood out because of the detailed story behind it was that of Pasquale's and Tommaso's paternal grandparents, Francesco and Gelsomina Di Salvo. At its center, there are two seated women, elegantly dressed, holding hands. On the extremes of the portrait are two men, also elegantly dressed, at the side of each woman, facing unyieldingly towards the camera, almost as if to avoid making eye contact with each other. Tommaso described the people in the portrait to me as Gelsomina and her husband Francesco on the right and Gelsomina's sister and her husband Joe on the left. As the story goes, Gelsomina's sister had married Joe (both from the province of Avellino, near Naples, not from Sicily like the Di Salvos) and it was Joe's intention for his brother to marry Gelsomina. This idea did not sit well with Gelsomina, who declared that, at sixteen, she was not yet ready to be married. Eventually, the family made its way to Port Henry, New York—as the back of the Di Salvo's Trattoria menu notes, "[I]n 1909, Miss Gelsomina Botillo arrived from Italy" while Francesco Di Salvo had already "left Italy in 1907 and settled in Port Henry, NY" (Di Salvo's).

Upon her arrival in New York, Tommaso told me that Gelsomina had already received three wedding proposals, but she turned each one down, saying she wanted to marry a Sicilian. Once the family was settled in New York and was working at a steel factory (which consisted mostly of Neapolitan workers, from the same general region as Gelsomina's family), Gelsomina met the future Sicilian husband she was hoping for in Francesco Di Salvo. He lived in the same apartment building as the other workers from the steel factory, which included some of Gelsomina's in-laws. Naturally, Gelsomina's interest in Francesco incensed her in-laws in America and they found a way to not-so-subtly persuade Francesco to leave the apartments where the rest of the steel workers were housed.

Francesco's and Gelsomina's love eventually found a solution, however, in Francesco's friend, who lived in a different apartment building and offered to trade rooms with him, which they did. Then, this friend served as intermediary between Francesco and Gelsomina, allowing their courtship to continue without incurring the ire of Gelsomina's family. As the family history on the back of the menu at Di Salvo's notes, one year after her arrival in 1910, Francesco and Gelsomina married and had three children before returning to Italy and getting delayed there by the First World War. The bad blood between the two families continued even in Italy, and when Francesco was conscripted into the Italian army during the war, Gelsomina—pregnant with her fourth child, Paolo—returned to her home in Avellino because her family preferred that she stay with them during the war rather than go to Francesco's town in Sicily and Gelsomina was not any more welcome in Francesco's family than he was in hers, as Francesco's family also had its own designs for him to marry a Sicilian girl from their town.

The fact that this bad blood existed between the two families is important because, as a result of it, Paolo—Pasquale's and Tomasso's father—was born in Avellino and his name was inscribed in his birth certificate as Paolo Francesco *De* Salvo, rather than *Di* Salvo—a preposition more commonly used in the surnames of central-southern Italy than in Sicily. This caused Paolo Di Salvo's family some trouble when it came time to immigrate to America because he spent three months trying to get the error rectified, and thus, Paolo and Rosa Di Salvo were the last of the Di Salvo clan to arrive in America, a fact also noted on the back of the menu at the restaurant. Tommaso beautifully weaves this almost Shakespearean story of love conquering all odds out of the portrait on the wall of the wedding room at Di Salvo's Trattoria, in which Gelsomina's brother-in-law Joe and her husband Francesco refuse to look in each other's direction and in which the somber looks on their faces tell the story of the Botillo family's disapproval of Gelsomina's choice of Francesco.

Thus, Di Salvo's Trattoria as a household shrine serves the same function as the memory boxes created by B. Amore in that the entire history of a family is displayed through the use of family artifacts and, especially, photographs and images which are loaded with anecdotes, stories and the immigration experience of a family which is trying to pay homage to the forebears who sacrificed so much by telling their history through this family altar. Furthermore, as Viscusi notes above and as is evident in B. Amore's use of some *generic* Italian artifacts, not necessarily linked to family histories like the ravioli cutter, the Italian basket and the *caffettiera napoletana*, these shrines may also include these general, public representations of Italian culture (Viscusi 60).

In the case of Di Salvo's Trattoria, these *generic* items of Italian culture are mostly represented by pictures on the wall throughout the restaurant of famous Italian and Italian American personalities. From the moment one enters the restaurant, one can see pictures of Frank Sinatra, promotional posters of Francis Ford Coppola's 1972 epic family saga, *The Godfather*, and pictures of the royalty of Italian cinema in the 1960s, like Sofia Loren. There is even a picture, at the entrance of Di Salvo's, of Pasquale dressed in a tuxedo and seated in an elegant leather chair, legs crossed and holding a glass in his left hand, reminiscent of the style of Old Blue Eyes. In addition to pictures which make allusions to general Italian culture, however, Pasquale has added an additional—more modern—trope to this representation of *italianità*, that of film. There are a number of flat-panel televisions throughout the restaurant which project images from famous Italian or Italian American films. On my second visit to Di Salvo's Trattoria, one of the big screens was streaming a movie starring the beloved Neapolitan comedian Antonio De Curtis, better known as Totò, a personality loved by Italians young and old and a true symbol of Italian cinema.

MENUS AND FAMILY RECIPES:
THE EXPERIENTIAL SIDE OF THE DOMESTIC *EX VOTO*

The items that make up the household shrine can also involve other senses, and thus, the recipes included in a family restaurant's menu say much about the level of ethnicity of such a restaurant and about the degree to which the family intends it to be a tribute to the family members who passed those recipes down through the generations. Adherence to the traditions and values of the particular family can be attempted through the very name of the restaurant. Hermann W. Haller's topical study entitled "L'italiano nei nomi dei ristoranti di New York," as the name implies, takes a sample of New York restaurants and attempts to determine their level of *italianità* by taking a cursory look at their names. It is interesting to look at Haller's division of the nomenclature of Italian restaurants into meaningful semantic categories, which include names and surnames, gastronomic or geographical references and cultural allusions (339). About the first category, that of names and surnames, Haller notes that "in the majority of cases it will be the name or surname of the owner, of a person in the family of the restaurants" (340). He then focuses specifically on surnames and notes that "among the surnames present on the signs of restaurants, almost half can be identified with an area or a region," as noted above that *De* Salvo indicated a more central Italian surname than the correct family name, Di Salvo (342). Therefore, one can assume that such names are intended to indicate to the viewer of such a sign that the restaurant will serve recipes passed down from generation to generation, making even the dishes served at a restaurant like Di Salvo's Trattoria part of the family shrine.

Another element in the context of the family restaurant which can be considered a tribute to the family and thus can be looked at as a part of these household shrines is the menu and the dishes and recipes contained therein. A subsequent study undertaken by Hermann Haller entitled "Shrimp Fra Diavolo *e* Chicken Scarpariello: *Italiano e Italianismi nella Lingua dei Menu dei Ristoranti Newyorkesi*," emphasizes the importance of the menus in Italian American restaurants, the naming of dishes and the recipes themselves. In the study, Haller notes that in Italian American menus, "the ethnic substratum is manifest even more" than in the use of Italian names for the dishes, "in the emphasis on home cooking [*la cucina casalinga*], with...simple, nostalgic, reliable dishes" (706). Localisms also bring a sense of authenticity to the restaurant and thus lend credence to the argument that Italian American restaurants can be tributes to the families of their owners. Haller also notes that "not only does a large part of the gastronomic lexicon derive from dialects, but the names of many regional dishes in use still today are also dialectical," such that "we find in our texts *scungille*, a term integrated in Anglo-American, the already-cited *Scarpariello*, and occasionally *Sciallatelli / Sciallatielli, Pastafurno, Penne con Cuccuzzi, Pasta e Fasoi, Spigola al Marichiaro*" (707-08).

These two elements contained in Haller's study—that of home cooking and recipes passed down from generation to generation, and the use of dialect and regional references in the naming of dishes—are particularly visible in the menu at Di Salvo's Trattoria. Already referenced above for the comprehensive family history contained on its reverse side, the menu at Di Salvo's contains a number of closely-guarded family recipes which are glossed with a description of their provenance, and in some cases even bear the name of the particular family member who developed the recipe. For instance, beginning with the Flatbreads section, one can easily see the family and regional influences in the recipes and in their designations. The first item in the section is "Pasquale's Flatbreat," followed by two regional references in the Sicilian and Palermo flatbreads, and the final item in the section is a local reference to the family's hometown and is named the "Bagheria Flatbread" (Di Salvo's).

Towards the back of the menu is a section entitled *Specialità DiSalvo*, which is followed by a brief gloss stating: "Our house specials are among the family's personal favorites. Closely guarded recipes originated in Sicily and have been passed down through several generations" (Di Salvo's). Upon viewing the items in the section, one can clearly see the influence of many generations of Di Salvos. The first item is "Pasquale's Anneli con Salsiccia," followed by "Nonna's Sunday Pork Sauce" with an accompanying gloss describing the dish as "[f]resh rigatoni with Nonna's special pork sauce, pork and ricotta impastata," a name and a description which immediately evoke images of a Sunday afternoon dinner with the entire family in attendance (Di Salvo's). Finally, there is a dish in this section called "Zio Tomaso's Spitini," to whose authenticity I can personally attest. On my first visit to Di Salvo's, the family, who graciously invited us to eat with them, ordered—among many other items—Tommaso's spitini. As we all savored the delicious beef filets, Tommaso described the recipe to us and why he used a certain kind of cheese and abhorred substituting it with any other. All of these instances reinforce Haller's argument about the emphasis in Italian American restaurants on this idea of *la cucina casalinga*. His argument about the dialectical naming of certain dishes, especially in southern Italian American restaurants, is also lent credence by Di Salvo's Trattoria in the dialectical use of dishes such as "Chicken Scarpiello" (even omitting the *a* between the *r* and the *p*) and "Veal Saltimbocca" (Di Salvo's). It also reinforces my own thesis that even the items on a menu at a family-owned Italian restaurant can become part of the *family artifacts* which make up these household shrines or domestic *ex voto* in tribute to the family name and history.

Conclusions: A Dream Realized

As is evident from the story of the Di Salvo family, the immigration experience is full of hardship and sacrifice. There is always a dream to be realized—the pursuit of which brings the family ancestors to the New World in the first place—but this dream is not achieved easily, and sometimes is deferred for years or even generations. When this dream is finally achieved—and *if* it is achieved, as so many of the Italian American literary greats like Pietro Di Donato and John Fante admonish that its realization is not always guaranteed—it becomes a tribute, a sort of shrine to those who sacrificed so much so that subsequent generations could achieve what their progenitors wanted them to have. These tributes can be offered through a variety of media—art, literature, and film, for example—or the achievement of success itself can serve as the shrine to the family's forebears.

In the case of the Di Salvo family, the achievement of success is manifest in a very concrete, very visible way. To begin with, Pasquale has succeeded with his real estate development firm and his accounting firm in creating a small commercial empire of which his children have also become a part. Tommaso has made a name for himself as a successful and talented artist, opening his own gallery in the same plaza that houses the other family businesses. These concrete signs of success are worthy tributes to the Di Salvo family; however, the most visible and overt tribute to these ancestors—the *ex voto* offered in gratitude of their many sacrifices—is the family restaurant, Di Salvo's Trattoria.

A dream of both Paolo's and Rosa's, the restaurant is a completion of an emigration story, as noted above, always based on a dream. Paolo, the *piccolo imprenditore*, wished to open his own restaurant and, as noted in an article published for the Palm Beach Post, it was Rosa Di Salvo's dream as well, as Pasquale Di Salvo describes it as "a tribute to my mom" (Balmaseda). Tommaso also attests to his mother's desire to realize Paolo's dream of opening a restaurant. Unfortunately, Paolo would never see his dream realized, as he passed away in 1998, and although Mamma Rosa saw the restaurant at ninety percent completion and even attended a family event there prior to its opening, sadly, she too passed away before the restaurant was officially opened less than a year ago in the summer of 2010.

The beautiful tribute the Di Salvo family has built for its ancestors, however, seeks to carry forward the spirit of the Di Salvos and honor Paolo and Rosa and their parents in a very real way. As Pasquale told the Palm Beach Post, "[She] lives through us, through the recipes she left, through the restaurant and our sense of family" (Balmaseda). This is the true achievement of Di Salvo's Trattoria, to provide a lasting tribute to family, to thank the parents and grandparents who sacrificed so much for the future generations of the family, to create a *household shrine* to honor the story of and the love shared by the Di Salvo family.

Works Cited

Amore, B. *An Italian American Odyssey, Life line—filo della vita: Through Ellis Isle and Beyond.* 2006. Photograph, artifacts and text. Center for Migration Studies, New York.

Balmaseda, Liz. "An Easter Legacy of Family and Fine Food." *Palm Beach Post.* Palm Beach Post, 20 Apr. 2011. Web. 27 Apr. 2011.

Barolini, Helen. *Umbertina.* New York: The Feminist Press, 2008. Print.

Di Donato, Pietro. *Christ in Concrete.* New York: New American Library, 2004. Print.

Fortes, Meyer. "*Pietas* in Ancestor Worship." *The Journal of the Royal Anthropological Institute of Great Britain and Ireland* 91 (1961): 166-91. Web. 27 Apr. 2011.

Haller, Hermann W. "L'Italiano nei Nomi dei Ristoranti di New York." *Lingua Italiana d'Oggi* 2 (2005): 331-52. Print.

Haller, Hermann W. 2009. "*Shrimp Fra Diavolo* e *Chicken Scarpariello*: Italiano e Italianismi nella Lingua dei Menu dei Ristoranti Newyorkesi." *Proceedings of Storia della Lingua e Storia della Cucina: Atti del Convegno ASLI Associazione della Storia della Lingua Italiana, Modena, September 20-22, 2007.* Ed. Cecilia Robustelli and Giovanna Frosini. Florence: Franco Cesati Editore. 703-715. Print.

Nelson, John. "Household Altars in Contemporary Japan: Rectifying Buddhist 'Ancestor Worship' with Home Décor and Consumer Choice." *Japanese Journal of Religious Studies* 35.2 (2008): 305-30. Web. 27 Apr. 2011.

Pavese, Cesare. *La Luna e i falò.* Manchester: Manchester UP, 1994. Print.

Pampalone, Antonella. "Gli Ex Voto del Santuario di Gallinaro: Riflessioni sui Rapporti fra Immagine Culta e Immagine Popolare." *La Ricerca Folklorica* 24 (1991): 83-9. Web. 27 Apr. 2011.

Scarpaci, Vincenza. *The Journey of the Italians in America.* La Gretna: Pelican Publishing Co., 2008. Print.

Spera, Enzo. "Fotografia ed Ex Voto: Le Nuove Immagini e le Rappresentazioni della Devozione Popolare Contemporanea." *La Ricerca Folklorica* 24 (1991): 91-8. Web. 27 Apr. 2011.

Steadman, Lyle B., Craig T. Palmer and Christopher F. Tilley. "The Universality of Ancestor Worship." *Ethnology* 35.1 (1996): 63-76. Web. 27 Apr. 2011.

Viscusi, Robert. *Buried Caesars, and Other Secrets of Italian American Writing.* Albany: State University of New York, 2006. Print.

WHO ARE ITALIAN AMERICANS?

THE ASSIMILATIONISTS
SARAH WOOL MOORE AND THE SOCIETY FOR THE PROTECTION OF ITALIAN IMMIGRANTS

Teresa Fava Thomas

Perhaps the earliest concerted effort by American reformers to aid Italian immigrants began in New York City, led by a woman who was determined to aid Italians but to remain in the background of the institution she established and to which she devoted her life's work. Sarah Wool Moore had lived in Europe and knew Italy and Italians firsthand. But later in life she witnessed the Italian immigrants she encountered working on railroad projects in New York as the objects of mistreatment and derision. She devoted the remainder of her life to their assimilation into American life. Gino Speranza, who worked with Moore in the Society for the Protection of Italian Immigrants, wrote that Americans could not ignore the problem of assimilation: "[I]f [Italian immigrants] herd into great and menacing city colonies, if they do not learn your language, if they know little about your country, the fault is as much yours as theirs" (Speranza, "How" 458). Sarah Wool Moore's remarkable career began in Plattsburgh, New York, where she was born in 1846 to a branch of the Dedham family of Massachusetts. Educated first in New York City, she studied art in Vienna and elsewhere in Europe. There she developed great skill as a painter. She became an early advocate of arts education in American schools, and in 1884 a university professor of art in Nebraska. In 1888 she became the driving force for the organization of the Society of Fine Arts in Lincoln, Nebraska with the aim of encouraging youth and establishing a museum, the University of Nebraska's arts historian termed her "as dedicated a disciple of the visual arts as ever wielded a crayon or a camel's hair brush." She taught at the university until 1892, having been head of the Art Department (Wells).

At some point she abandoned her life in the arts and returned to New York City, where she was one of the founders of the Society for the Protection of Italian Immigrants, along with Charles Eliot and Gino Speranza, in 1901. Speranza termed the Society's founders "that type of men and women whom many would have classified as 'dreamers'—settlement workers, reformers, philanthropists!" In 1903 Richard W. Gilder, a member, wrote an open letter to the editor of the *New York Times* to solicit support, arguing the "great increase of Italian immigration" necessitated the formation of the Society and their success in protecting "numberless bewildered Italians" and giving "a favorable start" to persons who "will shape largely the physical, mental, and moral future of our countrymen." Gilder observed they sought a new life "in a land discovered by one Italian and named after another" (Gilder).

The Society's objectives were first "to offer advice, information, aid and protection" to Italian immigrants, to assist those "unfamiliar with the language and customs" of the USA, to help them find "remunerative occupation" and to go about "investigating and remedying...all abuses to which Italian immigrants are exposed." Their final goal was to familiarize Italian immigrants with their "rights and duties" under the Constitution" (Speranza, "Solving").

Their first goal was achieved with the opening of an office at 17 Pearl Street, where immigrants could be brought once they left Ellis Island. This sounds easier than the reality of boarding house runners, "sharpers," and others who formed a gauntlet. The Society established what they called "a corps of uniformed watchers" who "put tags of identification" on the Italians and marched them, literally under guard, to the office. One Society pamphlet featured a photo of the group along with a NYC police officer headed with determination to the office and another showing the gates of the Battery in New York with the caption "Here 'Runners' formerly fleeced the Newcomers." The pamphlet's most poignant illustration showed an Agent standing by two children "Two Orphans cared for – Their Father died in Italy and their Mother Drowned Herself in Mid Ocean" ("Society").

On one particularly difficult trip, Speranza recalled, the Society's agents took thirty-six immigrants from the Battery gates headed to 17 Pearl Street; but only seventeen made it to the Society's office ("Solving"). Once they arrived immigrants were aided through the society's Labor Bureau. This was a formidable challenge to the well-established *padrone* system. Speranza observed the *padrone* of New York "are actively using their great influence against the Italian Labor Bureau."

The Society's aim to investigate and remedy labor abuses proved far more dangerous, especially on one investigative trip to West Virginia. Speranza noted "the power of friendliness as an assimilative force" with immigrants, and conversely "the surprise among officials and contractors at the idea that an American society should be taking so much trouble for a few 'dago' shovelers." For the Italians, there was some disbelief. As Speranza observed, "They could not conceive of private citizens arraying themselves against those whom they feared...." In the end the Italian laborers aided the Society's investigation and offered testimony against their abusers, going so far as to protect Speranza's team, having "mounted guard over our shanty" ("Solving").

The Society was funded by member contributions, dues, and a grant from the Italian government ("Solving"). Although rooted in volunteerism, it also reflected the Italian government's recognition they could no longer go it alone after the recent closure of their Italian Bureau inside the Ellis Island complex. Moore's role was so little-known that the editor of *The New Outlook* wrote the society had been established "through the efforts of one patient and devoted American woman who, knowing the Italian people, believed that the qualities of character [they bring] are of value to our national life." The Society, however, also viewed Italian immigrants as little able to defend or fend for themselves: "Almost all of them are very ignorant, very child-like and wholly unfamiliar with the ways, customs and language of this country...." But the Society was also concerned what happened to them after they had been safely escorted out of New York City. Their final goal was educate the Italians in America and to begin "rectifying the bad condition of Italian laborers at contractors' camps" and that "the Society has undertaken as an experiment to run such camps" (Speranza, "Solving").

It was on their last objective that Sarah Wool Moore took the lead and quietly built her legacy. She determined that education for the Italian adults must be at the job site and proposed to test that policy in Pennsylvania. She was invited to settle in Aspinwall near the Pittsburgh Filtration Plant job site, where she established her first "Camp School" for workers. She focused on teaching English to adults, and then labored to expand the Society's educational outreach to other job sites in upstate New York.

In 1907 the New York *Times* described how Moore opened her school in a shanty after having "personal experience with the business methods of the *padrone* near her home in Mount Vernon, NY," while Italian laborers did the pick and shovel work on the New York Central railroad. She was invited to establish her school after "an appeal was made to the Society" when the original workers' settlement "proved such a menace" that neighboring homes were shuttered. Intrepid in building support, she later convinced the president of the Pittsburg Stock Exchange to become "the backer of the camp school movement in Pennsylvania" ("Camp Schools").

The Camp Schools were expanded to Wappingers Falls, New York and to the Ashokan Dam project in the Catskills. The impact of large numbers of immigrant laborers obviously worried the neighbors of other projects as well. The $161 million Ashokan Project was planned to last seven years, 1908-1915, and the *New York Times* reported all workers were required to leave, and the site "will be depopulated and eventually all the buildings will be demolished." The Society issued a circular claiming their plans would "forestall the demoralization of drink and gaming...and the many tragedies of the lonely labor camp." Construction of housing included facilities for families, a hospital and company store, and Miss Moore's school, which would educate children as well as adults. The design, the Society claimed, would appeal to "the sense of beauty [which] is never lost on the Italian" ("Italian Society").

A year later the *Times* reporter revisited the site and found both a kindergarten for the children and a night school for adults were busy, there were daily "health inspections" a school garden and clubhouses established. Referring to it as "the model camp" and noting that Moore had also funded the educational project for the first year. The *Times* also headlined "Camp has a playwright"— Giaquinto Malpezzi, a stonemason, had taken up philosophy and had created a new play on the topic "What is Man?"

Soon other major job sites had small schoolhouses and resident women teachers. By 1910 the *Times* had grown even more enthusiastic, telling its reader in "Italian Society Uplifts Immigrants" that the Society for the Protection of Italian Immigrants had not only expanded its work in New York city but established "Casa per gli Italiani," a five story shelter for immigrants, able to offer them refuge in 200 rooms as "scrupulously clean as a hospital ward." The article noted, "For work outside the city the camp school movement, started and supported by the Society under the guidance of Miss Sarah Wool Moore [these were] the first schools for adult immigrants." Moore had also expanded the camp schools to other work sites and established a multi-lingual workingman's library. Perhaps of most interest to New Yorkers the camp school had led to a "decrease in police" and "lessens the number of accidents" on the site. The strategy was to train Italians in their native language and in English the words of warning used while pouring concrete "in the hole" – the most dangerous operation on the dam ("Italian Society").

The most lasting effort of the reclusive Miss Moore was an instructional text, *Libro Illustrato di Lingua Inglese: An Illustrated English-Italian Language Book,* which she wrote in 1908. After having observed Italian workers she identified the fundamental terms and phrases that an immigrant needed to survive in the workplace. She wrote and illustrated a grammar which included Reading Lessons with useful moral lessons: A Brave Man, Petty Larceny, Work About the House, A Letter to Italy, The Drunkard, and The Trial, a few paragraphs describing how a poor and drunken immigrant fought with his boss and ended up in Sing Sing.

In one of the readings, "The Night School," Moore described what she recognized as the Italian immigrants' goal: "to learn English because they do not desire to live in America like strangers in a strange land." The final lesson, "A Word of Advice From a Naturalized American," offered advice from an imaginary immigrant who asked the reader rhetorically, "Do you wish to live well in America? Then learn the English language, honor the laws of the land, respect yourselves, aid your brothers and never oppress them, have faith in God, bear your troubles bravely, never seek a vendetta, and do nothing to dishonor the good name of Italy" (Moore). This paragraph summed up what Sarah Wool Moore wanted to convey to every Italian immigrant she could reach with her message.

Looking back on the opening years of their efforts, Speranza argued that much had been achieved "by Americans who knew little, if anything, of immigration work, with little money at their command, and still less moral support to aid them" ("Solving").

The end of Moore's career was as modestly recorded as the rest of her life. A brief death notice appeared in the New York newspapers describing her passing but offering no details. She had died while in residence at one of the Camp Schools in New York State. She left no other record of her career—no collection of personal letters has so far been found, save for a cache of childhood correspondence.[1] Her life reflected her devotion to both education and

---

[1] The authors of a 2009 catalog for a University of Nebraska exhibition on women artists seem to have been unaware that Moore had a second career with the Society for Protection of Italian Immigrants. http://www.unl.edu/plains/gallery

the betterment of Italian immigrants. On May 19, 1911 she died at the Camp School, after a brief funeral, she was buried nearby under a grave marker with the simple epitaph: "She lived for others."

A SANE, SIMPLE AND PRACTICAL PLAN: THE YMCA & ASSIMILATION

Not long after her passing a much larger organization than the Society for the Protection of Italian Immigrants became interested in the plight of the immigrant. In 1914 the Young Men's Christian Association argued that America should help immigrants become assimilated. They argued that America needed "a sane, simple, and practical plan to meet the foreigner's needs...to take the foreigner by the hand and teach him." The YMCA's Peter Roberts described the new plan that they had developed to solve what they called the "Immigrant Problem." Their focus was on the states where immigration was having the greatest impact, Massachusetts and Rhode Island.

The leader of their new Immigrant Department was a central Massachusetts mayor and reformer, Frederick Fosdick of Fitchburg. He lived in a town which had attracted large numbers of immigrants to work in its factories, and where 74% of the population was either foreign born or the children of the foreign born.

In 1914 the population of Massachusetts was 3.6 million, of which 64% were either foreign born or their children. One half of immigrants arriving in 1912 settled in four states: Massachusetts, New York, Pennsylvania and Illinois. Those destinations were then industrial centers, and Tupper of the YMCA in a report called "The Immigrant Problem" concluded it was in the interest of businessmen to support assimilation of immigrants through an educational and civic training program: "Ignorant labor is always expensive. Morality in the workingman is a valuable asset" (21). The

---

/.shtml The Moore family correspondence is at the Feinberg Library SUNY Plattsburgh.

YMCA's program differed greatly from the Ford Motor Company and International Harvester programs, which were grounded in control of the worker in the factory.[2]

The Young Men's Christian Association proposed in 1914 to launch a program of assimilation, focused on English language skills for the workplace and civics training for naturalization. The YMCA promoted their program in *Foreign Born Neighbors*, a book that presented their rationale for helping to assimilate immigrants, as a means to recruit young college men to do the work. Their focus was entirely on male immigrant labor, who they argued would become a significant proportion of the next generation of voters.

Charles W. Eliot introduced the YMCA plan by tackling the restrictionist's most potent argument, as he quoted "a high authority on heredity and eugenics" [very likely Madison Grant], expressing the IRL's worst fears: "A Harvard Class does not reproduce itself…whereas from a thousand Roumanians entering Boston today…there will come a hundred thousand descendants two hundred years hence." Eliot countered that "present rates of reproduction" may change and that Americans "have no good reason, physical or mental, for despising the recent immigrant races." He also noted that workingmen feared immigrant labor. "This competition they dread." (Tupper xiii).

The YMCA countered by arguing for assimilation, which they defined as, "the blending of the best ideals of the Old World with the best ideals of the New" (Tupper). Arguing that since their founding in 1844 the watchword was "service," they called upon members and young university men to volunteer as teachers. But the numbers of immigrants were rising. They would, however, need more than volunteerism: they also sought financial support

---

[2] For comparison see Stephen Meyer, "Adapting the Immigrant to the Line: Americanization in the Ford Factory, 1914-21" in *Journal of Social History*, 1980, 67-82. Also Gerd Korman, "Americanization at the Factory Gate," in *Industrial and Labor Relations Review*, vol 18, #3, April 1965, 396-419. Korman describe how a linguist in the YMCA program, Peter Roberts, later established factory-based programs.

from the business and financial community for their nascent program.

What had they established so far? The YMCA program was both local and international: in thirteen embarkation ports around the world they dispatched teams to connect with emigrants and City Associations developing programs throughout major destination cities. Earlier observations by the Society for Protection of Italian Immigrants and the Italian Ambassador were echoed here: Tupper argued the immigrant without English language skills required what he called "First Aid," because he was "bereft of speech" and a victim, as "runners and sharpers, American and foreign-born, pounce upon him." As an international organization, well established in Europe, the Society soon established a volunteer network in European ports, including Le Havre and Naples—both key exit points for Italians. YMCA volunteers in the USA then met the same immigrants when they arrived at Ellis Island, East Boston and elsewhere.

But their best work was being done at the local level. Since 1908 civic-minded YMCA members had been recruited to run evening English classes and courses to prepare immigrants for naturalization. The YMCA defined civic education for immigrants as "education which fits a foreign-born man to enjoy the privileges and share the obligation incident to citizenship in the US" and their goal to "weld into one American civic body the diverse interests represented by many incoming nationalities" (83). Tupper did not see "the lure of freedom and liberty" as enough to accomplish this, but instead their program demanded an immigrant's full commitment: "[I]t presupposes and demands patriotic conviction, intelligent plans and systematic efforts." To that end the YMCA needed to establish support programs. In western Massachusetts they identified cities where there were no evening schools [Massachusetts law required them in cities above 10,000 population], and organized volunteers to establish classes. By 1910 these programs expanded eastward into Worcester county and greater Boston.

In 1911 the focus shifted to one of the 25 cities with the highest foreign born population: the former mayor of Fitchburg, Frederick Fosdick, became the national leader of the YMCA's Immigrant Department but also an activist on the ground in Fitchburg. Fosdick, a business owner and committed Bull Moose reformer, devoted years of his life to promoting the YMCA program and teaching evening classes for immigrants. He was the son of a Unitarian minister and had been long-time supporter of Christian Endeavour and other missionary efforts. Fosdick's brother, Charles, a local temperance leader and co-owner of the Fitchburg Steam Engine Company, and his niece were involved in developing the YMCA's immigration program in Fitchburg. The YMCA program not only taught English but prepared immigrants for the naturalization process.[3]

Nationally the YMCA created what they called "Schools for Citizenship." These were developed as part of a four-week course to explain the fundamentals of American government at the local, state and federal levels. Instructors came armed with materials which included a set of oral examinations to prepare the candidate for the hurdles of the naturalization process.

Much like Sarah Wool Moore, who feared that immigrants' lack of language skill posed life-threatening risks in the workplace, the YMCA also focused on factory communication. English-language courses focused on dangers in the workplace and communication around safety issues. Tupper observed "where five to twenty different tongues spoken in a single factory... foreman cannot, effectively, instruct all his men as to dangers which must be avoided." And he recognized, given the high rates of illiteracy, "the inadequacy of trying to warn them by means of signs printed, even in their own language...." The YMCA presented a series of public presentations entitled "The Prevention of Accidents" for managers

---

[3] Quotations from obituaries "Frederick Fosdick, ex-mayor is dead" Fitchburg *Sentinel*, July 7, 1924 and "Charles Fosdick, Long Active in Business and Civic Life of City..." Fitchburg *Sentinel*, June 11, 1925.

struggling with high foreign-born populations, noting that one eastern Massachusetts mill had a staff of 75-80% foreign-born laborers, while another had 2,000 employees unable to speak English. (Tupper, 85-86, and 97).

When Charles Fosdick died in 1925, his obituary highlighted his commitment to mentoring "those who entered his shop as young men" and that he "went a long way in helping them to develop...both in and out of the shop..." Fosdick had spent several years as an evening course instructor, while managing both the Fitchburg Steam Engine Company and the Willard Screen Plate Company.

But what results were achieved? There was little record of the program remaining. I interviewed the daughter of an Italian immigrant who arrived in Fitchburg in 1907, from the Veneto. She recalled how her father attended evening school to learn English from a young woman he happily referred to as "Bella, bella Miss Fosdick." She encouraged him to learn English and guided his transition to American life. Miss Fosdick particularly encouraged him to establish some small business and begin the naturalization process. Giovanni Moretto applied himself to English classes and worked as a tailor. In 1922 he took out first papers for citizenship and by 1926 was a naturalized American citizen with a grocery store, who later owned a men's custom tailoring business, and had seven children (Moretto).

Once begun on the path, Italian immigrants could establish their own means of aiding others. Many communities in Massachusetts had Italian American Clubs (many founded in the 1930s) and many more *mutuo succorso* (mutual benefit) clubs. But, quite a bit earlier, in neighboring Leominster, Massachusetts a small group of Italian immigrants organized a club devoted to encouraging naturalization and full participation in American society.

Giovanni Antonucci and a small group of immigrants from Corfinio, Italy worked together to establish the Italian American Citizens Club in Leominster, Massachusetts in 1910. Their goal, in establishing one of the earliest organizations of its kind, was to encourage and guide their fellow Italians on the road to naturalization and citizenship, and also to build their community's political influence. By the 1930s the group had a 25-man Political Committee and was actively sponsoring Italian candidates for City Council and mayoral races. Candidates actively sought their support, and the committee helped a number of Italian Americans to positions on the City Council. After World War II they went to work guiding the next generation, young veterans, into civil-service jobs. Many became businessmen and Italian "firsts" as members of the fire department and police force (Antonucci).

In conclusion, Italians desperately needed help from Americans when they first arrived. In 1904 Sarah Wool Moore's collaborator, Speranza, criticized Americans' assumption that assimilation would naturally occur: "Many imagine that the record and strength of the American democracy suffice of themselves to make the foreigner love the new land and engender in him a desire to serve it; that, in other words, assimilation is the natural tendency." But Speranza argued that assimilation required effort on both sides: "Assimilation is a dual process of forces interacting one upon the other. Economically, this country can act like a magnet in drawing the foreigner to these shores, but you cannot rely on its magnetic force to make the foreign an *American*. To bring about assimilation the larger mass should not remain passive" ("How," 458). He concluded that assimilation would fail unless action Americans took action to integrate them: "[I]f [immigrants] herd into great and menacing city colonies, if they do not learn your language, if they know little about your country, the fault is as much yours as theirs" (458).

Sarah Wool Moore's life work stands as the model of the American as assimilationist. She created the Society for the Protection of Italian Immigrants, helping to build an organization that literally took the Italians under guard to safety. She then wrote a textbook to teach them the language skills they desperately needed, and organized volunteers and financial support to integrate them into the educational system. She lived the life of sacrifice she encouraged others to follow. In the efforts of the Fosdicks and the YMCA program lie the furtherance and national expansion of Moore's early efforts.

At a time when restrictionists encouraged fear and lobbied Congress to shut the "unguarded gates" at Ellis Island, Sarah Wool Moore quietly built a model of assimilation that helped many Italians to find their way into American life and ultimately put them on the path to citizenship.

Works Cited

Abbott, Ernest Hamlin and Lyman Abbott. "The Establishment of Night Schools in the Great Labor Camps." *The Outlook*, 88, 24 January 1908, 244-248.

Antonucci, Robert V. President, Fitchburg State University. Personal interview. 6 November 2012.

"Camp Schools for Italian Laborers." *American Educational Review*, 28, #1, October 1906.

"Camp School for Italian Laborers to be Installed Among Erie Canal Workers..." *New York Times* 6 October 1907.

"City to be Built at Ashokan Dam...Workers to go to School." *New York Times*, 7 September 1908.

Corfinio Club Records, Leominster Historical Society, Leominster, Massachusetts.

Einaudi, Luigi, translator. "La Distribuzione Della Ricchezza nel Massachusetts" *Giornale degli Economisti*, XIV, Bologna: Tipografia Alfonso Garagnani e figli, Marzo 1897.

Ferraris, Prof. Carlo. *Il Movimento Generale dell'Emigrazione Italiana: suoi caratteri ed effeti*. Estratto dal Bollettino dell'Emigrazione, 5, anno 1909, Roma, 1909.

Gilder, Richard W. "Letter to the editor re: Society for the Protection of Italian Immigrants." *New York Times* 23 March 1903.

Hall, Robert C. "Camp Schools and the State." *Charities and the Commons*, XVII, #20, New York, 16 February1907, 892-893.

"Italian Society Uplifts Immigrants." *New York Times* 20 February 1910.

Immigration Restriction League manuscript collection. Houghton Library, Harvard University, Cambridge, Mass.

Immigration Restriction League. "The Present Italian Influx, Its Striking Illiteracy." [undated].

Italian American Citizens' Club records, Leominster, Massachusetts, 1910-1964, Fitchburg State University Amelia Gallucci-Cirio Library Archives, MS 27, boxes 1 and 2.

Kennedy, Sharon L. "Artists as Teachers: Sarah Wool Moore, Cora Parker and Sarah Sewell Hayden." University of Nebraska, Lincoln. n.d. Web. September 2010. Publications of the Immigration Restriction League, No. 14, 1896. Houghton Library, Harvard University, Cambridge, Mass.

Kennedy, Sharon. "Early Nebraska Women Artists, 1880-1950." Web accessed Resource Library, http://www.unl.edu/plains/gallery/gallery.shtml

Korman, Gerd. "Americanization at the Factory Gate." [electronic version] *Industrial and Labor Relations Review*, 18, 1965, 396-419.

"Model Camp Built at Ashokan Dam." *New York Times* 2 May 1909.

Moore, Sarah Wool. *An Illustrated English-Italian Language Book and Reader*. Boston: D.C. Heath Publishers, 1902. Alternate title of 1908 reprint: *Libro illustrato di lingua inglese*.

_____. "Near Recollections: Notes on Camp School, No. 1 Aspinwall, Penn." *Charities and the Commons: A Weekly Journal of Philanthropy and Social Advance*, XVII, 20, 16 February 1907.

_____. "School in Camps—The Teaching of Foreigners." *Survey*, 24, 4 June 1910, 386-391.

Moore family papers, Special Collections, Benjamin F. Feinberg Library, State University of New York, Plattsburgh, NY

Moorhead, Elizabeth. "A School for Italian Laborers." *The Outlook A Weekly Newspaper*, LXXXVIII, New York: The Outlook Company, 29 February 1908, 499-504.

Moretto, Bianca. Personal interview. 28 June 2012.

Obituary of Sarah Wool Moore. *Bible Society Record*. 56-58, Astor Place, NY: American Bible Society, [unsigned, undated].

Obituary of Sarah Wool Moore [unsigned]. *New York Times* 21 May 1911.

Prince, Prof. J. Dyneley. "Educating the Adult Immigrant." *Charities and the Commons*, XVII, #20, New York, 16 February 1907, 890-891.

"Society for the Protection of Italian Immigrants." Editorial by William B. Howland, *The Outlook*, 16 April 1904, 911-912.

Speranza, Gino. "The Alien in Relation to Our Laws." *Annals of the American Academy of Political and Social Science*, 52, March 1914, 169-176.

_____. "How It Feels to Be a Problem: A Consideration of Certain Causes Which Prevent or Retard Assimilation." *Charities*, XII, #18, May 1904, 457-463.

_____. "Solving the Immigration Problem." *New Outlook*, 16 April 1904, 928-933.

Tupper, George William. *Foreign-Born Neighbors*, Boston: The Taylor Press, 1914.

Wells, Fred N. "The Nebraska Art Association," web resource, published 1972, the Regents of the University of Nebraska.

Early Deaths in the Italian Enclaves at the Turn of the 20th Century
A Great Granddaughter's Perspective

Alexandra de Luise

On Christmas morning in the year 1896, a three-month-old baby by the name Gaetano, surrounded by his mother and father, dies of a gastrointestinal ailmrent in the Italian enclave of East Harlem, New York. Three years later in 1899, also on Christmas day, a second son is born into this family and is given the same name, Gaetano. The mother and father are my great grandparents, immigrants from the Campania region of Italy. So begins my undertaking into the sad history of infant mortality and mourning rituals by southern Italian immigrants living in New York City during the turn of the twentieth century.

Italian Americans follow rituals of remembrance and honor initiated by their Italian descendants who came before them. Some Italian rituals that began in the late Roman era still continue today, including one by southern Italians of baking small cookies shaped like bones called *ossa dei morti*. On All Saints Day, they place them on the graves of their loved ones. In this same spirit of commemoration, this essay will consider the babies born to the first wave of Italian immigrants who did not live beyond their second birthdays and who died in the Italian enclaves of New York City between 1890 and 1910. My focus is to understand the then-prevalent attitudes toward infant mortality. I will reflect on the babies' illnesses and the parents' ritualized expressions of grief, and the possible folk remedies used which might have even contributed to their babies' decline and early deaths.

It is estimated that roughly half a million Italians, including those children born to them in the U.S., were living in the greater New York area by 1903.[5] Newspaper accounts of that time noted that contagious diseases ravaged entire blocks in the Italian enclaves, where tenements held large families living in close quarters and in unsanitary conditions. Discouraged by their faith to practice birth control, large Italian families were common. Those with many children often experienced the death of a few, a pattern I uncovered within my own family. Having another baby soon after one had died helped comfort the grieving households. The deaths of these earlier offspring were not spoken of, their names not mentioned, their simple burial plot locations not divulged. Why the silence? Was it cultural, religious, or as the writer Mary Jo Bona put it, part of a survival mentality? (176)

What we do know is that babies of Italian immigrants received a warm welcome into the world. Few could rival Italian immigrants in their family celebration of the birth of a baby. Neighbors were invited over to feast at this happy event. When more children were born, it was often the older but still young daughter who cared for her baby brother or sister, often taking on the babysitting duties of the mother. Before the older daughter had a chance to achieve maturity, she became a bride.

Many Italian immigrant girls at the turn of the twentieth century were married and pregnant with their first baby by age 15. The burdens of having children so young and in such rapid a succession were great for them, so much so that they already were considered little old women by the time they reached adulthood. In order to escape this cycle, a young girl needed to attend school, which would lead to better opportunities in life. Unfortunately, many Italian girls of this first generation were relegated to assisting with housekeeping or family-run businesses or had parents who

---

[5] These figures are an estimate owing to the frequent back and forth by Italians ("birds of passage"), as well as unreliable census report figures, and the tendency to hide the real number of occupants living a dwelling. See Mangano 8.

regarded school as alien, and thus did not receive adequate educations. Their only option was to marry at a young age, trapping them inside their familiar, closed surroundings.

Living in the tenements would have an affect on their own health. Early chroniclers of Italian immigrants such as Eliot Lord, noted that young Italian females went from the fresh open air of their rural Italian villages to the oppressive, small tenements of urban America. The change would result in damage to their bodies, making them susceptible to intestinal problems, thus negatively impacting their children (200)

In many Italian communities in America, a large number of babies and small children succumbed to respiratory and gastrointestinal illnesses. In the summer especially, with its terrible heat, it took little for ill children to die. Newspaper accounts of the time noted that fresh air and sunlight, obtained simply by utilizing the tenement roofs upstairs, would have would have been a great defense against certain illnesses.

In spite of the immigrants' inherent distrust of doctors—some who might have insisted that a family be quarantined, or who were believed to be the ones responsible for spreading germs—several Italian-born and trained physicians catered specifically to this group living in the enclaves of New York City. These Italian doctors were critical of the southern Italian immigrant mentality that taught them "to accept death as the inexorable will of God" (Serra 139). Through listening to the immigrants' personal stories the physicians sought to change their thinking. They encouraged these southern Italians to give up their folk remedies and accept western medicine. They were, in Alan Kraut's words, "vocal and active adversaries of the poverty and congestion that allowed disease to breed and spread..." (108).

One doctor in particular, the tuberculosis specialist Dr. Antonio Stella, made a series of very public pronouncements about the Italians during the first decade of the twentieth century. He examined New York City's Italian enclaves of Little Italy and East Harlem where the death rate was particularly high. He reported that the children of Italian immigrants under five years old had the highest death rate from diseases of the respiratory tract and diarrheal diseases, five and three times respectively that of the entire city (Stella 14). American reformers tried to convince the public that inherent enfeeblement was the root cause of Italians' bad health in America. Instead, Stella faulted the lack of fresh air and crowded conditions as the basis for the babies' deteriorating health (21).

Despite this, the public perception was that Italian immigrants living in the tenements were unfit to care for their babies. Jacob Riis, the renowned photographer and social reformer wrote that southern Italians were often victims of ignorance, who refused to go to the hospital. Infant mortality would be seen as a problem of uneducated mothers.

Collected data from the 1900 United States Federal Census indicated a relationship between child mortality and literacy of both parents. Child mortality was higher for the illiterate and highest when both spouses were illiterate. The husband's literacy could have an effect on his children's mortality, reflecting his own economic status (Preston and Haines 150). Taking in boarders in the tenements also affected a child's survival. Boarders (lodgers who rented a room or a space) were a source of infection and a "burden on the mother's time" (168).

Italians exported to America their own ways of doing things, including the superstitions and rituals that were part of southern Italy's culture. Many of the *contadini* or farmers, who came to America, arrived with some basic notions about death. These were a blend of religion and folk beliefs, of going to a promised land (Heaven), reward for a life well lived, and punishment for not having lived a good life. Fatalism to not expect much out of life pervaded their thinking. *Pazienza* (or patience) said aloud, "assumed one should not expect a great deal from life and disappointment (would) therefore be minimized"(Kraut, 130).

Folk beliefs contributed to some of the unhealthy decisions made by southern Italian immigrants once in America. One of them was keeping the tenement windows closed shut to not let air circulate. There was the belief that the soul of the recently departed would try to return home through an open window. Another suspicion was that evil spirits would enter through open windows and cast spells on the family. With such beliefs accepted as fact, windows were kept closed, foul air was breathed in and lack of ventilation caused illnesses to spread.

The folk tradition that certain Italian immigrant women followed was in the *malocchio* (evil eye), used to counter perceived envy by others. Phyllis Williams noted how those who did not say *"Dio benedica"* ("God bless you") after any acknowledgement of a pretty baby or a talent or achievement, were branded as having the evil eye (143).

The following narrative underscored this belief;

> A story is told of a group who was meeting at a friend's house where a woman was also attending suspected of having the evil eye. A young mother with her baby was there, too. Everyone said something complimentary about the baby, except the woman. After all went home, the mother went into despair, suspecting that that the baby had been given the evil eye by the other woman. She went to the doctor who prescribed a change in diet, which the mother halfheartedly followed for the baby. She depended more on the advice of Italian women skilled in the art of folk medicine. Lemons were pierced with pins with their ends cut off, strings were knotted, and sacred cakes were baked and placed at the feet of a patron saint. It was of no use; the baby died (154).

The culture in post Victorian-era America was not to weep for the death of a child, but to keep one's self control. The sense of loss was overtaken by the reasoning that the child had achieved a far better destiny than he or she might have had on earth. Customs concerning the death and burial of a child brought about a conflict between cultural norms and sadness felt by the bereaved parents. Resisting the urge to cry could not help but move one's neighbors.

Since most Italian immigrant families experienced one, if not several, such baby losses, there was a shared sympathy amongst those living close by. The overwhelming sense of loss gave way to a survivalist mentality that helped ease the grief.

Italians' coping abilities and sense of sorrow were no different in Italy during this same time period. Giuseppe Pitrè, the Italian folklorist, described how seated before the dead baby with female family and friends nearby, the Italian mother wouldn't cry; to do otherwise would be an offense to God who called the child to heaven. The announcement of the death of a child was received with a consolatory exclamation, "Glory and Paradise!" Rituals like these derived from the Roman period. Pitrè recounted how bells would ring merrily and joyous music would accompany the funeral procession to the cemetery to commemorate the child's death and short life (241)

Another way to channel grief was to reuse the names of babies. This was a way to honor the deceased who had died very young. In the case of my great grandmother, the second son was named after the deceased first son, and having been born on the same day as his death seemed to also suggest the hope for a rebirth into his body.

During this period when baby mortality was high, and extreme poverty common, many were buried simply and in the same plots. It was cheaper to bury children together, because they took up so much less space than adults. In some instances, babies were buried with their parents in a family plot. If there was a gravestone, it might only be inscribed with the names of the mother and father, not the babies buried along with them, a situation I uncovered in the case of my great-great uncle and aunt buried in Calvary Cemetery in Woodside, N.Y. with their five babies whose internment record I obtained. Other times it was the funeral home or the cemetery itself that donated the plot, but not a gravestone, leaving behind only a patch of grass.

After more than a century, these short lives are coming to light. One could wish it were on account of the discovery of diaries, letters or family stories carried down generation to generation, but to this writer's opinion, it would not be the case. Such an idea would run counter to the Italian character of not talking about the past, particularly a sad one. Instead, these babies' existences have come to light through the easy availability of online genealogy programs (ie, Ancestry.com and Italiangen.org.).

From these descriptions, it is evident that there was a combination of factors contributing to the early deaths of Italian immigrant babies in the tenements: the health and welfare of the mother; the overcrowded and unventilated conditions of the tenements that led to spread of diseases; the reliance on folk remedies; the lack of faith in medical institutions and its practitioners; and the Italian parents' illiteracy and the unawareness of social services. These all were all strikes against the baby. Eventually, southern Italian immigrants living in the U.S. conformed and accepted American standards of hygiene and health. As Alan Kraut notes:

> The path to conformity was neither short nor straight, sometimes taking more than a generation or two. Strong cultural ties bound Italians to their unique definitions of health, and to a belief system that was a synthesis of Christian and pagan traditions... Italian immigrants' resistance to alien ways and intrusions from those unrelated to them by blood or Old World regional bonds proved a powerful obstacle... (134)

In the late nineteenth century in New York City, southern Italian immigrants endured many hardships while trying to adapt and survive in American society. Although modern historians might easily conclude that Italians were a group whose babies' deaths went largely "passed over, with little ceremony or not even marked at all" (Davies 159), it is evident the apparent indifference was a matter of limited resources, the mother's attention needed by the family and show of strength for those who still lived and carried on. In spite of the appalling conditions in which they found themselves, most Italian immigrant families went to great lengths to protect and save their children, wishing for a different outcome than death. The emotional and social role children had in Italian immigrants' lives would have demanded nothing less.

WORKS CITED

Bona, Mary Jo."What They Talk About When They Talk About Death." *By the Breath of Their Mouths: Narratives of Resistance in Italian America*. SUNY series in Italian/American Culture. Albany: State University of New York Press, 2010. 175-209. Print.

Davies, Douglas James. *A brief history of death*. Malden, MA: Blackwell Pub., 2005. Print.

Kraut, Alan M. "That is the American Way and in America you should do as Americans do," *Silent Travelers: Germs, Genes and the 'Immigrant Menace.'* Baltimore: Johns Hopkins University Press, 1995. 105-135. Print.

Lord, Eliot, John J. D. Trenor, and Samuel J. Barrows. *The Italian in America*. New York: B.F. Buck & Co., 1905. Print.

Mangano, Antonio. "The Italian Colonies of New York City." *Italians in the City: Health and Related Social Needs*. 1903 reprint ed. New York: Arno 1975. 1-57. Print. Pitrè, Giuseppe, *Usi e Costume, Credenze e Pregiudizi del Popolo Siciliano*, v.2. Florence, G. Barbera, 1939. Print.

Preston, Samuel H., and Michael R. Haines. *Fatal years: Child Mortality in Late Nineteenth-Century America*. Princeton, N.J.: Princeton University Press, 1991. Print.

Serra, Ilaria. *The Value of Worthless Lives: Writing Italian American Immigrant Autobiographies*. New York: Fordham University Press, 2007. Print.

Staffa, Antonio. "The Effects of Urban Congestion on Italian Women and Children.' *Italians in the City: Health and Related Social Needs*. 1903 reprint ed. New York: Arno, 1975. 3-36. Print. The Italian American Experience.

Williams, Phyllis H.. *South Italian Folkways in Europe and America. A Handbook for Social Workers, Visiting Nurses, School Teachers, and Physicians*. New York: Russell & Russell, 1938. Print.

Italianità Americana: A Study of Ethnic Identity Among Second-, Third-, and Third-Plus-Generation Italian Americans

Angelyn Balodimas-Bartolomei

For decades, social scientists have studied the ethnic identity of immigrants and their offspring. In seeking to explain the complex processes and degrees of generational ethnicity, frequent debates have occurred regarding the dichotomy of assimilation versus pluralism. Although Alba and Chamlin claimed in 1983 that ethnic identity issues had received little attention in empirical literature, numerous works were and still are being published on various groups including the Italian Americans. Such studies continuously attempt to examine the distinctive ethnic traits, characteristics, experiences and identity of the Italian Americans. Fred Gardaphè ("Identical") explains:

> For more than one hundred years, Italian American artists have been defining and documenting the Italian experience in America; yet Italian Americans are still very much at a loss for who they are. In less than three generations, Italian Americans have assimilated so rapidly and so well into the American way that they have become strangers, not only to contemporary Italians, but strangers unto themselves. This alienation can be observed in the experience of many Italian American writers.

One of the first to write about Italian Americans was Philip Marshman Rose. In 1922, his manuscript "The Italians in America" appeared in the Interchurch World Movement's New American series. In the book's introduction, it is noted that the series consisted of studies on various "racial groups"—the term used to describe and categorize different ethnic groups during that time period. Among the studied groups were the Albanian, Bulgarian, Armenian, Assyrian, Chaldean, Czecho-Slovak, Greek, Italian, Jewish, Jugo-Slav (Croatian, Servian, Slovenian) Magyar, Polish, Russian and Ruthenian, or Ukrainian, Spanish (Spaniards) Portuguese, and Syrian and additionally, the Eastern Orthodox Church. It was believed that the publications would "help America appreciate and appropriate the spiritual wealth represented by the vast body of new Americans, each group having its own peculiarities and potentialities" (Rose).

In a section on intermarriage (76), Rose provides the 1915 U.S. Bureau of Census percentages of second generation Italian Americans born to Italian fathers in Connecticut, New York, Rhode Island, Massachusetts and Pennsylvania. Rose marvels at how "the second generation Italian stock is a great asset to the United States." In discussing their second generation identity he writes:

> It is difficult to follow them as a separate group. Yet some things we know of them. It has been observed of them that many belong to a detached group, "neither really Italians nor yet Americans" (Rev. F. G. Urbano quoted by Mangano)

Rose describes their newly formed affection for Italy and Italian identity as:

> Many a provincial Italian, who never knew of or cared aught for the ideal of native land at home, finds developing early a new affection for Italy and his *"Italianità"* or racial heritage. (Marshman Rose 72)

One of the first books to extensively examine Italian American Identity was *Blood of My Blood*, published in 1974. The author, Richard Gambino, refers to third and fourth-generation Italian Americans who had entered the third stage of their ethnic journey. He explains that they could take one of two paths—one in which they would become jellyfish Americans having transparent souls and a non-identity or the other path that would allow them to revitalize and transform their old traditions—*la via vecchia*, into modern terms. He insisted that the latter could enrich American culture but would require an educated ethnic awareness or consciousness for this to happen.

While Krase states that most social scientists would agree that Italian Americans have integrated well into American society, Iorrizo and Rossi maintain that there are still those "elites" who believe in the "pluralist" version of assimilation, holding on to memory, desire, and nostalgia, and a quantity of *Italianità*. Such Italian Americans continue to carry on old customs, cuisine, and religion—all qualities that influence the broader American community. Many still recognize cultural differences rooted in the distinctive regional cultures of northern, central, and southern Italy, and Sicily (Quagliata); however, as contemporary studies have shown, the aforementioned are rare examples.

Today's Italian Americans are completely immersed into the American mainstream and fully participating in the American social, economic, and political systems. While several still maintain links to Italy and socialize with other Italian Americans in the United States, they are firmly tied to this country with their bonds growing stronger to America and weaker to Italy every day (Iorrizo & Rossi; Quagliata). Although the majority belong to the Roman Catholic Church, almost half of recent generations have intermarried with Catholics of other ethnic backgrounds or with people from different denominations, such as American Protestants and Jews (Quagliata). Church attendance is often nominal (Monti). They are marrying at a later age and divorcing more (Mangione & Morreale). Many no longer speak the Italian language, read Italian literature, follow Italian politics, uphold traditional beliefs or belong to Italian cultural organizations in the United States (Iorrizo & Rossi; Quagliata; Monti). Claiming that all of these declining characteristics are normal and expected, Iorizzo & Rossi are confident that as long as ethnic groups remain a distinctive feature of

America, the Italian Americans will continue to be represented as a group in modified form (Iorizzo & Rossi).

Several contemporary scholars have confirmed how the new "ethnogenesis" that assimilated Italian Americans have adopted is an ethnic identity quite different than that what their Italian ancestors brought over from the old country (Ferraro; Gardaphè, "Identical"; Iorizzo & Rossi; Tamburri, qtd. in Giorgi). When analyzing the terms "Italians" and "Italian Americans," Fred Gardaphè states that although there is a familiar word connecting the two, "Italian Americans are as different from Italians as the egg is different from the eggplant" (Gardaphè 4). It is rather difficult to provide a definition for the Italian American identity since there are many characterizations and different types of Italian Americans. Ferraro explains that feeling Italian has a double meaning, for one can feel like an Italian in ways that Italians in Italy feel, while also having recognizable or non-recognizable Italian or "Italianate" types of feelings. One can also feel that his/her identity is Italian or Italian-like without taking into consideration origin or ancestry. Renowned sociologist, Herbert Gans ("Making") states that the term "Italian" has become shorthand for "Italian American" since many, especially those living in large cities with Italian communities, tend to identify themselves as Italian without reference to the United States. Ferraro questions what it means to be an Italian American today, in this age of political correctness and virtual reality, and after the so-called twilight of ethnicity, which Alba claimed Italian Americans had reached several years ago (Ferraro).

A number of present-day scholars have provided a new interpretation of the Italian American identity while challenging Alba's twilight of ethnicity and/or Gans' Symbolic Identity theories. According to Marie-Christine Michaud, Italian Americans have transformed their original identity into an ethnic identity called "Italian-Americanness"—something quite different from the Italian identity of their ancestors. She states that Italian Americans are products of this country, even though they do not speak the language and many have not visited the ancestral country, they feel extremely Italian! Being born in this country without feeling marginalized allows them to use their symbols of ethnicity, which Michaud claims are more than Gans's "mere tokens of feeling." She claims that their symbolic ethnicity is a form of updated memory or usable past as described by Anagnostou. Through personal choice or option, a concept coined by Mary Waters, they are able to use their symbols to display their pride, ethnicity and Italian identity appropriately. Vecoli also reasons that such ethnic symbols are significant for keeping the heritage alive. Michaud maintains that Italian-Americanness has reached its "zenith" and has not faded into the twilight as Alba implied.

Boscia-Mulè finds Gans's "leisure-time ethnicity" hypothesis problematic. Throughout her study on third-generation Italian Americans, her respondents' ethnicity did not appear to be symbolic, individualistic, acontextual or leisure time as Gans suggested. Even though their understanding of the Italian American culture was limited, they had a strong sense of ethnic identity, which is logically sustained through a network of primary and family ties. Ethnicity plays a more significant role in their private lives. They live "diverse" styles of Italianness.

According to Monti, Gans's formulation draws too sharp a distinction between the successful middle class and the less fortunate who have not yet succeeded and probably never will. It is the latter group that is expected to carry on the traditions. Arguing that an ethnic group might display signs of assimilation while retaining signs of ethnic character, Monti points out that there are many middle-class Italian Americans who mirror Gans's symbolic ethnicity. They have married non-Italians and do not speak the language or carry on the customs, but they greatly contribute to the Italian community through their involvement in ethnic organizations. Then again, there are many working-class Italian Americans who, while still upholding the Italian traditions, are not interested in community involvement. Thus, both sets of Italian Americans are contributing to the Italian community. Monti asserts that ethnic people can and should have their feet in two worlds simultaneously.

Consequently, Italian American ethnicity has been transformed, reborn and reinvented as Gambino proposed forty years ago. Judging from the increased interest of ethnicity among the third and fourth-generation Italian Americans in Chicago, Domenic Candeloro believes that future generations of Italians may have an even stronger and more sophisticated ethnic identity than their second-generation grandparents.

Whereas numerous works have been published on Italian Americans, there is a need to examine and gather first-hand information through interviews and questionnaires from Italian Americans on their current Italian American identity. The present study investigates the stances and views of second, third and third-plus Italian Americans on issues regarding Italianness or *Italianità Americana*.

The Present Study

The present study was conducted on 135 Italian Americans in Chicago from 2009-2012. The majority of the participants were from Illinois with a small number from other states. All participants were at least eighteen years old at the time of the study. Thirty-three participants were second-generation Italian Americans, sixty were third-generation and forty-two were third/third-plus-generation. In order to have a more balanced study, the third generation and third-plus were placed in the same category.

In this study, the generations are categorized according to the U.S. Census report:

SECOND GENERATION: Born in the USA; a US citizen by birth; having at least one foreign born parent
THIRD or THIRD-PLUS GENERATION: Born in USA; a US citizen by birth; having both parents and grandparents born in the USA

Through the distribution of a questionnaire designed for the Italian community, the project attempted to analyze previous theories and determine what correlations exist with data on current second, third, and third-plus-generation Italian Americans. The participants were chosen randomly from advertisements in Italian ethnic newspapers and organizations, American universities, and word of mouth, especially through the Internet.

The results of the study provide the participants' interpretations on various views and issues affecting the community and ethnicity. The questionnaire is divided into seven sections:

- Section I: Socio-demographic information of the participants
- Section II: Involvement in Italian community
- Section III: Viewpoints on ethnic identity and heritage
- Section IV: Contact with Italy through travel and media
- Section V: Religion, holidays and marriage
- Section VI: Ethnic customs, traditions, cuisine, music and dance
- Section VII: Italian language and instruction

SECTION 1: SOCIO-DEMOGRAPHICS
RESULTS FROM TABLE 1:

GENDER: The study was slightly tilted in the direction of females within the second-generation (63.9%) and third/third-plus-generation (54.1%) categories.

AGE: The age spread was roughly divided among generations. Forty percent of second generation participants were between twenty and thirty nine years old, followed by 37.1 percent between sixty and eighty nine years old. In the third/third plus category, 51.9 percent were between twenty and thirty nine years old, followed by those between forty and fifty-nine years old (29.2%).

HERITAGE: More than half of the second generation respondents (61.1%) had parents with Italian heritage on both sides, with fewer in the third/third plus group (45%). Heritage only on the side of the fathers was somewhat higher among the third/third plus generation.

MARITAL STATUS: Around half of all participants were married. Very few were divorced or widowed, although the percentage was doubled among second generation.

EDUCATION: Around half of the second generation (47.2%) and third/third plus participants (56.0%) had only obtained a high school degree, associate degree or some type of certificate as their highest level of education. Nearly one third of the second generation (30.6%) and one fifth (22.9%) of the third/third plus had earned a bachelor's degree. Master's degrees and PhDs were earned by 22.2 percent of the second-generation and 21.1 percent of the third/third plus-generation groups.

DUAL CITIZENSHIP: Only 19.4 percent of second generation had dual citizenship with barely any among the third/third plus group (2.8%).

TOP THREE PROFESSIONS OF PARTICIPANTS (NOT IN TABLE): The top three professions among the participants were: Teacher, Student, and Attorney, followed by Professor, Sales/Retail Manager.

Section II—Involvement in Italian Community
Summary of Section 2: Table 2

INVOLVEMENT IN ITALIAN COMMUNITY: Over half of second generation (61.1%) and third/third plus (51.4) respondents consider themselves a part of the Italian community. Participants specifying such proceeded to answer the next eight questions concerning ethnic community involvement. Fifty-nine percent are currently active in the Italian community. Participants in both groups with slightly more in the third/third plus, believe that Italian community involvement is very important. Slightly lower percentages of both groups gain much satisfaction when being involved in Italian social events. The majority of second- (85.7 %) and third/third plus-participants (69.2%) are satisfied with their level of involvement, although many second generation (66.7%) and third/third plus (72.7%) would like to be more involved.

SOCIALIZING IN NON-ITALIAN CIRCLES: Although over half of the second generation, and even more from the third/third plus group are satisfied when engaging in Italian community social events, only one third responded that the majority of their friends are Italian Americans. Neither the second- nor the third/third plus-generation participants feel left out when socializing in non-Italian circles of acquaintances.

Section III—Ethnic Identity and Culture
Summary of Section 3: Table 3

ETHNIC IDENTITY: 80 percent of second-generation participants are very conscious or preoccupied with their Italian identity; however, there is a decrease of about 14 percent among third/third plus generations. At least 65 percent of all participants refer to themselves as Italian Americans when asked to define their nationality. An overwhelming majority is very proud of its Italian identity.

PROMOTING AND SUPPORTING ITALIANISM: Over half of all participants and even more in the third/third plus group believe that Italian Americans should participate as fully as possible in their ethnic community and that they also have a duty to educate others about Italian culture, heritage and history. Over half of the second generation and nearly three fourths of the third/third plus believe that Italian Americans should stay together as a closely-knit group in order to keep the culture alive. Very few respondents believe that uninvolved Italian Americans are less respected by fellow Italians.

ITALIAN FAMILY: Nearly all of the participants strongly believe that the family is very important in keeping the Italian heritage alive.

SECTION IV-CONTACT WITH ITALY THROUGH TRAVEL AND MEDIA
SUMMARY OF SECTION 4: TABLE 4

RELATIVES IN ITALY: Nearly all (91.7%) second-generation participants still have relatives in Italy, as do 72.4 percent of the third/third plus group.
INTEREST IN ITALY: The majority of participants are somewhat interested in Italy's future with only a mere six percent expressing their indifference.
VISITS TO ITALY: Most second- (88.6%) and third/third plus-generation (69.7%) participants believe that Italian Americans should visit Italy at least once in their lifetimes. Half of the second-generation participants travel to Italy every four to ten years, with only 38.5 percent from the third/third plus group doing so. Very few participants travel to Italy every two to four years and barely any visit every year. Most second-generation Italian Americans have traveled at least once to Italy whereas nearly half of the third/third plus participants have never visited.

CONTACTS WITH ITALY: Over half of the second generation, but very few from the third/third plus group corresponds frequently or occasionally with someone in Italy via email or by telephone.

ITALIAN MEDIA: Italian Americans do not appear to follow media: nearly 70 percent of the participants never listen to Italian radio; only half of the second generation and few from the third/third plus group occasionally watch Italian TV programs and hardly any subscribe to Italian satellite. Whereas only about half of the participants still read Italian newspapers and magazines, the majority stays informed about Italy through the internet.

SECTION V-RELIGION, HOLIDAYS & MARRIAGE
SUMMARY OF SECTION 5: TABLE 5

CATHOLICISM: Nearly all participants celebrate Catholic holidays to some extents. Third/third plus-generation Italian Americans supposedly attend church more frequently than the second generation group. Very few third/third plus never attend; however, a higher percentage admitted to attending only to please the parents. Involvement in other faiths was not polled.
ITALIAN TRADITIONS & CUSTOMS: Italian traditions and customs are intertwined in most participants' celebration of American holidays, with numbers slightly declining among the third/third plus group.

INTERMARRIAGE: Less than half of the respondents feel that intermarriage has influenced their practice of Catholicism. Very few participants believe that it is important to marry a fellow Italian American.

Section VI-Ethnic Customs, Traditions, Cuisine, Music and Dance
Summary of Section 6: Table 6

ITALIAN TRADITIONS, CUSTOMS & CELEBRATIONS: Whereas nearly all of the participants still retain many Italian customs and traditions, the majority and especially the third/third plus group admitted that the maintenance of such has somewhat changed or weakened over the years due to intermarriage. Although there is a decrease among the third/third plus generation in celebrating the birth of a child and a wedding traditionally, the death of a loved one is still intertwined with Italian traditions and customs by 85 percent of all participants.

ITALIAN DÉCOR & ARTIFACTS: Italian Americans and especially those from the second generation still appear to decorate their houses with Italian artifacts.

ITALIAN CUISINE: The Italian cuisine is still strongly maintained by all of the participants.

ITALIAN MUSIC AND DANCING: A strong 89 percent of all participants enjoy listening to Italian music. Whereas the majority of the second generation group enjoy traditional Italian dancing the percentage declines greatly among the third/third plus group.

Section VII-Ethnic Language
Summary of Section 7: Table 7

VIEWS ABOUT SPEAKING ITALIAN: Whereas more than half of the second generation participants feel that Italian Americans should speak Italian among their peers and at home, the percentages drop greatly among the third/third plus group.

VIEWS ABOUT ITALIAN SCHOOL: Nearly half of all participants desire to raise their children in an Italian environment. Over half of the second-generation participants feel that children should attend Italian school with only one third of the third/third plus group agreeing.

ITALIAN LANGUAGE SKILLS & USAGE OF LANGUAGE: Very few participants attended Italian school as children. More than half of the second-generation participants and a mere 9.3 percent of the third/third plus grew up speaking Italian. Only 27.8 percent of second-generation and 4.7 percent of the third/third plus-generation speak Italian at home today. The majority of second- (70%) and third/third plus-generation (89%) participants never spoke Italian among friends. Thus it is understandable that whereas 58.3 percent of second generation feels comfortable speaking Italian, only 21.5 percent of the third/third plus participants do.

ITALIAN LANGUAGE INSTRUCTION IN HIGHER LEARNING INSTITUTIONS: There has been an increase of those studying Italian at an institution of higher learning as indicated from the percentages among second- (22.9) and third/third plus-generation (41.1%) participants. The lower percentage among the second generation group is understandable since over half of these participants already speak Italian. The higher percentage of the third/third plus group can be attributed to the many higher learning institutions that offer Italian-language instruction. An overwhelming majority of second (69.4%) and third/third plus participants (85%) indicated that they would like to study Italian.

ITALIAN PRIDE OF LANGUAGE: Whether the individuals in this study speak Italian or not, the majority are very proud of their heritage language. For the non-speaking Italians, 34.5 percent of the second generation group and 68.2 percent of third/third plus still feel Italian oriented.

FINDINGS

The present study has demonstrated a marked generational decrease of Italian cultural and ethnic identity in several categories among third/third plus-generation Italian Americans along with a slight third-generation revival in a few others. What must be noted is that these conclusions were based on Americans who still consider themselves as Italians, whether being involved or uninvolved in the Italian community. In that sense, this case study reveals the patterns in Italian American society among those who already show some commitment to the community through their very participation in this effort. Another point that must be taken into consideration is that this is a small study representing participants mainly from one area of the country. A limited study as such cannot make a decisive statement for all Italian Americans per se. Thus the results represent those who took part in this study.

Whereas the majority of second-generation participants had Italian heritage on both sides of the family, the percentages of those having it on only one side were much higher among the third/third plus generation indicating that more of their fathers had married non-Italian women. Nearly half of the participants, with a slight rise among the third/third plus generation, had only obtained a high school diploma, a two-year associate's degree, or another type of certificate of license as their highest level of education. The other half had attained a bachelor's degree with a small percentage having earned a master's degree or PhD.

Having a recognized place and participating in the Italian community is important to many. At least half of the respondents consider themselves part of the Italian community, with many claiming to be currently active in some Italian organization. Although fewer third/third plus generation participants claimed to be as active, a higher percentage appears to gain somewhat more satisfaction when involved and engaged in Italian social activities. Several third/third plus participants are dissatisfied with their minimal involvement and would like to become more involved. While the majority of participants' friends are not Italian Americans, they do not feel left out from the Italian community when socializing with others.

All of the participants are very proud of their Italian identity, and at least sixty-five percent still refer to themselves as "Italian Americans." Although there is a significant drop among the third/third plus-generation respondents who are conscious of or preoccupied with their Italian identity, a higher percentage feels that it is their duty to educate others about the Italian culture, heritage and history. Over half of all participants believe that it is important for Italian Americans to stay together as a closed knit group in order to keep the culture alive, with an overwhelming majority considering the family as being the most important mechanism in doing so. Very few participants regard uninvolved Italian Americans as being less respected within the community.

While most second-generation participants still have relatives in Italy, the percentage considerably decreases among the third/third plus generation group. Nearly all respondents strongly believe that Italian Americans should visit Italy at least once in their lifetime with half of the second generation but fewer third/third plus participants visiting every four to ten years. A small number of participants visit every two to three years but hardly any visit every year. Unfortunately, nearly one half of third/third plus-generation Italian Americans have never visited Italy.

Although a high percentage of participants are interested in the future of Italy, media contact and communication with Italy appear to be declining, especially within the third/third plus group. Over half of the second-generation participants still telephone or email with people in Italy, but a minimal number of third/third plus do so. When considering that the latter group has fewer relatives and friends in Italy, these responses are understandable. Few second-generation and even fewer third/third plus participants listen to Italian radio. Over half of the second generation but very few from the third/third plus group watch Italian TV programs, with hardly any subscribing to Italian satellite. Although only about half of the participants read Italian magazines or newspapers, more than half stay informed about Italy through the internet.

Religious beliefs and practices play an important role among most participants. The majority still observe Catholic holidays while also integrating ethnic Italian and religious traditions into American holiday observances. A much higher percentage of third/third plus-generation participants attend church more frequently than the second generation; however, nearly forty percent of the latter admitted to doing so only to please their parents. One third of the second-generation participants never attend church. More than half of all participants stated that intermarriage has not influenced the religion that their families' practice and that marrying a fellow Italian is not a priority.

Although slightly decreasing among third/third plus generations, Italian traditions and customs influence the way that the majority celebrate the birth of a child and marriage. Most participants still retain several Italian traditions and customs however, at least half and especially those from the third/third plus group, admitted that these traditions have somewhat weakened or changed over the years due to intermarriage. While the practices have waned to some extent among the third/third plus group, most participants still adorn their houses with Italian cultural artifacts, maintain an Italian cuisine and enjoy listening to Italian music. Although more than half of the participants stated that they liked traditional Italian dancing to some extent, several third/third plus participants indicated their dislike of it.

Clearly the area which demonstrated the highest percentage of diminishing *Italianità* was that of language. with an enormous number of third/third-generation Italian Americans having never been exposed to Italian. Although over half of the second generation grew up speaking Italian not even a third currently speaks it today. Mostly all of the participants do, however, believe that Italian Americans should speak Italian among themselves. While very few participants attended an Italian language school as youngsters, over half of the second generation and one third of the third/third plus group believe that children should attend such schools. More than half of the participants but fewer among the third/third plus group want their children to be raised in an Italian environment. Over two thirds of both groups want to study Italian. While it is rather disturbing that the Italian language is not being spoken at home, statistics demonstrating that there is an increase of those currently studying the language are quite impressive. These percentages most likely represent the popularity of the Italian language and the accessibility to numerous Italian-language programs in American universities and organizations. Despite this linguistic anemia, nearly all of the participants are very proud of their Italian heritage language. More than 65 percent of the third/third plus generation respondents claimed to feeling very ethnic oriented, even if they do not speak Italian.

The results from this study support and contradict various theories of assimilation, symbolic identity and third-generation ethnic revival. Although the collected data confirmed a generational decrease among the third/third plus generation concerning ethnic involvement, identity, contact with Italy, and language, *Italianità* is nevertheless present with the majority of participants still maintaining many traditions and religious observances along with upholding strong beliefs and pride in identifying as Italian Americans. Whereas Joseph Conforti mentions in *Italian Americans as Ethnics*, that not a single fourth-generation person in his family identified as an Italian American (41), sixty five percent of this study's third/third plus-generation respondents refer to themselves as such. Most respondents still regard the family as the continuing unit of communal solidarity as found in Alba's study (2). Similarly as in Herbert Gans's study on the Italian cuisine among Italian Americans in Boston's West End, Italian cooking still prevails among this study's participants. Alba attributes that the continuation of the Italian American cuisine is due to its acceptance and integration within the American cuisine (133).

Just as previous studies demonstrated groups expressing a positive attitude towards the Catholic Church, most third-generation Italian Americans in this study appear to attend church more than second generation participants. However according to Barone since Italian immigrant Catholics were not building their own ethnic churches, they became more conventionally Catholic by approaching the Irish Catholic norm. Within time, second-generation and even more third-generation Italian Americans appeared to attend church more frequently than the first-generation group (136). When considering the above reasoning, one could question whether Catholicism is considered to be an attribute of ethnic identity for these participants.

There is definitely a third-generation revival, as Hansen suggested, in the area of language learning (Bender and Kagiwada 360). Considering that the majority of third/third plus-generation Italian Americans expressed a strong interest in studying Italian, this study's results can serve as a tool for the advancement of modern Italian studies programs. Additional Italian studies and language programs at higher education institutions and scholarships for organized study programs to Italy seem critical to preserving Italian American involvement in Italian events and activities, especially with so many third/third plus Italian Americans lacking the opportunity to visit Italy. Such programs could also be vital to keeping students connected to contemporary Italian culture.

In conclusion, although the data appear to verify a portion of the assimilation theory that concludes that by the third generation, grandchildren of immigrants have completely assimilated into the American society and have become less ethnic, the study also indicates that third/third plus-generation Italian Americans have not left behind all traces of ethnicity. In considering Gans's Symbolic Identity theory claiming that third generation ethnics are detached from ethno-religious culture; are not strongly committed to their ethnicity; and have daily lifestyles that "ethnic" culture does not penetrate, this study's results demonstrated that third/third plus-generation Italian Americans are still rather committed to their ethnicity and that *Italianità* is significant among them.

The present study has demonstrated that *Italianità* has taken on a new meaning among the participants. Although the assimilated, twenty-first century second, third and third plus Italian Americans no longer speak the language and have little contact with Italy through media and correspondence, their ethnic pride helps them surpass linguistic and geographical barriers. It is this same pride that keeps them involved and interested in the Italian community and is pushing them to learn their ancestral language. In reiterating Fred Gardaphè's assertion that "future Italian Americans will no doubt look very different from what we consider the Italian American is today," this study has proven that they already are different and so is their *Italianità Americana*.

WORKS CITED

Alba, Richard and Chamlin, Mitchell. "A Preliminary Examination of Ethnic Identification among Whites". *American Sociological Review.* Vol. 48, No. 2 (Apr. 1983). Print.

Alba, Richard. *Italian Americans. Into the Twilight of Ethnicity.* Englewood Cliffs. N.J. 1985. Print.

Bender, Eugene and Kagiwada, George. "Hansen's Law of "Third-Generation Return" and the Study of American Religio-Ethnic Groups." *Pylon.* Vol. 29, No. 4 (4th Qtr., 1968), 360-370 Print.

Bosce-Mulè, P. (1999). *Authentic Ethnicities. The Interaction of Ideology, Gender Power and Class in the Italian-American Experience.* Connecticut: Greenwood Press. Print.

Candeloro, Dominic. *Voices of America. Italians in Chicago.* Chicago: Arcadia Publishing, 2001. Print.

Conforti, Joseph. "Italian Americans as ethnics." *Italian Americans in a Multicultural Society.* Eds. Krase, Jerome & DeSena, Judith. New York: Forum Italicum, 1994. 35-43. Print.

Ferraro, Thomas . *Feeling Italian. The Art of Ethnicity in America.* New York: University Press, 2005. Print.

Gans, Herbert. *Making Sense of America: Sociological Analyses and Essay.* Maryland: Rowman & Littlefield, 1999. Print

Gans, Herbert. *The Urban Villagers: Group and Class in the Life of Italian Americans.* New York: Free Press, 1982. Print.

Gardaphè, Fred L. "Identical Difference: Notes on Italian and Italian American Identities." *The Essence of Italian Culture and the Challenge of a Global Age (Cultural Heritage and Contemporary Change Series IV)* Eds. Janni, Paolo & McLean, George. New Zealand: Corner Brook Press, 2002. Print.

Gardaphè, Fred L. Interview by Michele Reale. "Italian Americans." *Sempre Sicilia,* Online. Web. 21 October 2012.

Gardaphè, Fred L. *Leaving Little Italy.* New York: State University of New York Press, 2004. Print.

Hansen, Marcus Lee. *The Problem of the Third Generation Immigrant.* Illinois: Augustana Historical Society. 1938. Print

Iorizzo, Luciano & Rossi, Ernest. *Italian American. Bridges to America.* New York: Teneo Press, 2010. Kindle AZW file.

Iorizzo, Lucciano & Mondello, Salvatore. *The Italian Americans.* 3rd Edition. New York: Cambria Press, 2006. Kindle AZW file.

Krase, Jerome. Italian American Urban Landscapes. Images of Social and Cultural Capital. *Italian Americana.* 21 Winter 2003: 17- 44. Print.

Krase, Jerome & DeSena Judith. *Italians in a Multicultural Society.* New York: Forum Italicum. 1994. Print.

Mangione, Jerre & Morreale, Ben. *La Storia. Five Centuries of the Italian American Experience.* New York: Harper Collins Publishing, 1993. Print.

Michaud, Marie-Christine. (N.D.). *Nowadays' Italian-American Identity: between Hypothesis and Definition.* Web. 12 December 2013.

Monti, Daniel. (1993). Some sort of Americans. The Working and Reworking of Italian-American Ethnicity in the United States. Eds. Jerome Krase and Judidth N. Desena. *Italian Americans in a Multicultural Society.* New York: Forum Italicum.1994. 19-34. Print.

Parenti, Michael. (2009). *Italian American Identity: To Be or Not To Be.* Web. 28 December 2013.

Quagliata, Michael. "Italian American History." *The Quagliata Family.* (2001-2009). Web.13 September. 2012

Rose, Philip, M. *The Italians in America.* New York: George H. Doran Company. 1922. Reprints form the collection of the University of Michigan. Print.

Song, Miri. *Choosing Ethnic Identity.* MA: Blackwell Publishing, 2003. Print.

Tamburri, Anthony. "Italian Identity and Italian Americans in the Third Millennium." Azzurra Giorgi. I-Italy. Life and People. 29 October 2012. Web. 28 December 2013.

Waters, Mary. *Ethnic Options. Choosing Identities in America.* California: University of California Press. 1990. Print.

Vecoli, Rudolph. "The Search for an Italian American Identity Continuity and Change." *Italian Americans: New Perspectives in Italian Migration and Ethnicity.* Ed. Lydio F. Tomasi. New York: Center for Migration Studies of New York, Inc.1985. 88-118. Print

Appendix

Section 1: Socio-demographics
Table 1

	2nd Gen. Italian	3rd Gen. Italian
Gender-Female	63.9%	54.1%
Gender-Male	36.1%	45.9%
Age: 1900-1950 (Ages 60 - 110)	37.1%	18.9%
Age: 1951-1970 (Ages 59-40)	22.9%	29.2%
Age: 1971-1990 (Ages 39-20)	40.0%	51.9%
Heritage on Mother's Side	13.9%	24.8%
Heritage on Father's Side	25.0%	30.2%
Heritage on Both Sides	61.1%	45.0%
Marital Status: Single	30.6%	45.9%
Marital Status: Married	52.8%	46.8%
Marital Status: Divorced/Widowed	16.7%	7.3%
Education: High School, Associates, Other	47.2%	56.0%
BA/BS	30.6%	22.9%
MA/PhD	22.2%	21.1%
Dual Citizenship-Yes	19.4%	2.8%
Dual Citizenship-No	80.6%	97.2%

Section II-Involvement in Italian Community

Table 2

Do you consider yourself a part of your Italian community:	2nd Generation	3rd/3rd+ Generation
Yes	61.1%	51.4%
No	38.9%	48.6%
I am currently active in some organization in the Italian community:		
Agree	59.1%	59.3%
Disagree	40.9%	40.7%
Having a recognized place in the Italian community is important to me:		
Agree	77.3%	81.5%
Disagree	22.7%	18.5%
I gain much satisfaction from my involvement in my ethnic community:		
Agree	72.7%	77.8%
Disagree	27.3%	22.2%
I feel satisfied with my involvement in my Italian community:		
Agree	85.7%	69.2%
Disagree	14.3%	30.8%
I would like to become more involved in my Italian community:		
Agree	66.7%	72.7%
Disagree	33.3%	27.3%
I feel most satisfied when I am engaged in social activities within my Italian community:		
Agree	52.4%	64.8%
Disagree	47.6%	35.2%
I feel "left out" when I am in circles other than my Italian circle of acquaintances:		
Agree	4.8%	3.6%
Disagree	95.2%	96.4%
The majority of my friends are from my Italian community:		
Agree	31.8%	34.5%
Disagree	68.2%	65.5%

Section III-Ethnic Identity and Culture

Table 3

	2nd Generation	3rd/3rd+ Generation
I am very conscious of or preoccupied with my Italian identity:		
Agree	80.6%	66.7%
Disagree	19.4%	33.3%
I am very proud of my Italian identity:		
Agree	100.0%	99.1%
Disagree	.0%	.9%
When people ask me what my nationality is, I always place Italian before the word "American":		
Yes	69.4%	65.1%
No	30.6%	34.9%
In order to keep the Italian culture alive in North America, Italian Americans should participate as fully as possible in the Italian community:		
Agree	66.7%	72.5%
Disagree	33.3%	27.5%
It is important that Americans be made aware of my ancestors' fight for freedom for their homeland:		
Agree	57.1%	67.3%
Disagree	42.9%	32.7%
I have a duty to educate others about my Italian culture and heritage:		
Agree	54.3%	53.7%
Disagree	45.7%	46.3%
It is important for Italian Americans to stay together as a closely-knit group for the purpose of keeping the culture alive and growing outside the homeland:		
Agree	57.1%	67.3%
Disagree	42.9%	32.7%
Those Italian Americans who move away from involvement in the ethnic community are less respected by fellow Italians than those who stay within:		
Agree	19.4%	24.8%
Disagree	80.6%	75.2%
I believe that the family is important in keeping the Italian heritage alive:		
Agree	100.0%	96.2%
Disagree	.0%	3.8%

Section IV-Contact with Italy through Travel and Media

Table 4

	2nd Generation	3rd/3rd+ Generation
I still have relatives in Italy:		
Yes	91.7%	72.4%
No	8.3%	27.6%
I am interested in the future of Italy:		
Always	47.2%	44.0%
Sometimes	47.2%	50.5%
Never	5.6%	5.5%
I believe that it is important that Italian Americans visit Italy at least once in their lifetime:		
Always	88.6%	69.7%
Sometimes	11.4%	23.9%
Never	.0%	6.4%
How often do you visit Italy:		
Every Year	11.1%	4.8%
Every 2-3 Years	25.0%	9.6%
Every 4-10 Years	50.0%	38.5%
Never Have	13.9%	47.1%
I correspond via mail/email with people in Italy:		
Always	36.1%	13.8%
Sometimes	33.3%	26.6%
Never	30.6%	59.6%
I telephone people in Italy:		
Always	22.2%	11.9%
Sometimes	38.9%	16.5%
Never	38.9%	71.6%
I listen to Italian radio programs:		
Always	.0%	2.8%
Sometimes	33.3%	20.2%
Never	66.7%	77.0%
I watch Italian programs on TV:		
Always	2.8%	3.7%
Sometimes	55.6%	34.8%
Never	41.6%	61.5%
I subscribe to a Italian satellite program:		
Always	5.6%	.9%
Sometimes	8.3%	1.8%
Never	86.1%	97.3%
I read Italian newspapers/magazines:		
Always	5.6%	8.3%
Sometimes	44.4%	33.9%
Never	50.0%	57.8%
I stay informed about Italy through the internet:		
Always	16.7%	16.7%
Sometimes	55.6%	47.2%
Never	27.7%	36.1%

Section V-Religion, Holidays & Marriage

Table 5

	2nd Generation	3rd/3rd+ Generation
I celebrate Catholic religious holidays. My religious holidays are influenced by my ethnic traditions:		
Always	72.2%	53.2%
Sometimes	22.2%	37.6%
Never	5.6%	9.2%
I attend Catholic services at a Catholic church:		
Always	44.4%	57.8%
Sometimes	22.3%	22.9%
Never	33.3%	19.3%
I attend Catholic services at a Catholic church only as an obligation I am fulfilling for my parents:		
Always	5.7%	11.1%
Sometimes	14.3%	26.9%
Never	80.0%	62.0%
Ethnic Italian and religious traditions from Italy are integrated in my observance of American holidays:		
Always	47.2%	34.9%
Sometimes	50.0%	50.5%
Never	2.8%	14.6%
Intermarriage has influenced the religion that my family practices:		
Always	19.4%	19.3%
Sometimes	13.9%	25.7%
Never	66.7%	55.0%
I believe that it is important to date and marry a person from my ethnic Italian background:		
Always	8.3%	2.8%
Sometimes	25.0%	32.4%
Never	66.7%	64.8%

Section V-Religion, Holidays & Marriage
Table 5

	2nd Generation	3rd/3rd+ Generation
I celebrate Catholic religious holidays. My religious holidays are influenced by my ethnic traditions:		
Always	72.2%	53.2%
Sometimes	22.2%	37.6%
Never	5.6%	9.2%
I attend Catholic services at a Catholic church:		
Always	44.4%	57.8%
Sometimes	22.3%	22.9%
Never	33.3%	19.3%
I attend Catholic services at a Catholic church only as an obligation I am fulfilling for my parents:		
Always	5.7%	11.1%
Sometimes	14.3%	26.9%
Never	80.0%	62.0%
Ethnic Italian and religious traditions from Italy are integrated in my observance of American holidays:		
Always	47.2%	34.9%
Sometimes	50.0%	50.5%
Never	2.8%	14.6%
Intermarriage has influenced the religion that my family practices:		
Always	19.4%	19.3%
Sometimes	13.9%	25.7%
Never	66.7%	55.0%
I believe that it is important to date and marry a person from my ethnic Italian background:		
Always	8.3%	2.8%
Sometimes	25.0%	32.4%
Never	66.7%	64.8%

Section VI-Ethnic Customs, Traditions, Cuisine, Music and Dance

Table 6

	2nd Generation	3rd/3rd+ Generation
Italian traditions and customs influence the way I celebrate the birth of a child:		
Always	47.2%	29.4%
Sometimes	38.9%	44.0%
Never	13.9%	29.6%
Italian traditions and customs influence the way I celebrate a wedding:		
Always	52.8%	45.9%
Sometimes	41.6%	43.1%
Never	5.6%	11.0%
Italian traditions and customs influence the way I celebrate the death of a loved one:		
Always	50.0%	43.1%
Sometimes	33.3%	42.2%
Never	16.7%	14.7%
Many of my Italian traditions and customs have changed over the years:		
Always	8.3%	10.3%
Sometimes	72.3%	65.4%
Never	19.4%	24.3%
My family has retained many of our ethnic Italian traditions and customs:		
Always	47.2%	33.0%
Sometimes	50.0%	58.7%
Never	2.8%	8.3%
Intermarriage has influenced the way that my family celebrates and observes Italian customs and traditions:		
Always	8.6%	18.3%
Sometimes	45.7%	51.4%
Never	45.7%	30.3%
There are several Italian cultural artifacts displayed in my house:		
Always	58.3%	39.4%
Sometimes	33.3%	42.2%
Never	8.4%	18.4%
My cuisine is strongly influenced by my Italian heritage:		
Always	77.8%	71.3%
Sometimes	22.2%	26.9%
Never	.0%	1.8%
I enjoy listening to Italian music:		
Always	47.2%	40.4%
Sometimes	41.7%	48.6%
Never	11.1%	11.0%
I enjoy Italian dancing:		
Always	22.2%	17.4%
Sometimes	50.0%	42.2%
Never	27.8%	40.4%

Section VII-Ethnic Language

Table 7

	2nd Generation	3rd/3rd+ Generation
Italian Americans should speak Italian among themselves:		
Agree	57.1%	42.1%
Disagree	42.9%	57.9%
I feel it is important that Italian Americans respect their parents' wishes to speak Italian at home:		
Yes	88.6%	68.2%
No	11.4%	31.8%
I feel it is important that Italian American children attend Italian school:		
Yes	62.9%	36.4%
No	37.1%	63.6%
I would want my children to be raised in an Italian environment (i.e., attend Italian school, speak Italian in the home, socialize with other Italian children, participate in Italian clubs and organizations, visit Italy):		
Yes	50.0%	46.8%
No	50.0%	53.2%
I attended Italian school as a child:		
Yes	11.1%	3.7%
No	88.9%	96.3%
I grew up speaking Italian:		
Yes	57.1%	9.3%
No	42.9%	90.7%
I currently speak Italian at home:		
Yes	27.8%	4.7%
No	72.2%	95.3%
I frequently speak my Italian with my friends:		
Yes	30.6%	11.1%
No	69.4%	88.9%
I feel comfortable speaking Italian:		
Yes	58.3%	21.5%
No	41.7%	78.5%
I am currently studying Italian at an institution of higher education:		
Yes	22.9%	41.1%
No	77.1%	58.9%
I would like to study and learn Italian:		
Yes	69.4%	85.0%
No	30.6%	15.0%
I do not speak Italian but feel very ethnic oriented:		
Yes	69.4%	85.0%
No	30.6%	15.0%
I do not speak Italian but feel very ethnic oriented:		
Yes	34.5%	68.2%
No	65.5%	31.8%
I am very proud of the Italian language:		
Yes	97.2%	88.8%
No	2.8%	11.2%

A KNOWLEDGE MANAGEMENT SYSTEM (KMS) FOR THE ITALIAN HISTORICAL EMIGRATION[1]

Fabio Capocaccia and Carlo Stiaccini

"DAL PORTO AL MONDO"
FROM THE HARBOUR TO THE WORLD

Since its foundation in 2006, CISEI—International Center for Studies on Italian Emigration— has had among its main objectives to retrieve lists of emigrants departing from the port of Genoa to the Americas, with the purpose of creating a national database that contains names and destinations of emigrants. The name given from the start to this database—*"Dal porto al mondo" from the Harbor to the World*—later became the motto of many CISEI activities: under this name, for example, five books on Italian emigration have been published by CISEI ever since. The first objective was to start from Italian sources, public and private archives, local and national. Such research did not produce significant results, except for lists of passenger ships contained in the records of *Sanità Marittima* (Maritime Health) stored at Archivio di Stato di Genova. These documents, as shown later, bear the names of the passengers leaving Genoa harbor in the period 1793-1852, with prominent destinations of the Mediterranean ports but also overseas.

For the period after 1852, when Genoa became one of the main ports of departure for North and South America, some exploratory surveys have been made in past years at Archivio Centrale dello Stato in Rome, in order to definitely exclude the possibil-

---

[1] The section *"Dal porto al mondo* from the Harbour to the World" is by Carlo Stiaccini; the section "From database to KMS – Knowledge Management System" is by Fabio Capocaccia.

ity, however remote, that the archive of *Marina Mercantile, Direzione Generale della marina, Gente di mare* (Merchant Marine, Directorate-General of the Navy, Seafarers), not completely cleared up and devoid of any analytical inventory, could contain partial series of boarding lists from the Italian ports. These surveys have firmly established the indications collected by CISEI that lists, delivered according to the regulations of the emigration inspectorates of the ports of Genoa and Naples (at least from 1901) as peripheral organs of the Emigration Authority, have been destroyed in recent times as a result of dumping, most likely authorized by the Ministries of Transport, Interior and Foreign Affairs.

Having lost any reasonable chance of finding in local archives the lists of passengers departed from Genoa and other Italian ports after the unification of Italy, CISEI's attention has shifted to alternative sources represented by landing lists, preserved even today in national or state archives of the reception centers for immigrants of the main American landing ports (Di Comite and Glazier 78-90).

Available Landing Logs and Databases

Landing logs and databases compiled by North American authorities with the names of passengers landed in New York (Battery Park and Ellis Island) and lists of arrivals delivered by Italian ship captains to consular authorities in the Brazilian port of Santos (São Paulo - Memorial do Imigrante) or Buenos Aires in Argentina (CEMLA - Centro de Estudios Migratorios Latinoamericano) have been used in past years to build extensive databases (Monteverdi 54-112; Glazier and Kleiner 115-125; Favero 126-138). The older and better known are undoubtedly the New York centers of Castle Garden and Ellis Island: The first has collected in a data bank about 10 million names, registered from 1830 to 1912; the second has made available online since 2002 over 22 million names of people landed in New York between 1892 and 1924. These evolving databases offer the visitor/researcher the possibility to recover, through passenger names, additional data such as age, year of arrival, country of origin, profession, name of the vessel, and departure harbor. The Ellis Island database, upon registration, also offers the possibility of direct access to digital images of original log sheets, through which general information on passengers can be obtained, but also allows checks on the many inconsistencies, errors and omissions in relation to data entry. Simple operations make it possible to explore the reproduction of the original passenger list of, for example, one of the many steamers departed from the port of Genoa.

Interesting projects of cooperation, with mutual exchanges of researchers, information and experiences between CISEI and Castel Garden have made it possible in recent years to initiate targeted efforts to normalize and restructure data already contained in American databases, some of which contain obvious errors of transcription or normalization, deriving in part from the first registrations by the authorities responsible for the supervision of immigrants arriving in America. A useful example in this direction can be done by extracting data from the departure database and comparing them with the list of passengers arrived in New York on July 16, 1907 with the Italian steamer *Città di Milano*. Certainly not a casual choice, since of that trip the Archivio di Stato di Genova preserves the nautical logbook compiled by Captain Francesco Schiaffino. In this case it was possible to compare two very different documents, stored in two ports, for two different operations: departure and arrival. The nautical logbook, is a document drawn up by the ship's commander during navigation and does not contain the list of passengers boarded but records different information to verify, and often complement, those already present in existing databases available on the Web (Stiaccini 165-186).

One obvious difference between the lists of departures and arrivals is that the first contains the names of people who died during the voyage, while the second carries the names of those born on board. This difference might seem irrelevant if you do not take into account that both deaths and births on board during the voyage at that time were numerically relevant, the ship commander being obliged by law to record any change in ship occupancy. Thanks to nautical newspapers, as we will see later, a detailed list of deserters on board can be obtained. These deserters were often recruited among the emigrants upon departure and bound to enter America illegally: here again the nautical papers reveal information not available at the departure.

Beyond the possible additions, the databases currently available have a remarkable number of transcription errors. Apart from those concerning places of origin of passengers (Gossalto instead of Fossalto, Milasso/Milazzo, Catama/Catania, Casenso/Cosenza, Tone Greco/Torre del Greco, Salermo/Salerno, Frafani/Trapani, Zoggia/Foggia) in some cases, as mentioned above, already transcribed incorrectly by the official during the compilation of the register, the most common errors include names of passengers entered in the database: Istr'Antonio (surname) Benjamin (name) instead of Asti (surname) Antonio Benjamin (name), Juliani Luigi anziché Zuliani Luigi, Ginsto Guiliano/Giusto Giuliano, Santagato Maria Giuseppa/Santagata Maria Giuseppa, Aposito Antonio/Esposito Antonio, Oliurio Tommaso/Oliverio Tommaso, Insagna Vito/Insigna Vito. Eight surnames, over thirty present on a log page taken at random, reveal a high percentage of error, and the consequent difficulties in using a database that does not return the exact names of many people arriving at their destination, unless the visitor knows the name of the ship used by the person sought, the day of arrival, and has the patience to go through the full passenger list as we did to produce this example.

Among the many other omissions, the most obvious, in terms of using the records in the database to get a list of people from Genoa or from Italy, is undoubtedly that the database does not distinguish among 945 passengers landed at New York the 27 boarded in Genoa. For the database, all passengers off the steamer *Città di Milano* were boarded in Naples, despite the original register clearly stating the boarding of 27 people in Genoa: a figure confirmed inter alia by the Commander Schiaffino's report on departure from Genoa, on his nautical logbook. Among other omissions, 12 passengers regularly surveyed upon arrival and present in the register of landings are incomprehensibly "forgotten" in the database. Twelve of a thousand passengers represents a negligible percentage, statistically a physiological error, but that percentage applied to the total number of names placed in the data bank results in something like three hundred thousand names of people regularly landed in New York. Among the twelve "forgotten" is a certain Joseph Desiato di Lentini (province of Syracuse) husband of Maria Mastrarrigo (and not Maitrarrigo, as erroneously reported by the database) and father of Salvatore Desiato (and not Deziato). In this family the database does not return as mentioned the name of the father and falsely reports the names of the mother and son, furthermore establishing no relation between the last two. The original log instead not only shows the correct names of all three but with some signs—in this case a bracket, in other cases the compiler makes explicit the relationships—allows the researcher to easily reconstruct parental relationships between passengers and then add essential information and links between people. In some cases, database errors, as already noted, add up to those introduced by American landing officials. Amedeo Franchini, for example, according to the database, is loaded in Naples and comes from an unlikely San Bomano, while in the logs departs from Genoa and comes from San Romano in Garfagnana (Lucca). To errors made in the transition to digital form, you must add errors introduced in New York: For the official record of landing, and consequently for the database, Amedeo Franchini would be ethnically *Italian North* instead of *Italian South* as were all Italians coming from regions south of river Po (including those from Garfagnana), at least according to the strict rules of compilation *Instructions for Filling Alien Manifests* printed on the back of each sheet of record of landing.

There are countless cases of passengers rejected by US authorities and taken back to Italy, often on the same steamer used for the outward journey: these passengers are regularly present in the database without having ever set foot outside New York Reception Centers. In practice the databank makes no distinction between those who managed to get into America and those who were rejected and forced to return to Italy. Landing lists display the stamp "Deported" next to the name, and very often the back pages record a list with the names of the persons detained, subjected to additional checks, admitted in the Ellis Island Hospital, rejected, with motivation and steamer name assigned ex officio for the repatriation. All these valuable data are completely ignored by the database but appear clearly in the registry. Paolo Caliendo, to take another example for the passenger list of the *Città di Milano*, is a 44-year old peasant from the province of Caserta and according to the information in the database is regularly landed in New York along with other townsfolk. The registry leaves no doubt that Caliendo is among immigrants rejected. The log-book kept by the *Città di Milano* commander at the departure from New York indicates Caliendo among passengers on board who were forced return to Italy. Apart from these inaccuracies in the compilation, landing lists provide information that the current database does not record, such as employment, education, and networks of relationships, which might be derived from final destinations declared by migrants on landing, in addition to data that would allow to reconstruct the composition of the family as well as the reasons, as mentioned above, for forced repatriation.

THE FIRST DATABASE

This information, already present online, may be then supplemented with other data from Italian sources still almost completely unused, which are the subject of the KMS project, as explained later. These are the so-called *Registri Spedizione Passeggeri* (Passenger Boarding Registers), preserved in the Archivio di Stato di Genova, inside the *Fondo Sanità Marittima* (Maritime Health Fund), until now scarcely used and almost unknown to most students of Italian emigration. The Fund is composed of two distinct series of registers: the first series consists of 45 records compiled in the port of Genoa during the period from October 25, 1793 and August 31, 1833, albeit with some gaps or overlapping of dates among registers. Within this first series, 7 registers are written in French (exactly those from 1808 to 1814), produced during the period in which Genoa and its port were annexed to France (1805-1814). The second series is composed of 34 records compiled during the period from July 31, 1823 and December 24, 1852, with some gaps and overlapping of dates. On this block a project of digitization and data entry is already underway (CISEI has digital copy of all series of registers and has already uploaded into KMS a small portion). These logs provide for each passenger last name, first name, sex, age or year of birth, the country and the nation or the state of birth, the destination and the name and type of ship, the name and surname of the master of the ship (which in many cases, at that time, coincides with the owner), the flag of the vessel, the Lewy Council's decision (position on mandatory conscription). Through some pictures already on the CISEI database the peculiarity of these documents may be appreciated: documents that, by reference to the time of their recording, can be regarded as the oldest, if not the earliest, examples of passenger lists.

Data stored in research centers in New York start from 1820, with several gaps at least for passengers coming from Italy, as demonstrated by the following example: In a randomly selected record, a long list of *Sardi* (Kingdom of Sardinia) passengers is registered in the port of Genoa on May 5, 1849, before their embarkation for New York aboard the Brig *Cerere* under the *Sarda* flag, commanded by Nicolò Pitto. Among the passenger names are Lagomarsino Giovanni, Molinari Giacomo, Bacigalupo Giuseppe, Brizzolari Maria Celestina. Making a comparison with the data contained in databases, the first Lagomarsino Giovanni is found for example on the site of Castle Garden on May 3, 1886, and the first Molinari Giacomo is registered on May 4, 1882. No earlier data are present in New York databases. Another example regards departures from the port of Genoa on March 22, 1849. Destinations are Porto Torres, Bastia, New York and Livorno. Significant in this case the nationality stated by passengers (today it would be "Italian" for all of them): "Sardo" (Kingdom of Sardinia), "Lucchese" (Duchy of Lucca, before it was annexed to the Grand Duchy of Tuscany), "Toscano" (Grand Duchy of Tuscany), "Romano" (Papal). This nomenclature explains not just the Italian reality during the Kingdom of ancient Italian States, but rather the reasons, for example, that in America for many years after the unification of Italy, Italian immigrants continued to call themselves and to be called by the natives "genovesi", "lucchesi", "parmigiani", "romani", "napolitani" or "siciliani", precisely because this was often the way they defined themselves upon arrival in America.

From Database to KMS
Knowledge Management System

On the basis of the first projects launched, as described above, CISEI for at least five years has been working on the creation of a digital archive containing information about Italian emigrants (www.ciseionline.it), an ambitious project considering that since the unification of Italy no fewer than 30 million people have left Italy, and at least 20 million did not return to their homeland. Initial efforts of this project focused on the search for the names of that percentage of those 30 million emigrants (less than half) who preferred, to the European alternative, the American continents, leaving many traces of their passage in the main departure ports, including Genoa, and in the arrival ports of New York, Rio de Janeiro, Santos, Montevideo and Buenos Aires (Capocaccia 186-205).

CISEI has picked up this challenge and has begun to develop a system (thanks to a financial support by Compagnia di San Paolo) starting initially from information taken from the documentation, as mentioned above, still now kept in the places of departure, mainly concerning public safety practices, containing the personal data of passengers. In a second phase, CISEI has launched collaborative programs with some of the most important American museums and research centers, including Memorial do Imigrante in São Paulo for the data on Brazil, Castle Garden-Battery Conservancy in New York for arrivals in the United States, and CEM-

LA for arrivals in Buenos Aires. This project responds to a need that has been growing over the years. CISEI, and, earlier, the Genoa Port Authority, receives dozens of requests daily from people on the other side of the ocean looking for information on their ancestors. A trend also seen in Italy, is a shift from a database audience of research professionals to one of enthusiastic amateurs often struggling to reconstruct their family history. Not to mention the genealogical research market, vital in America and expanding in the last several years in Europe and in Italy. Or the publishing world, for more than a decade more and more attentive to the issue of migration. This is probably not the right place to recall the series dedicated to the subject; periodicals, movies, publications and everything in these years was produced in Italy (Prencipe and Sanfilippo 44-141). It is not possible here to discuss all the exhibitions and the museums opened in recent years on the subject of emigration, at a local level, and the meetings, conferences and seminars held in Italy. Evidence of a particular attention to the issue of migration is the recent expansion into collateral themes such as food, food culture, ethnic, music, theater and all cultural expressions related to emigration on both sides of the ocean.

In light of all this, KMS is a project that wants to offer an innovative solution to the need to relate and integrate as much of the knowledge and the various databases of information about people who over the past two centuries have moved from one side of the ocean to the other. This is particularly important at this time, since until a few years ago, it should be remembered, no unified archive existed in Italy covering the entire period of the so-called Great Italian Diaspora the one that occurred in the late nineteenth and twentieth centuries. Existing databases were mostly partial and sectorial, mostly dedicated to specific historical periods and to a limited number of travel destinations, or in many cases concerning only persons from a specific and circumscribed geographical area that could correspond to a province or to a region of Italy, in most cases the village from which the "donor" of the Museum came. Local stores offer in fact, very often, collections of names of emigrants and of related documents restricted to limited geographic areas, regions, cities or even countries. State archives have significant information of wider geographical relevance, but are focused on specific aspects of the migration process. There are lists of passports, registers of shipping companies, or the aforementioned logbooks or maritime health registers. Destination countries of Italian emigration preserve instead, in most cases, immigration registers containing relevant information on the arrivals, but hardly integrated with each other, if not through the construction of dedicated computing platforms.

Starting from this heterogeneous collection of databases and documentation, CISEI intended, from the beginning of its activity, to build up the first national unified system of access to information that includes all sources from the past two centuries. This project, launched in 2006, was oriented, as explained above, toward two main lines of action: The first concerned the census data sources at local and national as well as state archives; the second, a study and partial acquisition of data concerning the main destinations of Italian emigration, with particular reference to the great ports of arrival: New York, Sao Paulo and Buenos Aires. A part of the registers of the Archivio di Stato di Genova has been selected, photographed and converted into digital format. A complex process and intrinsically slow, but it has been a path that has laid the foundations for new technological approaches to access and consultation of information related to the Italian Diaspora. The available data at the ports of arrival were normalized and corrected (Errors of transcription of Italian emigrants' accounts by officials of immigration of the offices of destination are, as mentioned above, the norm and not the exception) and, when available, with other information concerning places of departure. This approach has not only facilitated our task, but has also resulted in the development of fruitful processes of cooperation with the US, with Memorial do Imigrante in Sao Paulo and CEMLA in Buenos Aires

The subsequent development of the KMS was the natural continuation of this first approach. The information collected in databases of CISEI is subject to continuous updating and expansion in both quantitative and qualitative form. This process results in an increase in the diversity of information and growing difficulties of access, integration and comparison. At the same time it creates new and original analyses and enhancement opportunities. In order to efficiently address this new evolutionary phase of the archiving process, we decided to migrate the information from traditional database to a more modern and innovative Knowledge Management System (Choucri 9-12; Baets 89-112).

Unlike a database, the Knowledge Management System allows you to identify, capture, organize, and develop all forms of knowledge that are generated during the use of the archive. The KMS is able to store, integrate and put at the disposal of users any trace or comments left, in their consultation of the system, by experts, scholars and even by amateurs or occasional users. This is an open knowledge system, especially relevant to the access and use of information: comments, exchanges of views and opinions, evaluations, reports, requests for clarification, provision of original documentation. It is therefore a form of articulated knowledge allowing the researcher to access any data contained in the archive alongside new information from actual users. This new information simplifies the complex task of integration and standardization of information deriving from databases intrinsically heterogeneous in nature (Maier 15-87). This approach suggests an evolutionary path of the archive philosophy perfectly integrated in principle with the phenomenon of social networks on the Web, which have become the new universal storage systems of knowledge (Google, Wikipedia).

The design and development of a KMS is a very complex initiative both from a methodological and technological point of view, requiring an approach to innovative and advanced knowledge, emphasizing the process of generating and sharing new information. The main challenge is to keep a constant stream of relationships between data and users, since in a KMS an important source of information is generated by users. In this respect the traditional technological solutions—for example, a database published on a traditional Website—may soon became obsolete. Researchers must follow the paths of knowledge, flexible methodologies and technologies in constant evolution.

CISEI KMS adopts this methodology; its purpose is to correlate all data available, through processes of standardization and scientific content validation by experts, using technological systems for the generation of semantic networks able to associate among them different contents: expert analyses, data lists, pictures, maps, animations, music and multimedia materials, social networking profiles and web links, books, reviews, mailing lists, lists of researchers, and other information. Each user who logs on can ask for clarifications, and can propose corrections, additions of information, ideas and materials. Each proposal will be evaluated on its scientific merit and validated by a team of experts in the project. After this process is complete, the new knowledge will be ranked for reliability and accessibility, related to KMS, and made available to users in appropriate sections. KMS development aims to broaden and enhance the relationship between content and users under the supervision of a qualified team of experts and researchers, not necessarily belonging to a single country or a single research center. This cooperative process should encourage the growth of a large community of interest on the topic of migration and more specifically on the subject of Italian emigration.

At this stage the KMS has 2,725,000 name-cards (With the next update it will reach 3,741,906 cards), equivalent to over 55 million pieces of information (with updates more than 75 million). The information concerns people who left Italy during the last two centuries and arrived in the United States (1,427,589), Brazil (772,451) and Argentina (504,618, which with updates will rise to 1,541,866). The first level of search returns the researcher some essential information: emigrant's name, age, date and place of registration. This search of course may also include for any single name multiple targets in different periods, allowing the user to understand immediately whether or not the person sought has made more than one trip in his life and for which destination. Once the name has been selected, a second phase of the search returns other general information for the person, depending on the place of registration, place of birth and origin, the profession, the ship used for the trip, the name of the shipping company, the family relations to other passengers, the official destination declared to authorities, and the professed religion. This information sis accompanied by a series of themed screens, thanks to which the researcher can expand the number and type of person-related data: for example, migration statistics relating to the period in which the person has traveled and how many people have left Italy in that year, how many reached the planned destination, which regions of Italy they came from, and how many people in the same year decided to return to Italy. Information is complemented by legal regulations on the subject of immigration in force in that particular year in the countries of departure and arrival. Essentially these reported regulations comprise a first legal aid statistical framework to contextualize the migratory experience of the person sought, and to better understand the experience of the individual within a much broader context, with the ability to compare one year statistics with those of other years, depending on their interests. At this level, the reference bibliography is also supplied, with a selection of books, essays, articles and publications related to the migratory experience of the person sought, then studies of the countries of departure and of arrival, or of other aspects relating to the economic, political and social issues found by the emigrant once arrived at destination.

Information on the historical context is complemented with data on the ship used for the journey, its image, information on the steamship and shipping company, detailed route carried out by the ship, and the journal/logbook written by Commander during that trip. The latter information links to a long list of journals/diaries available to the researcher who can have access, if the single diary of that trip were not available, to other diaries related to other ships in the same period.

On the other hand, the possibility of relying on a place of deposit and consultation, safe and protected from possible damage or disturbances, may induce users to deliver the story and the documents of their ancestors: in the long run this source of information may become the main asset for expanding the size of the database.

The activity of CISEI stands in the long wake of outstanding studies made in recent decades on both sides of the Atlantic, demonstrating, once more, that the relationship between the United States and Italians (and Italy as a country) is indeed a very special relationship. In the year 2000 nearly 16 million Americans claimed to have Italian ancestors, and descend in various ways from the approximately 6 million Italians who arrived in the United States between 1850 and 2000. Not to mention those who came before—in the period of the ancient Italian States—for the purpose of helping build the first American towns, certainly far from the conventional model of the. Consider, for instance, the first settlers, entrepreneurs or political refugees, fled from Italy following the failure of insurgencies for Italian Unity. Or else the most glamorous gold prospectors. When the Italian Diaspora in America is considered, one rarely thinks of this type of migration, the so-called pioneers of the early California immigration, or even of the many young researchers who now live and work in the major American research centers. These emigrations are quite different from the 800,000 Italians that, between 1876 and 1900, swarmed the decks and the third class of ships departing from Europe. Most of them, it should be remembered, had in their minds to return home with as many dollars as possible, to pay off debts and make new investments in Italy.

The expansion of the database, and even more the inclusion of the additional information on the historical context made possible by the structure of KMS, may be instrumental in avoiding the risks of generalizing this phenomenon of mobility, and passively accepting the conventional models on Italian emigration. On this basis, CISEI is also wondering if it is still possible to add significant pieces of this mosaic and make sharper and more readable images of parts that have remained in shadow so far; and to rewrite the sotry of emigration in years to come.

WORKS CITED

Baets, Walter R.J, ed., *Knowledge management and management learning: extending the horizons of knowledge-based management*, New York; London: Springer, 2005. Print.

Capocaccia, Fabio, "Il viaggio dell'Emigrante. Verso un archivio nazionale informatizzato." *Museo Nazionale Emigrazione Italiana.* eds. Nicosia, Alessandro, and Lorenzo Prencipe, Roma: Ministero degli Affari Esteri, 2009. 186-205. Print.

Choucri, Nazli, *The Politics of Knowledge Management*, Massachusetts Institute of Technology: The UNESCO Forum on Higher Education, Research and Knowledge, 2007. Print.

Di Comite, Luigi, and Ira A. Glazier. "Sociodemographic Characteristics of Italian Emigration to the United States from Ship Passenger Lists: 1880-1914." *Ethnic Forum* 4, 1-2 (1984): 78-90. Print.

Favero, Luigi. "Le liste di sbarco degli immigrati in Argentina." *Altreitalie* 7 (1992): 126–138. Print.

Glazier, Ira A., and Robert Kleiner. "Analisi comparata degli emigranti dall'Europa meridionale e orientale attraverso le liste passeggeri delle navi statunitensi." *Altreitalie* 7 (1992): 115-125. Print.

Maier, Ronald, *Knowledge management systems: information and communication technologies for knowledge* management, Berlin: Springer, 2007. Print.

Monteverdi Alessandro. "Aspetti demografici e socio-professionali dell'emigrazione italiana negli Stati Uniti (1880-1891): un'indagine esplorativa basata sui registri di bordo." *Altreitalie* 29 (2004): 54–112. Print.

Prencipe, Lorenzo, and Matteo Sanfilippo, "Per una storia dell'emigrazione italiana: prospettiva nazionale e regionale." *Museo Nazionale Emigrazione Italiana.* eds. Nicosia, Alessandro, and Lorenzo Prencipe, Roma: Ministero degli Affari Esteri, 2009. 44–141. Print.

Stiaccini, Carlo, "Racconti di emigrazione nei diari di bordo dei piroscafi italiani." *Scritture migranti. Uno sguardo italo-spagnolo/Escrituras migrantes: una mirada ítalo-española*, eds. Caffarena, Fabio and Laura Martínez Martín, Milano: Franco Angeli, 2012. 165–186. Print.

What Is Italian American Politics?

The Heyday of Italian-American Congressional Politics in East Harlem
La Guardia, Lanzetta, and Marcantonio in the Races for the US House of Representatives[1]

Stefano Luconi

INTRODUCTION

Parties are not only the elitist organizations by which, according to John Aldrich, small cadres pursue their own goals in government.[2] In Robert A. Dahl's view, they are also prominent vehicles that facilitate the political incorporation of ethnic groups by the allotment of candidacies for elective offices among the representatives of such minorities.[3]

Although Italian newcomers and their children long failed to gain considerable recognition in elections after the beginning of their mass immigration to the United States in the late 1870s, some of their leaders, too, eventually managed to secure slots on the ballots and to make inroads into the political establishment. Salvatore J. LaGumina has generally placed the assertive period of candidates from Italian background "in the years immediately following World War II."[4] Nonetheless New York City's East Harlem was a locale where Italian Americans had already loomed considerably on the political horizon a decade earlier. From 1923

---
[1] Research for this essay was made possible in part by a grant from the Roosevelt Study Center, Middelburg, the Netherlands.
[2] John Aldrich, *Why Parties? The Origin and Transformation of Political Parties in America* (Chicago: University of Chicago Press, 1995).
[3] Robert A. Dahl, *Who Governs? Democracy and Power in an American City* (New Haven, CT: Yale UP, 1961) 34-36.
[4] Salvatore J. LaGumina, "Politics," *The Italian American Experience: An Encyclopedia*, ed. Salvatore J. LaGumina et al. (New York: Garland, 2000) 483.

What is Italian America? (New York: IASA, 2015)

through 1950, the member of the US House of Representative from East Harlem (initially the Twentieth District, which changed to the Eighteenth after New York State's 1944 reapportionment) was always a politician of Italian ancestry: Fiorello H. La Guardia (from 1923 to 1933), James Lanzetta (in 1933-1934 and 1937-1938), and Vito Marcantonio (in 1935-1936 and from 1939 to 1950). Furthermore, from 1930 through 1942 all the candidates of both major parties in East Harlem's Twentieth District were of Italian extraction.[5] This essay examines the latter races, their context, and their implication for Italian Americans' accommodation within New York City's politics.

Andrew Rolle has pointed out that "Harlem's electorate once sent more Congressmen of Italian origin to Washington than did any other district in the United States."[6] No other constituency in the United States could have more properly let Italian Americans exert their hold on a Congressional seat than East Harlem. In 1930, at the peak of the Italian presence in the neighborhood, East Harlem was home to about 89,000 Italian Americans. They made up more than 80 percent of the total population and concentrated in the eastern areas. The western section was inhabited mainly by Puerto Ricans and, to a lesser extent, by African Americans and the remnants of a previously sizeable Jewish community.[7]

La Guardia Sets a Precedent

It was La Guardia who became the first Italian-American can-

---

[5] *Biographical Directory of the American Congress, 1774-1961* (Washington: GPO, 1961) 652, 660, 676, 772, 1184-85, 1193, 1262, 1561-62, 1690, 1639.

[6] Andrew Rolle, *Italian Americans: Troubled Roots* (Norman: U of Oklahoma P, 1980) 141.

[7] Gerald Meyer, "Italian Harlem: Portrait of a Community," *The Italians of New York: Five Centuries of Struggle and Achievement*, ed. Philip V. Cannistraro (New York: New York Historical Society and John D. Calandra Italian American Institute, 1999) 57-58; Nadia Vanturini, *Neri e italiani ad Harlem: Gli anni Trenta e la Guerra d'Etiopia* (Rome: Edizioni Lavoro, 1990) 45-59; Jeffrey S. Gurock, *When Harlem Was Jewish, 1870-1930* (New York: Columbia UP, 1979).

didate to get a place on the ballot for Congress in East Harlem. He had already been a member of the House in the late 1910s, after securing election in Manhattan's Greenwich Village in both 1916 and 1918.[8] La Guardia's entry into the political arena had been almost accidental. Greenwich Village was a Democratic stronghold and no Republican wished to waste his time and money in an allegedly hopeless campaign. Therefore, almost nobody in the GOP objected when La Guardia volunteered to run on the Republican ticket in 1914.[9] Despite his eventual defeat, he made an impressive showing, which entitled him to a second bid two years later. This time he won and, thereby, the 1914 fortuitous candidate became a US Representative in 1916 and remained in Washington until he began to serve his term as president of New York City's Board of Aldermen in 1920.[10]

The GOP slated La Guardia again for Congress in 1922, this time in East Harlem, as part of a deal to prevent him from running for Governor of New York State and spoiling the chances of the Republican incumbent for another term.[11] The son of an Italian father and a Jewish mother, La Guardia seemed the fittest candidate to appeal to the two largest immigrant groups in East Harlem which, at that time, were Italian Americans and Jews.[12]

La Guardia's campaign focused on issues that were of particular interests to the Italian-American electorate, such as the repeal of prohibition and the liberalization of the US restrictive legislation

---

[8] Thomas Kessner, *Fiorello H. La Guardia and the Making of Modern New York* (New York: McGraw-Hill, 1989) 38-40, 57-59.
[9] Fiorello H. La Guardia, *The Making of an Insurgent: An Autobiography, 1882-1919* (Philadelphia: Lippincott, 1948) 103.
[10] Howard Zinn, *La Guardia in Congress* (New York: Norton, 1959) 7-10.
[11] Lowell M. Lympus and Burr W. Leyson, *This Man LaGuardia* (New York: Dutton, 1938) 133.
[12] Louis Rittenberg, "La Guardia Pays Tribute to His Mother," *American Hebrew and Jewish Tribune*, 12 January 1934, 183; Gemma La Guardia Gluck, *My Story* (New York: McKay, 1961) 13-14; Edward Corsi, "My Neighborhood," *Outlook*, 16 September 1925, 90-92.

on immigration that had begun to be enforced since the enactment of the 1921 Quota Law.¹³ Yet, according to New York City's Italian-language daily *Il Bollettino della Sera*, La Guardia's ethnic background would be sufficient per se in order to enable the candidate to carry the Italian-American vote: "For the Italians, Major La Guardia has no need of an expressed program. His name is the entire program."¹⁴ Even the more authoritative *New York Times* agreed that "Mr. LaGuardia, an Italian, [...] is expected to get the entire Italian vote."¹⁵

La Guardia played the ethnic card with the Jewish electorate, too. For instance, he challenged his 1922 opponent, Democratic lawyer Henry Frank, to debate with him in Yiddish. La Guardia knew that Frank could not speak this language and felt confident that his own linguistic skills would make Jewish voters in East Harlem see him as one of their own.¹⁶ He also took care of the specific requests of Jewish organizations in his district such as the Hebrew Home for the Aged of Harlem.¹⁷

La Guardia's impressively victorious campaigns in the following years persuaded Tammany Hall's Irish-dominated Democratic machine to give up its traditional ostracism toward Italian-American politicians and to match his ethnic appeal by pitting a candidate of Italian extraction against him. The first and unsuccessful choice was Vincent H. Auleta, a member of New York

---

[13] "LaGuardia Opens Congress Campaign," *New York Times*, 6 September 1922, 7.

[14] *Il Bollettino della Sera*, 7 September 1922, as quoted in Arthur Mann, *La Guardia: A Fighter against His Times, 1882-1933* (Philadelphia: Lippincott, 1959) 153.

[15] "LaGuardia Placed on Congress Ticket," *New York Times*, 30 August 1922, 12.

[16] Mann, *La Guardia: A Fighter against His Times* 156-57.

[17] I. Spira, superintendent, Hebrew Home for the Aged of Harlem, to Fiorello H. La Guardia, New York, 24 August 1927, Fiorello H. La Guardia Papers, microfilm edition, reel 1, folder "General Corr. 1927, A-Z," Roosevelt Study Center.

State Assembly, in 1930.[18] The second was Lanzetta, a young second-generation lawyer who represented East Harlem on New York City's Board of Aldermen, in 1932.[19]

Auleta was unable to counter La Guardia's incumbency factor as an effective legislator and an even more efficient provider of patronage.[20] Indeed, as in the case of numerous residents in East Harlem, a few months before the 1930 election, Auleta himself had benefitted from the political assistance of La Guardia, who had successfully recommended his future challenger's son, August Auleta, as a midshipman to the US Naval Academy at Annapolis, thanks to his own Congressional privileges.[21]

Conversely, the outcome of the 1932 campaign was a reversal of the 1930 race and Lanzetta unseated La Guardia by 16,447 votes to 15,227. The Democratic candidate profited by Franklin D. Roosevelt's coattails at a time when the economic depression had made Republicans anathema to most voters. Lanzetta also reached out to a growing cohort of Puerto Ricans that La Guardia had in part overlooked. But, while New York City was still under a Democratic administration, it was Tammany Hall's distribution of local jobs and assistance among the destitute that eventually enabled Lanzetta to defeat La Guardia. In particular, voters were threatened with the loss of the municipal relief unless they voted for the whole Democratic ticket.[22]

---

[18] "Republicans Map Fight on Sirovich," *New York Times*, 24 August 1930, 17. For Tammany Hall's hostility against Italian-American politicians, see Sergio Bugiardini, "'Stretti tra gli irlandesi e la non partecipazione...': Gli italo-americani di New York City e l'accesso in politica," *Storia e Problemi Contemporanei* 19.46 (2006): 115-35.

[19] "Farley Aide Slated to Run for Sheriff," *New York Times*, 19 August 1932, 7.

[20] "Record Plurality for Governor Here," *New York Times*, 5 November 1930, 3.

[21] Fiorello H. La Guardia to Albert [sic for August] Auleta, Washington, 20 February 1930, La Guardia Papers, reel 2, folder "General Correspondence, 1930, A-C."

[22] Ernest Cuneo, *Life with Fiorello: A Memoir* (New York: Macmillan, 1955) 106; Cleveland Rodgers and Rebecca B. Rankin, *New York: The World's Capital City* (New York: Harper, 1948) 118; Mann, *La Guardia: A Fighter* 319; Ronald

THE ELECTION OF 1934

La Guardia's election to City Hall in 1933 ruled out a rematch with Lanzetta in 1934.[23] Yet the new mayor wanted to select his heir as the Republican candidate in the Twentieth Congressional District. Since Italian Americans were the largest cohort of voters in East Harlem and complained that they were "not represented politically in proportion to their numerical and moral strength,"[24] there was no objection to slating another member of their community on the Republican ticket against Lanzetta. La Guardia designated Marcantonio and maneuvered to place him on the GOP slate.[25]

Marcantonio was a close associate of La Guardia and deserved a political reward after he had brought out the Italian-American vote for the mayor in the 1933 race, showing his skills as an effective campaigner. Conventional wisdom has it that La Guardia met Marcantonio when the latter was still a high school student, was fascinated by his oratory skills in a speech advocating social security and old-age pensions, and established a long political relationship with him. Marcantonio was a labor lawyer as well as a social worker involved in adult education at Haarlem House, a center of cultural activism in East Harlem, where he taught classes in English and other subjects for immigrants who planned to apply for US citizenship. He was also a dynamic member of the neighborhood's Italian-American ethnic association Il Circolo Italiano. Marcantonio was placed in charge of the allocation of La Guardia's Congressional patronage and laid the foundation of his mentor's

---

H. Bayor, *La Guardia: Ethnicity and Reform* (Arlington Heights, IL: Harlan Davidson, 1993) 79.

[23] Arthur Mann, *La Guardia Comes to Power, 1933* (Philadelphia: Lippincott, 1965).

[24] Evelyn M. Bacigalupi, "The Italian Americans in the Political Arena," *Atlantica* 4 (1933): 216.

[25] Alan Schaffer, *Vito Marcantonio: Radical in Congress* (Syracuse: Syracuse UP, 1966) 24.

personal machine, the Fiorello La Guardia Political Club, which operated independently from the parties its leader happened to be affiliated with.[26]

Against the backdrop of the early achievements of the New Deal, 1934 was a Democratic year.[27] Therefore, Lanzetta's defeat of Marcantonio could sound anti-climatic. The bulk of the midterm campaign centered on the impact of the legislative accomplishments of the Roosevelt administration.[28] Yet Lanzetta had quite a controversial record as a Congressman. As a Democratic legislator, he was supposed to back Roosevelt's New Deal, but in fact he voted some of its provisions or was absent from the House of Representatives when others were addressed. Lanzetta's major attainment in Congress was an amendment to the Federal Home Loan Bill, which aimed at protecting the interests of tenement landlords by enabling them to borrow money from the federal government in order to repair their properties. During the debate, Lanzetta even pitied homeowners who had not evicted their tenants despite the latter's failure to pay their rent.[29]

East Harlem was a working-class district, where most voters were slum dwellers and subjected to eviction in the Depression years. What Lanzetta's constituents had long been interested in was the protection of tenants against the claims of the landlords, not the plight of the homeowners, and resentment toward proprie-

---

[26] Leonard Covello, *The Heart Is the Teacher* (New York: McGraw-Hill, 1958) 152-54; Vito Marcantonio, *I Vote My Conscience: Debates, Speeches and Writings of Vito Marcantonio*, ed. Annette T. Rubinstein (New York: Vito Marcantonio Memorial, 1956) 314-15; H.C. Leslie, report for the Federal Bureau of Investigation, New York, 4 August 1930, FBI file no. 100-28126, "Vito Marcantonio," part 1, New York Public Library, New York; Gerald Meyer, *Vito Marcantonio: Radical Politician, 1902-1954* (Albany: State U of New York P, 1989) 15-17.
[27] Andrew E. Busch, *Horses in Midstream: US Midterm Elections and Their Consequences, 1894-1998* (Pittsburgh: U of Pittsburgh P, 1999) 138-45.
[28] Edgar Eugene Robinson, *The Roosevelt Leadership* (New York: Da Capo, 1972) 147.
[29] Schaffer 23; Meyer, *Vito Marcantonio* 23.

tors was strong and widespread.[30] Consequently, the Democratic candidate found himself on the wrong side of the social and political divide in his own district.[31] Actually, in spite of Lanzetta's Democratic affiliation, numerous unions endorsed Marcantonio.[32] These labor organizations included the powerful International Ladies' Garment Workers' Union (ILGWU), which had a large membership among Jews and Italian Americans. In particular, Luigi Antonini—the head of Local 89 and first vice president of the ILGWU—repeatedly came out for Marcantonio.[33]

Moreover, La Guardia placed his own machine behind Marcantonio's campaign. With La Guardia as mayor, the Democratic Party was short of patronage, and people in East Harlem relied on the city administration to cope with the economic crisis. New York City's welfare commissioner, William Hodson, and the director of the Home Relief Bureau, Edward Corsi, allegedly mobilized their resources to seek votes for Marcantonio within East Harlem's sizeable cohort of the unemployed.[34] Besides committing himself to the New Deal, Marcantonio based his successful campaign strategy on Lanzetta's supposed failure to deliver services to his constitu-

---

[30] "Roosevelt ha firmato ieri l'Home Mortage Relief Bill," *Il Progresso Italo-Americano*, 14 June 1933, 1, 10; "Il problema degli sfratti," *La Stampa Libera*, 16 June 1933, 4.

[31] "Lanzetta illustra i suoi precedenti," *Il Progresso Italo-Americano*, 2 November 1934, 2.

[32] "Le Unioni dei sarti per la candidatura di Marcantonio," *Il Progresso Italo-Americano*, 18 October 1934, 8.

[33] "Ieri i messaggi della Locale 89, ILGWU," *La Stampa Libera*, 14 October 1934, 2; "Il messaggio settimanale della Locale 89," *Il Progresso Italo-Americano*, 21 October 1934, 2; "Un appello di L. Antonini per l'avv. V. Marcantonio," ibid., 30 October 1934, 2; "Un discorso elettorale di Antonini," ibid., 2 November 1934, 13; "Nel campo del lavoro," ibid., 4 November 1934, 2; "Antonini per Marcantonio," ibid., 5 November 1934, 2.

[34] "Hodson Is Accused of Relief Politics," *New York Times*, 31 August 1934, 1-2; James J. Lanzetta to Fiorello H. La Guardia, Washington, 8 October 1934, La Guardia Papers, reel 17, folder "L;" "Relief Politics Charged," *New York Times*, 10 October 1934, 3.

ents. He dubbed the incumbent Congressman "Jimmy Next Week," claiming that his Democratic opponent routinely answered "I'll take care of it next week" to people asking for his help, and eventually did nothing for them.[35]

THE ELECTION OF 1936

In 1936, in the wake of the president's landslide reelection, Roosevelt's coattails again helped Lanzetta win back his seat in a replica of the 1932 race. Indeed, historian Alan Schaffer has maintained that "it was undoubtedly Roosevelt, not Lanzetta, to whom Marcantonio lost in 1936."[36] Yet, beyond the trend of national politics, defections among Marcantonio's 1934 backers contributed to the outcome of the 1936 contest.

In the span of two years the support of labor unions for Marcantonio waned. In particular, Antonini and the ILGWU turned their back on him. On the one hand, Marcantonio's stand in Congress was so radical that, contrary to his campaign pledge, he refused to play the New Deal legislator. For instance, he abstained on some public works provisions because they stipulated for a minimum-wage threshold that, in his opinion, was too low to ensure workers decent living standards.[37] On the other, enhancing his own radicalism, Marcantonio undertook a gradual approach to communism that lost him the support of Antonini and his anti-Communist union. During Marcantonio's early weeks in Washington, Antonini already advised the Congressman to disavow his apparent connections to communism if he longed for the endorse-

---

[35] "Vito Marcantonio ed il 'New Deal,'" *Il Progresso Italo-Americano*, 26 October 1934, 2; Vito Marcantonio, "My Answer to a Very Filthy and False Attack Made on Me by Luigi Antonini, Emperor Tripe Tyrant of New York Dressmakers and Labor Racketeer," n.d. [but 1940], 5, Vito Marcantonio Papers, box 1, folder "Anonymous Letters," New York Public Library; Meyer, *Vito Marcantonio* 23, 100-1.

[36] Schaffer 55.

[37] "L'On. Marcantonio contro i progetti che ribassano il tenore degli operai," *La Stampa Libera*, 3 April 1935, 4; Schaffer 32-34.

ment of the ILGWU.³⁸ "One cannot stand by the Devil and the holy water at the same time," the union leader warned Marcantonio in August 1935.³⁹ Undaunted, Marcantonio continued to appear at rallies along with prominent Communists such as the party's secretary general Earl Browder.⁴⁰

As the labor movement was one of the main vehicles for the mobilization of the theretofore inactive voters in 1936, it can be reasonably assumed that Marcantonio suffered from his break with Antonini.⁴¹ Allegedly, the latter even intimidated ILGWU members to prevent them from casting their ballots for Marantonio.⁴²

Nonetheless ethnic politics also played a role in Marcantonio's defeat. Several Italian-American voters distanced themselves from him because they resented the Congressman's critical attitude toward the Fascist regime.

After enduring prejudice in their adoptive land on the grounds that they belonged to an inferior people, many Italian Americans took pride in the alleged accomplishments of their native country during Benito Mussolini's dictatorship.⁴³ The prominent international status Italy achieved under the *Duce* allowed numerous individuals of Italian ancestry bask in the glory of their national origin. This sense of ethnic satisfaction peaked when Italy invaded Ethiopia in 1935 and established her own colonial empire in May of the following year. At that time, many Italian Americans made a point

---

³⁸ Luigi Antonini to Vito Marcantonio, New York, 25 April 1935, Marcantonio Papers, box 52, folder "International Ladies' Garment Workers' Union."
³⁹ Luigi Antonini to Vito Marcantonio, New York, 12 August 1935, Marcantonio Papers, box 1, folder "Antonini, Luigi."
⁴⁰ "Browder, Marcantonio, Butler to Speak on Bonus Bill," *Daily Worker*, 11 June 1935, 4. For the details of Marcantonio's complex relationship with the Communist Party, see Meyer, *Vito Marcantonio* 53-86.
⁴¹ Harvey Klehr, *The Heyday of American Communism: The Depression Decade* (New York: Basic Books, 1984) 293-94.
⁴² "Un gruppo della Local 89" to Marcantonio, Brooklyn, n.d. [but 1936], Marcantonio Papers, box 52, folder "International Ladies' Garment Workers' Union."
⁴³ Matteo Pretelli, *Il fascismo e gli italiani all'estero* (Bologna: Clueb, 2010).

of financing the Fascist military machinery and lobbying Congress against economic sanctions that could interfere with Mussolini's colonial venture. In particular, New Yorkers of Italian extraction collected more than $700,000 for the *Duce*'s war chest, besides donating wedding rings and other gold objects.[44]

Only a handful of radicals were impervious to that jingoistic atmosphere.[45] Marcantonio was among them and refused to endorse the Fascist unprovoked attack on Ethiopia. Specifically, he declined to join a mass rally at the Madison Square Garden to boost donations for the Fascist regime. In the Fall, his stand on Mussolini's colonialism became a campaign issue among Italian-American voters. Pro-Fascist Italian-language newspapers urged their readers to cast their ballots for Lanzetta because, as *Il Grido della Stirpe* put it, "while Italy was struggling to gain her place in the sun, while our vigorous youth was covering itself with glory in eastern Africa in a heroic fight, while Italian blood was shed on the sun-burnt Ethiopian land to strengthen the prestige of our nation in the world, Vito Marcantonio, who now unashamedly claims the Italian vote, stabbed Italy in the back."[46]

THE ELECTION OF 1938

In 1938 Lanzetta and Marcantonio faced each other for the third time in a row. In an off-year election Lanzetta could not rely on the voters' tendency to cast straight Democratic ballots to support Roosevelt. Moreover, Marcantonio ran both on the Republi-

---

[44] Fiorello B. Ventresco, "Italian Americans and the Ethiopian Crisis," *Italian Americana* 6 (1980): 4-27; Gian Giacomo Migone, *Gli Stati Uniti e il fascismo: Alle origini dell'egemonia americana in Italia* (Milan: Feltrinelli, 1980) 343-57; Leo Kanawada, Jr., *Franklin D. Roosevelt Diplomacy and American Catholics, Italians, and Jews* (Ann Arbor: UMI Research P, 1982) 81-89; Venturini 137-38.

[45] Jennifer Guglielmo, *Living the Revolution: Italian Women's Resistance and Radicalism in New York City, 1880-1945* (Chapel Hill: U of North Carolina P, 2010) 217-18.

[46] "L'antitalianità di Vito Marcantonio," *Il Grido della Stirpe*, 31 October 1936, 1.

can slate and on the ticket of the American Labor Party, a partisan house for workers who supported Roosevelt but refused to endorse the Democratic candidates for other offices.[47]

In 1936 the most enthusiastic backing for Marcantonio had come from groups of unemployed and destitute voters who were also the backbone of the Fiorello La Guardia Political Club in East Harlem.[48] Therefore, after his own defeat, planning to reclaim his seat in the House in 1938, Marcantonio did not discontinue his services to the residents of the Twentieth Congressional District in the following two years. His law practice as an attorney often interwove with the mechanics of his political organization.[49] Marcantonio obviously also exploited La Guardia's aid to the hilt. The patronage of the city administration continued to be a key to the people's welfare in East Harlem. Roughly three quarters of the residents of the district depended on the Home Relief Bureau to make a living in 1938.[50]

The Fiorello La Guardia Political Club had reached 5,000 members by 1938 and could, thereby, determine the results of the midterm elections in the Twentieth Congressional District, where the number of votes cast hardly exceeded 30,000 ballots.[51] The adherents to this organization could easily perceive that their own access to relief, welfare programs, and personal assistance was the outcome of Marcantonio's commitment to the plight of the destitute in his constituency. Reminding residents who could hardly

---

[47] Shaffer 59.
[48] See, e.g., "Calde accoglienza al Congressman Vito Marcantonio," *Il Progresso Italo-Americano*, 30 September 1936, 2; "Comizio dei disoccupati per l'On. Marcantonio," ibid., 17 October 1936, 2; "Una riunione in favore di Vito Marcantonio," ibid., 27 October 1936, 3
[49] See, e.g., Vito Marcantonio to David Marcus, New York, 30 June 1937, Marcantonio Papers, box 2, folder "F."
[50] Leonard Covello, "Community-Centered School (1938-39)," Leonard Covello Papers, box 18, folder 2, Balch Institute Collection, Historical Society of Pennsylvania, Philadelphia.
[51] Workers of the Federal Writers' Project, *The Italians of New York* (New York: Random House, 1938) 98.

make ends meet of the benefits of Marcantonio's election was the task of the Communist volunteers who had taken over the American Labor Party in East Harlem and mobilized to bring out the vote for Marcantonio especially among Puerto Ricans and African Americans, who were more likely to welcome Marxist activists than Italian Americans.[52]

It was this grass-roots recruitment of voters that enabled Marcantonio to win the day. Lanzetta's political following remained stable between 1934 and 1938, as he polled 12,483 and 12,376 votes, respectively, in these two years. Conversely, support for Marcantonio on the Republican ticket fell from 12,428 to 10,059 ballots. But, in 1938, Marcantonio also received 8,901 votes on the slate of the American Labor Party.[53] As for the Italian-American electorate, which remained the leading force in East Harlem, Edward Corsi's candidacy for the U.S. Senate in New York State on the Republican ticket stanched the drain of voters from the GOP. Many Italian Americans cast straight Republican ballots in the eventually fruitless effort to help Corsi conquer the highest political position for which one of their fellow ethnics had been ever slated by either major party.[54]

THE ELECTION OF 1940

In anticipation of the resurgence of the coattails effect when Roosevelt's name appeared again on the Democratic ticket, in 1940 Lanzetta succeeded again in receiving Tammany Hall's endorsement for Congress despite his 1938 defeat. The choice was reasonable because Lanzetta had won in the previous two presidential years.[55] Yet the repercussions of the outbreak of World War II in

---

[52] Klehr 294; George Charney, *A Long Journey* (Chicago: Quadrangle, 1968) 113.

[53] Meyer, *Vito Marcantonio* 45.

[54] "L'Ordine Ind. Figli d'Italia per Dewey e l'On. Corsi," *Il Progresso Italo-Americano*, 24 October 1938, 2; Cosimo Masillo, "Per le elezioni," ibid., 8 November 1938, 6.

[55] "Marcantonio Files for Primary Race," *New York Times*, 14 August 1940, 23.

Europe upset the Democratic plans, and Marcantonio managed to secure a third term.

Throughout the previous three years, Marcantonio had made a point of cultivating Italian-American voters, including Mussolini's fellow travelers, whom he would blame for his 1936 defeat against Lanzetta.[56] Softening his attacks on the *Duce*'s dictatorship was part of such a scheme. For instance, his protest against the Fascist anti-Semitic legislation was almost negligible. Specifically, at a rally to protest the passing of Mussolini's anti-Jewish measures Marcantonio spoke at length about the German situation and made only cursory remarks about what was happening in Italy.[57] He also excused himself from greeting the convention of the Committee for United Action Against Fascism and Anti-Semitism.[58]

Paradoxically, however, it was Marcantonio's pro-Communist stand on World War II that eventually reconciled him with the pro-Fascist Italian-American voters in 1940. Until Germany invaded the Soviet Union in June 1941 and Moscow needed the US arms supplies of the Lend Lease Program, in Congress Marcantonio was the staunchest advocate of Washington's neutrality in the conflict, following a line that closely reflected the position of the Communists and their denunciation of the fighting as an "imperialistic war."[59]

Though Communist-induced, Marcantonio's views of US foreign policy made him extremely popular with Italian Americans, who feared a war between their native and adoptive countries and

---

[56] "Both A.L.P. Wings Voice Confidence," *New York Times*, 10 August 1942, 9.
[57] Gaetano Vecchiotti to Giuseppe Cosmelli, officer of Italy's Ministry of the Interior, New York, 21 November 1938, Records of the Ministry of the Interior, Casellario Politico Centrale, box 160, folder 2113, Archivio Centrale dello Stato, Rome, Italy.
[58] M. Gertner to Vito Marcantonio, New York, 5 December 1938, Marcantonio Papers, box 3 folder "Jewish People Committee;" Vito Marcantonio to R. Gertner, New York, 8 December 1938, ibid.
[59] Fraser M. Ottanelli, *The Communist Party of the United States: From the Depression to World War II* (New Brunswick, NJ: Rutgers UP, 1991) 185-92.

did not want to fight against their own relatives and friends who had remained in the motherland.[60] Roosevelt's stigmatization of Italy's declaration of war on France in June 1940, by means of the derogatory metaphor "the hand that held the dagger has struck it into the back of its neighbor," drew additional Italian-American votes from the Democratic column into Marcantonio's camp.[61] As reporter Warren Moscow remarked, "the Italian did not have to be a rooter for Mussolini to feel that his own pride was involved."[62] Furthermore, the president's words sounded like an anti-Italian ethnic slur that was likely to trigger a wave of discrimination because the prejudicial stereotype of Italian immigrants as stiletto-prone people seemed to have inspired Roosevelt's statement.[63] Italian-American animosity toward Roosevelt was so strong that, in their neighborhoods, the workers of the Democratic Party needed police escort to campaign in the Fall of 1940.[64]

Recipients of federal relief were potentially the largest cohort of Democrats within the Italian-American electorate. Still, sociologists Nathan Glazer and Daniel Patrick Moynihan have pointed out that "the Italian Americans became probably the most anti-Roosevelt of all low-income groups" in the wake of the president's criticism of the Fascist entry into World War II.[65] Indeed, the Ital-

---

[60] Sergio Campailla, "Little Italy," *Il sogno italo-americano: Realtà e immaginario dell'emigrazione negli Stati Uniti*, ed. Sebastiano Martelli (Naples: Cuen, 1998) 61; Meyer, *Vito Marcantonio* 119-20.

[61] *The Public Papers and Addresses of Franklin D. Roosevelt: War and Aid to Democracies* (New York: Macmillan, 1941) 63.

[62] Warren Moscow, *What Have You Done for Me Lately? The Ins and Outs of New York City Politics* (Englewood Cliffs, NJ: Prentice Hall, 1967) 132.

[63] Salvatore J. LaGumina, "Introduction," *Wop! A Documentary History of Anti-Italian Discrimination in the United States*, ed. Salvatore J. LaGumina (San Francisco: Straight Arrow, 1973) 13.

[64] *F.D.R.: His Personal Letters, 1928-1945*, ed. Elliott Roosevelt (New York: Duell, Sloane and Pearce, 1950) 1072.

[65] Nathan Glazer and Daniel Patrick Moynihan, *Beyond the Melting Pot: The Negroes, Puerto Ricans, Jews, Italians, and Irish of New York City* (Cambridge, MA: MIT P, 1963) 214.

ian-American vote for Roosevelt fell from 78.7 percent in 1936 to 42.2 percent in 1940.[66] Conversely, in the same years, the votes for Marcantonio on the Republican ticket increased from 12,116 to 14,737.[67]

Not all voters in East Harlem, however, were of Italian heritage; nor was foreign policy the only issue in the 1940 campaign for Congress. With unemployment rate as high as 29 percent in the district,[68] relief and welfare were paramount matters in the political debate. Yet this was another field from which Marcantonio could draw more benefits than Lanzetta. The Congressman's services were still important to the everyday lives of many of his constituents. In his campaign literature, Marcantonio boasted that "I have been in my district every single Sunday, and have devoted every Sunday dealing with the problems of the people of my district. I have made their problems my problems, and I have handled over 12,000 of such cases."[69] In particular, the relief rolls of New York City's Department of Welfare for East Harlem and the membership of the Fiorello La Guardia Political Club revealed similarities and overlap.[70] The gratitude of East Harlem's residents had obvious electoral implications. For example, in recognition for all that Marcantonio had done for the unemployed, Ferrer Marchini, president of the Italian Welfare Association, in East Harlem, committed his organization "to assure that the House of Representatives is honored again with your presence in the crucial coming two years."[71] Against this backdrop, since Mayor La Guardia and Roo-

---

[66] Ronald H. Bayor, *Neighbors in Conflict: The Irish, Germans, Jews, and Italians of New York City, 1929-1941* (Baltimore, MD: Johns Hopkins UP, 1978) 147.
[67] Meyer, *Vito Marcantonio* 45-46.
[68] Kenneth Alan Waltzer, "The American Labor Party: Third Party Politics in New York, 1936-1954," Ph.D. diss., Harvard U, 1978, 191.
[69] Vito Marcantonio, circular letter to East Harlem voters, n.p., 27 October 1940, box 44, folder "East Harlem Italian Organizations."
[70] Meyer, *Vito Marcantonio* 91.
[71] Ferrer Marchini to Vito Marcantonio, New York, 8 July 1940, Marcantonio Papers, box 3, folder "Italian Associations (American) (1 of 2)."

sevelt prevented the access of Tammany Hall to the bulk of patronage, Lanzetta had little in his hands to lure voters and managed to poll just 37.5 percent of the ballots, even though he ran in a presidential year,[72]

CONCLUSION

Lanzetta's 1940 defeat swept him away forever from East Harlem's politics. Nonetheless his retirement did not mark the demise of Italian Americans' hegemony in the district. In 1942 Marcantonio was re-elected unopposed after securing the nominations of the Republican, Democratic, and American Labor parties against other Italian-American contenders. His power seemed absolute and unchallengeable. As a coeval political analyst observed, "In East Harlem Marcantonio's name is a legend as 'the man who does things for people.' There is a joke that he would win if he ran on a laundry ticket. In his 'home territory' he is a political saint who intercedes with the bureaucratic gods, a Solon, a poor man's lawyer and an oracle of wisdom."[73]

Italian-American control of East Harlem politics appeared indisputable and unassailable, too. For example, in 1942 both Marcantonio's contenders in the primaries—Frank J. Ricca for the Democratic nomination and A. Charles Mucciolo for the Republican as well as American Labor nominations—were of Italian extraction.[74] Yet Italian Americans' monopoly over candidacies in the Twentieth Congressional District resulted from the fact that they were the largest ethnic group there. Consequently, their hold over politics did not survive a major transformation in the local political geography.

---

[72] Meyer, *Vito Marcantonio* 46.

[73] J. H. Stephenson, "Political Sociology of the Eighteenth Congressional District, New York City," n.d. [but mid 1940s], Marcantonio Papers, box 44, folder "Campaign, 1940 – Hdqrs. Corresp. (1 of 2)."

[74] "Barry Nominated," *New York Times*, 12 August 1942, 1, 3; tabulation of the 1942 primary election returns, Marcantonio Papers, box 44, folder "Campaign Primary Results—1942".

In an alleged attempt at gerrymandering Marcantonio out of office,[75] in 1944 most of East Harlem was added to Yorkville in the reapportioned Eighteenth Congressional District. Such efforts were in vain. Thanks to the strengthening of his political machine, Marcantonio retained his seat until his opposition to the US intervention in the Korean War caused his defeat in 1950.[76] But the merger of East Harlem and Yorkville radically changed the demography of his constituency, as the area was home to a significant number of Irish and German Americans, besides Puerto Ricans and African Americans. Italian Americans were no longer the most numerous cohort of voters in the district.[77] Consequently, Marcantonio's challengers in both the primaries and elections were not of Italian ancestry any longer.[78]

In 1950 New Yorkers of Italian extraction reached the climax of their political power. Carmine DeSapio had been the new boss of Tammany Hall since the previous year, and three of their fellow ethnics ran for City Hall. Corsi received the nomination of the GOP, Ferdinand Pecora was slated by the Democratic Party, and acting mayor Vincent Impellitteri made an independent and eventually successful bid.[79] Yet, as the ratio of Italian Americans was watered down by the 1944 reapportionment of East Harlem, so was their political clout in the Eighteenth District. In the Con-

---

[75] This is the opinion of Annette T. Rubinstein ("Vito Marcantonio, Congressman," Marcantonio, *I Vote My Conscience* 5) and Alan Schaffer (142), but Gerald Meyer has rejected this interpretation (*Vito Marcantonio* 207).

[76] Marcantonio, *I Vote My Conscience* 352-55.

[77] Salvatore J. LaGumina, *Vito Marcantonio: The People's Politician* (Dubuque, IA: Kendall Hunt, 1969) 85; Peter Jackson, "Vito Marcantonio and Ethnic Politics in New York," *Ethnic and Racial Studies* 6 (1983): 62-63.

[78] Meyer, *Vito Marcantonio* 46-47.

[79] Warren Moscow, *The Last of Big-Time Bosses: The Life and Times of Carmine DeSapio and the Decline of Tammany Hall* (New York: Stein and Day, 1971); Steven P. Eire, *Rainbow's End: Irish Americans and the Dilemmas of Urban Machine Politics, 1840-1985* (Berkeley: U of California P, 1988) 122, 150, 171; Salvatore J. LaGumina, *New York at Mid-Century: The Impellitteri Years* (Westport, CT: Greenwood, 1992) 106-30.

gressional races that followed Marcantonio's 1950 defeat, no candidates of both major party were from Italian background until Alfred Santangelo received the Democratic nomination and won election to the House in 1956.[80] Moreover, in both 1948 and 1950, even Marcantonio himself was rejected by the establishment of the Republican and Democratic parties and was forced to run only on the ticket of the American Labor Party.[81]

---

[80] Betty L. Santangelo, *Lucky Corner: The Biography of Congressman Alfred E. Santangelo and the Rise of Italian Americans in Politics* (New York: Center for Migration Studies, 1999).
[81] Meyer, *Vito Marcantonio* 47.

Italy's Postwar Migration and the Campaign for the Reform of the U. S. National-Origins Quota System, 1950-53

Stefano Luconi

INTRODUCTION

It was not so long ago that Andreina De Clementi remarked that historiography had overlooked Italian postwar migration. In 2003 she pointed out that the revitalization of the exodus from the peninsula after the end of World War II had until then aroused little scholarly attention. In her opinion, the prewar decades of the mass fluxes and Italy's more recent partial transformation from an emigration into an immigration country had theretofore seemed more valuable fields for research to the detriment of the intervening events.[1]

In the following decade, however, the state of the art has significantly changed, as studies about Italian migrations have given birth to an "endless production" that has also addressed previously neglected periods and themes.[2] Consequently, also thanks to a major contribution by De Clementi herself, scholarship has progressively begun to fill the gap of the postwar years.[3] Yet historiography has focused mainly on Italian postwar migrants to European

---

[1] Andreina De Clementi, "Curare il mal di testa con le decapitazioni? L'emigrazione italiana nel secondo dopoguerra: I primi dieci anni," *'900* 8-9 (2003): 11.

[2] Matteo Sanfilippo, "Una produzione sterminata: 2009-2010," *Archivio Storico dell'Emigrazione Italiana* 7 (2011): 150-56.

[3] Andreina De Clementi, *Il prezzo della ricostruzione: L'emigrazione italiana nel secondo dopoguerra* (Rome and Bari: Laterza, 2010).

destinations and, though to a lesser extent, to such transoceanic countries as Argentina, Canada, and Australia.[4]

The United States has remained the Cinderella of this relatively new trend of research, probably because Washington's restrictive legislation continued to stifle the number of Italian newcomers to that country after World War II. In particular, works on the post-war pro-Italy lobby in the United States have usually overlooked the issue of Italian immigration.[5] On the few occasions they have tackled this matter, they have also adopted a dubious approach. For instance, a recent study has dealt with Italian Americans' attempts at promoting a reform of the existing laws against the backdrop of the Cold War. Its author, however, has drawn almost exclusively on U. S. sources and has implicitly assumed that Italian Americans operated in a sort of vacuum insulated from the policies and interests of the Italian government. Indeed, she has argued for the existence of a not-too-hidden agenda for Italian-American activism on immigration reform. Specifically, in her view, the paramount interest of the largest and most dynamic Italian-American organization in that campaign—the American Committee on Italian Migration—was not the resumption of mass influxes from Italy. Rather this association was concerned with demonstrating that Italian immigrants should be welcome because they would make good U. S. citizens. The primary purpose of the initiative, therefore, was to dispel the fear that Italians were undesirable as well as inassimilable people, and to remove an ethnic stigma that continued to prevent the full accommodation of Italian Americans within U. S. society. In other words, the main beneficiaries of the liberalization of the U. S. immigration legislation would not be the pro-

---

[4] For a review article, see Dario Carta, "L'emigrazione italiana nel secondo dopoguerra," *Studi e Ricerche di Storia Contemporanea* 71 (2009): 114-19.

[5] See, e.g., James Edward Miller, *The United States and Italy, 1940-1950: The Politics and Diplomacy of Stabilization* (Chapel Hill: U of North Carolina P, 1986); Domenico Fracchiolla, "L'ambasciatore Tarchiani e la lobby italiana: La diplomazia italiana a Washington nell'immediato dopoguerra, 1945-1947," *Nuova Storia Contemporanea* 13.3 (2009): 45-66.

spective Italian newcomers and their homeland affected by overpopulation, but the Italian Americans themselves.[6]

Focusing on the years between the end of World War II and the passing of the 1952 McCarran-Walter Act, this brief essay intends to place Italian Americans' efforts to soften the U. S. immigration policies within a transnational perspective that highlights the deliberate interactions between their initiatives and an analogous campaign of the Italian government. In particular, this research outlines how both Rome and Italian Americans appropriated the anti-communism rhetoric of the early Cold War and used it in the attempt at achieving their goal.

ITALIAN MIGRATION IN THE POSTWAR INTERNATIONAL PERSPECTIVE

The postwar years witnessed a paradox. On the one side, the end of World War II saw the early steps toward the liberalization of the international political economy in the western world during the initial stages of what nowadays is called globalization. On the other, while they were progressively overcoming the protectionist approach of the prewar decades, the single states generally stuck to policies of immigration restriction and control that prevented workers from enjoying the same benefits that—in spite of a few surviving curbs, for instance in the textile industry—were reserved for the circulation of goods and capitals among non-Communist nations.[7]

This inconsistency deeply affected overpopulated countries, such as Italy, that had been hardly able to provide for their unemployed people even before the devastations of the war further impaired their economic resources and job opportunities. Italy had

---

[6] Danielle Battisti, "The American Committee on Italian Migration, Anti-Communism, and Immigration Reform," *Journal of American Ethnic History* 31 (2012): 11-40.

[7] Leah Haus, "Migration and International Economic Institutions," *Global Migrants, Global Refugees: Problems and Solutions*, ed. Aristide R. Zolberg and Peter Benda (New York: Berghahn, 2001) 271-73.

been an emigrant nation even before her 1861 political unification.[8] After the Fascist regime had suffocated the exodus in order to embark itself on a policy of demographic power in 1927 and to reorient the outgoing fluxes toward the Italian colonies in Africa in the mid 1930s,[9] the postwar governments aimed at facilitating the expatriation of the country's surplus population, to prevent social unrest and to speed up the economic reconstruction. In 1949, in one of his best-known statements on this issue, Prime Minister Alcide De Gasperi advised Italians to learn foreign languages and to "walk again the paths of the world," so as to flee an uncertain future of unemployment and other hardships in their native land.[10] In the face of a yearly increase in population of about 400,000 individuals, Italy had "a metropolitan territory, for a considerable extent mountainous and barren" and was "a poor country, lacking all essential raw materials," Ambassador Alberto Tarchiani reported to U. S. President Harry S. Truman as early as 1945.[11] Expatria-

---

[8] Paola Corti and Matteo Sanfilippo, *L'Italia e le migrazioni* (Rome and Bari: Laterza, 2012).
[9] Philip V. Cannistraro and Gianfausto Rosoli, "Fascist Emigration Policy in the 1920: An Interpretative Framework," *International Migration Review* 13 (1979): 673-92. The only exception was the migration of Italian workers to Germany between 1938 and 1943 in compliance with the terms of a treaty between the Fascist and Nazi regimes. See Brunello Mantelli, *"Camerati del lavoro": I lavoratori italiani emigrati nel Terzo Reich nel periodo dell'Asse, 1938-1943* (Florence: La Nuova Italia, 1992).
[10] Alcide De Gasperi, "Intervento al III Congresso nazionale della Democrazia Cristiana," Venice, 5 June 1949, Alcide De Gasperi, *Scritti e discorsi politici: Alcide De Gasperi e la stabilizzazione della Repubblica*, ed. Sara Lorenzini and Barbara Taverni, vol. 2 (Bologna: il Mulino, 2009) 1240.
[11] Alberto Tarchiani to Harry S. Truman, Washington, 6 July 1945, Harry S. Truman Papers, President's Secretary's Files, box 181, folder 60, Harry S. Truman Presidential Library, Independence, MO. Research at the Truman Library was made possible by a grant from the Harry S. Truman Library Institute, which is gratefully acknowledged. For Tarchiani, see Daniela Felisini and Elena Aga-Rossi, "Alberto Tarchiani: Politica, diplomazia ed economia di un liberale atipico," *I liberali italiani dall'antifascismo alla Repubblica*, ed. Giampietro Berti,

tion was, therefore, an unavoidable necessity. Still, to mark the discontinuity between the policy of the postwar democratic government and the expansionistic dreams of the Fascist regime, De Gasperi argued that Italy's new colonialism was "the imperialism of work and culture" pursued not by her soldiers but by her emigrants.[12]

Significantly enough, until the dynamic of the Cold War caused the exclusion of the Communist and Socialist ministers from the Italian cabinet in May 1947, the Left generally shared this approach, although it made a point of calling for the safeguard of workers abroad with more emphasis than the moderate parties such as De Gasperi's Christian Democratic Party did. For instance, *l'Unità*, the mouthpiece of the Communist Party, hailed a 1946 deal between Paris and Rome enabling 20,000 Italian workers to immigrate to France as a "success."[13] Few month later, Socialist leader Pietro Nenni—then the minister of foreign affairs—asked for international solidarity in order to let two million jobless or underemployed Italians expatriate by 1949.[14] To the labor movement, too, emigration was the lesser of two evils, as opposed to unemployment and the ensuing starvation.[15]

Against such a backdrop, Italian emigrants became a double resource. On the one hand, their remittances contributed to financing the postwar economic recovery of their motherland. On the

---

Eugenio Capozzi, and Piero Craveri (Soveria Mannelli: Rubbettino, 2010) 209-56, esp. 216-31, 236-52 for his diplomatic activities in Washington.

[12] Alcide De Gasperi, "Agli italiani perché ricerchino le vie dell'Europa," Rome, 9 June 1949, Alcide De Gasperi, *Scritti e discorsi politici: Alcide De Gasperi e la stabilizzazione della Repubblica*, ed. Sara Lorenzini and Barbara Taverni, vol. 3 (Bologna: il Mulino, 2009) 2242.

[13] "Lavoro per ventimila italiani," *l'Unità* 30 April 1946: 1.

[14] Pietro Nenni, "Dichiarazioni del Ministro Nenni," *Relazioni internazionali* 10.22 (1946): 10.

[15] Paola Salvatori, "Politica sindacale per l'emigrazione nel secondo dopoguerra," *La riscoperta delle Americhe: Lavoratori e sindacato nell'emigrazione italiana in America Latina, 1870-1970*, ed. Vanni Blengino, Emilio Franzina, and Adolfo Pepe (Milan: Teti, 1994) 132-46.

other, Italy signed treaties with a number of European countries by which she provided workers in exchange for raw materials and fuels, primarily coal, that the nation lacked. For example, Belgium sold Italy 200 kilos of coal per day for each Italian immigrant who worked in a Belgian mine.[16] Between 1946 and 1955 bilateral agreements to that effect were reached with a number of European countries which, besides Belgium, included France, Switzerland, Great Britain, the Federal Republic of Germany, and even such a Soviet satellite as Czechoslovakia.[17] Italy also relied on her membership in the Organization for European Economic Cooperation, whose purpose was to help administer the Marshall Plan, to encourage the liberalization of migration in western Europe.[18] In addition, the De Gasperi government endeavored to play upon the beginning of the process of European integration, to have workers' rights to employment abroad recognized in order to secure a further avenue to emigration for her surplus population.[19] As a result, for instance, article 69 of the Treaty of Paris, which established the European Steel and Coal Community in 1951, allowed the free circulation among member countries on the part of certified skilled workers in both fields; while article 48 of the Treaty of Rome, which created the European Economic Community six years later, extended such a right to all laborers, providing that workforce shortages affected the receiving countries.[20]

---

[16] Vittorio Briani, *L'emigrazione italiana ieri e oggi: Verso la libera circolazione del lavoro nella Comunità Economica Europea* (Rome: La Navicella, 1959) 97-100.

[17] Claudio Besana, "Accordi internazionali ed emigrazione della mano d'opera italiana tra ricostruzione e sviluppo," *Il lavoro come fattore produttivo e come risorsa nella storia economica italiana*, ed. Sergio Zaninelli and Mario Taccolini (Milan: Vita e Pensiero, 2001) 3-17; Michele Colucci, *Lavoro in movimento: L'emigrazione italiana in Europa, 1945-1957* (Rome: Donzelli, 2008).

[18] Antonio Varsori, *La Cenerentola d'Europa? L'Italia e l'integrazione europea dal 1947 a oggi* (Soveria Mannelli: Rubbettino, 2010) 44-45.

[19] Federico Romero, *Emigrazione e integrazione europea, 1945-1973* (Rome: Edizioni Lavoro, 1991).

[20] Gemma del Gaudio, "Libera circolazione e priorità comunitaria del lavoratori nei paesi della CEE," *Il movimento migratorio italiano dall'Unità nazionale ai*

ITALY AND THE U. S. IMMIGRATION RESTRICTION

There were several shortcomings and delays in the enforcement of those agreements. For example, the Italian miners who pursued job opportunities in Great Britain in 1951 and 1952, in compliance with the Collective Recruiting Plan agreement between London and Rome, suffered from so much hostility and discrimination that they were eventually repatriated.[21] Likewise, both Italy's slowness in identifying possible emigrant workers and the Federal Republic of Germany's rigorous health checks interfered with the exodus to that country.[22] Nevertheless the attempts of the Italian government at revitalizing emigration to European destinations met some success. After all, from 1946 to 1955, about 1,300,000 Italians, namely 52.6 percent of the total number of the expatriates, moved to European countries.[23] Following an additional bilateral treaty, which was signed on 21 February 1947, the main receiving country outside Europe was Argentina, which became home to 274,523 Italian newcomers between 1946 and 1950, as opposed to their 66,068 fellow citizens who settled in the United States in the same

---

giorni nostri, ed. Franca Assante, vol. 2 (Genève: Droz, 1978) 147-53; Luciano Tosi, "La tutela internazionale dell'emigrazione," *Storia dell'emigrazione italiana: Arrivi*, ed. Piero Bevilacqua, Andreina De Clementi, and Emilio Franzina (Rome: Donzelli, 2002) 452-54; Maria Pina Giaquinto, "Emigrare nell'Europa del carbone e dell'acciaio: Il problema della manodopera italiana nei primi negoziati per l'integrazione europea," MA thesis, U of Rome "Tor Vergata," 2008.

[21] Michele Colucci, *Emigrazione e ricostruzione: Italiani in Gran Bretagna dopo la Seconda guerra mondiale* (Foligno: Editoriale Umbra, 2009) 91-109.

[22] Roberto Sala, "Il controllo statale sull'immigrazione di manodopera italiana nella Germania federale," *Annali dell'Istituto Storico Italo-Germanico di Trento* 30 (2004): 119-52; Elia Morandi, *Governare l'emigrazione: Lavoratori italiani verso la Germania nel secondo dopoguerra* (Turin: Rosenberg & Sellier, 2011).

[23] Antonio Golini e Flavia Amato, "Uno sguardo a un secolo e mezzo di emigrazione italiana," *Storia dell'emigrazione italiana: Partenze*, ed. Piero Bevilacqua, Andreina De Clementi, and Emilio Franzina (Rome: Donzelli, 2001) 50.

period.[24] Still Italy's prospective emigrants continued to think of the latter country as the destination of their dreams.[25] The U. S. restrictive legislation of the 1920s allotted Italy a maximum of as few as 5,802 immigrant visas per year.[26] The national-origins quota system heavily discriminated against the prospective Italian newcomers. The 1924 Johnson-Reed Act stipulated that each European country was entitled to the admission of a number of its nationals equaling 2 percent of its immigrants residing in the United States according to the 1890 federal census. No fewer than 29,000 Italians had entered the country between the end of World War I and the enactment of this measure.[27] But the year 1890 was only the dawn of Italian mass immigration. Consequently, Italy was underrepresented in the distribution of visas under the provisions of the Johnson-Reed Act.[28]

Nonetheless Italians made significant efforts to dodge the existing legislation. About 2,000 women, for instance, married American soldiers who had occupied Italy during World War II, to benefit from the 1945 War Brides Act that allowed the alien spouses of military personnel to move to the United States as non-quota immigrants. Another 3,500 Italian women got engaged to U. S. enlisted men and similarly entered the country under the

---

[24] Fernando J. Devoto, *Storia degli italiani in Argentina* (Rome: Donzelli, 2006) 411-19; Patrizia Audenino and Maddalena Tirabassi, *Migrazioni italiane: Storia e storie dall'Ancien régime a oggi* (Milan: Bruno Mondadori, 2008) 138.

[25] Sandro Rinauro, "Sognando l'America: Mete dell'emigrazione italiana negli anni della Ricostruzione tra desiderio e realtà," *Città, regione, territorio: Studi in memoria di Roberto Mainardi*, ed. Guglielmo Scaramellini (Milan: Cisalpino, 2003) 201-30.

[26] US Bureau of the Census, *Statistical Abstract of the United States* (Washington: GPO, 1966) 92.

[27] Anna Maria Martellone, "Italian Mass Emigration to the United States, 1876-1930: An Historical Survey," *Perspectives in American History* 1 (1984): 392.

[28] Matteo Pretelli, *L'emigrazione italiana negli Stati Uniti* (Bologna: il Mulino, 2011) 75.

provisions of the 1946 Alien Fiancées and Fiancés Act.[29] The fact that roughly half of such marriages had ended in divorce by the fifth year since the settlement of the couples in the United States offers quantitative evidence of the expedient convenience of the bulk of these liaisons.[30] A few Italians did not even refrain from embarking as stowaways on ships sailing for the United States, in the most often fruitless attempt at avoiding immigration control.[31]

It is hardly by chance that *Il Popolo*, the mouthpiece of De Gasperi's Christian Democratic Party, carefully reported the introduction of any bill aiming at reforming the U. S. immigrant legislation, and closely followed its Congressional procedures. The newspaper paid special attention to six slightly different bills that, if they had not been tabled, would have granted Italy the immigrant visas she had been unable to use during World War II.[32] These bills were introduced by U. S. representatives with a significant number of constituents of Italian background in their districts, under pressure from Italian-American ethnic associations that operated in cooperation with Italy's consular personnel.[33] Most prominent among such organizations was the Order Sons of Italy in America (OSIA), the largest and most influential Italian-American mutual-aid society nationwide, which had encouraged its own

---

[29] Silvia Cassamagnaghi, "Relax Girls, US Will Treat You Right: Le spose italiane dei GI della Seconda guerra mondiale," *Altreitalie* 38-39 (2009): 109-32; Maria Porzio, *Arrivano gli Alleati: Amori e violenze nell'Italia liberata* (Rome and Bari: Laterza, 2011) 142-66.

[30] Oriana Fallaci, "America dolce-amara per le spose di guerra," *Epoca* 17 novembre 1951: 26-31.

[31] Sandro Rinauro, *Il cammino della speranza: L'emigrazione clandestina degli italiani nel secondo dopoguerra* (Turin: Einaudi, 2009) 101.

[32] "Il sistema delle quote nell'emigrazione italiana in USA," *Il Popolo* 26 October 1951: 3.

[33] See, e.g., Alberto Tarchiani to Leonard Pasqualicchio, Washington, 3 February 1950, Records of the Ministry of Foreign Affairs, Series Ambasciata a Washington, box 56, folder 1613, Archivio Storico del Ministero degli Affari Esteri, Rome, Italy; Giovanni Battista Cuneo to Italian Embassy, Chicago, 28 January 1950, ibidem.

members to lobby their Congressmen for the liberalization of the existing measures since the resumption of immigration from Italy to the United States, following the demise of hostilities between the two countries in World War II.[34] The campaign, however, gained momentum in 1950, when Leonard Pasqualicchio—the first national deputy of the OSIA and its chief lobbyist on Capitol Hill—convinced Representatives William Barrett (D-PA) and Gary Clemente (D-NY) to draw similar bills for the purpose of granting Italy the about 37,000 immigrant visas that the country had lost between 1940 and 1945 because of the war.[35]

The early postwar years seemed a most promising time to advocate for the reform of U. S. immigration legislation. At the end of World War II, within its broader grand design to develop institutions that could encourage the global liberalization of economic relations, the United States did not rule out its own adherence to some limited forms of international cooperation on migration issues, under the auspices of the International Labor Organization (ILO), an agency of the former League of Nations that had subsequently become part of the United Nations. Against this backdrop, the creation of a Migration Administration was planned, to help negotiate agreements between sending and receiving countries. Nonetheless, after the consolidation of the Cold War, Washington decided to avoid any commitment to an agency in which Communist nations could play a role, contributed to killing the proposal

---

[34] Ernest L. Biagi, *The Purple Aster: A History of the Order Sons of Italy in America* (New York: Veritas, 1961) 86-91; E. Michael Del Papa, "The Order Sons of Italy in America and Its Campaign to Revise and Liberalize the Immigration Laws of the United States," MA thesis, Assumption College, Worcester, 1968, 19. For the Order Sons of Italy in America, see Jennifer Guglielmo and John Andreozzi, "The Order Sons of Italy in America: Historical Summary," *Guide to the Records of the Order Sons of Italy in America*, ed. Jennifer Guglielmo and John Andreozzi (Minneapolis: Immigration History Research Center, 2004) xix-xxx.
[35] Alberto Tarchiani to Ministry of Foreign Affairs, Washington, 26 April 1950; Leonard Pasqualicchio to William Barrett, Washington, 15 June 1950, both in Records of the Italian Ministry of Foreign Affairs, series Ambasciata a Washington, box 56, folder 1613.

for the Migration Administration, and redirected the ILO to focus on practical assistance to migrants, leaving aside any auxiliary stimulus for people's mobility.[36] Rejecting compliance with international regulations that could somehow interfere with national sovereignty over the admission of individuals to the United States, Washington even declined to ratify the conventions for the treatment of immigrant workers that the ILO eventually drew.[37]

The Truman administration initially pointed to the ILO as a possible venue to address the overpopulation problems of many European countries. A preliminary conference on migration—which was attended by delegates from twenty-nine countries, including the United States, and convened in Geneva, Switzerland, under the auspices of the ILO in 1950—acknowledged that Italy's "surplus of manpower" was a "serious problem," and conceived a program to facilitate international migrations that pleased Rome.[38] As late as June 1951 the draft for a proposed U. S. position paper on overpopulation called the ILO "a most promising" "instrument of international cooperation for emigration."[39] Therefore, the refusal of the United States to finance the establishment of the Migration Administration at a conference of the ILO held in Naples the following October and Washington's progressive decoupling from the UN agency were major setbacks to De Gasperi's attempts at persuading the Truman administration to facilitate international migrations.[40] Indeed, the United States preferred to promote the

---

[36] Ernst B. Haas, *Beyond the Nation-State: Functionalism and International Organizations* (Stanford: Stanford UP, 1964) 172-73.

[37] Haus 282-83.

[38] "Migration and Economic Development," *International Labour Review* 62 (1950): 91-115 (quotes 91, 92). For the evaluation of the Italian government and diplomats, see Records of the Ministry of Foreign Affairs, Series Ambasciata a Washington, box 56, folder 1612.

[39] Robert West, "Surplus Population in Western Europe: Proposed US Action," 19 June 1951, Truman Papers, Files of David D. Lloyd, box 3, folder "Immigration Memoranda 4."

[40] Patrizia Rontini, "Il governo italiano e il problema dell'emigrazione negli anni '50," *L'Italia e la politica di potenza in Europa, 1950-60*, ed. Ennio Di Nolfo,

establishment of the Geneva-based Provisional Committee for the Movement of Migrants from Europe, later renamed the Intergovernmental Committee for European Migration (ICEM). Headed by Hugh S. Gibson, an experienced U. S. Foreign Service senior officer, the ICEM accepted only "governments with a demonstrated interest in the principle of free movement of persons" for membership, to exclude Communist countries.[41] With about one third of its nearly thirty-four-million-dollar budget funded by Washington, it also encouraged the resettlement of European migrants mainly to Canada and Latin America, but purportedly not to the United States. Consequently, the ICEM enabled Washington to make its own contribution to easing the overpopulation problems of the Old World while continuing to keep the American gates only ajar for such European immigrants as the Italians.[42]

The Cold War was also responsible for the introduction of further restrictions to the U. S. immigration legislation. For instance, the 1950 McCarran Internal Security Act set affiliation with totalitarian organizations as ground for denying admission to the United States. The measure was conceived to ban Communist aliens, and even authorized the deportation of those who had already entered the country prior to the enactment of the new law.[43] Yet the Italian government was worried that the provision could apply to adherents to the already dissolved National Fascist Party, because the latter's membership had included the great bulk of the Italian pop-

---

Romain H. Rainero, and Brunello Vigezzi (Milan: Marzorati, 1992) 531-32; Richard T. Griffiths, *The Economic Development of the EEC* (Lyme: Elgar, 1997) 246-48.

[41] ICEM charter as quoted in Freda Hawkins, *Canada and Immigration: Public Policy and Public Concern* (Kingston: McGill-Queen's UP, 1988) 19.

[42] Murrey Marder, "Truman Hears Plan to Move Migrants," unidentified and undated newspaper clipping, Hugh S. Gibson Papers, box 36, folder "Migration # 1," Truman Library; Carl J. Bon Tempo, *Americans at the Gate: The United States and Refugees during the Cold War* (Princeton: Princeton UP, 2008) 37.

[43] Christopher Rudolph, *National Security and Immigration: Policy Developments in the United States and Western Europe Since 1950* (Stanford: Stanford UP, 2006) 50.

ulation—which had joined the party and its youth organizations less out of choice than of necessity under the pressures of a dictatorship – before the fall of Benito Mussolini's regime on 25 July 1943.[44] This expectation proved to be correct, as not only immigrants but also temporary visitors ran into trouble entering the United States, following the enforcement of the act. The most illustrious victims were shipping magnate Enrico Costa, who was planning to attend an international conference on silk trade in New York in the Fall of 1950, and Victor De Sabata, a conductor of Milan's La Scala orchestra, who was briefly detained when he arrived in the United States for a few concerts in the same period.[45]

THE LOBBY AGAINST THE NATIONAL-ORIGINS QUOTA SYSTEM

If the Cold War caused the United States to make a partial retreat from the issue of cooperation in the field of international migration, anti-communism was not only a drawback but also an opportunity as for the attempts at having Washington soften its restrictive legislation for prospective Italian newcomers. Actually, both the De Gasperi government and the Italian-American ethnic organizations exploited the Cold War rhetoric while encouraging a liberalization of the U. S. measures. The two parties had already resorted to a similar strategy in 1948, to pressure Washington into making concessions to Italy that would speed up the economic recovery of the country and her reinstatement to the status of a medium Mediterranean power, after her devastating defeat in World War II. Actually, on the one hand, Italian Americans embraced the anti-communist approach of the Truman administration and

---

[44] Rosaria Quartararo, *Italia e Stati Uniti: Gli anni difficili, 1945-1952* (Naples: Edizioni Scientifiche Italiane, 1986) 386-88.
[45] Gino Tomajuoli, "100 passeggeri italiani fermati allo sbarco a New York," *La Stampa* 11 October 1950: 1; "Maestro of La Scala Is Detained with 30 Others Under Alien Act," *New York Times* 13 October 1950: 14; "Fermati al loro arrivo a New York anche il Maestro De Sabata e l'armatore Costa," *La Stampa* 13 October 1950: 1; "L'azione del Governo italiano per i fermi di italiani negli Stati Uniti," *Il Popolo* 19 October 1950: 4.

participated in a massive letter-writing campaign to persuade their relatives and friends who still lived in their native land not to vote for the candidates of the Communist-Socialist fusionist ticket—the Fronte Democratico Popolare (People's Democratic Front)—on the occasion of Italy's 1948 parliamentary elections. Consequently, they demonstrated their allegiance to their adoptive country and won political credit that they intended to spend to the benefit of Italy. On the other hand, the De Gasperi government and the leading Italian-American ethnic organizations and newspapers joined forces in warning Washington that, unless Italy was included in the Marshall Plan, could establish again her sovereignty over the port city of Trieste, and was allowed to retain her pre-Fascist colonies in northern and eastern Africa, the disappointment of the Italian people would cause a protest vote against the United States that would enable the Communist Party to win the elections.[46]

The campaign against the national-origins quota system between 1950 and 1952 followed the same course. In June of 1950 Fortune Pope—the publisher of *Il Progresso Italo-Americano*, the most authoritative Italian-language daily in the United States—and his two brothers, Anthony and Generoso Jr., prepared a memorandum for President Truman in support of the bills that aimed at awarding Italy her wartime unused immigrant visas. According to the Popes, the resumption of sizeable immigration to the United States would "deal a direct blow to communism in Italy and not only aid those forces fighting for democracy as we understand it, but also defeat Communist attempts to nullify the salutary effects of the Marshall Plan aid to Italy made possible by American taxpayers."[47] They also made their way to the White House to further elaborate their point in person. No sooner was their meeting with

---

[46] Stefano Luconi, "Anticommunism, Americanization, and Ethnic Identity: Italian Americans and the 1948 Parliamentary Elections in Italy," *Historian* 62 (2000): 285-302.

[47] Fortune R. Pope, Anthony J. Pope, and Generoso Pope, Jr., to Harry S. Truman, New York, 14 June 1950, Truman Papers, Official File 233, folder "Italy, Misc. (1950-53)."

Truman over than the president received Italian Ambassador Tarchiani, to discuss the same issue. The sequence of the talks can easily suggest one more time the interaction between Italy's diplomatic pressures and the Italian-American lobbying efforts.[48]

The quotation from the Popes' memorandum aptly shows how supporters of the liberalization of Italian immigration to the United States—both among Italian statesmen and Italian Americans—endeavored to exploit anti-communism to achieve their aim. Their best argument was that, if restrictions on the number of Italian newcomers were not lifted in the near future, the Communist Party would capitalize on overpopulation and unemployment in the country, as well as on the ensuing social unrest and voters' dissatisfaction with Washington, and would seize power in Italy by legal means. The stand of *Il Progresso Italo-Americano* on the McCarran Internal Security Act sheds light on both the contents of this strategy and the connections between the Italian government and Italian Americans. After Congress passed the law, the daily justified its "draconian restrictions" on the grounds that the sacrifice of a few individual freedoms were necessary to prevent Communist infiltrations into the United States.[49] But as soon as Carlo Sforza, Italy's minister for foreign affairs, criticized the new piece of legislation because it interfered with the admission of Italians to the United States, the newspaper took on its provisions by arguing that "nazism and fascism are dead and buried. Reviving them out of over-precaution means playing into the hands of communism."[50]

These pressures were not in vain. In March 1951 the McCarran Internal Security Act was amended to the effect that Washington would no longer bar individuals who could prove that their membership in the National Fascist Party and its various organiza-

---

[48] "Truman discute con i fratelli Pope l'immigrazione italiana negli S.U.," *Il Progresso Italo-Americano* 15 June 1950: 1, 3.

[49] "L'Internal Security Act," *Il Progresso Italo-Americano* 26 September 1950: 6.

[50] "96 Italiani giunti col 'Vulcania e l' 'Italia' inviati ad Ellis Island," *Il Progresso Italo-Americano* 11 October 1950: 1, 9; "Il McCarran Act," ibid. 12 October 1950: 6 (to which the quotation refers).

tion had been only nominal.⁵¹ As a result, the Italian government thought that the anti-Communist rhetoric would reap additional fruits. During a visit to the United States in September of 1951, both at official and at less formal events, De Gasperi himself resorted to the thesis that U. S. immigration restriction helped the Communist Party in Italy.⁵² For example, in a meeting with President Truman behind closed doors, he contended that "Italy is not able to solve her unemployment problem by herself. Unemployment is a critical problem that has to be settled because unemployment is a breeder of communism." In his opinion, "an extraordinary program is needed to encourage and help a large number of Italians to emigrate" and, therefore, the Prime Minister expected the United States to lift restrictions on prospective Italian newcomers.⁵³ On his way back from the White House, De Gasperi reiterated the same points, speaking to reporters at the National Press Club in Washington. Specifically, he held that "we have too much [sic] people for the size of our country, and its availabilities. [...] Many of the people in our country who voted communist are not followers of Marx and Lenin. They are simply people who do not have enough to eat or people who do not feel secure about work and their standard of life."⁵⁴

This strategy came to a head after the introduction of companion bills by Senator Pat McCarran (D-NV) and Representative Francis E. Walter (D-PA), which were eventually merged into the 1952 McCarran-Walter Bill. Contrary to the hopes of both the Italian government and Italian Americans, the proposed piece of

---

⁵¹ "Immigration Bill Signed," *New York Times* 29 March 1951: 23.
⁵² For De Gasperi's visit, see Quartararo 462-71; Giancarlo Giordano, "Il secondo viaggio di De Gasperi a Washington (settembre 1951)," *Clio* 20 (1984): 79-93.
⁵³ "Meeting of the President and Prime Minister De Gasperi," 25 September 1951, George M. Elsey Papers, box 113, folder "De Gasperi, Italian Prime Minister Alcide – Visit to the United States, September 1951," Truman Library.
⁵⁴ Alcide De Gasperi, "Address to the National Press Club," Washington, 25 September 1951, De Gasperi 3:2421-22.

legislation not only reaffirmed the national origins system and its preferential treatment for newcomers from northern Europe, it also further reduced Italy's annual quota to 5,645 immigrant visas per year, while 32,107 Italian citizens applied to enter the United States as permanent residents in 1952 alone.[55]

Protesting against the anti-Italian discrimination underlying the bill, the ethnic press campaigned against it. Specifically, newspapers such as *Il Progresso Italo-Americano* and *Ordine Nuovo*—the mouthpiece of the Order of the Sons of Italy in Pennsylvania—launched a letter campaign among their readers. They called on Italian Americans to write their representatives and senators and to warn them that Congressmen would both lose electoral support and strengthen the Communist Party in Italy if they supported the reform.[56] In particular, *Il Progresso Italo-Americano* suggested that, with reference to the retention of discriminatory quotas in the immigration legislation, Italian Americans should emphasize that "the persistence in this crass injustice...unnecessarily provide valuable grist for the mills of the Communists in Italy....It makes it...terribly hard to enhance American prestige and the cause of democracy inside Italy."[57]

Italian-American associations, too, took on the McCarran-Walter Bill. Italian diplomats, for instance, mobilized a few local chapters of the recently-established American Committee on Italian Migration, whose national secretary—Judge Juvenal Marchisio of New York City's Domestic Relations Court—had already embraced anti-communist rhetoric in the struggle to soften the U. S.

---

[55] Robert A. Divine, *American Immigration Policy, 1924-1952* (New Haven: Yale UP, 1957) 164-91; President's Commission on Immigration and Naturalization, *Whom We Shall Welcome* (Washington: GPO, 1953) 100, 104.

[56] "Uniamoci nella lotta per umanizzare le leggi immigratorie," *Il Progresso Italo-Americano* 13 April 1952: 5; "Le nuove leggi d'immigrazione e di naturalizzazione nel Congresso degli S.U.," *Ordine Nuovo* 31 May 1952: 1.

[57] "Protestate per il McCarran Bill," *Il Progresso Italo-Americano* 11 May 1952: 7.

immigration legislation.[58] For example, the previous year, while advocating less strict rules for Italian prospective newcomers, he had stated at a joint hearing of the Senate and House Subcommittees on Immigration and Naturalization, "At no cost to ourselves and with much profit to our economy and culture, we can, by some increase and/or liberalization of the Italian immigration quota, increase faith in the political and democratic strength of our way of life at a strategic point in the combat between Democracy and Communism."[59]

The dailies published in Italy—even those that sided with the Christian Democratic Party such as *La Stampa*, *Il Popolo*, and the *Corriere della Sera*—did not mention any contribution on the part of Washington's immigration restriction to the enhancement of communism while discussing all the possible drawbacks of the McCarran-Walter Bill and stressing the nativist intent of such a piece of legislation. Therefore, one can easily conclude that this issue was brought up in the United States for the sole purpose of scaring the Truman administration and Congress into again opening American doors to a significant influx of Italians.[60] The fact that the harshest critics of the national-origins quota system in Italy included the Jesuit journal *La Civiltà Cattolica* further points to

---

[58] Enrico Aillaud to Alberto Tarchiani, New Orleans, 22 September 1952, Records of the Italian Ministry of Foreign Affairs, series Ambasciata a Washington, box 23, folder 607. For Marchisio, see Frank Cavaioli, "Juvenal Marchisio: Distinguished Italian-American Citizen," *Italian Americans in the Professions*, ed. Remigio U. Pane (Staten Island: American Italian Historical Association, 1983) 143-52.

[59] Juvenal Marchisio, "Memorandum Submitted to the Joint Hearings of the Subcommittee on Immigration and Naturalization of the US Senate and the Subcommittee on Immigration and Naturalization of the House of Representatives," 9 April 1951, Records of the American Committee on Italian Migration, microfilm edition, reel 1, Biblioteca di Storia e Letteratura Nordamericana, University of Florence, Florence, Italy.

[60] Gino Tomajuoli, "Un progetto americano per gli emigranti e gli stranieri," *La Stampa* 21 May 1952: 1; "La legge McCarran," *Il Popolo* 29 June 1952: 1; "La legge americana sull'emigrazione," *Corriere della Sera* 4 luglio 1952: 1.

the expediency in linking immigration restriction to the Italian people's pro-Communist feelings.[61]

Italy's 1952 local elections offered an additional and timely opportunity to use anti-communism as a trump card in the pursuit of a partial liberalization of immigration to the United States. On the eve of the vote, Providence's Italian-American weekly *Italian Echo* argued that all the efforts to keep Italy within the western bloc risked being wasted if the Communist party was given the chance of exploiting the economic hardships and unemployment resulting from the country's demographic pressure because of "our discriminatory immigration laws."[62] Furthermore, claimed the Rhode Island daily, *Il Progresso Italo-Americano* profited by a modest increase in the Communist vote and a slight decline in the following of the Christian Democratic Party at the polls.[63] This political outcome was presented as a demonstration of the hypothesis that the extreme Left benefited from the dissatisfaction of the unemployed who could not leave the country to pursue better economic opportunities, especially opportunities in the United States. The newspaper argued that an effective means to helping Italy fight communism was to "solve her problem of overpopulation."[64] Similarly, the *Italian Echo* contended that Communist candidates cashed in on the voters' awareness that, with the Marshall Plan, the United States had only thrown the Italian people "a bone in the form of financial help" without making significant efforts to solve the nation's structural problems such as surplus population.[65]

---

[61] Giorgio Rumi, "Un antiamericanismo di *La Civiltà Cattolica?*," *L'antiamericanismo in Italia e in Europa nel secondo dopoguerra*, ed. Piero Craveri and Gaetano Quagliariello (Soveria Mannelli: Rubbettino, 2004) 316-17.

[62] "Apprehension for Italy," *Italian Echo* 16 May 1952: 1.

[63] Giuseppe Mammarella, *L'Italia contemporanea, 1943-1985* (Bologna: il Mulino, 1985) 190-91.

[64] "Un sintomatico monito," *Il Progresso Italo-Americano* 1 June 1952: 1.

[65] "Our Paesani Vote," *Italian Echo* 30 May 1952: 1.

CONCLUSION

Of course, it cannot be ruled out that the debate about the McCarran-Walter Bill had other implications in the eyes of the Italian statesmen. For instance, De Gasperi did fear that the failure of his own government to secure concessions for Italian migrants from the Truman administration would curb the following of the Christian Democratic Party and its allies in the 1953 parliamentary elections and prevent them from obtaining 50 percent of the votes plus one, which would ensure the ruling coalition 65 percent of the seats, although the Prime Minister did not think that it could cause their defeat at the polls.[66] After all, the Italian press analyzed De Gasperi's 1951 visit to the United States against the backdrop of its contribution to strengthening or weakening the Prime Minister and his government.[67] Likewise, as Danielle Battisti has suggested, a few Italian-American individuals and organizations that lobbied against immigration restriction might have had a primarily domestic agenda, which aimed at improving the status of their own ethnic minority in the United States instead of offering people in their ancestral land more opportunities to leave the country and to enjoy a presumably better life on the other shore of the Atlantic.[68] In any case, the joint strategy of the De Gasperi government and its counterparts in the Italian-American community was definitely part of a larger attitude toward Washington that scholarship has called "tyrannical weakness," namely the overemphasis by the ruling Christian Democratic Party on a supposed Communist threat

---

[66] Alcide De Gasperi to Alberto Tarchiani, Rome, 5 November 1951, *De Gasperi scrive: Corrispondenza con capi di Stato, cardinali, uomini politici, giornalisti, diplomatici*, ed. Maria Romana De Gasperi, vol. 2 (Brescia: Morcelliana, 1974) 142.
[67] Barbara Taverni, "Da Ottawa a Washington: Il secondo viaggio in America di De Gasperi nella stampa italiana," *Quaderni Degasperiani per la Storia dell'Italia Contemporanea* 4 (2012): 111-46.
[68] Battisti 12, 21, 24-26, 30.

that could be defused only if the United States made significant concessions to fortify an allegedly frail cabinet.[69]

In 1948 Italy had obtained 1,387 million dollars in U. S. economic aids for a period of five years under the provisions of the Marshall Plan—in spite of the British opposition to her inclusion among the beneficiaries of American assistance—and a joint declaration by the United States, Great Britain, and France supporting the return of Trieste under Rome's jurisdiction.[70] But, in the subsequent years, the "tyrannical weakness" was to no avail as for the reform of immigration legislation, except for the amendment to the McCarran Internal Security Act. De Gasperi came out empty handed from his 1951 meeting with Truman. The president made it clear that, notwithstanding his personal willingness to accept a larger number of European immigrants, the matter was under Congressional jurisdiction and a majority of the legislators opposed modifications to the national-origins quota system or even the temporary introduction of significant exemptions for Italians.[71] U. S. Secretary of State Dean Acheson even rejected De Gasperi's argument that "Italy's overpopulation was a common problem, which we should help solve by easing our immigration laws." According to Acheson "if Italy wished to regard birth control from the medieval point of view of what was then Vatican policy, she had only herself to blame. To ask others to mitigate her own blindness seemed to me wholly unwarranted. So we refused to make any

---

[69] Alessandro Brogi, *L'Italia e l'egemonia americana nel Mediterraneo* (Scandicci: La Nuova Italia, 1999) 36-44; Mario Del Pero, *L'alleato scomodo: Gli USA e la DC negli anni del centrismo (1948-1955)* (Rome: Carocci, 2001) 291.

[70] Federico Romero, "Gli Stati Uniti in Italia: Il Piano Marshall e il Patto Atlantico," *Storia dell'Italia Repubblicana: La costruzione della democrazia: Dalla caduta del fascismo agli anni Cinquanta*, ed. Francesco Barbagallo (Turin: Einaudi, 1994) 261 (to which the figure refers); Antonio Varsori, *L'Italia nelle relazioni internazionali dal 1943 al 1992* (Rome and Bari: Laterza, 1998) 52-54, 63-64.

[71] "Minutes of the Meeting of the President with Prime Minister De Gasperi at the White House, 25 September 1951," Dean Acheson Papers, box 69, folder "October 1951," Truman Library.

commitments."[72] As a result, the final joint communiqué on De Gasperi's visit confined itself to vaguely mentioning the intent of the Truman administration to "cooperate with other governments...and put into effect concrete plans for the solution of the related problems of Italian and European overpopulation," without listing any sort of commitment to the liberalization of the U. S. immigration legislation.[73] Similarly, one year later, Congress passed the McCarran-Walter Bill over Truman's veto, despite the intense lobbying efforts of both the Italian government and Italian-American voters against the measure, which included "close to 11,000 telegrams, letters and cards" backing the president's decision.[74]

On the eve of Italy's 1953 parliamentary elections, De Gasperi resorted one more time to the Cold War rhetoric. In an interview with the *US News and World Report*, he stated that overpopulation was the main explanation for the Communist strength in his country and that the McCarran-Walter Act had contributed to it, impairing the chances of the victory of the Christian Democratic Party at the polls.[75] Yet the Prime Minister's words were again to no avail. Notwithstanding the campaigns of both Rome and Italian Americans against this piece of legislation in 1952 and 1953, it took a long time to have the new law repealed, which happened only in 1965.[76]

---

[72] Dean Acheson, *Present at the Creation: My Years in the State Department* (New York: Norton, 1969) 733-34.

[73] US Department of State, Communiqué no. 869, 26 September 1951, Elsey Papers, box 113, folder "De Gasperi, Italian Prime Minister Alcide – Visit to the United States, September 1951."

[74] Alberto Tarchiani, *Dieci anni tra Roma e Washington* (Milan: Mondadori, 1955) 132; William J. Hopkins, "Memorandum," Washington, 20 June 1952, Truman Papers, President's Secretary's File, box 111, folder "McCarran-Walter Bill" (to which the quotation refers).

[75] Robert Kleiman, "A Divided Europe Means War: De Gasperi of Italy," *US News and World Report* 15 May 1953: 30-32.

[76] Leonard Dinnerstein and David M. Reimers, *Ethnic Americans: A History of Immigration* (New York: Columbia UP, 2009) 120; Frank J. Cavaioli, "Italian

Italy's unsuccessful efforts to play upon anti-communism in order to soften the national-origins quota system in the early 1950s offer a case in point of what historian Roger Daniel has remarked about the implications of the Cold War for U. S. immigration policy. As he has pointed out, the American postwar legislation turned out to be more flexible than it seemed, and the United States was willing to ease immigration restriction under the stimuli of its worldwide confrontation with the Soviet Union. But Washington was motivated mainly by propaganda purposes aiming at the exposition of the lack of freedom in nations under Moscow's yoke. Therefore, the United States confined changes to its strict immigration rules almost exclusively for the benefit of refugees from Communist countries.[77]

Americans Slay the Immigration Dragon: The National-Origins Quota System," *Italian Americana* 5 (1979): 71-100.

[77] Roger Daniels, *Coming to America: A History of Immigration and Ethnicity in American Life* (New York: Harper Collins, 2002) 335-37, 347-49.

ITALIAN-AMERICAN POLITICAL LEADERSHIP IN THE TEA PARTY ERA
CONSERVATIVE, PROGRESSIVE, REACTIONARY?

Laurie Buonanno and Michael Buonnano

Having cut our teeth as students of Italian American culture on Rudolph Vecoli's *Italian-American Radicalism: Old World Origins and New World Developments* and having experienced the radical tradition there described first-hand in the discourses of our own Italian-American community, we couldn't help but wonder about the other end of the political spectrum that seems every bit as much the reality of Italian American politics: For every Italian-American radical—for instance, the anarchist who notoriously named his daughters *Fame*, *Miseria* and *Rivoluzione*—there is the conservative jurist who clucks his disapproval of Barack Obama at the State of the Union Address. For each Nancy Pelosi or Andrew Cuomo there is a Tom Tancredo or a Susan Molinari. Where once Patterson, New Jersey and Lowell, Massachusetts defined our political affiliation, too often ugly events in Boston, Bensonhurst, or Howard Beach, have driven external perceptions of Italian American culture and its political manifestations.

Italian Americans, once considered a key constituency in the Democratic party, now are almost equally divided between the two major parties—36 percent Republican, 37 percent Democratic—with a healthy 30 percent claiming themselves to be independents (figures from Tamburri). Thus, we can no longer speak of Italian Americans as solid Democratic voters, if—that is—we ever could. And, then, when we turn to questions of identity, we often do so with very few allusion to politics—but certainly political affiliation must provide at least one facet of Italian-American identity. Other

American ethnic groups have demonstrated clearly recognizable voting patterns, with the two main political parties vying fervently for the African-American, Latino/Latina, and Jewish-American votes. Do Italian-American party identification and voting patterns reveal anything about Italian America identity? To put names to our query we might ask how Italian American families in New York State could produce both a Carl Paladino and an Andrew Cuomo.

Our task, then, is the exploration of the origins of Italian political identity in America. And, as a corollary to this, it is our desire to ascertain if there was a historical bias in the formulation of such identity. In other words, were the radical and reactionary traditions that have so assiduously been charted by Vecoli and others being irrevocably displaced by another, more conformist, impulse, driving both toward more centrist but nonetheless polarized positions? And, if so, what was driving the transformation? Or, conversely, was the conservative bent found among some Italian Americans carried, like the radical tradition, from Italy—Vecoli's 'Old World Origins' thesis with a conservative twist—to find voice in the America's center-right party and movements? After all, three-quarters of Italian migrants to America came from the south and—despite the periodic outbreak of peasant revolt or rural labor activism in the years between the *Risorgimento* and Benito Mussolini's March on Rome—the postwar *Mezzogiorno* has been a reliably conservative voting bloc for the *Democrazia Christiana* and its successor center-right party, *Il Popolo della Libertà* (PdL), a grown-up version of *Forza Italia* joined with the sanitized neo-fascist party *Alleanza Nazionale* (NA) (when, of course, the leading politicians of these parties see an advantage in forming governing coalitions).

OLD WORLD AND U.S. POLITICS AND IDEOLOGY

American scholars have produced a number of studies chronicling Italian American extremism on both the Right and the Left. The underlying idea of these analyses is that Italian immigrants to America, coming mainly from pre-industrial societies in the south, were suspicious of *laissez-faire* economics, and, thus attracted to ideologies that proposed to either abolish the market (socialism) or put the market at the service of the state (corporate fascism). A number of such studies have explored the Italian American flirtation with the Far Right manifested in the cult of personality—best represented in a public admiration for Benito Mussolini—where it was common for the *prominenti* (the leaders of Italian American communities) to hang photos of *Il Duce* in their business establishments and for Italian language newspapers published in the United States (notably *Il Progresso Italo-Americano*) to extol Mussolini's virtues.

Thus, Rossi (160) concluded that while the total number of Italian Americans actually joining the Fascist Party was small, "latent support remained high throughout the 1930s."[1] In retrospect, it can be understood that in Italy and among America's governing class there might originally have been some degree of misinformation regarding the level of sympathy for fascism among Italian Americans. So, for example, Gaetano Salvemini (an exile from Fascist Italy and a Harvard professor) kept a continuous drumbeat warning Americans of fascism's deleterious effect on Italian society and of the infiltration of fascists in Italian American organizations, colorfully labeling the Sons of Italy, the Dante Alighieri Society, and the Italy-American Society "fascist transmission belts." Most Italian Americans well understand that such organizations have long had as their foremost goal the acceptance and appreciation of Italian culture as every bit as civilized (or, actually more so) than that of English-speaking countries. Even the *prominent*—who did, in fact, tend more toward the right of center on the political continuum—often confused the desire for their homeland to be taken seriously in the eyes of English speakers (Mussolinianism[2]) with

---

[1] See Gaetano Salvemini, "Italian Fascist Activities in the United States," ed. Philip V. Cannistraro (New York: Center for Migration Studies, 1977).
[2] See especially, Chapter 5 'Italian-Americans and Mussolini's Italy in John P. Diggins, *Mussolini and Fascism: The View from America* (Princeton: Princeton University Press, 1972).

support for fascist ideology. Our interviews tend to confirm the view that fascist sympathy tended to be a first-generation (and mainly an "upper-class"[3]) phenomenon. The Italian language paper with the widest circulation and decidedly pro-Mussolini views, Generoso Pope's *Il Progresso Italo-Americano*, was read not by second-generation Italian Americans (much less third generation, even if a copy was always seen to be lying on our grandmother's kitchen table) but rather by their Italian reading fathers and mothers.[4] Second-generation Italian Americans, following a pattern typical of all second-generation immigrants, were decidedly American, with little or no nostalgia for Italy or, at least, not its politics. When the photos of Mussolini and the Italian flags were hastily pulled down on December 7, 1941 (when the Japanese bombed Pearl Harbor)[5], Italian-Americans openly taunted their neighborhood Mussolini apologists and volunteered in droves for the US armed forces.[6]

---

[3] Whether an Italian-American was considered "upper-class" was naturally subjective. In very poor Italian-American neighborhoods in both large and small cities, a prominent man could simply be a fellow who owned a pool hall or restaurant and played the part by never inserting his sleeves into his overcoat!

[4] Even here, as Salvatore LaGumina points out, Italian-American *prominenti* were not obsequiously enthralled to Mussolini. So, for example, Pope's editorials vehemently opposed Mussolini's anti-Semitic laws promulgated in 1938. See Diggins, *Mussolini and Fascism: The View from America* 342-43. Italian Americans can still be rather sensitive about this brief flirtation with fascism. At least one Italian-American Republican—during the 1992 Abrams-D'Amato campaign for the New York State U.S. Senate seat—has interpreted the characterization of 'fascist' by a political rival as an ethnic slur: see Todd S. Purdum, "Abrams Apologizes for Calling Rival 'Fascist'," *The New York Times* October 16 1992, Catherine S. Manegold, "Abrams Calls Sen. D'amato 'a Fascist'," *The New York Times* October 13 1992.

[5] Mussolini declared war on the US on December 11, 1941.

[6] In one interview with Italian-Americans who were pre-teens and teenagers when the Japanese bombed Pearl Harbor, they related a story of a local shop owner in their neighborhood who had a large photo of Mussolini hanging behind the counter. The boys used to ask when he was going to take down the photo of "that pig." He would shout that he would kill anyone who touched the photo. On December 8th, with the photo down and the Italian flag removed

Countering what at one time had been a rather pervasive view that Italian Americans gravitated toward Far Right extremism, there is substantial scholarship documenting radicalism among the Italian American immigrant communities—anarchism, socialism, or communism—and the so-called '*sovversivi*,' or subversives, who ascribed to it (See Bencivenni; Pernicone; Cannistraro and Meyer).[7] Nunzio Pernicone argues that anarchism among Italian-Americans was not homegrown in Italy: "The growth of the movement during the first two decades of the 20th Century must be attributed principally to the social and economic conditions that confronted the immigrant, for it is certain that the majority of Italians who became anarchists did so *after* their arrival in the United States (emphasis in original) (2). The lack of organized action previous to emigration has been attributed to a number of factors, particularly the isolation of southern mountain villages, the related development of *campanilismo*, and Banfield's famous or (more accurately) infamous—choose your perspective—pronouncement of amoral familism. Countering this thesis, Bencivenni points out that "as an increasing number of revisionist works have shown, [these factors] did not prevent [southern Italians] from organizing themselves, cooperating with fellow workers, or understanding the principles of unionism and socialism" (10). Significantly, Bencivenni reports that "Italian rural society was not fixed, immutable, and static" and that there was much greater geographic mobility than is commonly assumed among the *contadini*, many of whom practiced trades as masons, blacksmiths, weavers, spinners, shoemakers, and joiners in the off-season often "hundreds of kilometers

---

from outside the shop, the boys popped into the shop throughout the day, taunting the man with, "Who died?"
[7] The particular case of Sacco and Vanzetti has produced no end of contemporary scholarly analyses investigating not only the innocence of these two men, but also the larger anarchist milieu which they inhabited. See especially, Paul Avrich, *Sacco and Vanzetti: The Anarchist Background* (Princeton: Princeton University Press, 1991). and, Bruce Watson, *Sacco and Vanzetti: The Men, the Murders, and the Judgment of Mankind* (New York: Viking, 2007).

away from their homes" (ibid). In sum, first-generation Italian Americans, whether from the North or the South, would have had some experience with unconventional political activities and were at times exposed to radical ideologies.

Yet between fascism and radicalism, there was always a middle ground in Italy before the Church and Mussolini undermined Italy's nascent democracy.[8] Significantly, during the peak years of Italian emigration, 1880 and 1920, Italy was a constitutional monarchy—an electoral democracy, albeit one with corrupt elections and scheming multiple parties governing in coalitions from the center in a system, *"trasformismo,"* in which politicians switched parties or parties dropped in and out of coalitions not for ideological reasons but in order to keep seats or gain cabinet posts. There were two major political movements in this period. The liberal party[9] (center right)—*Giovane Italia* (GI)—was founded by Giuseppe Mazzini and other liberals exiled in France in 1831 as a mass

---

[8] During the Fascist period the Vatican made an alliance with the Fascists (e.g. 1929 Lateran Treaties) and was rewarded with the abolition of the *Partito Popolare Italiano* (the center-right, mainstream Catholic political party which the Church despised).

[9] "Liberal" in the European sense—laissez faire economics without social meddling. In the US, this would be Republicans without the Christian Right. This was the political reality before the era of "confessional parties" took hold in Italy. The term confessional party is used to describe parties whose main organizing philosophy is based on adherence to (typically) the state religion. Originally applied to Europe and specifically to Roman s influence, contemporary usage has broadened to include all religious-based parties in democratic systems. The principal confessional party (*Democrazia Cristiana*-DC) governed postwar Italy from the center in the Pentapartito (five-party coalition) system, but lost its kingpin status and eventually disbanded in the wake of the *Mani pulite* (clean hands) investigations of the early 1990s that revealed rampant corruption. Europe's confessional parties, which support market capitalism (with a little pinch of Christian socialism), maintain that the government has the authority to uphold the "social order." Silvio Berlusconi's *Il Popolo della Libertà* (The People of Liberty) is essentially Italy's confessional party (albeit in a sometimes uneasy alliance with liberals (again, in the European sense) and social conservatives.

movement (rather than a cadre party[10])—which was to change its name on several occasions (to *Partito d'Azione* and then to *Alleanza Repubblicana Umanitaria*). Its major opponent was the *Partito Socialista Italiano* (PSI), which had been founded in 1892 to unite workers, artisans and rural laborers into a national party linked to organized labor (Morisi 310).

The GI was active in Naples and Sicily and was 'the first national organization to penetrate the southern regions and link them to broader political concerns' (314). Similarly, by 1904 *Avanti*, PSI's national newspaper, enjoyed wide circulation in Italy, with Naples being one of six major cities where over 1000 copies were distributed daily (314). While it is true that PSI sections were most active in northern and central Italy, inroads had been made in the south in the late 19th and early 20th centuries. Indeed, PSI contested local elections throughout Italy and by 1902 had won seats in all but one region, Basilicata (314). Thus, even early Italian immigrants (1880-1900) would have been exposed to party politics: while some certainly would have belonged to political clubs, others would have voted in local and national elections.

At the end of World War I (1913), the Italian government introduced universal suffrage for adult males,[11] expanding the electorate from 3 to 8.5 million voters, which meant that many first-generation Italian Americans had voted and participated in a democratic system that had a full range of political parties represented before emigration; therefore, Italian immigrants came to America with the experience of elections, parliamentary democracy, and party politics (One could belong to the PSI even if he couldn't

---

[10] Cadre parties are pre-mass suffrage parties formed out of legislative bodies to contest elections and are limited to participation by a small power elite. Mass parties (such as Socialist and Communist parties) arise with universal suffrage, are ideologically based, and recruit paying members. When Italians emigrated to the US, the Democrats and Republicans had been transforming from cadre mass-based parties (mainly during the Progressive era and as a result of the demand for primaries and less bossism).

[11] Italian women were not granted the vote for national elections until 1945.

vote). Moreover, even landless *contadini* who emigrated after World War I would have voted in national elections. This political reality meant that Italian Americans were not monolithic in their political ideologies—Some were liberals, some were socialists, and so0me belonged to confessional parties. In Italy religious affiliation was linked with market capitalism (center right), but with support for institutions and policies that softened the harsher effects of the market (so long as such organizations—such as unions or worker cooperatives—were linked to the Church). It also suggests that many Italian Americans would have formed their political and economic ideologies *prior* to emigration and would have found in the Republican and Democratic parties the familiar left/right bifurcation with respect to the proper role of government in the economy that defined their political allegiance back home in Italy. The major difference that they would have discovered in the American system was Protestant dominance of the Republican Party, which naturally alienated those Italian Americans from the confessional tradition (as it had earlier alienated Irish Americans). In other words, religious Italians who would have been natural recruits for the Republican Party were alienated by its lingering anti-Catholic rhetoric and membership. This is an important point, because as Italian-American Catholicism adapted to a more Northern European (German and Irish) brand of Catholicism in the United States, the Republican Party's willingness to champion order (especially maintaining the established social order) over individual freedom, and to support religious rights (for example, a less strict separation of Church and State) attracted Italian Americans to the Republican Party.[12] In fact, both Italian liberals and Italian

---

[12] This point is important for devout Catholics, because Republican support for public tax dollars to be used for school vouchers directly benefited Catholic parish schools in the urban centers of the Northeast and Midwest. Democrats oppose voucher schemes, preferring to increase the distribution of tax dollars to poorly-performing schools in poor cities. Similarly, government "outsourcing"—accelerated under Republicans—

confessionals were ideologically closer to the Republican Party. Some PSI members would have initially joined the American Socialist Party but—due to the winner-take-all party system that has produced two-party systems[13] in Canada, the UK, and the US—Italian Americans soon accepted the fact that voting for Norm Thomas was getting them nowhere—that they had, in fact, to vote Democratic and join Democratic clubs if they were to have any say in selecting local, state and national politicians. Still, it remains unclear whether or not this early formation of party identification, often shaped back home in Italy, helped in any way to shape patterns of party identification among Italian Americans today.

FORMATION AND ENDURANCE OF
POLITICAL PARTY IDENTIFICATION

Political parties, while not synonymous with ideology, can undoubtedly act as a proxy for establishing ideological affiliation—and thus serve as an indicator of sociocultural identity. And although not a perfect indicator, years of polling have shown that party identification is, in fact, a good predictor of long-term voter choices. Therefore, political scientists naturally seek to understand how voters form party identification. Political science offers two rival theories which may shed light on this process. One of the two main continuums of conflict in modern political life, for instance, is that which pits freedom and order against freedom and equality. The Republican Party, on the one hand, monopolizes the center-right position (favoring order over freedom and freedom over equality). The Democratic Party, on the other, owns the center-left position (favoring freedom over order and equality over freedom). But the extent to which a voter first forms an attachment to

---

of social welfare functions to non-profit and many times religious-based agencies, has poured millions of tax dollars into programs run by Catholic entities—from Catholic-run health care systems to Catholic Charities.

[13] Duverger's Law: proportional representation electoral systems produce multi-party systems; winner-take-all electoral systems produce two-party systems.

a political party based on its ideological stances on issues is a matter of considerable controversy.

One school— Rational Choice—thinks voters do not have psychological attachments to political parties but rather believe that the parties are proxies for a voter's utilitarian interests. For instance, no one would believe a Republican would strongly support universal health care (equality over freedom) and promote a more expansive view of civil liberties (freedom over order). Hence, political parties represent a time-economizing device for voters. Rather than voting against universal health care and in favor of law and order solutions to crime, one could simply vote Republican. The rival school—the Party Identification Model—often referred to as the "Michigan Model," after the team of political scientists at the University of Michigan who developed it in the early 1950s—rather posits that party identification begins at a young age, viewing the formation of party identification as pre-rational—or consisting of early party attachment rather than party attachment based on ideological positions (See Campbell et al.). This model is illustrated in Figure 1.

Figure 1: Formation of Party Identification (Michigan Model)

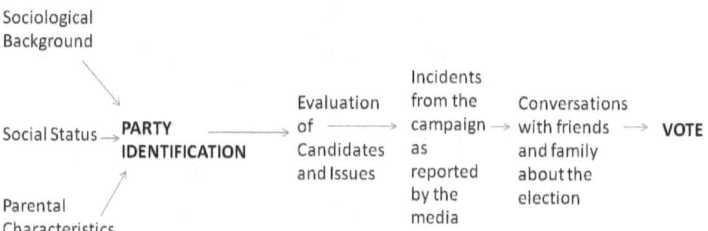

The extent to which the variables—sociological background, social status, parental characteristics—affect party identification varies. So, for example, party identification with the party of one's parents depends upon the child knowing the father's and/or mother's party identification. Analysis of party identification by seven social groupings found that cultural factors, such as race and religion, have more effect on party preference than do socioeconomic factors, which in turn are more important than region. The critical idea here is that party identification is formed at a very early age through a number of socio-psychological influences: sociological background (ethnicity, race, religion, region); social status (education, occupation, class) of one's family and referent groups; and parental characteristics (class, partisanship). These taken together are considered long-term influences on the vote. They are pre-rational, meaning "First I know I'm a Democrat, and later I find out why." Forming a party identification is not so very different, then, from how one forms a religious attachment: "First I know I'm Catholic and later I find out why." Party Identification, in turn, shapes the short-term influences on the vote. All of the variables that fall between party identification and the vote pertain to the immediate election cycle. What this means is that while a voter may not vote for the candidate who is a member of the voter's self-identified party, this is a short-term decision shaped by the voter's evaluation of the candidate and issues, incidents from the campaign, and conversations with family and friends about the election.

A key implication of this model is that party identification is durable: Most electors remain attached to their party throughout life. The minority of voters who change attachments do so from a combination of the following circumstances: (1) an absence or weakness of personal attachments; (2) the fact that one's family and one's own initial attachments differ from those of one's adult reference groups; and/or (3) large-scale economic, social, and political change.

PARTY IDENTIFICATION AND ITALIAN AMERICANS

How might the Michigan Model enhance our understanding of Italian-American voting patterns?

First, it can be suggested that first-generation Italian parents—especially fathers—with strong political affiliations/ideologies in Italy, would have passed on these ideologies to their children. Those on the Right (or in the liberal camp in Italy) would with time gravitate to the Republican Party, those on the Left, to the Democrats.

Second, the Michigan Model also suggests that social and economic upheaval can affect the party identification formation (as well as switching among those voters who have already formed party attachments). This circumstance naturally figures in the formation of Italian-American political party identification because the Great Depression occurred in a time period when the vast second-generation of Italian Americans was coming into its own as political actors. The "official" unemployment rate during the Great Depression grew to 25 percent, and had to be higher for young Italian-American men (who swelled the ranks of the Works Progress Administration and the Civilian Conservation Corps). As with other urban dwellers living in European ethnic enclaves, many second-generation Italian Americans were joining the polity as voters when Franklin Roosevelt realigned the party to confront the poverty and joblessness of America's urban poor. Similarly, unions gained the right to collective bargaining in the Roosevelt era. Union protections benefited the many Italian Americans who were members of the United Mine Workers, the Amalgamated Clothing Workers, the International Ladies Garment Workers Union, and the United Steelworkers, among others (Luconi "Italian Americans"). The Michigan Model would then predict that the children and grandchildren of working class Italian Americans would identify as Democrats, even as they became wealthy businessmen, chemists, and attorneys.

But the fact that party identification is durable does not mean it is immutable. Not all children of Democrats can be expected to identify with the party of their poor parents and neighbors. The Michigan Model suggests party identification can alter among family members experiencing upward mobility. Given the storied upward mobility of Italian Americans from poor circumstances who have achieved a higher social status (through education, marriage, a successful business career or a combination of these circumstances), some of these individuals who left their poor urban neighborhoods behind would be expected to "abandon" the socialist leanings or Democratic Party of their parents for those of their adult referent groups (the familiar Italian- American assimilation pattern of becoming "white").

Obviously not all Italian Americans would gravitate to the Democratic Party. This is because some first- and second- generation Italian Americans would have been more inclined to identify with the Republican Party due to their socioeconomic situation. The self-employed running small- and medium-sized businesses often tend to gravitate toward the Republican Party. Thus, Italian-American conservatism is animated by the same impulse as that of the petit bourgeoisie the world over who view the "government" as meddlesome pickpockets that protect the "shiftless" worker at the expense of "hard-working" entrepreneurs. Thus, Italian-American identification with the Republican Party could be rooted in and reinforced by the millions of Italian-American restaurateurs, commercial and residential landlords, building contractors, and shopkeepers.

So the Michigan Model can help us to understand why Italian Americans are not a monolithic voting bloc; however, the Michigan Model misses the "instrumental" piece that several scholars of Italian-American politics have pointed to explain the prevalence of Italian-Americans in both the Democratic and Republican parties.

ETHNIC VOTING BLOCS, PATRONAGE POLITICS,
AND POLITICAL AMBITIONS

Italian American also voted and affiliated with one of the two major political parties for instrumental reasons—to gain a place on a ticket, for instance, or to keep their jobs; to obtain coveted patronage jobs, perhaps, or to augment their sense of ethnic pride and strengthen their bonds within the Italian-American community and beyond. The idea here is that whichever party best met these goals, Italian Americans would support.

Gaining a place on a ticket is a case in point: of the few Italian Americans who ran as Republicans in the first years that Italian Americans began running for political office, many did not join the Republican Party for ideological reasons but because Irish American political bosses would not put Italians on a Democratic ticket.

This was famously the reason Fiorello H. LaGuardia (East Harlem's congressman and later New York City's mayor) was a Republican despite his progressive politics.

Another case in point: Italian Americans needed to support the party that was in a position to dispense patronage—this despite their outrage at discovering that America, like Italy, was a flawed democracy in which, despite the legend that adhered to the Declaration of Independence—not all men were created equal in America's urban centers. These were also the days of machine politics and company towns.[14] In those areas where Italian Americans were dependent upon Republican employers for work, tallies for Republican presidential candidates were notably higher than in large urban centers where there were more jobs available or many Italian Americans were self-employed. Those Italian Americans interested in patronage jobs had little choice but to affiliate with the local machine or the political club that had a chance of challenging the local party bosses.[15]

By the time Al Smith[16] ran for president in 1928, the national parties had begun to recognize the importance of the Italian-

---

[14] See, for example, Salvatore LaGumina, "Italians in Glen Cove: A Case Study of Ethnic Politics," *Italian Americans: The Search for a Usable Past*, eds. Richard N. Juliani and Philip V. Cannistraro (Staten Island: American Italian Historical Association, 1989), Stefano Luconi, "The Political Dimension of Multcultural Society: Italian Americans and Ethnically Balanced Tickets in Philadelphia During the New Deal," *Italian Americans in a Multicultural Society*, eds. Jerome Krase and Judith DeSena (Stony Brook, NY: Forum Italicum, 1994), Sandra Featherman, "Italian American Voting in Local Elections: The Philadelphia Case," *Italian Americans: The Search for a Usable Past*, eds. Richard N. Juliani and Philip V. Cannistraro (Staten Island: American Italian Historical Association, 1989), Salvatore LaGumina, "March and Vaccarelli: Turn-of-the-Century Political Bosses," *Italian Americans in a Multicultural Society*, eds. Jerome Krase and Judith DeSena (Stony Brook, NY: Forum Italicum, 1994).

[15] Where Republicans did not control patronage jobs, a greater percentage of votes in Italian American wards went to Democratic presidential candidates (Luconi "Italian Americans and the New Deal Coalition").

[16] Governor Al Smith was a practicing Roman Catholic and claimed Italian-American ancestry (one of his grandparents).

American voting bloc in several key states. Naturally, the electoral college system of 51 separate elections works to the advantage of ethnic groups concentrated in states—making Italian Americans (although less so today than in the past) a key voting constituency in Connecticut, Massachusetts, New York, New Jersey, Pennsylvania, and Rhode Island (each with over 10 percent of the population self-identifying as Italian American in the 2010 US Census)[17] and to a lesser extent Florida and Ohio (but more pivotal than they otherwise would be due to the fact that these two are perennial swing states).

Franklin Delano Roosevelt assiduously cultivated the Italian-American vote.[18] In 1940 when FDR's patina began to wear off as the Depression hung on, his biggest losses were not in locales where working class Italian Americans predominated but in cities where Republicans controlled patronage (for example, San Francisco and New York) and in more middle class Italian American neighborhoods (Luconi "Italian Americans"). FDR's administration also sees the beginning of a trend in which high-profile federal posts have been distributed to Italian Americans (Luconi "Italian Americans"). Indeed, the Kennedy Administration attempt to compile a list of Italian Americans whom the president appointed to federal posts (John F. Kennedy Archives).[19] In 1962, JFK appointed Anthony Celebrezze, Secretary of Health, Education and Welfare (HEW); in 1965 President Lyndon Johnson appointed

---

[17] See http://www.niaf.org/research/2000_census_5.asp for easy view tables of 2000 US Census. To view data for 2010 US Census, click map of state. On individual state tables, such as NYS at http://factfinder2.census.gov/faces/tableservices/jsf/pages/productview.xhtml?src=bkmk (click, for example, tab "More New York data sets" and "Social Characteristics" to obtain breakdown for "Ancestry."

[18] Italian Americans overwhelmingly supported FDR's presidential bids despite the fears of first-generation Italian Americans that FDR would drag the US into war against Italy.

[19] Archives housed at the JFK Presidential Library reveal that the Kennedy Administration attempted to determine Italian-American pedigree by name—and, as is the case today—this was far from an exact exercise.

Celebrezze to the United States Court of Appeals for the Sixth Circuit. For his part, Johnson appointed Joseph Califano to HEW. Richard Nixon, acutely aware of the role played by Italian Americans in JFK's 1960 victory, actively wooed Italian American voters. He brought John Volpe (during his third term as Republican governor of Massachusetts) into his administration as Secretary of Transportation and in 1973 he appointed him to be America's first Italian-American ambassador to Italy.

BETWIXT AND BETWEEN: LIMINALITY, POLITICAL
PATHOLOGIES, AND ITALIAN AMERICAN IDENTITIES

One thing that we find intriguing in the delineation of Italian American political identity is the fact that media commentators never fail to make mention of the ethnic background of Italian American political leaders, cuing the audience to a set of generalizations—a short-cut, if you will—into their supposed worldview and expected political outputs. Thus, we wonder to what extent there is an identifiable brand of Italian-American political leadership in the contemporary American political landscape. One of the leading assumptions, we believe, is that Italian-American politicians, the majority of them practicing Roman Catholics, have never had an easy alliance with the Christian (Protestant) Right in American politics, mainly because while they could often agree on "morality" issues, they parted company on social democracy (or the tradition of Christian democracy that they had imbibed as children of Italian households and of the Church).

We further wonder if the conservative and, by some accounts, reactionary brand of Italian American politics can be traced, rather than to religious affiliation, to conflicted constructs of ethnicity: in essence, an "othering" by the perennial "other." Such constructs may arise, in part, from a desire not to be included in one of America's many underclasses but rather to "pass for white." If so, we might be able to find explanatory mechanisms for the seemingly incongruous Samuel Alitos, Howard Beaches, Bensonhursts, and— most certainly—Tom Tancredos of the Italian-American political landscape. On the other hand, we wonder as well what explains the continuing progressive politics of many prominent Italian-American politicians. There are many important examples in the contemporary political landscape. Governor Andrew Cuomo—who is more personally responsible than any other politician for legalizing same-sex marriage in his state—deftly turned the Roman Catholic hierarchy's "morality" issue into one of "social equality." Nancy Pelosi, as Speaker of the House and, currently, House Minority leader, has been a forceful and effective champion of the Democratic Party's core.

Inasmuch as Italians in America are neither a part of the dominant class—the rolling vowels with which our names terminate tended to preclude that until quite recently—nor clearly a part of the underclass—our hue in a society whose very history is so dominated by race that that one factor almost singly-handedly can still determine the outcome of a presidential election (particularly, but not only, in the south), we perennially abide in a bifurcated locus of American political identity. We are, to put it in the words of anthropologist Victor Turner, betwixt and between, liminal (or threshold) agents in the drama that is American politics, and—as such—characterized by much ambiguity and frank ambivalence. Under such conditions, we don't find it particularly remarkable that we are pretty equally allotted to the New Deal Democrats, the Reagan Republicans, and the completely unaffiliated and uninterested (take Snookie, please!). There are those whom we have interviewed, like Sal—a second-generation Italian from western New York—who willingly recognize their class origins—his family being the first in the community to receive welfare. And then there are those like Sal's older brother, Tommy, who is torn between his affection for the Little Italy of his youth and the rarefied air of the Anglo-Saxon corporate boardroom which he successfully infiltrated. To this day, he affects a brute silence if Sal reminds him (in public) that each year they received a note from the welfare office permitting them to go *en masse* to the local shoe store and each pick out their new pair of shoes.

Is there a "singular history" of Italian American political identity?[20] Our reply is that just as the Italian American experience was shaped by American diversity in a far-flung federal system, there are several factors that have shaped the political behavior of Italian Americans. First, there are likely "Old World" origins in the political party identity and the ideological leanings of Italian Americans. Second, there are instrumental origins (patronage, political ambition) that have factored into political party identity that later crystallized into familial patterns of political identification (pre-rational formation). Finally, there are Italian Americans who have selected their party identification based on referent class (upward mobility) and a desire to pass for "white." Only the continuing charting—through archival research and exhaustive interviewing—will our question finally be, if not answered, at least clarified.

WORKS CITED

Avrich, Paul. *Sacco and Vanzetti: The Anarchist Background*. Princeton: Princeton University Press, 1991. Print.

Banfield, Edward. *The Moral Basis of a Backward Society*. New York: Free Press, 1958. Print.

Bencivenni, Marcella. *Italian Immigrant Radical Culture : The Idealism of the Sovversivi in the United States, 1890-1940*. New York, NY, USA: NYU Press, 2011. Print.

Campbell, Angus, et al. *The American Voter*. Chicago: University of Chicago Press, 1980-originally published 1960. Print.

Cannistraro, Philip V., and Gerald Meyer, eds. *The Lost World of Italian American Radicalism: Politics, Labor, and Culture*. Westport, CT: Greenwood Publishing Group, 2003. Print.

Diggins, John P. *Mussolini and Fascism: The View from America*. Princeton: Princeton University Press, 1972. Print.

Featherman, Sandra. "Italian American Voting in Local Elections: The Philadelphia Case." *Italian Americans: The Search for a Usable Past.*

---

[20] This is the subject of our forthcoming book—*A Singular History: The Shaping of Italian-American Identity*. Gainsville: University of Florida Press.

Eds. Juliani, Richard N. and Philip V. Cannistraro. Staten Island: American Italian Historical Association, 1989. 43-54. Print.

John F. Kennedy Archives. "Italian-Americans: Partial List of President John F. Kennedy's Federal Service Appointments for Americans of Italian Descent." 1961. June 26. <http://www.jfklibrary.org/Asset-Viewer/Archives/JFKPOF-101-016.aspx>.

LaGumina, Salvatore. "Italians in Glen Cove: A Case Study of Ethnic Politics." *Italian Americans: The Search for a Usable Past*. Eds. Juliani, Richard N. and Philip V. Cannistraro. Staten Island: American Italian Historical Association, 1989. 92-105. Print.

———. "March and Vaccarelli: Turn-of-the-Century Political Bosses." *Italian Americans in a Multicultural Society*. Eds. Krase, Jerome and Judith DeSena. Stony Brook, NY: Forum Italicum, 1994. 200-16. Print.

Luconi, Stefano. "Italian Americans and the New Deal Coalition." *Transatlantica* (2006). <http://transatlantica.revues.org/212>.

———. "The Political Dimension of Multcultural Society: Italian Americans and Ethnically Balanced Tickets in Philadelphia During the New Deal." *Italian Americans in a Multicultural Society*. Eds. Krase, Jerome and Judith DeSena. Stony Brook, NY: Forum Italicum, 1994. 184-99. Print.

Manegold, Catherine S. "Abrams Calls Sen. D'amato 'a Fascist'." *The New York Times* October 13 1992. Print.

Morisi, Paolo. "Republicans and Socialists and the Origins of Italian Political Parties." *Modern Italy* 12.3 (2007): 309-25. Print.

Pernicone, Nunzio. "Anarchism in Italy: 1872-1900." *Italian American Radicalism Old World Origins and New World Developments*. Ed. Vecoli, Rudolph .J.: American Italian Historical Association, 1972. Print.

Purdum, Todd S. "Abrams Apologizes for Calling Rival 'Fascist'." *The New York Times* October 16 1992. Print.

Salvemini, Gaetano. "Italian Fascist Activities in the United States." Ed. Cannistraro, Philip V. New York: Center for Migration Studies, 1977. Print.

Tamburri, Anthony. "Niaf. Two Days of Italian/American Affairs." *i-Italy* October 14 2007. Print.

Vecoli, Rudolph .J. *Italian American Radicalism Old World Origins and New World Developments*. American Italian Historical Association, 1972. Print.

Watson, Bruce. *Sacco and Vanzetti: The Men, the Murders, and the Judgment of Mankind*. New York: Viking, 2007. Print.

What are The Italian American Arts?

"The performance of it all"
Lady Gaga and a Legacy of Female Italian American Pop Icons

Roseanne Giannini Quinn

for Mario and David...

I could begin my essay with a multivalent analysis of Lady Gaga from the overlapping theoretical perspectives of, say, Susan Sontag and her infamous essay on camp (275); or of Donna Haraway and her treatment of cyborgs (149); or Judith Butler and her troubling of gender (101); or perhaps Jennifer Baumgardner and Amy Richards with their Third Wave approaches to female expression (227). When thinking about Stefani Joanne Angelina Germanotta, aka Lady Gaga, from an historically ethnic cultural perspective, however, I would like to situate her here as coming from a long, and recognizable, legacy of Italian American female musical artists who have prominently occupied the cultural imagination of Italian America—including how their public ethnic identification has been performed and mitigated under wider mainstream demands.

What are the images of Italian American women in popular culture that have shaped Italian American identity performance and ethnic consciousness? Prevalent circulating images of Italian Americans (both female and male) as stupid, criminal, underemployed, drunken and over-determined in their gender and hetero-sexuality are very much alive and well for, at least, many of my students who do not think critically about what they are viewing—unless perhaps they are of Italian descent. In fact, these representations have only increased in number. For example, the current VH1 series, *Mob Wives*, entrenches the compulsory stereotype that, not only are Italian American women married to criminals, but they are themselves also complicitly criminal and persistently violent with each other. In the long-running *Housewives of New Jersey*, these women are coded as more concerned about the size of their granite kitchen countertops than the genuine-well being of their families. Like many Italian American scholars, I am interested in tracing the sources of these images and the many ways in which they have been reinforced, transgressed, and reconstituted—in this case by female performance icons in Italian American culture. To that end, I would like to examine Lady Gaga by starting with her predecessors: Connie Francis from the 1950s and 1960s; Liza Minnelli from the 1970s; and Madonna from the 1980s to the present.

Born Concetta Rosa Maria Franconero, in 1938 in Newark's Little Italy, Connie Francis was of Calabrese and Napolitano ancestry. Concetta, an accordion prodigy, was famous throughout her childhood. Arthur Godfrey, the host of the *Arthur Godfrey's Talent Scouts* radio and television variety show for CBS, could not pronounce her name when she appeared. In response, he told her that the studio needed to give her an easy-to-pronounce Irish name, and the Connie Francis stage persona came into being (Francis, *Who's Sorry* 35). Notably, Connie Francis has never officially changed her name and still goes by Concetta Franconero in her personal life.

She was, and continues to be, an absolutely beloved figure in Italian American households. As a teenager, Francis insisted that she wanted to sing not only in Italian and English but in as many languages as she could learn. Her vocal fluency in 13 languages, and her genuine interest and appreciation of cultures in addition to her own, led to her transnational stardom. By 1960, surveys rated her "Favorite Female Recording Star" in several countries, including Australia, Hong Kong, Italy, Japan, the Netherlands, and India, as well as in Hawaii and the continent of Europe (Francis, *Who's Sorry* 244). By 1984, the same year that an unpolished new recording artist Madonna Louise Ciccone was twirling awkwardly around the Live Aid Stage, Connie Francis was the number one female recording artist of all time, with over 80 million copies of her records sold around the world, including the iconic "Who's Sorry Now?"; country cross-over single "Everybody's Somebody's Fool"; and the Italian American single standards "Mama," and *"Al di lá."* In the wake of Francis's success, at Billboard's latest count, Madonna Louise Veronica Ciccone became not only the number one female recording artist of all time, but the number one solo artist: with 75 million U.S. CD sales and 200 million world-wide sales (Madonna, "List"np).

In her best-selling autobiography, Connie Francis writes of her mother, "Like many Italian wives of her generation, she was, at best, unappreciated. She was simply taken for granted. "(To be taken for granted is simply not to be seen.)" (Francis, *Who's Sorry* 21). This emphasis on the visual is a common one in Italian American culture. The concept of *"La bella figura"* ". . . the Italian cultural phenomenon which translates literally as 'beautiful figure,' which means scrupulous attention to all aspects of outward appearance" has been well defined by Gloria Nardini in her study of filmmaker Nancy Savoca (19). How Connie Francis was seen became a very important issue in her debut film, *Where the Boys Are*. Considered too physically unattractive and ethnic to play the lead, Francis was given the role of Angie (no last name), a comic foil to the women who are considered beautiful in the film: i.e., the two blondes, Dolores Hart (who would soon after famously leave Hollywood to become a nun) and Yvette Mimieux, as well as a young Paula Prentiss (who would infamously end up stabbing herself over and over again in her spotless kitchen in the original *Stepford Wives*). Connie's character, Angie, is the only one of the quartet who is unable to find a college man during Fort Lauderdale spring break and is called "short" and a "criminal." Only as a joke, is Connie/Angie addressed as a "beautiful girl" by the Beatnik Jazz musician played by Frank Gorshin, when he is not wearing his eyeglasses. It is also suggested, throughout the film, that perhaps that her problem (not having a boyfriend) is that she is a lesbian. At one point, Angie tells the other women, "Maybe I should stop playing on the girls' hockey team." Originally, MGM put Connie Francis in the film to sing—and sing she does in a scene-stealing performance. More importantly, she is heard to be singing the film's theme over the opening and closing credits:

> Where the Boys Are, someone waits for me,
> a smilin' face,
> a warm embrace,
> two arms to hold me tenderly

Significantly, the studio never made her alter her voice, but they did her embodied self. Bowing to corporate scrutiny, Connie Francis would go on to have plastic surgery to fix her "pudgy Italian nose" in order to be seen as less Italian on screen. This extreme act of erasure would be one that she would regret the rest of her life. In large measure, because of her effective film and vocal performance, the movie would go on to become a classic of gay camp, and Francis would welcome its sustained popularity. In 2010, for the film's 50th anniversary, the city of Ft. Lauderdale renamed its main street after her (Piccoli np).

Like Connie Francis, Stefani Germanotta was born in New Jersey and was also a musical prodigy. In print and new media, she has variously been described as "ugly," a "hermaphrodite," a "man," a "gay man trapped in a woman's body" (Strauss 68); and even a female-to-female drag queen (Jaffe np). Her performances in various states of radical haute couture clothing and then not much clothing have allowed for alternating states of visual display that some would say gives permission for such critics to attempt to denigrate her. From a psycho-dynamic perspective is has been asserted that Lady Gaga's willingness to show her body—and dress it across unexpected gender lines—is enacting some exhibitionist, confused fantasy. In other words, there is an identifiable push to pathologize her and disclaim her. Accounts such as these from mainstream critics clearly dismiss Lady Gaga's gender-fluid role-play. They instead measure her by a conventional aesthetic that calls for her actual body to be more acceptably feminine. Within this misogynist paradigm, there is more occurring than simply subjecting Lady Gaga to the scrutiny of a random, idealized feminine form. After she was dropped by Island/Def Jam Records, Germanotta was signed by Interscope, whose Chair Jimmy Iovine said of her, "'When she first came in here, she looked like one of my cousins. You know, like an Italian girl from New York'" (Robinson 329). Again, it's the ethnic embodiment accompanies mainstream objection to the female Italian American pop star..

Much continues to be been made about how Lady Gaga looks, including the public debate between philosopher Nancy Bauer and Camille Paglia for the latter's trashing of Lady Gaga in the London *Sunday Times*. Paglia describes, "Photos of Stefani Germanotta just a few years ago show a bubbly brunette with a glowing complexion…despite showing acres of pallid flesh in the fetish-bondage garb of urban prostitution, Gaga isn't sexy at all—she's like a gangly marionette or plasticized android" (np). No matter what you might think of Paglia, in general or in her commentary on Gaga, she is getting at the change in appearance hoped for by the corporate mainstream imperatives of Interscope records—and MGM before them—no more Italian girls. Even in the performance of fashion the several well-known influences on Gaga—Isabella Blow, Alexander McQueen, Ziggy Stardust, and Freddy Mercury—are all British. Interestingly, Madonna, when asked how she felt about comparisons between them, "has said she is 'very flattered' by Lady Gaga." [And] "'She looks like she is going to a carnival in Venice, very beautiful'" (McLean 57). In direct response to Paglia, Judith Jack Halberstam writes in *Bully Pulpit*, the queer identified blog, "We liked her in leather, in chains, in a wheelchair, in bed, in a sandwich, in a pussy wagon, on the phone, in jail, under meat" (np).

There has even been further online consternation about Lady Gaga's vagina and whether or not she has one—to which she has responded, "My vagina is offended. I think it's society's reaction to a strong woman...the idea that we equate strength with men and a penis is a symbol of male strength" (Britney np). To be certain, current critiques have also been fueled by Gaga's instance of a rather hapless gender-crossing—in her clumsy MTV Musical Awards portrayal of heart throb Joe Calderone, in whose persona she actually first appeared on the cover of Japanese men's *Vogue* (Scott np). As a mode of explanation, she later explained her portrayal as an example of "performance art." It is important to underscore that within this cross-gendered performance, she maintains a narrative of Sicilian American identity for her Calderone doppelganger.

What do we make of these evident sexual and sexy (or not) embodiments of Lady Gaga in a feminist context? In her essay *The Erotic Woman Writer: A Special Case of Hypokrites*, Italian feminist semiotician Viola Papetti writes, "the authoress of erotica finds she must needs be a hypocrite in the same way as an actress: the representation of the female body that they stage tends to slip and fuse with the body of the individual woman who has enunciated the representation, who has put on, so to speak, the mimesis" (56). I do think this type of theoretical approach applies to Lady Gaga, as well as to Madonna, Connie Francis and Liza Minnelli. What is sexy, and therefore empowering about all four, across decades and contexts, is their serving up of sexual expression and female empowerment amid Italian American tropes and queer culture, at the same time as they are sometimes making fun of their own eroticized selves.

One attribute applied to Francis, Madonna, and Lady Gaga is their continued ability to adapt their images across time, an idea Madonna herself played with during her "Reinvention Tour" in 2004. During that concert, Madonna had models dressed up in her various past public personae spinning around on a giant reflective mirror from which the "real" Madonna would step off to the front of the stage. In the cover interview of an issue of *Vanity Fair*, Lady Gaga talks about what she identifies as the worst day of her life when Island/Def Jam dropped her. There follows an extended section when she visits her 82 year-old wise *Nonna* for solace. Lady Gaga reports her response, "I'm gonna let you cry for a few more hours. And then after those few hours are up, you're gonna stop crying, you're gonna pick yourself up, you're gonna go back to New York, and you're gonna kick some ass'" (Robinson 329-330). This isn't just some hokey vignette. Rather, it represents the immigrant Italian cultural value of *sempre avanti*: the idea that the previous generation moves forward for the next generation's sake within a dominant culture that is going to try to annihilate the foreign. The cultural imperative of needing to acknowledge the past and then adapt as a survival strategy is a lesson not just learned through *Nonna*.

It does not take a musicologist to hear that Lady Gaga does clearly borrow from Madonna's music. *The New Yorker* critic Sasha Frere-Jones makes those links explicit in his discussion of "Born this Way" sounding like "Express Yourself"; and of "Alejandro" resembling "*La Isla Bonita*" (72, 75). She also direct samples Madonna in the song "Bad Romance." In her MDNA World Tour during 2012, in direct response to calls of Lady Gaga being derivative of her, during one of her sets, Madonna begins singing Lady Gaga's *Born this Way*, and then suddenly morphs into her own *Express Yourself*. It is not difficult to see this musical gesture as finger-wagging. While I was attending one of her MDNA concerts, the audience cheered when, unexpectedly, Madonna starting singing part of the chorus to a song from her CD *Hard Candy*, entitled, "She's Not Me." With each vocalization of the lyric "she's not me," the audience erupted as if to say, knowingly and perhaps conspiratorially, we know you are not the imitative Lady Gaga, and that you're the truest diva. In one of her tracks from the MDNA record, called "I Don't Give A," guest artist Nicki Minaj pays respect to Madonna. While rapping the lyrics, Minaj vocalizes in terms that convey status upon Madonna as premier performer. She does so via decidedly Italian material markers:

In the Bugatti: ten grand, one tire

Aye yo, Madonna (Yes, Nicki), may I say you original Don Dada
In that, yeah Gabbana, and the, ah yeah, Prada

At the same time as Lady Gaga has been gratefully acknowledging her debt to Madonna, on television and in print interviews, Madonna has been less inclined to reciprocate. In a full hour interview with Ellen on *The Ellen Degeneres Show*, when asked about Lady Gaga, Madonna hesitated for over fifteen seconds, and then begrudgingly said, "Good voice." Again, and in yet another type of entertainment venue, Madonna asserts herself as *la prima donna*.

I want to re-emphasize, though, that Madonna is not Lady Gaga's only influence. When some mainstream music critics were having a terrible time trying to understand the origin of the fascist imagery in her music video *Alejandro*, I was wondering whether or not they had seen Liza Minnelli in the film *Cabaret*? In the video, Lady Gaga, replete with bobbed hair and a nouveau black chic outfit—twirling with arms over her head—is meant to look like Liza during the *Cabaret* era: at the top of her game when she was Liza-with-a-Z and world famous. Liza Minnelli, the daughter of Hollywood legend Judy Garland and innovative film director Vincente Minnelli, is one of the most accomplished musical artists of all time, Italian American or otherwise. She is the rare entertainer who has been acknowledged in the four major entertainment award categories by earning two Tony Awards for Best Actress in a Musical; an Emmy for her television special *Liza With a Z*; a Grammy Legend award; and, of course, the Oscar for Best Actress in *Cabaret*.

Vocally and stylistically, it is apparent that Minnelli is her mother's daughter. Their voices share a poignant vulnerability that surfaces in renditions of American standards. Aesthetically, she recognizes her father, who is the grandson of Sicilian revolutionary Vincenzo Minnelli, for his influence on her focused attention to the mise-en-scene of performance itself (Perusse np). In the Emmy nominated documentary, *Minelli on Minnelli: Liza Remembers Vincente*, Minnelli says admiringly of her father, "He so cared about how things looked. No detail was ever too small to matter." In addition to her numerous accolades, she was awarded the prestigious Ella Fitzgerald Award from the Montreal International Music Festival in 2012 . In an interview for the event, Minnelli cited her father's influence, once again discussing their shared artistic interest in, as she phrased it, "the presentation of it all" (Perusse np). Gaga's referencing of Lize Minelli may move younger audiences to watch *Cabaret* and begin to discover the considerable weight of Liza's own legacy and take into account that Lady Gaga's own artistic bent leans back to the past but is very much in flux.

Equally intriguing, Lady Gaga no doubt reaches further back than the 1970s and 1980s. She does not just borrow the imagery or melodies of those eras. Consider the opening lyrics of the famous gimmick-parlor song "*Mambo Italiano*" from 1954, made beloved by Rosemary Clooney, and then the opening of Gaga's "*Americano*" from 2011. The melodies overlap:

> A girl went back to Napoli
> Because she missed the scenery
> The native dances and the charming songs
> But wait a minute, something's wrong!
> . . .
> I met a girl in East LA
> In floral shorts—as sweet as May
> She sang in eighths and two Barrio chords
> We fell in love, but not in court

Homages such as these to the more distant and recent past are absolutely purposeful musical/performance allusions on Lady Gaga's part, and they are often multi-valent. (For example, The Canadian film *Mambo Italiano*, about a gay character named Nino, has Connie Francis singing on the soundtrack.) As Madonna has continually asserted her Italian-ness in her art (as in the video *Papa Don't Preach*—winner of the MTV Best Female Video Award in 1987—

and with her "Italians Do It Better" tee shirt), Gaga has followed suit. In an amusing YouTube video, *Lady GaGa's Italian,* a three-minute, fan-created montage features Gaga in various American and Italian television appearances saying some version of "I'm Italian" over and over again (Marjol). What is significant about their ethnic enunciation is that both Madonna and Lady Gaga have from their career beginnings emphasized that they are Italian and/or Italian American during their interviews even when their art at the time may or may not be culturally Italian or Italian American. There is a way in which these moments of Madonna and Gaga feel, and therefore can be read, as *non*-performative and, therefore, understood as being their more authentic selves.

Lady Gaga's most recent cd, *ARTPOP,* pushes the boundaries of music and performance art further than her past work—arguably not as effectively as previously albums. In his review, "What's Going Wrong with Gaga?," music critic Chuck Arnold tries to explain the relative lack of popular and critical acclaim for *ARTPOP,* asking the reader, why is Lady Gaga "now getting upstaged by the likes of Miley Cyrus?" He answers, "All stunts, gimmicks and costumes aside, it goes back to the music. I went back and Listened to Artpop before writing this, and it hasn't held up well. It feels dated and frustrating..." (Arnold np). The music, as a whole, is a concept album on which Lady Gaga employs not simply the dominant subject of fame and its consequence, as in her other two cds, but also fashion and popular. Several of the individual songs are funny at face value but have since taken on unintended (or perhaps intended) irony. In the song, "Donatella," a tribute to the dynamic leader of the House of Versace, Lady Gaga directs the song lyrics to either imagined fashion models, or Donatella herself, mocking, "Walk down the runway, but don't puke, it's okay/you just had a salad today." The evocation of the fashion industry's acceptance of anorexia has taken an unfortunate turn with what Lady Gaga just orchestrated at the recent South-by-Southwest Music Festival. While on stage, she had a self-defined "vomit artist" named Millie Brown throw-up on her, spewing colored dye as if Lady Gaga's body were a canvas. The resulting negative criticism, in particular from the young singer Demi Lovato, contends that this act has revealed that Lady Gaga herself endorses eating disorders. Gaga, who has in the past discussed her own history of bulimia and anorexia, rejects this criticism (Maresca np).

To make matters more complicated, or conflicted, Lady Gaga is the official "Face of Versace" and represents the company in their advertisements. In them, she is styled to look like a Donatella replica and is blonder, skinnier, non-smiling, and more spray-tanned than her own usual presentation. More to the musical point, she is in perfect keeping with the image evoked in the opening lyrics of her song "Donatella." She speaks the beginning lines, "I'm blonde, I'm skinny, and I'm a bit of a bitch." It is difficult to tell what Lady Gaga is doing. Is this fashioned irony? If it is, on her part, then what is to be made of the absolute sincerity with which Donatella Versace announces of Gaga, "She is like family to me, the embodiment of the Versace DNA" (Milligan np). For *ARTPOP*, the intertexual combinations of the music with the realities beyond the music are difficult to embrace, which makes listening to ARTPOP a challenge. As a listener, just when you might have a handle on her artistic intent, Lady Gaga resorts to "stunts and gimmicks."

In the video of the newest *ARTPOP* single entitled "G.U.Y.," Lady Gaga directs herself and a cast of backup dancers at Hearst Castle in San Simeon, California. The gender-bending song title stands for "Girl Under You" and is meant to cause purposeful confusion as to the sexuality and gender of the singer and the object of desire. The video begins with Lady Gaga as a classical winged Phoenix, who has risen from the usual ashes, but fallen into the lush outdoor pool at Hearst Castle. The visual images and choreography reflect Lady Gaga's previous preoccupations with sex, death, mythology, and sexuality. In this sense the song and video may be called "vintage" Lady Gaga. In addition, as the video continues, there are women in pink shown in long-shot, singing along with her, who may look vaguely familiar. As the camera moves closer and lights over each of their faces, it reveals that these are the female reality television stars of Bravo's *The Housewives of Beverly Hills* including the show's recognized dueling divas, Lisa Vanderpump and Kyle Richards.

Again, it can be asked, as with ARTPOP in general, is the inclusion of the *Housewives* just another popular culture reference that is mostly over-determined and derailing? Gaga herself phoned into Andy Cohen's Bravo television talk show, *Watch What Happens Live*, to tell the audience that the intent of having the women appear was to confirm, as she explains: "I am snapped back to reality by reality television." Yes. This explanation is funny and serves to justify the camp trajectory of the video. Alas, and with some measure of disappointment, one wants to take her aside and plead with her just to sing. Of course, I am not trying to be naïve here or too old-school; Lady Gaga's performative stances are about image making and controlling how the public is to supposed to consume the videos and react to her songs. Just as Connie Francis sang "Goldfinger," while styled in a floor length, gold lame dress in a memorable appearance on *The Ed Sullivan Show*, Lady Gaga plays with the so-called "fame monster." From an Italian American critic's eye, there is the desire to see every reference possible that Gaga uses in her videos as some cultural endpoint. After all, along with the *Housewives*, there is Venus (the Roman goddess of spring, love, and beauty) who is evoked in the video for G.U.Y. too. Isn't Gaga as Venus another example of artistically embracing her Italian heritage?

Part of the dilemma of how to read, listen to, and understand Lady Gaga's art-infused pop music or pop-music infused art may rest in the perception of what clinical and research psychologist Elizabeth G. Messina has so valuably underscored: "Italian Americans still remain conceptually invisible in psychological and psychoanalytic research literature" (88). In other words, there is much work to be done in formulating how Italian American values, media projected stereotypes, and a history of limited opportunities has impacted what and how artists of Italian American descent work (as in production of art and as in psychological states of being). In this vein, there is also much room to further explore tensions between past emigrant Italian culture with the progress of immigrant Italian American cultural values—as expressed, repressed, accepted, and/or rejected by artists such as Francis, Minnelli, Madonna, and Gaga.

What is recognizably common to all four of the Italian American vocal performers is their political commitment to the realities of women's and LGBT lives. The political activism of Minnelli, Madonna, and Lady Gaga is well documented. For example, Minnelli is one of the original supporters of the American Foundation for AIDS Research (amfAR) since its inception in 1983. Madonna has been involved in more than twenty philanthropic organizations, including being an early AIDS activist working with the late artist Keith Haring. In 2006 she-co founded *Raising Malawi* with Michael Berg. In 2011 Lady Gaga co-founded the *Born this Way Foundation* with her mother Cynthia Germanotta as a resource for at-risk youth, and the foundation has received the Lennon Grant for Peace from Yoko Ono. It is also important to consider the invaluable, and perhaps lesser-known activism that Connie Francis has pioneered to improve sexual assault laws during the past four decades. Raped in a Howard Johnson's motel after a concert in 1974, Francis would go on to win a $2.5 million dollar lawsuit against the chain for failure to provide adequate security (Bevacqua 129). It remains one of the largest awards related to a sexual assault case in U.S. legal history. She was one of the first celebrities ever to appear on television to advocate for the rights of rape survivors throughout the country. As a result, in 1982, she was asked to become the head of the first-ever President's Task Force on Victims of Crime for the Reagan White House, and has continued her advocacy over forty years later.

The oft-discussed *Harper's* cover story, "American Electra: Feminism's ritual matricide," by journalist Susan Faludi, makes much of tensions arising amongst today's generations of feminists: including those between women of the Second and Third Waves, women of color and white women, straight women and lesbians, transgender and bio women, of turmoil amid what some would describe today as an era of post-post feminism (34). By the end of the long article, Faludi appears to take a rather dismissive view of Professor Judith Jack Halberstam's appreciation of Lady Gaga as representative of the current generation of young feminists who may be more united across differences than Faludi allows (41-2). (Halberstam will go on to employ Lady Gaga's as the launching point for a wider cultural analysis in her book *Gaga Feminism: Sex, Gender, and the End of Normal.*) As a Second Waver, one who teaches Women's Studies, I can tell you that many of my students declare their appreciation of Stefani Joanne Angelina Germanotta, not so much for her amusing retelling of the film *Thelma and Louise* in her *Telephone* video with Beyoncé, but to many politically progressive students, more for her role as their generation's spokesperson for Lesbian/Gay/Bisexual/Transgender/Questioning/Intersex (LGBTQI) rights.

This is just one promising point of liberation that they tell me is important to them as today's feminists. Yes, the music and fashion are fun and often funny, but my students were not laughing as they reported to class on Lady Gaga's speech in Maine, urging the repeal of the government's absurd policy of Don't Ask/Don't Tell, and which helped turn the tide for its eventual repeal in 2011. When Connie Francis sings *Where the Boys Are* in concert, she introduces the song by saying, "This is the Gay National Anthem" (Chonin np). When Gaga sings the song "Boys, Boys, Boys," in concert, a clear nod to Connie Francis, she pauses before starting to talk to the audience about the perils of being young and LGBTQI in a too often rabidly homo- and transphobic culture.

If an older constituency does not view Lady Gaga as an Italian American feminist (even while she herself says she is), it may be because of what Gaga and Madonna and Liza and Connie have all contributed to gay and lesbian culture (not just female culture), and the resulting heightening of public visibility that has been gained. There is also a thriving female performance world of New York

Neo-burlesque with notable Italian American women such as Dirty Martini and Penny Arcade (Sciorra 187-8). In a fascinating on-line interview, Connie Francis muses, "I always thought God was a woman, but now…now I believe God is gay" (ellipses hers). She continues, "I much rather spend an evening with gay people; female or male, any day of the week, than with straight people. They are much more creative, exciting, introspective, sensitive, and empathetic, and they have experienced pain as I have. They are much hipper; they know what's going on. I mean, *come on!* They're much more interesting people—and talented" (Ybarra 19). Such an enthusiastic coupling of the Italian American aesthetic of *bella figura* with queer culture is anything but a "bad romance." To whit, the body of work produced by Lady Gaga and her iconic foremothers/sisters has continued to defy and transform expectations of what a female performer can and should and will continue to embody for future generations of Italian Americans like me—born in this way to an ethnic culture that demands performance in all of its many told and untold forms.[1]

WORKS CITED

American Foundation for AIDS Research. 1983-present. www.amfAR.org.
Alejandro. Dir. Steven Klein. Perf. Lady Gaga. Interscope, 2010.
Arnold, Chuck. "What's Going Wrong with Gaga?" *People* 20 March 2014. 22 Mar. 2014. http://www.people.com.
Arthur Godfrey's Talent Scouts. Dir. David Rich and Robert Steven. Perf. Arthur Godfrey. CBS, 1946-1958.
Bauer, Nancy. "Lady Power." *New York Times* 20 June 2010. 14 Nov. 2010. http://nytimes.com.
Baumgardner, Jennifer and Amy Richards. *Manifesta: Young Women, Feminism, and the Future*. New York: Farrar, Straus and Giroux, 2000.
Bevacqua, Maria. *Rape on the Public Agenda: Feminist and the Politics of Sexual Assault*. Boston, MA: Northeastern UP, 2000.
Behar, Joy. *The Joy Behar Show*. New York, NY: Headline News Net-

---

[1] I would like to thank Elizabeth G. Messina and Dawn Esposito for their valuable feedback on previous versions of this essay.

work. 26 Dec. 2010. *Born this Way Foundation*. 2011-present. www.bornthisway.org.

Britney, Free. "Lady Gaga Addresses Hermaphrodite Rumor." *The Hollywood Gossip* 5 Sept. 2009. 12 Dec. 2010. http://thehollywoodgossip.com.

Cabaret. Dir. Bob Fosse. Perf. Liza Minnelli, Joel Grey. ABC Pictures, 1972.

Clooney, Rosemary. "*Mambo Italiano*." Columbia Records, 1954.

Butler, Judith. *Gender Trouble: Feminism and the Subversion of Identity*. New York: Routledge, 1990.

Chonin, Nancy. (2007 March). "The crowd loves Connie Francis." *San Francisco Chronicle* 6 Mar. 2007. 10 Mar. 2007. http://www.sfgate.com.

DeGeneres, Ellen. *The Ellen DeGeneres Show*. NBC Universal. 29 Oct. 2012.

Ed Sullivan Show, The. Prod. Ed Sullivan. Perf. Ed Sullivan, Connie Francis, Tony Bennett. CBS. 21 Mar. 1965.

Faludi, Susan. "American Electra: feminism's ritual matricide." *Harper's* Oct. 2010. 29-42, 192, 321.

Francis, Connie. "Al di lá." *Connie Francis Sings Modern Italian Hits*. MGM Records, 1963.

———. "Everybody's Somebody's Fool. *More Greatest Hits*. MGM Records, 1961.

———. "Mama." *Connie Francis Sings Italian Favorites*. MGM Records, 1960.

———. "Where the Boys Are." *Where the Boys Are*. Dir. Henry Levin. MGM, 1960.

———. *Who's Sorry Now?* New York: St. Martin's, 1984.

———. "Who's Sorry Now?" *Who's Sorry Now?* MGM Records, 1958.

Franklin, Nancy. "Jersey Jetsam: MTV goes to the beach." *The New Yorker* 18 Jan. 2010: 70-2.

Gaga, Lady. "Alejandro." *The Fame Monster*. Interscope, 2009.

———. "Bad Romance." *The Fame Monster*. Interscope, 2009.

———. "Born this Way." *Born this Way*. Interscope, 2011.

———. "Boys, Boys, Boys." *The Fame*. Interscope, 2008.

Frere-Jones, Sasha. "Show Rumors: The Women of Pop." *The New Yorker* 27 June 2008: 72-5.

Halberstam, J. Jack. "What's Paglia got to do with it?" *Bully Bloggers* 14

Sept. 2010. Dec. 2010. http://bullybloggers.wordpress.com.

_____. *Gaga Feminism: Sex, Gender and the End of Normal*. Boston: Beacon, 2012.

Haraway, Donna. "A Cyborg Manifesto: Science, Technology, and Socialist-Feminism in the Late Twentieth Century." *Simians, Cyborgs, and Women: The Reinvention of Nature*. New York: Routledge. 149-81.

Jaffe, Sarah. "Lady Gaga: Pop star for a country and an empire in decline. *AlterNet* 26 July 2010. 1 Dec. 2010. http:// www.alternet.org.

Jersey Shore. Prod. SallyAnn Salsano. Perf. Nicole Polizzi, Michael Sorrentino, and Paul DelVecchio. MTV, 2009-2012.

Levy, Michael. "Is Lady Gaga a feminist? 5 questions for philosopher Nancy Bauer." *Britannica Blog* 26 July 2010. 1 Dec. 2012. http://www.brittanica.com.

Liza with a Z. Dir. Bob Fosse. Perf. Liza Minnelli. NBC. 10 Sept. 1972.

Madonna. "Express Yourself." *Like a Prayer*. Sire Records, 1989.

_____. "I Don't Give A." *MDNA*. Interscope, 2012.

_____. "La Isla Bonita." *True Blue*. Sire Records, 1987.

_____. MDNA World Tour. HP Pavilion, San José, CA. 7 Oct. 2012.

_____. Reinvention World Tour. HP Pavilion, San José, CA. 6 June 2004.

_____. "She's Not Me." *Hard Candy*. Warner Bros., 2008.

Mambo Italiano. Dir. Èmile Gaudreault. Perf. Luke Kirby, Claudia Ferri, and Paul Sorvino. Equinox Films, 2003.

Maresca, Rachel. "Lady Gaga responds to vomit performance controversy: It 'was art in art in its purest form.'" *New York Daily News* 21 Mar. 2014. 22 Mar. 2014. www.nydailynews.com/entertaintment.

Marjol. "Lady GaGa is Italian." *YouTube*. 15 Dec. 2011. 15 Aug. 2012. <http.www.youtube.com/watch>.

McLean, P. "Madonna: I see myself in Lady Gaga." *Faces* Oct. 2010: 56-7.

Messina, Elizabeth, G. (2004). "Psychological Perspectives on the Stigmatization of Italian Americans in the American Media." *Saints and Rogues: Conflict and Convergence in Psychotherapy*. Eds. Robert B. Marchesani and E. Mark Sterr. New York, Howarth. 87-121.

Milligan, Lauren. "Becoming Donatella: Lady Gaga for Versace. *Vogue News* 25 Nov. 2013. 14 mar. 2014. <www.vogue.co.uk/news/>.

Mob Wives. Prod. Jennifer Graziano. Perf. Karen Gravano, Renee Graziano. VH1 Productions, 2011-present.

Nardini, Gloria. "Is it true love? Or not? Patterns of Ethnicity and Gender in Nancy Savoca." *Voices in Italian Americana* 2.1 (1991): 9-17.
Papa Don't Preach. Dir. James Foley. Perf. Madonna, Alex McArthur, and DannyAiello, Sire Records, 1986.
Paglia, Camille. "Lady Gaga and the death of sex." *Sunday Times Magazine* 12 Sept. 2010. 4 Oct. 2012.
Papetti, Viola. "The erotic woman writer: A special case of hypokrites." Trans. Meriam Soopee. *The Lonely Mirror: Italian Perspectives on Feminist Theory*. Eds. Sandra Kemp and Paolo Bono. London: Routledge. 55-63. 1993.
Perusse, Bernard. (2012, July 5). "Montreal International Jazz Festival 2012: Liza Minnelli Protects the Family Business." *Montreal Gazette* 5 July 2012. 6 Oct. 2012. http://www.montrealgazette.com /Minnelli.
Piccoli, Sean. "Back where the boys are." *Sun Sentinel* 31 Jan. 2010. 1 Mar. 2014. <http://articles.sun-sentinel.com>.
Powers, Ann. "Critic's notebook: *Lady Gaga, sexuality, and 21st century pop: Speaking truth to Camille Paglia*." *LA Times* 16 Sept. 2010. 14. Nov. 2010. http://latimes.com.
Raising Malawi. 2006-present. <www.raisingmalawi.org >.
Robinson, Lisa. "Lady Gaga's Cultural Revolution." *Vanity Fair* Sept. 2010: 281-286, & 329-331.
Minnelli on Minnelli: Liza Remembers Vincente. Dir. Richard Schickel, Richard. PBS. KCET, Burbank, CA. 18 Mar. 1987.
Sciorra, Joseph. "A Lived History Under Scrutiny: Italian American Performance
Art. *Teaching Italian American Literature, Film, and Popular Culture*. Eds. Edvige Giunta and Kathleen Zamboni McCormick. New York: MLA. 182-99.
Scott, Elizabeth. "Lady Gaga Poses as a Man for *Vogue*." *SkyNews*. 27 Aug. 2010. Nov. 11 2012. news.sky.com.
Sontag, Susan. (1966). "Notes on 'Camp.'" *Against Interpretation and Other Essays*. New York: Picador, 275-92.
Stepford Wives, The. Dir. Bryan Forbes. Per. Katherine Ross, Paula Prentiss. Columbia Pictures, 1975.
Strauss, Neil. "The Broken Heart and Violent Fantasies of Lady Gaga." *Rolling Stone* 12 July 2010: 66-74.
Telephone. Dir. Jonas Akerland. Perf. Lady Gaga and Beyoncé. Darkchild Studios, 2010.

Thelma and Louise. Dir. Ridley Scott. Perf. Susan Sarandon, Geena Davis, and Brad Pitt. MGM, 1991.
Watch What Happens Live. Prod. Andy Cohen. Perf. Andy Cohen. 24 Mar. 2014.
Where the Boys Are. Dir. Henry Levin. Perf. Dolores Hart, Connie Francis, and Yvette Mimieux. MGM, 1960.
Ybarra, David. "*La Bella Concetta*: The Connie Francis interview." *DAEIDA Magazine* Dec. 2009: 18-27. http://www.daida.com.

Is Tony Manero Gay?
Masculinity, Sexuality, and Ethnicity in *Saturday Night Fever*

Stelios Christodoulou

In her review of *Saturday Night Fever* (1977), Pauline Kael notices in John Travolta's portrayal of Tony Manero, "a feeling of the sexiness of young boys who are bursting their britches with energy and desire ... which recalls Kenneth Anger's short film *Scorpio Rising* (1963)." Kael immediately proceeds to clarify that, whereas *Scorpio Rising* is a "homoerotic fantasy of toughness," *Fever* is a decisively "straight heterosexual film" (59-60). Kael's comment represents a common tendency in analyses of the film to acknowledge the seemingly obvious signifiers of homosexuality in the representation of Tony Manero, while adding the disclaimer that these signifiers do not perform their expected function. For a film that has overall attracted little interpretive interest, its representation of gender and sexuality has received considerable scrutiny (see, for example, Bordo, Yanc, Nystrom). The attention is certainly not surprising. *Fever* seems consciously to expose Tony Manero's masculinity as a patchwork of inconsistent gender and sexual signifiers that invite audiences to question whether he is gay—or, to be more precise, how he manages not to be.

While agreeing with Kael's description of *Fever* as a "straight heterosexual film," this paper attempts to problematize the often unstated assumptions underpinning this conclusion. Rather than seeking to discover how suggestions of homosexuality are remedied or balanced, I attempt to situate them as intrinsic parts of a homogeneous masculine identity. The analysis that follows negotiates the limitations of a purely textual approach and examines *Fever*'s representation of masculinity in the context of late 1970s American culture. I consider intertextual connections embedded in the film as well as connections to contextual knowledge circulating in the public sphere.

The discussion concentrates on Tony Manero's two favorite activities, disco dancing and self-grooming, which are usually cited as evidence of challenges to his heterosexuality. In the case of the former, the assumed link between disco and homosexuality does not withstand historical scrutiny. In the case of the latter, Tony's narcissism and tendency for displaying his body as erotic spectacle fit uneasily with both heterosexual and homosexual masculine models of the late 1970s. They can be reconciled, however, if examined through the interrelation of masculinity and ethnicity, which the film presents in terms of geography, a difference between Brooklyn and Manhattan. I argue that Tony Manero exemplifies a historically specific representation of Italian American heterosexual machismo, a re-imagined version of the Guido stereotype that speaks to the anxieties and desires of middle class, heterosexual, WASP men of the era. Ethnic difference allows the film not only to incorporate in the representation of Tony Manero styles and behaviors that would have otherwise signified homosexuality, but also to render the outcome plausible and believable.

DISCO

Disco has not only defined *Fever*'s place in popular memory, but it has also posed the greatest challenges to Tony Manero's heterosexuality. Discussions of the film often rely on the assumption of an inherent link between disco and homosexuality. Echoing Kael's disclaimer, Derek Nystrom begins his recent analysis of the film with the observation that "the importance of disco to gay male self-understanding in the 1970s is well established," before proceeding to explore how the film overcomes disco's "hurdles" and manages to "craft a heterosexual narrative" (114). Such assumptions, however, do not adequately appreciate the trajectory that disco traversed through the 1970s, from underground gay clubs at the beginning of the decade to mainstream discotheques at the time *Fever* was released.

Disco began in the late 1960s as a marginalized form of music associated with cultural difference—including, but not restricted to, sexual difference. A 1979 article in *The Washington Post* traces disco's origins back to "the bayous and backfields of the cultural landscape, the gay clubs and black clubs where long nights of non-stop motion counterpointed the long days of getting by" (Darling). Disco attracted anyone who felt excluded from mainstream forms of entertainment, primarily gay men and African Americans, but also Latino Americans, communist students, and former and current Hippies. As Tim Lawrence has recently argued, disco in the 1970s was not so much gay as queer, in an anachronistic use of the term to mean socially subversive (231). Under the mesmerizing, repetitive beat, disco dancers could declare freedom and cultural centrality. In his 1979 essay "In Defence of Disco," Richard Dyer discovers in disco a "whole body eroticism" that is distinctly different from rock's eroticism, which he indicatively describes as "thrusting," "grinding," and "indelibly phallocentric." Whereas rock music is a predominantly live medium, with an emphasis on the relationship between the performers and the audience, disco is organized in terms of dancers and recorded, deejay-performed music. "Rock's repeated phrases," Dyer explains, "trap you in their relentless push," while disco "releas[es] you in an open-ended succession of repetitions" (22).

Nevertheless, Dyer's association of disco with "an openness to sexuality that is not defined in terms of cock" (22) must have undeniably been a bold argument in 1979, a time when *Fever* epitomized disco culture. Lawrence holds *Fever* responsible for almost single-handedly destroying disco's queer potential and turning it into "a space for straight men to display their prowess and hunt for a partner of the opposite sex" (241). Tony's solo dance for "You Should Be Dancing" provides an indicative example of disco's entry into the hetero-normative mainstream. The song has all the qualities that Dyer finds conducive to "whole body eroticism"—

repetitive beat, falsetto vocals, and a primal cry of "yeah" after every lyric. Yet, Tony constrains the song's liberating potential into a calculated and purposeful choreography meant to impress female onlookers. His dance combines the flashiest disco moves with imitations of easily recognizable acts, such as combing his hair and wiping sweat off his forehead, which suggest a conscious preparation to put his body on display, not instinctive liberation. Tony never misses a chance to strike a pose, flirt with girls, and nod in affirmation of his own skill. With lips slightly pursed and minimal facial expressions, he constantly keeps his cool and never compromises the performance. His move that receives most attention involves the rhythmical "thrusting and grinding" of his hips in an imitation of sexual penetration.

Dyer's essay defends a very particular version of disco that is clearly reflected in the title of the periodical for which he is writing, *Gay Left*. Dyer defends disco's liberating potential against the common Marxist position equating pleasure with capitalist infiltration. His defense, however, applies to the early days of the strictly non-mainstream, non-bourgeois disco that played in gay clubs. By the late 1970s, this type of disco had already been overwhelmed by a more commercialized version. On one side of the spectrum were the gospel-charged disco of the black divas and the sequined gay falsetto of Carl Bean's "I Was Born this Way." On the other side were the Bee Gees and Tony Manero projecting an image of whiteness and heterosexuality that, in *Newsweek*'s estimation, provided "disco's ticket to respectability" (Graustark *et al.*). The Village People, formed in the same year that *Fever* was released, provide an indicative example of disco's journey from the cultural margins to the center. The group remains today the most readily available example of disco's ties to the increasingly vocal gay communities of the disco era. These ties, however, manifest in the Village People as an exuberant and somewhat silly style, strictly within the bounds of hetero-normative entertainment. The group's meticulously choreographed performances and manifestly phallocentric costumes could not diverge further from Dyer's argument for instinctual corporeality and whole body eroticism. "It depresses me," Dyer admits, "that such phallic forms of disco as Village People should be so gay identified" (22). Indeed, as Peter Shapiro points out, the Village People were from the very start "*personae non gratae* in the gay clubs" (220).

As disco crossed over into the mainstream, American culture also experienced a virulent rise in homophobia, the supporters of which readily pointed to the popularity of disco as evidence of a spreading gay threat. The backlash culminated in what became known as Disco Demolition Night on July 12, 1979, a massive destruction of disco records during a baseball game between the Chicago White Sox and the Detroit Tigers. Clad in images of heterosexual machismo towering over disco, the event was led by rock radio deejay Steve Dahl, who drove into the field in a military jeep and set off explosions that destroyed disco records. Disco Demolition Night was hardly a spontaneous and isolated event. Gillian Frank considers it to be the most expressive and evocative articulation of a pervasive homophobia in the late 1970s. Coming on the heels of a widespread legislative and electoral backlash against gay civil rights, the backlash against a form of sexual and musical expression marks "the conscious evacuation of gays from popular culture" (Frank 279). Considered in retrospect, the rise in homophobia through the decade of disco belongs to same set of developments as the backlash against feminism and African Americans' civil rights. Though comprising disparate and often extreme events, these changes collectively serve as evidence of America's gradual shift toward the right by the dawn of the 1980s, which would find its clearest expression in Reagan's election and the rise of neo-conservatism.

Fever was released at that opportune time after disco was commercialized, but before the radical backlash against it had peaked. This was a time when WASP disco dancers could escape from the margins of suburbia and their corporate cubicles and claim cultural centrality on the dance floor. As Norma Jean's 1978 hit "Saturday" spells out, disco was a reward and a remedy for a boring job: "All I do is work. I'm no robot. Let's go disco." Tom Wolfe succinctly captures the status of disco for middle class WASPs in his contribution to the November 1978 issue of *Harper's*, a sketch of an elderly man in a suit dancing frantically on the disco floor. Wolfe accompanies the sketch with a poem for a caption, which ends,

> I grow old the 1970s way:
> Deaf, but from a Max Q octaphonic beat,
> Stroked out, but on my own two feet,
> Disco macho!—for you, my New Cookie.

A heterosexual man's visit to the disco may have been frowned upon, but it was hardly an indication of his coming out of the closet. On the contrary, it is considered a macho, albeit desperate attempt to impress his "new cookie."

In 1975, *Rolling Stone* published the pressbook *Dancing Madness*, an analysis of disco's popularity and an instruction manual for neophytes. *Dancing Madness* includes an interview with Tony Magano, a teenager from Staten Island who frequents Le Jardin, an elite Manhattan disco, on the weekends. "What my old man doesn't understand," Magano tells Ed McCormack , "is that you don't have to be a fag to be into this scene....It doesn't mean you want to fuck a broad or a guy if you dance with them. You're just doing what comes natural" (13). The fictional Tony Manero shares Tony Magano's social background. They are both young, heterosexual, Italian American men, who live with their parents in boroughs outside Manhattan. From McCormack's middle-class, WASP perspective, they both belong to "the Italian drinking class" (13). Yet, Tony Magano's experience in Le Jardin is fundamentally different from Tony Manero's experience in the Odyssey 2011. The former is looking to lose himself in the liberating anonymity of Le Jardin; the latter wants to be recognized and admired as the disco king, both in and out of the Odyssey. Le Jardin offers Magano a symbolic form of social elevation, a chance to join the

Manhattan crowd and leave his ethnic, working-class family home behind. The Odyssey is the locus of an all-encompassing subculture in Brooklyn's Bay Ridge neighborhood. Its patrons come almost exclusively from the local Italian American youth. They live close to each other, frequent the same fast food restaurants, belong to the same gangs, and share rides to the disco on Saturday nights.

Fever's representation of disco can be succinctly described in the title of Nik Cohn's article "Tribal Rites of the New Saturday Night," which was published in the June 7, 1976 issue of *New York* magazine and provided the inspiration for the film's script. Cohn describes Bay Ridge's tribal rites as a pseudo-ethnographic guide, written from the perspective of an uninitiated Manhattanite. "Over the past few months," he writes,

> much of my time has been spent in watching this new generation. Moving from neighborhood to neighborhood, from disco to disco, an explorer out of my depth, I have tried to learn the patterns, the old/new tribal rites....Everything described in this article is factual and was either witnessed by me or told to me directly by the people involved. (31)

The film incorporates Cohn's perspective to present Bay Ridge as the home of a more authentic, but strictly heterosexual, disco. At a telling instance, as Tony walks into Pete's dance studio for his usual practice before the competition, he encounters a class of budding middle-aged dancers, who stand in line and follow his instructions with equal amounts of eagerness and clumsiness. Though the film does not clarify who these students are, we can safely assume that they are not Bay Ridge residents. Based on what we know about Tony's friends and family, people in Bay Ridge neither require, nor can afford disco lessons. Pete's students belong to the same demographic as the man in Wolfe's illustration, Manhattanites who seek a break from their WASP routine and take a trip to the exotic world of ethnic Brooklyn for a taste of disco fever.

As Cohn revealed on the film's twentieth anniversary, his claims to authenticity were blatant lies. A British music journalist fresh to New York, Cohn needed a subject for his first story and, after a brief visit to Brooklyn, made up the story of Vincent (the film's Tony Manero) and his disco escapades. Cohn filled in the details based on his childhood experience of witnessing a gang fight in his hometown of Derry and his familiarity with London's Mods ("Saturday" 48). Cohn's may be an extreme example of a fiction being embraced as the reality of Brooklyn's Italian American culture (and, following the film's immense success, shaping the legacy of an entire decade), but it usefully highlights the cultural valence of Italian American ethnicity in the 1970s and its ability to open up a space for suspending disbelief. Before exploring *Fever*'s ethnic disco fantasy further, the film's Italian American hero warrants a closer look.

NARCISSISM

If Tony's fascination with disco is not enough to immediately signify him as gay, *Fever* infuses into his representation textual, intertextual, and contextual references to homoeroticism. Travolta's Tony Manero evokes the well-established stereotype of the Guido. In Peter Bondanella's taxonomy of Italian American stereotypes, the Guido is a cross between the Romeo (the Latin lover) and the Dago (the lazy laborer), a young man with the looks of charm of Rudolph Valentino but the brains of a buffoon (57). The four housemates on MTV's *Jersey Shore* are the latest well-known and self-proclaimed Guidos. Although the show has made it something of a requirement that Guidos pay meticulous attention to their appearance and remain naked from the waist up, Hollywood norms in the 70s expected them to be good-looking and swaggering, but always dressed. *Fever* shows off the Guido's objectification and good looks, inviting Susan Bordo's apt comment that "never before *Saturday Night Fever* had a heterosexual male movie hero spent so much time on his toilette" (198).

Sandwiched between the opening credit sequence and Tony's first night out at the disco, the scene of Tony's grooming ritual reverses a long-held Hollywood binary in representations of gender. Following Laura Mulvey's canonical thesis, Hollywood perpetuates patriarchal hegemony by equating the masculine position with power and the feminine position with passivity and objectification. This binary is most pronounced when it comes to erotic displays of the body, with men being the active owners of the erotic gaze and women the passive recipients. The male body cannot be marked explicitly as the erotic object of looking without upsetting this order. "It is one of the fundamental reasons," Steve Neale explains, "why the erotic elements involved in the relations between the spectator and the male image have constantly to be repressed and disavowed" (19).

Far from repressing the erotic display of the male body, *Fever*'s grooming scene does everything possible to highlight it. With the Bee Gees singing "Fever Night," the scene begins with the image of Tony's hand holding a hairdryer in what could have easily been an advertisement for the product. Framing the hairdryer in close-up, with the brand and model clearly visible, the camera gently moves leftwards to frame Tony's face in the center and reveal the hairbrush in his other hand. The inherent connotations of effeminacy in the activity of hairstyling are accentuated by a series of stylistic devices meant to emphasize the beauty of Travolta's face. The soft lighting, the out-focus background, the near perfect symmetry of the composition, the frontal angle of the camera, and the inclusion of just a hint of Travolta's bare shoulders in the frame create an image that resembles an advertising beauty shot. As the camera moves from the hairdryer to its user, Tony himself becomes the object on display. Following this dramatic opening, the rest of the scene unfolds as a series of fetishizing shots of Travolta's body: his hairy chest as he puts on his golden chains, his biceps as he flexes and poses, and his crotch as he pulls up his zip.

To be sure, *Fever*'s fascination with the naked male body as spectacle need not immediately code Tony Manero as gay. Neale expands on Mulvey's thesis to account for representational strategies that can "denigrate or deny" implications of homosexuality in erotic displays of the male body (19). In fact, Neale mentions *Fever* in a parenthetical reference as "a clear and interesting example" of the male body "unashamedly put on display," insinuating, as does Kael, that Tony's heterosexuality withstands the apparent challenges. Drawing on examples of male pin-ups, Dyer locates one such heterosexualizing strategy in the male model's refusal to acknowledge that he is being looked at, often by looking upwards and suggesting a preoccupation with loftier concerns ("Don't Look" 270). Bordo concurs that men "may display their beauty only if it is an unavoidable side effect of other 'business'" (198). In other instances, male models are portrayed under physical duress, holding their bodies taut and tightening their muscles to suggest some form of activity that counters the passivity of being looked at. Even accounting for these representational strategies, *Fever*'s grooming scene resists a "straight" reading. Tony shows none of the heterosexualizing casualness and unawareness in displaying his body, but voluntarily participates in the process. When he does flex his muscles and pose, it is not in a spontaneous manifestation of his masculinity, but in a conscious imitation of the Bruce Lee poster on his wall. Cutaway shots to the discotheque during the grooming scene, furthermore, remind us that the goal of the entire preparation is to turn his body into an alluring image and display it on the dance floor.

A historical approach to *Fever*'s depiction of the male body offers a more promising—but, as we shall see, equally problematic—means of negotiating the film's representational discrepancies. Whereas Mulvey draws her examples from Classical Hollywood, *Fever* was released at a time when patriarchy was facing increasing pressures to negotiate the bounds of hetero-normativity, most famously expressed in the development of a nascent male liberation movement. Quickly dubbed "men's lib," and counterbalancing women's lib, the movement championed a new model of masculinity, unencumbered by traditional masculine norms. In 1970, Jack

Sawyer, a young psychologist and former anti-war and civil rights activist, defined men's liberation as a call "for men to free themselves of the sex-role stereotypes that limit their ability to be human" (25). Published in 1974, Warren Farrell's *The Liberated Man* refashioned Sawyer's doctrines in the popular self-advancement language of Erhard Seminars Training. Borrowing Betty Friedan's language, Farrell sees men as trapped in the "masculine mystique" and diagnoses their "emotional constipation" (3). His prescribed remedy is for men to embrace their feminine side and free themselves from their roles as protectors and breadwinners.

Men's lib offered its followers the benefit of adopting behaviors and styles that had previously carried the stigma of effeminacy. In the name of liberation, for example, a heterosexual man could abandon the traditional standard requiring him to be indifferent about his appearance and begin paying attention to his clothing and grooming. "Male narcissism," Henry Allen observed in 1978, "has more than come out of the closet. It has prospered, burgeoned, bloated, overborn." While feminism trained heterosexual men to appreciate narcissism, gay liberation allowed them to do so without being suspected for sexual deviance. With the heightened cultural visibility of gay men and the development of distinct gay communities since the 1960s, the threat of homosexuality assumed a more concrete identity through the 1970s. It stopped being an indeterminate otherness, hidden potentially in every man. Liberated men could display their refined taste, indulge in self-grooming, and opt for fashionable dress, while remaining strictly within the boundaries of heterosexuality.

Nevertheless, liberated masculinity came at that cost of embracing feminism and rejecting homophobia. A man could confidently indulge in narcissism under the explicit condition that he understood and accepted the sources and requirements of this freedom. Whether genuinely believing in gender equality or simply trying to disassociate themselves from the evils of patriarchy, liberated men were always self-proclaimed feminists. The image of the liberated man found its epitome in the ascendency of Alan Alda's public persona. A proud friend of the women's movement, Alda confessed to *Ms.* magazine in 1976 that "where men work without women, there is just a little less warmth, a little less laughter, a little less relaxation." Men's liberation, on the other hand, makes for happier men, even allowing them to garner "the courage to stick a flower on their desks" (Alda 93).

Alda's brand of feminism may be evidently problematic, but Tony Manero is certainly far from the model of male liberation. Tony has no qualms in publically declaring that all women can be neatly divided into "good girls" and "cunts," and spends whatever time is left between dancing and styling his hair to displays of white bigotry and violent machismo. In a scene that is otherwise completely unconnected to the plot, Tony and his gang bully two stereotypically effeminate gay men. Their exaggerated display of prejudice interrupts their discussion of sexual exploits, as if to re-affirm heterosexuality through homophobic machismo. Tony's sartorial choices, furthermore, push the boundaries of his narcissism beyond what would even be permissible for liberated men. Men like Alda expressed in their stylistic choices the refinement and sensitivity of being in touch with their feminine side. They opted for pale hues, knits, and the ubiquitous earth-tone polyester, a sharp contrast to Tony Manero's preference for bold, contrasting colors, frilly lapels, and oversized platform shoes.

Much more than what Tony chooses to wear, it is what he does not wear that accentuates insinuations of closeted homosexuality. For much of the grooming scene Tony remains stripped down to his black bikini briefs. Though briefs were then still Hollywood's choice of male underwear, both the color and cut of Tony's briefs set him apart from the heterosexual norm. Before what Dyer calls "the revival of the boxer shorts," white, high-rising, Y-front, cotton briefs used to be the epitome of men's underwear ("The Matter" 124). Their design combined support and functionality through the frontal opening while their color and material allowed for hygienic care. Tony's tight, low-rising, black briefs sacrifice (masculine) practicality for the benefit of (feminine) style. More importantly, they draw attention to what they are supposed to conceal, the penis. Dyer explains that, although "the symbolism of male sexuality is that it is overwhelmingly centered on the genitals, the penis is mainly represented through the phallus. Phalli are unbending, sharp, sword-like, and seldom made of flesh and skin. They resemble nothing of the soft and imprecise form of the penis. As Dyer succinctly puts it, "the penis isn't a patch on the phallus" ("Male" 112). Following the same reasoning, D.A. Miller explains that the middle-class, heterosexual man's preference for boxer shorts reveals an attempt to conceal "the penis, which disappears into a cool rectangularity that ... only apotheosizes it as the phallus" (28). Though *Fever* does not actually show the penis, and hence avoids the box-office suicide of full frontal nudity, it evidently ignores Dyer's and Miller's precautions. The camera shoots Tony from extremely low angles, a spatial perspective that, as Jeff Yanc notes, "makes the crotch appear larger and more prominent than any other part of [his] body" (42).

The film, furthermore, invites us to question Tony's machismo through intertextual references to homosexuality. When Tony catches a glimpse of *Serpico* (1973), he remembers a girl's comment that kissing him felt like kissing Al Pacino. He celebrates the compliment by prancing around in his underwear, chanting "Al Pacino, Al Pacino" and "Attica, Attica." His imitation of Pacino does not refer to Frank Serpico, a heterosexual police officer, but Sonny Wortzik, the bisexual protagonist of *Dog Day Afternoon* (1975), who robs a bank to pay for his lover's sex change operation. Pacino's cry "Attica, Attica" in *Dog Day Afternoon* is yet another reference to the 1971 Attica Prison riots following the shooting of a radical African American inmate. When Tony Manero repeats the line in *Fever*, inspired by a woman's compliment on his kissing skills, his intended celebration of white heterosexual virility is undermined by a network of intertextual references to blackness, queerness, and left radicalism.

In addition to textual and intertextual suggestions, the grooming scene can assume contextual homoerotic meaning that is historically specific to the late 1970s. When Tony awakens on Sunday morning, he moves the sheets out of the way and reaches into his underwear to scratch himself. Viewing this image through an ahistorical lens, one can find both challenges and affirmations of Tony's heterosexuality. On the one hand, Tony's crude handling of his body would signal in Dyer's reasoning an alignment with the gay male "refusal ... *to closet our bodies*" ("The Matter" 125). On the other hand, clearly visible in the same shot are his hairdryer and a construction worker's hard-hat. The hard-hat could be seen as a reference to male physical labor and the upward pointing hairdryer as an obvious phallic symbol. In the light of Dyer's analysis, these two objects could be interpreted as representational strategies that counter the objectification of Travolta's naked body. While his nakedness and the visual emphasis on the penis objectify him, his heterosexual phallic power is simultaneously rescued on the left side of the frame.

In the context of 1977, however, the coupling of a naked young man and a hard-hat cannot but evoke the subculture of the gay clone. In Martin Levine's description, gay clones are those post-Stonewall gay men who "embrac[ed] the presentational image of the butch style, modifying it into a more stylized uniform." Exemplified in the image of the Village People, clones "favored the hood, athlete, and woodsman looks for everyday leisure attire. They wore the Western, leather, military, laborer, and uniform looks for going out or partying" (Levine 58-60). While reacting against the stereotype that associated homosexuality with the effeminacy and feebleness of an aristocratic upper class, clones also rejected the traditional male indifference toward outward appearance. They opted for carefully trimmed facial hair, evenly toned bodies, and well-tailored costumes. The hard-hat on Tony's dresser carries the same connotations of calculated machismo. It appears unworn and, based on what we already know about him, completely useless in his work at the hardware store.

This almost playful juxtaposition of signifiers of homosexuality and heterosexuality reaches its climax in an indicative sequence of images at the end of the grooming scene. A shot of the Bruce Lee poster on Tony's wall cuts to a reverse shot from the perspective of the poster as Tony looks in the mirror and imitates the same pose. This is followed by yet another dramatic low angle shot of Tony's crotch; however, just when the narcissistic display of Tony's body threatens to challenge his heterosexuality, the film cuts to a poster of Farah Fawcett. Her wide smile, presumably at the sight of Tony's penis, affirms its heterosexual use. Immediately afterwards, when Tony's father comes into the room, threats to heterosexuality surface once more, as the onlooker is no longer a poster, but another living man. We first see his father through his reflection in the mirror, next to Tony posing in his new shirt. In the context of a scene constructed around the fetishization of Tony's body, his father's gaze could even signify incestual homosexuality. In the following shot, however, Farrah Fawcett's poster appears next to the father to claim his gaze and rescue heterosexuality. Not only does he turn to look at the poster, but the camera even assumes his point-of-view for a close-up of Fawcett's cleavage. In a textbook-like example of the Mulveyian male gaze, Tony's father becomes the subject of the film, the heterosexual masculine position, and Farah Fawcett's body is objectified and fragmented under his gaze.

Fever assembles these contradictory signifiers and references with a playful and almost provocative lack of subtlety, as if confident that Tony Manero's heterosexual machismo is not actually threatened. Reviewers and interpreters seem to share this confidence. It underpins Neale's unqualified comment that the film provides an "interesting example" of an erotic display of the heterosexual male body (19). Similarly, Yanc elaborates on "the objectification of Travolta's body," but insists that his heterosexuality is "rescued" (39). The same confidence surfaces in Kael's suggestion that the film is a heterosexual version of *Scorpio Rising* (59). Attempting to explain what makes *Fever* different from Anger's film, Kael asserts that Tony is simply unaware of his conflicted masculinity (60), what Nystrom identifies as "a perceived disparity in critical self-consciousness" between Tony and the film's audiences

(127). Tony's sexism does not derive from hostility toward feminism, insofar as hostility presupposes knowledge. Rather, he simply remains oblivious to the demands of feminism and the constraints of male liberation.

This unselfconsciousness renders Tony's amalgam of masculinities qualitatively different from the homoeroticism of *Scorpio Rising*'s bikers, the costumed performances of the Village People, the overconfident feminism of Alan Alda, and especially the more recent parodies of 70s masculinity in films like *Starsky & Hutch* (2004) and *Semi-Pro* (2008). In all these cases, masculinity is a deliberate performance; it acknowledges the process of its construction and displays its mastery over the source material. Tony Manero, on the other hand, embodies his patchwork masculinity as if unaware of its seams. He can stare in the mirror for hours fixing his hair while remaining a sexist alpha male or borrow Pacino's "Attica, Attica" to celebrate a sexual compliment, but lacks a critical perspective on what each part of his masculine identity signifies and how uneasily they all fit together.

"WELCOME TO BROOKLYN"

The question that remains unanswered is what exactly allows Tony Manero the privilege of this unselfconsciousness. In his review of the film for *The Washington Post Magazine*, Allen conjectured that "[Tony] is too dumb to know about the obligations of the new sexuality. He's just a nice guy." What Allen identifies as dumbness and niceness in Tony is essentially an ethnic stereotype. From his socially and intellectually elevated perspective as a *Washington Post* writer and someone familiar with the obligations of the new sexuality, Allen recognizes Tony Manero as simply the Guido from Bay Ridge. Allen's explanation corresponds with descriptions of *Fever* as a "coming of age story" (Keeler 167) or a "tale of maturity" (Kupfer 171). Tony begins the film as the undisputed disco king and ends up giving up disco, resigning his job, and settling down in a monogamous relationship with Stephanie. Tony's personal growth, however, also involves a spatial, social, and even ethnic relocation, from Italian American Bay Ridge to WASP Manhattan. His hybrid masculinity can be similarly located in social geography. Until the film's final minutes, Tony does not inhabit the world of men's liberation, feminism, and gay clones, but the ethnic universe of Brooklyn. It is his identity as a white ethnic man that allows him to pick and choose elements of 1970s masculinities, ignore any compromises to his heterosexuality, combine them with more traditional masculine traits, and nonchalantly embody them as a believable masculine identity.

Men's liberation was from the start a strictly white, middle-class phenomenon. In one of the movement's earliest accounts, *Life* magazine describes the liberated man as "a healthy and intelligent young white American male" (B. Farrell 50). As the movement gradually took shape, the connections between its constituency and politics also became clear. As Messner describes, the movement walked a tightrope between two antithetical goals, a willingness to accept feminist demands and a parallel effort to emphasize the costs of patriarchy to men (256). Liberated men used the idea of oppression in a politically neutered sense, as a free-floating general condition that affects everyone equally, on a personal rather than a social level. Warren Farrell's diagnosis for masculine emotional constipation, for example, provided an ideal discursive package for promoting feminist ideas to men and lessening the guilt of patriarchal supremacy.

In its attempt to associate masculinity with victimhood, men's liberation was not an isolated phenomenon in the 1970s. From the uncontested cultural hegemons, middle-class, heterosexual, white men found themselves answerable for the repercussions of their hegemony. The civil rights and women's movements were the first to launch their attacks in the 1960s, with accusations of racism and sexism. Gay liberation soon followed with charges of homophobia. As *Life* put it, "not only was black beautiful and sisterhood powerful—now it was also groovy to be gay" (B. Farrell 53). The elderly, the disabled, the vegetarians, the nudists, and several other groups followed their lead through the decade to follow—not all with equally valid claims to victimhood. By asserting that patriarchy had symmetrical costs on men and women, men's liberation allowed middle class, heterosexual, white men to "join blacks, gays, and women in the ranks of the oppressed" (Kimmel 264).

In this climate, Italian American men found themselves in what was perceived to be an advantageous position, with ethnicity offering a readily available means for disassociating themselves from white privilege. After decades of enforced assimilation into an all-encompassing whiteness, the descendents of Italian and other European immigrants abandoned the melting pot and joined in what became known as the 1970s revival of ethnicity. By embracing their ethnic heritage, Italian Americans could simultaneously plead their innocence to the actual and symbolic charges facing white America. Whereas liberated men appealed to psychological self-advancement to claim a share of victimhood, the revival discourse invested in the popularity of biological determinism. Using the evocative language of ancestral roots and unbroken bloodlines, revived ethnics conceptualized the relationship between birthplace and ethnicity as analogous to that between genes and racial physiognomy. "Italian ethnicity," explained Richard Gambino, "comes with the blood if not through it. Its components are unique and strong" (375). Biological determinism offered Italian Americans a strong cultural privilege. They could enjoy all the benefits of whiteness and simultaneously claim an inalienable, primordial right to a guilt-free shade of whiteness. Micaela di Leonardo finds in ethnic revival "a distinct flavor of a Three Bears analogy,"

> White WASPs were "too cold"—bloodless, modern, and unencumbered—and blacks "too hot"—wild, primitive, and "over"-cumbered—white ethnics were "just right." For a hot minute in the 1970s, Italian Americans commandeered Baby Bear's chair. (177)

Fever invests in Tony's command of Baby Bear's chair to construct his hybrid masculinity. At a very suggestive moment in the film,

Joey, one of Tony's friends, spells out the privileges of Italian American ethnicity. As he catches his reflection in the car door window, Joey narcissistically remarks "Looking sharp, huh? Sharpest you can without turning into a nigger." Tony and his gang are ethnic enough to comfortably adopt the coolness of African American men and white enough to remain racist bigots. When Marsha Kinder criticized the film for being unable to decide if "Tony's style is a matter of personal expressiveness or racial identity" (40-41), she was unwittingly identifying that very ambivalence that makes his style possible. In the context of a culture that conceptualized Italian American whiteness as biologically distinct from WASP whiteness, Tony's style reflects precisely this racial in-betweeness. His flamboyantly macho strutting belongs to the stereotypical "pimp" representations of period blaxploitation films. At the same time, however, his outspoken bigotry reveals a faith in white supremacy that contradicts the new liberal and liberated Anglo-Saxon mores.

The same in-betweeness can also explain Tony's adoption of styles and behaviors that would have otherwise challenged his heterosexuality. To paraphrase Joey's comment, Tony can style his hair, display his naked body, and imitate Pacino in *Dog Day Afternoon* without turning gay. Whereas these behaviors have their referents in 1970s white, middle class models of masculinity, Tony's ethnic masculinity gives him the privilege of an unbroken connection to earlier models of aggressive heterosexual machismo. In his description of Italian American youth, Cohn conjectures that "this generation's real roots lie further back, in the fifties" ("Tribal" 31). Though Cohn probably has London's Mods in mind, his comment effectively captures the cultural valence of Italian American ethnicity of the *Fever* era. Tony can enjoy the behavioral and sartorial benefits of liberated men and gay clones while preserving the racism, sexism, and homophobia of a 1950s alpha male. As *The Village Voice* effectively put it, "in *Saturday Night Fever*, Travolta plays a kid who lives in a world where it's like the 60s never happened" (Rose 50). It is perhaps not surprising that six months after *Fever*'s release Travolta turned his 1970s Guido into a 1950s Greaser for *Grease* (1978).

While *Grease* locates Italian American masculinity in the past, *Fever* situates its distinctness in geographical terms. The film opens with extreme long shots of the two bridges that connect Brooklyn to Manhattan and Staten Island. Appearing right after the Paramount logo, the opening shots give the impression of a prologue that precedes the actual beginning of the film. The first shot shows the Brooklyn Bridge in the foreground, with the iconic Manhattan skyline in the background (figure 13). This is the view of Manhattan as the city of shiny, tall buildings, fast changes, and new possibilities, the cityscape view of Manhattan from Brooklyn's distant "out there." Apart from the basic narrative function of setting the story in Brooklyn, the film's opening also offers a very particular view of Brooklyn, as an enclosed, intermediary space between sophisticated Manhattan and suburban Staten Island. As audiences, we are being transported from the city and the suburbs to an exotic world where a hardware store employee can become disco king.

The slow retracting motion of the camera and low ambient noise are suddenly interrupted by the much louder sound of a train as it passes diagonally across the frame. The introduction of "Staying Alive" begins in the soundtrack and Travolta's credit is superimposed against the background of the train arriving in Brooklyn. Though Travolta's only other film credit in 1977 was a small part in *Carrie* (1976), his name was already recognizable as the star of the television series *Welcome Back, Kotter* (1975-79). According to *The Village Voice*, "as Vinnie Barbarino, Travolta draws about 10,000 pieces of fan mail per day" (Rose 49). In addition to elevating Travolta to stardom, *Kotter* established the connections between his star persona and Brooklyn's Italian American working class, which made him an ideal candidate for the role of Tony Manero. The greeting in the series title refers to Gabe Kotter's return to Buchanan High in Brooklyn, to teach a group of underachievers known as the sweathogs. An ex-sweathog himself, Kotter is welcomed back as a facetious but well-meaning teacher who realizes the sweathogs' true potential. Travolta's wisecracking Vinnie Barbarino is the leader of the sweathogs and the school's heartthrob. Vinnie is only the first articulation of the persona that elevated Travolta to stardom in the late 70s. It takes little effort to notice, as *Fever*'s contemporary reviewers invariably did, that Tony is essentially an R-rated version of Vinnie after graduation. *Newsweek* introduced a December 1977 tribute to Travolta with the title "From Sweathog to Disco King" and described the young star as having "specialized in playing kids from the wrong side of the tracks" (Orth 63). Both Vinnie and Tony are working class Italian Americans living in Brooklyn; Vinnie is the leader of the Sweathogs, Tony is the leader of the Faces.

Audiences expecting to see John Travolta's debut as a cinematic lead encounter not only a familiar character, but also a familiar space. The imagery of bridges and transport in the film's opening bears a striking resemblance to the opening titles of *Kotter*, which begin with a shot of a roadside sign "Welcome to Brooklyn." Images of trains, roads, and bridges are interspersed with travelling shots of Brooklyn shops and houses, presumably filmed from the window of a car or a train. In this respect, *Fever* assumes additional meaning through what Klinger calls audience digressions, "intertextual activations on reading that exceed intrinsic control" (7). Whereas the aforementioned intertextual reference to Pacino is incorporated in the text, the connection between Brooklyn and Italian American masculinity is reinforced through contextual knowledge of Travolta's role in *Kotter*. Like Cohn's story and *Fever*'s opening, *Kotter*'s credit sequence does not present Brooklyn as a place in our midst, but as a place one has to travel toward and warrant the greeting "welcome" upon arrival. As the credits appear on screen accompanied by the theme song "Welcome Back," every image emphasizes the idea of physically going to Brooklyn. The song's lyrics, furthermore, welcome Gabe Kotter back to the place from which "[his] dreams were [his] ticket out," suggesting that Brooklyn is a somewhat limiting place, conducive to cultivating your dreams or inspiring others to dream, but not for actually fulfilling your dreams.

Tony Manero ends the film in precisely this position, leaving Brooklyn to pursue his dreams in Manhattan. Though I have not focused on Tony's character development in this essay, it ought to be noted that *Fever* is not just about dancing and hairstyling. The film's most memorable scenes may take place on the dance floor, but its narrative is in fact carried forward by a series of dramatic and often violent events that force Tony to give up disco and leave Brooklyn. Unlike Vinnie in *Kotter*'s sitcom universe, Tony ventures outside high school in the R-rated *Fever* and encounters the less welcoming side of Brooklyn. Outside the discotheque and Tony's room, Brooklyn is infested with gang fights, unemployment, and obstacles to upward social mobility. At the end of the film, Tony realizes that his disco lifestyle is a dead-end and takes the midnight train out of Brooklyn. The final scene finds Tony and Stephanie in a borrowed Manhattan apartment. They sit by the window and hold hands, silhouetted against the light of the dawning new day. Tony seems determined to find a job with higher prospects and agrees with Stephanie to remain just friends, while the melodic "How Deep Is Your Love?" suggests the appeasing possibility of romance.

This conclusion seems to shatter the social and geographical foundation of Tony's masculine privileges. In the context of a film that has defined the interrelation between ethnicity and masculinity in a rigid geographical binary, Tony's Italian American masculinity will have to pay the price of his social elevation in Manhattan. A monogamous relationship with Stephanie will signal the end of his sexual adventures; a white-collar job will limit his time for dancing and grooming; sophisticated Manhattan friends will gradually tone down his racism and homophobia. Overall, Tony's hybrid masculinity will collapse and "then he'll be just like all the other male narcissists, and nobody will even notice him" (Allen). For white, middle class, male audiences in the 1970s, this must have been both a comforting and an alarming realization. On the one hand, the suggestion that even Brooklyn's disco king aspires to their lifestyle affirms middle-class "superiority over their working-class characters" (Nystrom 128). On the other hand, this conclusion also eliminates the pleasure in watching, and possibly identifying with, a white man unaffected by contemporary challenges to masculinity. Nevertheless, the brevity and romantic mood of the final scene conceal these implications. As the end credits begin to roll, the film makes certain that nobody ruminates too much on its conclusion by switching from "How Deep Is Your Love?" to the upbeat "Staying Alive." "I've been kicked around since I was born," the Bee Gees sing in their signature falsetto, echoing the darker side of Tony's life in Brooklyn. The following line, however, offers an assurance that could apply equally well to the male character in the film and the male viewers watching the film: "Now it's all right. It's OK. And you may look the other way."

CONCLUSION

Pauline Kael's unwillingness to qualify her comparison of Tony Manero with *Scorpio Rising*'s homosexual bikers reveals an almost instinctive reaction to what she perceives as an obvious fact: Tony Manero is a heterosexual man. Despite his sexist, homophobic, racist, and often violent brand of machismo, Tony also indulges in the traditionally feminizing activities of disco dancing and self-grooming. Yet, attempts to investigate this paradox from a purely textual perspective carry the risk of ignoring the "obviousness" of Tony's heterosexuality. My purpose in this essay has been to explore the historical discourses that underpin *Fever*'s visual strategies and to problematize the hypotheses that have guided their interpretation. The association between disco and homosexuality does not withstand historical scrutiny. By the time of *Fever*'s release, disco had already entered into the hetero-normative mainstream. Tony's narcissistic attention to his appearance, on the other hand, cannot be justified as the expression of a 1970s liberated man. Tony may benefit from developments that opened the doors of narcissism to heterosexual men, but he does not share their presumed feminism. Neither does the film employ any of the usual heterosexualizing techniques in displaying Tony's body as erotic spectacle. Immediately offset against Tony's hybrid masculinity is his intriguing unawareness of its inconsistencies. This combination of hybridity and unselfconsciousness can be reconciled by locating Tony's masculinity as a historically specific brand of Italian American heterosexual machismo. The 1970s understanding of white ethnicity as a primordial identity allows Tony to combine seamlessly the styles and behaviors of new masculinities with an older brand of aggressive heterosexual machismo. It is Tony Manero's identity as an Italian American man that warrants Kael's unequivocal description of *Fever* as "a straight, heterosexual film."

WORKS CITED

Alda, Alan. "Alan Alda on Era." *Ms*. July 1976: 48+. Print.

Allen, Henry. "The New Narcissism: The Male Narcissist." *The Washington Post Magazine* 10 June 1978: 21. *LexisNexis*. Web. 21 Aug. 2012.

Auster, Albert and Leonard Quart. Rev. of *Saturday Night Fever*. *Cineaste* 8.4 (1978): 36-37. Print.

Bondanella, Peter. *Hollywood Italians: Dagos, Palookas, Romeos, Wise Guys, and Sopranos*. New York: Continuum, 2004. Print.

Bordo, Susan. *The Male Body: A New Look at Men in Public and in Private*. New York: Farrar, Strauss and Giroux, 1999. Print.

Cohn, Nic. "Saturday Night's Big Bang." *New York* 8 Dec. 1997: 32+. *Google Books*. Web. 21 Aug. 2012.

_____. "Tribal Rites of the New Saturday Night." *New York* 7 June 1976: 31-43. *Google Books*. Web. 21 Aug. 2012.

Darling, Lynn. "The Prince of Disco: You Always Have to Have Something Happening in the Disco Business." *The Washington Post* 5 Aug. 1979: H1. *LexisNexis*. Web. 21 Aug. 2012.

di Leonardo, Micaela. "White Ethnicities, Identity Politics, and Baby Bear's Chair." *Social Text* 41 (1994): 165-91. *JSTOR*. Web. 21 Aug. 2012.

Dyer, Richard. "In Defence of Disco." *Gay Left* 8 (1979): 20-23. *Gay Left*. Web. 21 Aug. 2012.

     ―――. "Don't Look Now: The Male Pin-up." *The Sexual Subject: A Screen Reader in Sexuality.* Ed. *Screen.* London: Routledge, 1992. 265-76. Print.

     ―――. "Male Sexuality in the Media." *The Sexuality of Men.* Eds. Martin Humphries and Andy Metcalf. London: Pluto, 1985: 28-43. Print.

     ―――. *The Matter of Images: Essays on Representations.* London: Routledge, 1993. Print.

Frank, Gillian. "Discophobia: Antigay Prejudice and the 1979 Backlash against Disco." *Journal of the History of Sexuality* 16.2 (2007): 276-306. *JSTOR.* Web. 21 Aug. 2012.

Farrell, Barry. "You've Come a Long Way, Buddy." *Life* 27 Aug. 1971: 50-59. *Google Books.* Web. 21 Aug. 2012.

Farrell, Warren. *The Liberated Man: Beyond Masculinity: Freeing Men and Their Relationships with Women.* New York: Random House, 1974. Print.

Gambino, Richard. *Blood of My Blood.* New York: Anchor, 1974. Print.

Graustark, Barbara, Janet Huck, Peggy Clausen, and Ronald Henkoff. "Disco." *Newsweek* 2 Apr. 1979: 56. Print.

Jersey Shore. MTV, 2009-2012. Television.

Kael, Pauline. "Nirvana." Rev. of *Saturday Night Fever. The New Yorker* 26 Dec. 1977: 59-60. *The New Yorker Archives.* Web. 21 Aug. 2012.

Keeler, Greg. "*Saturday Night Fever*: Crossing the Verrazano Bridge." *Journal of Popular Film and Television* 7.2 (1979): 158-167. *ProQuest.* Web. 21 Aug. 2012.

Kimmel, Michael. *Manhood in America: A Cultural History.* New York: Free Press, 1996. Print.

Kinder, Marsha. Rev. of *Saturday Night Fever. Film Quarterly* 31.3 (1978): 40-42. *JSTOR.* Web. 21 Aug. 2012.

Klinger, Barbara. "Digressions at the Cinema: Reception and Mass Culture." *Cinema Journal* 28.4 (1989): 3-19. *JSTOR.* Web. 21 Aug. 2012.

Kupfer, Joseph. "'Stayin' Alive': Moral Growth and Personal Narrative in *Saturday Night Fever.*" *Journal of Popular Film and Television* 34.4 (2007): 170-78. *ProQuest.* Web. 21 Aug. 2012.

Lawrence, Tim. "Disco and the Queering of the Dance Floor." *Cultural Studies* 25.2 (2011): 230-43. *EBSCO.* Web. 21 Aug. 2012.

Levine, Martin P. *Gay Macho: The Life and Death of the Homosexual Clone.* Ed. Michael S. Kimmel. New York: New York UP, 1998. Print.
Messner, Michael A. "The Limits of 'The Male Sex Role': An Analysis of the Men's Liberation and Men's Rights Movements' Discourse." *Gender & Society* 12.3 (1998): 255-76. *JSTOR.* Web. 21 Aug. 2012.
Miller, D.A. *Bringing Out Roland Barthes.* Berkeley: U of California P, 1992. Print.
Mulvey, Laura. "Visual Pleasure and Narrative Cinema." *Screen* 16.3 (1975): 6-18. Print.
Neale, Steve. "Masculinity as Spectacle." *The Sexual Subject: A Screen Reader in Sexuality.* Ed. *Screen.* London: Routledge, 1992. 277-90. Print.
Nystrom, Derek. *Hard Hats, Rednecks, and Macho Men: Class in 1970s American Cinema.* Oxford: Oxford UP, 2009. Print.
Orth, Maureen. "From Sweathog to Disco King." *Newsweek* 19 Dec. 1977: 63-65. Print.
Rose, Frank. "Travolta Puts Out." *The Village Voice* 19 Dec. 1977: 49-50. *Google News.* Web. 21 Aug. 2012.
Saturday Night Fever. Dir. John Badham. 1977. Paramount Home Entertainment, 2007. DVD.
Sawyer, Jack. "On Male Liberation." *Liberation* 15 (1970): 32-33. Rpt. in *Feminism and Masculinities.* Ed. Peter F. Murphy. Oxford: Oxford UP, 2004. 25-27. Print.
Shapiro, Peter. *Turn the Beat Around: The Secret History of Disco.* New York: Faber, 2005. Print.
Welcome Back, Kotter. ABC, 1975–1979. Television. Warner Home Video, 2007. DVD.
Wolfe, Tom. "The New Cookie." *Harper's* Nov. 1978: 79. Print.
Yanc, Jeff. "'More than a Woman': Music, Masculinity and Male Spectacle in *Saturday Night Fever* and *Staying Alive.*" *Velvet Light Trap* 38 (1996): 39-50. *ProQuest.* Web. 21 Aug. 2012.

A History of the "Palooka"[1]

Courtney J. Ruffner Grieneisen

Because of the many negative associations that prizefighting has linked to the Italian-American, one of the most overlooked positive depictions of the Italian-American is that of the prize-fighter. Scholarship on the history of boxing and particularly prizefighting within the Italian-American ethnic group has been written by many critics of the Italian-American canon including Peter Bondanella and Fred Gardaphé. Scholars have emphasized the term "palooka" and its metamorphosis from a positive origin (ironically, one that has not been ascribed to any one ethnic background) to a negative association. Yet, this metamorphosis has not been examined closely. In reality, the change in this representation stems from a deep-seated hegemonic bias against the Italian-American and against the mentality of the prize-fighter. To help expose and to further explain the obvious unfairness that American viewing audiences have come to embrace when being challenged by films that depict Italian-Americans as less than whole characters, viewers can study not only films like *Rocky* (John G. Avildsen, 1976) and the *Raging Bull* (Martin Scorsese, 1980) but also autobiographical material from real fighters like Rocky Graziano and Jake LaMotta. At first glance, viewers can say that the directors' treatment of the boxers in these films is less than positive in terms of making strides against demonizing the Italian-American male, because the films call attention to associations with the mob,

---

[1] This essays derives from a portion of my dissertation chapter titled "'Hey Joe (Palooka)': Hollywood Prize Fighters On and Off Screen." In the larger work, the two main characters of the films *Rocky* (1976) and *Raging Bull* (1980) are analyzed extensively as palooka figures in an Inter-Colonial America.

heightened violent and displaced outbursts, and overbearing misogynist attitudes; however, upon closer analysis, viewers can distinguish depth within the images of these Italian-American males as they struggle through their identity issues and attempt to gain entrance into a culture into which they have not been born.

This paper explains how the prizefighter who was once referred to as a "large and stupid [...] oaf or lout" (qtd. in Bondanella 93) became synonymous with the term "palooka," meaning "an incompetent or easily defeated player, especially prize fighter" (qtd. in Bondanella 93).[2] The American public has come to view this term, "palooka," negatively, even though it once was used as a positive term to describe a fighter with heart, someone who earned a positive image even though he might not have been a champ. Although the definition of "palooka" is now obscure, its connotations have become tainted because of the stereotypes the media has associated with it. The definition of the term has morphed into yet another way in which the image of the Italian-American male can be distorted. The term "palooka" and Hollywood representations of "palookas" have changed extensively over the past ninety years to include more urbanized, ethnicized meanings, ignoring historical relevance and aiding today's marginalization of Italian-American heritage.

In addition to the historical / cultural significance of the term "palooka" and its transformative association with Italian-American men, American viewers must also acknowledge the Eurocentric paradigms that are most certainly attached to the Italian-American and, in this case, the Italian-American prizefighter. These structures of thought help to shape the image of the Italian-American "palooka" and what this image says about the culture that created it. Nearly four million Italians immigrated to the United States

---

[2] Ironically, the term palooka has little to do with the idea of male virility that so many critics draw attention to when writing on boxing. In fact, the definition, here, implies a lack of masculine characteristics associated with sports in general as the palooka is ultimately a loser of the match.

between 1880 and 1920, carrying with them a desire to succeed in life. When they made it to America, they began to develop colonies of Little Italys, where they could band together and form support systems for each other. They were met with the expectation that they "were incapable of assimilating into Anglo-Saxon society" (Aguirre 227). In part because of this prejudice, the men were not offered well-paying jobs. It was difficult to get out of the Little Italy they were born into unless they became a *somebody*. One legitimate way to do this was to become a prizefighter. In his chapter titled "Palookas: Hollywood Italian Prize Fighters," Bondanella writes:

> Juveniles growing up in the lower socioeconomic levels, who saw gang fights as a normal condition of life, entertained fantasies about "easy money," lacked real vocational opportunities, and remained generally isolated from middle-class culture, were as likely to become criminals as boxers: the major difference resided in the role model available for the youngster, whether criminal or prizefighter. (95)

Becoming a prizefighter was a reliable means of earning a good income, even though the sport was contaminated with criminality; ironically, the criminality associated with the sport was controlled by two Italian-Americans named Frankie Carbo and Blinky Palermo. These two men controlled the fight game for years, setting up fighters to take dives when the odds were in the fighter's favor in order to boost betting profits and manipulate the outcome of prizefighters' careers. These men preyed on their own ethnic group, because they knew they could manipulate these young men by promising them that they would be celebrities, something they themselves remembered desiring when they were younger. In addition, a certain group of young Italian-American men "saw boxing as a means of joining mainstream culture" (Bondanella 96), something that their parents were likely never invited to do because they were viewed as less-than-desirable, uneducated and non-fluent in

English. This desire for assimilation drove a number them to become fighters, even when they did not possess the poise a prizefighter needs. Because boxing had become a popular social event, promoters put anyone in the ring that would fight.

Fighters like Rocky Marciano, Rocky Graziano, and Jake LaMotta in the 1940s and 1950s came out of Little Italys, and these "[b]rawling fighters—those with heart" (Bondanella 94) perpetuated the stigma of the palooka and solidified the connection of the term with Italian-Americans. These fighters were crowd pleasers who could endure much more physical punishment than the average boxer could. They did not possess the speed or accuracy of boxers like Ali or Frazier, but they could punch their way into a win against an opponent who may not have had equal "bravery" or "courage."

Oates refers to these boxers as "interesting symbolic figures" who "[sought] physical pain" (qtd. in Bondanella 94). It is this symbol that Hollywood writers latched onto when they realized that boxing films were becoming as popular and as lucrative as films of the gangster genre. Boxing films go back to the beginning of cinema.[3] But I will concentrate on two that hail from the 1970s and 1980s, a time when Italian-American males were attempting to build a cultural identity beyond that of the gangster and the palooka. The symbol of the palooka became the center for such films as the *Rocky* franchise, a story about a boxer with heart, and *Raging Bull* (1980), a chronicle of boxer Jake LaMotta's downfall, where

---

[3] While analyzing films that encompass the many years that boxing has been depicted on-screen would detract from the overall basis of this chapter, it is important to point out a few important films that illustrate the tradition of cinematic representations of boxing. *Any Old Port!* (1932) directed by James Horne, *Kid Galahad* (1937) directed by Michael Curtiz, *Golden Boy* (1939) directed by Rouben Mamoulian, *Kid Dynamite* (1943) directed by Wallace Fox, *Body and Soul* (1947) directed by Robert Rossen, *The Ring* (1952) directed by Kurt Neumann, *Requiem for a Heavyweight* (1962) directed by Ralph Nelson, and *The Great White Hope* (1970) directed by Martin Ritt are amongst the body of work available.

the palooka character—the Italian-American boxer—has transformed the term into one that has none of its original definition and has been replaced with negative Italian-American stereotypes. These two films together represent a progression in the depictions of Italian-American males on film. With this background, viewers are closer to understanding the culture that has caused these males to make life decisions based, in part, on the way they have been perceived through American eyes and have been depicted through the Hollywood lens. More important, viewers are able to see a context for what I call Inter-Colonialism,[4] by reading the characters of Rocky and Jake against elements of masculinity, misogyny, and aggression, the very characteristics middle-America ascribes to Italian-American males in film and, often times, uses to define these characters on screen. Fortunately, both Rocky and Jake are able to transcend this demonization in ways that allow their identities to grow and shift positively.

In 1926, the most important boxing publication, *The Ring*, defined a "palooka" as "a tenth rater, a boxer without ability, a nobody" (qtd. in Bondanella 93); however, it was Ham Fisher in 1920, according to *The Oxford English Dictionary*, who popularized the term when he sketched "the comic-strip character Joe Palooka, a well-meaning but clumsy prizefighter" ("Palooka"). Although the image of Joe Palooka transformed from time to time to match the image of the current boxing champ, it is the first image of Joe Palooka that helps to explain the American public's connection of the character with Italian-Americans. It is common knowledge within sports arenas that the Joe Palooka character for the comic strip was modeled after a "big, burly, and inarticulate boxer" whom Fisher

---

[4] As a means to discuss the Italian-American ethnic group as an oppressed people after immigrating to America and while remaining within the borders of America, I have constructed a theoretical framework, Inter-Colonialism, to work inside so that an organized and well-rounded study can take place planted at the center of the field of Italian-American Studies. Inter-Colonialism is a post-colonial type oppression of a minority population that has migrated into the dominant culture of America.

met "outside a poolroom in [Fisher's] hometown of Wilkes-Barre, Pennsylvania" (Waters). In "Joe Palooka: A Comic Strip Character Goes to War," T. Wayne Waters suggests that the first image of the palooka character, one that "scored big with the American public," was "ugly, dark-haired, bug-eyed, and quite stupid" and a "dim-witted roustabout" (qtd. in Kashatus 25). By the time the character was being used by the American government as wartime propaganda, Palooka had been transformed into what Waters refers to as "handsome, blond, clear-eyed, and merely inarticulate," the opposite in almost entirety of the original Palooka character. In other words, to clean him up for presentation to the American public, Joe Palooka was made less ethnic. Cleaning the character up for war and sketching him as an "all-American bastion of honesty, humility, courage, and devotion to duty" (Waters) may have aided the US government in the acceptance and bolstering of national pride, but it certainly did nothing to help deflect the associations of the character with Italian-Americans in spite of the term's (palooka) unknown origin. Because the palooka had been directly linked to the Joe Palooka character when the character was said to have been sketched to emulate boxing champions like featherweight champion Tony Canzoneri,[5] for instance, naturally the comic character would share a physical likeness to the Italian boxer.

Even as a war hero, Joe Palooka's character ultimately remained questionable, as later in 1942, while fighting in North Africa, Palooka shot in the back a Nazi soldier who was attempting to escape. Waters explains that "this questionable act from the clean cut bastion of American fair play upset" a number of his American readers. Just as modern-day media constantly gain revenue by associating the Italian-American character with crime in one way or another, it can be said that Fisher, most likely, began the negative associations, albeit unconscious ones, when he sketched his newly-polished character as a shady soldier with criminal capability.

---

[5] Canzoneri beat Benny Bass for the championship on February 10, 1928.

Because Italian-American boxers predominately hailed form the northeastern areas of the United States and were known for their plodding, violent street-fighting style of boxing, mirroring Palooka's quick and intense anger, "thunder in his fist," and *luggish* demeanor (Kashatus 26), America, naturally, began to associate this character with the Italian-American boxer. Yet, in the early years of his portrayal, Palooka's "refreshing innocence" (Kashatus 23) was his most famous trait. Readers found this innocence humorous, and the humor is what connected the character with his readers in the company of the common man. In "Wilkes-Barre Boxing Legend With a National Punch," William C. Kashatas explains that it is Palooka's quick and intense anger and his name (meaning third-rate boxer) that "appealed to the common man, especially in northeastern Pennsylvania, where the immigrant's own experience of winding up as the patsy for those with less virtuous ambitions and plenty of guile seemed to mirror Palooka's innocence and sense of trust" (26). Herein the immediacy of the image of the palooka is compromised by what Kashatas implies, because he is simply stereotyping the northeastern Pennsylvanian common man as a dim-witted patsy, mirroring the palooka. Viewers could suggest that instead of highlighting the positive aspects of the character of Joe Palooka and his place in boxing, Kashatas increased the blemish of the image of the "palooka," by attaching it to that of the immigrant patsy. While referring to Joe Palooka as a patsy could simply be a way for Kashatas to sympathize with the plight of the less politically powerful immigrant, the term "patsy" implies a lack of swiftness or intelligence. In fact, the *Oxford English Dictionary* defines patsy as "[a] person who is easily taken advantage of, esp. by being deceived, cheated, or blamed for something; a dupe, a scapegoat." Viewers have to remember that at the time of the grand emergence of Italian immigration, Italians banded together in Little Italys so that families who were being oppressed because they were Italian immigrants could help one another by living together and working together, much as they did back in their old country. By forming these communities, exclusive to their own ethnic group, Italians appeared as if they did not desire to become part of everyday America, and as a result, were becoming a symbol of resistance to assimilation. This is one reason lower and middle class Italians had become threatening to WASPs, causing the white-collar non-Italian-Americans to blame Italian-Americans for activities like criminality in communities. The term palooka is now associated (*a priori*) with Italianità as it has expanded beyond simply being a clumsy, northeastern prizefighter to a lower/middle class individual associated with criminality.

In *Palookas: Hollywood Italian Prize Fighters*, Peter Bondanella explains that the film roles of Italian-American prizefighters have done little to change the "distorted images" of the Italian-American and "merely continue the identification of Italians with lower-class environments" (93). He goes on to say that boxers such as Rocky Graziano and Jake La Motta, who both have written autobiographies later used as stories for Hollywood depictions of Italian-American prizefighters, are to be viewed as palookas instead of dagos. Viewers are to assume from Bondanella's descriptions of the two fighters that he associated them with the palooka, a more pejorative term than "dago," because of its association with lower-class origins, a lack of education, a violent fighting style, and a violent profession. He indicates that there is a vast difference between the dago and the palooka (suggesting that there are four main categories of Italians: dago, palooka, romeo, wiseguy); however, viewers must distinguish the two terms, "dago" and "palooka," from one another in order to understand the origin of the palooka and the implications the palooka has on the American viewing audience. As Bondanella points out, even though "[t]he Hollywood Italian Palooka hails from the same urban, working class, and East coast background" as the dago, sharing "a number of anti-intellectual traits and behavior patterns," the language spoken by the palooka marks him as "a semi literate, anti-intellectual...whose brains are in [his] fists, not in [his] head" (130).

Viewers begin to distinguish the dago from the palooka at the outset of the Joe Palooka comic. The image of the Italian-American in the comic is different from those that were shown on Saturday morning cartoons[6] so popular from the 1940s to the 1960s. Something different is under attack. The image of the Italian-American has changed slightly to include now less of the mustache Pete stereotype and more of the second-generation characteristics, a little more assimilated yet still less literate than the typical boxer and uninitiated in terms of further education.

In the renowned sociological article written in 1952 titled "The Occupational Culture of the Boxer," Wienberg and Arond suggest that the phrase known in and amongst boxing arenas, "You have to live up to being a fighter," stands as a justification for the way in which boxers with a "fighting heart" persevere in the fight world. To have a "fighting heart" means to never admit defeat (462). Weinberg and Arond go on to suggest that this mindset is what

---

[6] *Racketeer Rabbit* is a 1946 animated short film in the Looney Tunes series produced by Warner Bros. Cartoons, Inc. It stars Bugs Bunny, who duels with a pair of racketeers or gangsters, Rocky and Hugo forerunners who resemble Edward G. Robinson (Rocky, not to be confused with the aforementioned Rocky) and Peter Lorre (Hugo). ("Racketeer Rabbit").

In the 1950 short *Golden Yeggs*, Porky Pig and Daffy Duck defy the mob. Creator Freleng "redesigned Rocky for this short, making him a more generalized caricature of the tough guy gangster rather than Robinson in particular" ("Rocky and Mugsy").

Several more episodes of the cartoon utilize the mob image and Italian characteristics. In 1953's *Catty Cornered*, Sylvester the Cat and Tweety Bird meet up with gang leader Rocky and his "hulking" simpleton named "Nick" ("Rocky and Mugsy"). In 1954's *Bugs and Thugs*, "Nick" is now "Mugsy", and "though his over-muscled body stays mostly the same, his hair is gone, and his facial expressions are decidedly less intelligent" ("Rocky and Mugsy"). The duo also appeared in *Bugsy and Mugsy* (1957) and *The Unmentionables* (1963). Mugsy also appeared in the 1956 short *Napoleon Bunny-Part*.

Note: Rocky and Mugsy are parodied in the South Park episode, *Crippled Summer*, where Nathan (Rocky) tries to arrange fatal accidents for Jimmy Vulmer (a counterpart to Bugs Bunny), but his plans are always ruined by Mimsy's (Mugsy's) stupidity ("Rocky and Mugsy").

characterizes the boxer/fighter as a crowd pleaser, a spectacle as such (462). It is obvious to the viewing audience that these boxers who enter the ring labeled as underdogs and who literally punch their way to a victory are viewed as virile and masculine as well as animalistic, Neanderthals, to say the least. The audience of such fights then becomes enamored with the boxer with heart, because they identify with the underdog in whom they tend to see themselves. The fact that the palooka was able to draw a crowd is exactly what allows him to continue in the sport of boxing regardless of whether he possesses the necessary skill and technique a boxer must have to win.

Once the managers see how many people the palooka draws to the fight, they begin selling the fighter to the promoters for a larger profit, which hypes the fight and begins the gambling ring associated with the sport of boxing. It is clear that the managers "regard boxing as a business and the fighter as a commodity" (Weinberg and Arond 466). Ethnic background does not matter when money is the object of the sport. Promoters are concerned with attracting a large audience; and managers, although they are expected to care about their boxers, seem to be more concerned with winning to promote themselves and gaining even more work in the field. To insure more control over the boxers, the promoter, who cannot legally be a manager, appoints certain managers to boxers. Thus, the boxer is powerless to direct his own career.

To this end, boxers are turned into products up for purchase in our country of consumerism. Actual fighters like Rocky Graziano, Rocky Marciano and Jake La Motta had to endure this constant demeaning exploitation even after they completed their careers in the ring. Graziano and LaMotta wrote autobiographies that were turned into films focusing on the events that could be sensationalized by the directors of the films. Ultimately, it is within the filmic representations of these Italian-American prizefighters, the palookas, that viewers are able to see what this image says about the culture that created it, that of the consumer. The image of the palooka became the center for many films chronicling these prizefighters, strengthening the negative association of Italian-Americans and crime that the media creates for the American viewing audience.

ON OUR WAY TO PALOOKA-VILLE

In "Italian-Americans in Prize Fighting in the USA," James Mancuso mentions that after viewing the film *The Hurricane* (1999) the audience is made to feel that Rubin Carter should have won a bout with Joey Giardello, because Giardello represents the idea of "[some] evil Italian-American machinery," a comment on his way of fighting, perhaps marking him as a palooka before the others. One interesting note in Mancuso's film is that "the writers and directors took advantage of the widely circulated and accepted Italian-American criminal imagery that Hollywood has assiduously cultivated" by portraying the law enforcement officers as Italian-Americans "who harbored racist ideologies." We can suggest that this is a negative portrayal of Italian-American, even though his occupation is not that of the traditionally stereotyped gangster or criminal. The creation may be because Hollywood has conventionally depicted members of this minority group as less than fully American, that is to say less moral and ethical than the average American.

Aiding in the further decline of Italian-American ethnic identity on and off screen is a film that showcases the life of 1940s middleweight champion Rocky Graziano. Graziano embodies all that has been associated with the term palooka and can be credited as one of the Italian-American males solidified the association between the term palooka and Italian ethnicity. Graziano's own history with crime and his personal drive to clean up his life and begin a new chapter mirrors the beginning of Ham Fisher's Joe Palooka strip and cinches the connection between the term and the Italian American boxer. In

Robert Wise's 1956 film, *Somebody Up There Likes Me*, Graziano's life of crime is glorified by the casting of Paul Newman in the lead role.[7] Newman was a relatively unknown actor when he took the role of Graziano in the film. It has been noted by director Josh Logan that Newman "carried no sexual threat" (qtd. in Levy 110) although he was much larger than Graziano, who only weighed between 144 and 165 pounds and stood a mere five feet, seven inches. Newman, therefore, decided to train at Stillman's Gym, the same gym Graziano trained in, and for six hours a day as Graziano did in order to transform from a slim frame to a muscular, more sexually threatening build, like Graziano's.

Newman spent a lot of time with Graziano, to absorb some of his personality. Newman was quoted as saying that "there were two things" that he learned about Graziano: "[O]ne was that there was very little thought connected with his responses; they were immediate and emotional. Another was that there was a terrific restlessness about him, a kind of urgency and a thrust" (qtd. in Levy 111). Of all the things for Newman to highlight about Graziano, he chose to call attention to Graziano's temperament, the temperament of a fighter. Instead of calling attention to Graziano's ability to keep personal information about his family to himself, for example, the author of Newman's biography chose to quote Newman's assessment of Graziano in these two sentences. Never mind that in Levy's book, Levy quotes Newman mentioning that one night he and the director of the film attempted to get Graziano "stoned so that he'd loosen up and talk about himself" (111). Newman mentioned in a short aside that it was really he and Wise who ended up talking about themselves to Rocky—"Rocky loosened *us* [sic] up. We told him *our* [sic] life stories" (111). The image of Graziano as a patient man listening to his friends' life stories is dropped in the book directly after this quote, when Levy goes right back to molding Graziano as a palooka. He writes that Newman said "he [Graziano] spits a lot" (111). Viewers associate spitting with the blue-collar worker, the less-than-desirable image

---

[7] James Dean was to play the role of Graziano in the film, but he died in 1955 before filming began.

that Hollywood likes to exploit when working with Italian-Americans. Levy goes so far as to mention in his book that Graziano played the part of "a punch-drunk palooka" (111) in public while Newman shadowed him for his part in *Somebody Up There Likes Me*. Newman wanted to get inside Graziano's soul, but was only able to truly adapt Graziano's physical demeanor and mannerisms.

This film is noted as making Newman's career; afterward Newman would be compared to Marlon Brando.[8] Bosley Crowther of the *New York Times* wrote, "Let it be said of Mr. Newman that he plays the role of Graziano well, making the pug[9] and Marlon Brando almost indistinguishable" (qtd in Levy 113). Here, again, Graziano is referred to by the media as something less than desirable, an ape. What viewers can take from Graziano's experience with Newman and *Somebody Up There Likes Me* is that Graziano is portrayed as the palooka figure Bondanella speaks of, and Newman and director Wise have benefitted from this commodification of the Italian-American fighter. Newman's career was launched and Wise made a lot of money as the film won two Oscars.

Even though the director and lead of *Somebody Up There Likes Me* portrayed Graziano as a broken, damaged man with a criminal and abusive past, who makes it to the top, the story of Graziano's life was, in fact, told. Out of this story, and something Graziano and Italian-Americans in general, can be proud of, is the inspiration that Graziano gave to other actors of the 1950s playing similar

---

[8] Marlon Brando, at the time a method actor, gave Rocky Graziano and his wife tickets to the show he was starring in on Broadway, *A Streetcar Named Desire*. When Graziano saw Brando's character, he said, "that kid is playin' *me* [sic]" (qtd. in Levy 112). Brando had watched Graziano work out at Stillman's for a few weeks prior to completing his role in *A Streetcar Named Desire*.

[9] A monkey, an ape. pug, n.2
Third edition, September 2007; online version June 2011.
<http://www.oed.com/view/Entry/154210>; accessed 23 June 2011. An entry for this word was first included in *New English Dictionary*, 1909.

roles of anti-social, rebellious youths like Marlon Brando in *The Wild One* and *On the Waterfront* and James Dean in *Rebel Without a Cause*. As Gerald Early states in "The Romance of Toughness: La Motta and Graziano," these new actors began "aping on screen the kind of mannerisms of the misunderstood, antisocial youth that Graziano had cultivated in real life.... Graziano became a kind of pathetic pop gestalt of the bad white urban kid turned establishment hip" (389). Graziano helped shape the contemporary definition of the palooka in its essence, by allowing the true image of his life story to be told through his autobiography and then through the film version of the autobiography. When Newman portrayed Graziano in *Somebody Up There Likes Me*, Newman brought to the "wily character" (Levy 111) a humanity that allowed the American viewing audience to root for the underdog; however, Wise, like other directors before him, softened the harshness of the Italian-American actor as well as the ugliness of his childhood so that the audience could find common ground with his character and connect with his plight.[10] Here, by casting a non-Italian to play the Italian Graziano, Wise began softening the ethnic harshness that Graziano carried with him. The director's softening of Graziano's character suggests that Italian-Americans like Graziano, palookas, need to be altered in some way before they can be accepted by mainstream culture.

Even though the character was softened, Newman was allowed to mimic Graziano's speech patterns and mannerisms in so far as he could use these adaptations to garner sympathy from the viewing audience. Of course, mainstream America feels badly for a semi-illiterate, disadvantaged immigrant who continually is abused by his father, because his father's own dream was squashed by economic realities of the time. Mainstream America also begins to root for Graziano, because his story "is the story of human reclamation" (Rubin 428). He is able to "learn to be somebody else"

---

[10] Also seen in films like *Cobra* directed by Joseph Henabery, and *The Gay Divorcee* directed by Mark Sandrich, for instance.

(Rubin 428). And this is ultimately what white-collar non-Italian-Americans want from immigrant ethnics, for them to assimilate into, and thus become something other than what they were when they came to America.

Works Cited

Aguirre, Thomas. *Generation Saved Hollywood*. New York: Touchstone, 1998.

Bondanella, Peter. *Hollywood Italians: Dagos, Palookas, Romeos, Wise Guys, and Sopranos*. New York: The Continuum International Publishing Group, Inc., 2004. Print.

Early, Gerald. "The Romance of Toughness: La Motta and Graziano." *The Antioch Review* 45, 4 (Autumn 1987) 385-408. 22 June 2011. Web.

Kashatus, William C., III. "Joe Palooka, Wilkes-Barre Boxing Legend With a National Punch." *Pennsylvania Heritage* 26 (Spring 2000): 22-29. Print.

Levy, Shawn. *Paul Newman: A Life*. New York: Three Rivers Press, 2009.

Mancuso, James C. "Italian-Americans in Prize Fighting in The USA." *Essays and Articles Relevant to the Great Italy-the-USA-immigration: L'Avventura*. September 2000. Updated: July 2002. Web. 7 June 2010.

"Palooka." Def. *The Oxford English Dictionary*. 3rd ed. *OED Online*. Web. 10 January 2010.

"Patsy." Def. *The Oxford English Dictionary*. 3rd ed. *OED Online*. Web. 21 June 2011.

"Pug", Def. n.2. *The Oxford English Dictionary*. 3rd ed. *OED Online*. Web. 2007. 23 June 2011.

Rubin Jr., Louis D. "The Manly Art of Modified Mayhem: Dempsey and Others." *The Sewanee Review* 108, 3 (Summer 2000) The Johns Hopkins University Press. 412-432. 26 July 2010. Web.

Waters, T. Wayne. "Joe Palooka: A Comic Strip Character Goes to War." *Weider History Network: HistoryNet*. 12 June 2006. Web. 15 June 2011.

Weinberg, S. Kirson, and Henry Arond. "The Occupational Culture of the Boxer." *The American Journal of Sociology* 57, 5 *The Sociological Study of Work* (Mar.1952) The University of Chicago Press, 460-469. 6 July 2010.

The Italian Tarantella

Vera Lynn Lentini

It is not the discovery, but the re-telling of the past histories that changes the ways we position ourselves.
—Stuart Hall

The average second, third, or fourth-generation Italian-American is finding it extremely difficult in attempting to rediscover his roots, heritage, tradition, etc. What he sees is a view vastly distorted by the American media of what is traditionally Italian. When he goes to Italy to see for himself, he discovers the Americanization of nearly every part of Italian traditional music.
—Celest P. DiPiertropaolo

Since its origin in the fourteenth century near Mount Vesuvius, the Italian Tarantella has been a dance of the common people. It captures the air of suspense, eruption, and passion from the people who sit at the foot of the active volcano. The dance was originally an integral part of a culture of peasants going about their everyday lives of planting grain, celebrating weddings, or performing elaborate healing rituals. And today, we as Italian-Americans are re-telling their story though performances and adaptations of this ancient ethnic tradition.

Considering the Tarantella as a dance of traditional or rural peoples helps position modern performances of the dance in American society, film and theater. Some contexts in which the original dances took place include line dances, couple dances, improvisational, carnival, courtship, social, weddings, religious, competition, games and singing dances. Obviously the original context of the dance was varied depending on the social situation in which the music and dance took place. Today, the Tarantella is more often performed in a theater rather than in any kind of traditional context—save for weddings and carnivals. Because of this change, part of the historical tradition may be lost in translation.

Taking the original folk practices out of the original context creates a problem for Italian-Americans looking to rediscover their roots, as independent scholar and folk dancer Celest DiPietropaolo notes. He claims that the average fourth and fifth-generation Italian-American is "finding it extremely difficult in attempting to rediscover his roots," because what he sees is a view that is vastly distorted by the Western media. For instance the reality TV show "Jersey Shore" represents the "guido" and "guidette" characters in extreme situations—which are not so flattering to the Italian American image. To what extent does the Italian-American take these cultural representations seriously? In the case of music and dance, to what extent does the spectator take the performance at face value?

In her 2004 New York University dissertation, Laura Biagio traces the origins of the Tarantella to Apulia, which was in 1735 incorporated into the Bourbon kingdom of Naples and Sicily (Biagio 6). Until the unification of Italy in 1861 the region was divided into different estates owned and exploited by a few rich barons (6). Biagio also mentions Ernesto De Martino's 1961 text *La terra del rimorso* to explain the struggle of the peasant working class of Southern Italy. The Italian Tarantella was born out of the context of this extreme class and economic struggle. De Martino noticed this class difference even in 1959, when he reported on the rituals of St. Paul and the "bitten" Tarantate dancers who engaged in the Tarantella ritual. He noticed that the population's attitude towards this ritual varied according to people's economic class and level of education (6).

These dark origins of the Tarantella are dissonant with the versions we might know of it in pop culture today, as a dance of celebration we might see at weddings. In this more popularized modern version, the Italian Tarantella is a lively part of Italian weddings and carnivals where friends and community gather in a circle to dance. The celebration of the Tarantella has roots in the Renaissance traditions of courtship, but the darker version of the dance has to do with dissatisfied women and the exploitation of the South (11). The ritual of St. Paul adapted a pagan ritual from Greek mythology—specifically having to do with a myth about Dionysus. The story is that there was a girl whose weaving rivaled that of the goddess Athena. Athena challenged the girl to a weaving dual. If the girl were to lose, she would be doomed to weave forever (like a spider), but if she were to win, she would become just as powerful as Athena. The girl agreed to the dual, and lost. She was doomed to weave forever, and the Tarantella dance was born out of a combination of that physical weaving motion.

The story of the spider bite is part of the dance because the spider must always weave its web like the girl who must weave forever. The word Tarantella actually comes from the word "tarantula." In this context, the dance was a way of curing the weaving disease and releasing the tension that came from constant weaving. This weaving story coupled with the myth of Dionysus, god of ecstasy and wine, makes up the origins of the Southern mythic dance. The dance released from the body the poison that came when the woman was bitten by the mythical spider (Biagio 79). Biagio claims that the maddening frenzy and anxiety these women expressed was related to political pressures and economic hardships.

With the rise of Christianity, the rituals were considered Pagan, since they involved sacrificial rights in honor of Dionysus. Christianity adopted these rights into the ritual of St. Paul, who became the sacred patron of the Tarantate. The Tarantate danced every year, to release the poison spider bite, and then St. Paul would bless them in keeping with the Christian tradition. Centuries later the Italian Tarantella is performed in different contexts. Cultural critic Sally Banes notes the difference we see here is between dancing in traditional societies and theatrical dancing in Western societies. This original social dance evolved into a dance of cultural production in the West.

The Tarantella music is in 6/8 time and is usually kept with a tambourine. The element of spinning and circles is essential to the choreography, as are the dancers being low to the ground and scuffing their feet. Although modern performances of the Tarantella keep some of these elements, Italian-Americans should consider that sometimes tradition revived is tradition invented. For example, there is a modern version of the Italian Tarantella on YouTube that differs from what peasants did in the South of Italy centuries ago. It is a performance of a serious Tarantella group in Canada called the Italian Dancers. The group performed at the 2004 Italian-American Festival in Duluth (YouTube). Ten girls execute precise choreography with flair, and it is clear that the instructors are serious about the Tarantella as a dance form. Each dancer holds a tambourine, which is already a departure from traditional versions, where only a few musicians hold tambourines. The dancers do leg crosses, make massive circles and ballet-style arm gestures. Each dancer slaps her hip in unison to the intense and quick downbeat. The audience seems quiet when compared to the loud and vibrant display on stage. The stage is in a gymnasium, and the audience is an audience of Italian-Americans, who seem to be marveling at the physical feats. The dance is an insistence on heritage at an Italian-American festival.

The choreography of the Italian Dancers is an amalgam of Renaissance Tarantella elements combined with folk and ballet. The iconic use of the tambourine and the sprinkling of grain on the ground through the drum recall peasant life, while at the same time they are completely out of context. The tambourine has become a symbol of performance, and is removed from the direct experience of economic hardship. It recalls the peasant life of the grandparents of the Italian-American families, but is an artificial reproduction for the sake of art. The authentic dance was less stylized than the new dance.

According to DiPietropaolo the working class did not have time to learn complex dances; instead complexity in traditional dances comes from the improvisational ability of the dancers. DiPietropaolo would be wary of highly stylized dance claiming to be authentic. He would rather ask what region gave rise to the dance instead of noting how impressive the steps look. The dancers at the

Italian-American festival promote cultural heritage but they may not be preserving history.

Another interesting example of tradition re-invented is La Notte Della Taranta, an annual festival in Taranta, the small province in Puglia where the audience participates in the Pizzica, Tarantella Napoletana, Tammuriata Nera and other dances. This kind of activity bridges the gap between performance and spectator, and the context may be closer to the original folk context because of the format of the performance. Musical composer Roberto De Simone agrees that the revival of tradition works as long as you don't claim that it is an exact reproduction.

De Simone says that the copy must remain close to the original in order for it to be authentic. He adapted traditional Neapolitan folk songs in the 1970s with his group la Nova Compagnia di Canto Popolare. His adaptations of popular songs use traditional arrangements and performance methods. He believes that context is important when attempting to recreate tradition, and you must call your production a recreation if it is that. Even la Notte Della Taranta is inauthentic for him because it is too cosmopolitan, even though for us it may seem closer to the original experience.

The Italian Tarantella can mean different things depending on cultural and political climate. For instance the story of the Tammuriata Nera is about a Neapolitan woman giving birth to an African child during World War II when Naples was in between the Axis and Allied forces. Keeping with the oral tradition, the song lyrics tell a story at a Mediterranean crossroads. The dance steps are more grounded and less celebratory than those of Renaissance courtship dances or Italian-American dance groups. They have Flamenco, belly-dancing and Spanish-Arabic elements. The existence and survival of variations like these reflect the variety of this iconic Italian music and dance over the centuries.

Thus adaptations of the Tarantella span centuries and locations. The dance has evolved from a peasant dance to a theatrical dance, while also still being a symbol of healing rituals. Modern adaptations include contexts that are political, celebratory, competitive, recreational, and healing—and embody different versions of history. Depending on the reason for the performance and the modern adaptation of the dance, the meaning to the dancers and the spectators also changes. American dance historian, editor and author of the *International Encyclopedia of Dance* (1998), Selma Cohen suggests that "ideas of what is essential to a dance will vary, depending on one's concept of its purpose." Since modern adaptations of the Tarantella serve various purposes, the essence of the dance becomes strangely elusive. Defining a set pattern of steps is more of an art than a science, and the researcher must take into account both modern context and original historical context in order to make a statement about a dance's authenticity.

The revival of the Tarantella in the Italian-American community is an attempt to create a historical narrative, to tell a story of immigration and a search for roots. The revival may have little to do with preserving original contexts but maybe more to do with the invention of tradition, a term coined by British Marxist historian Eric Hobsbawm. To understand the dance at its core, we must ask historical and cultural questions and find a narrative to re-tell the story that goes beyond only paying attention to representations in Western theater.

Works Cited

Banes, Sally. *Writing Dancing in the Age of Postmodernism*. Middletown, CT: Wesleyan University Press, 2011. *Project MUSE*. Web. 3 Apr. 2014. http://must.jhu.edu/.

Biagi, Laura. *Spider Dreams: Ritual and Performance in Apulian Tarantismo and Tarantella*. Diss. New York University, 2004. UMI Dissertations Publishing, 2004. Print.

Cohen, Selma. *International Encyclopedia of Dance*. Oxford University Press USA. 2004. Print.

De Simone, Roberto. Personal interview. 5 April. 2009.

DiPietropaolo, Celest. *Folk Dance Scene* 47.2 (2011): 8. Print.

Italiandancers. "Italian Tarantella." *YouTube*. Web. 3 April 2014.

Hobsbawm, Edward. *The Invention of Tradition*. Cambridge University Press, 1992. Print.

A Counter-Reading of Women's Stasis in the Family Sagas of Barolini and Mazzucco

> *Finding unfamiliar the familiar context in which a person is born is the experience of many people who have chosen another place to live. It does not mean that the new location is an ideal place. The new location is only outside one's past.*
>
> —Graziella Parati

Dennis Barone

Loretta Baldassar and Donna Gabaccia have written that "Most national cultures— certainly all the ones that migrants from Italy encountered in the course of their own migratory lives— accept that men will move, while imaging women as ensconced within the family or household and thus within a single nation" (6). In another essay, "Peopling 'Little Italy'," Gabaccia has said that "while sex ratios among Italians entering the United States remained relatively constant during the mass migration at two men for every one woman, women were closer to half of Italians living in New York City by 1910. Family groups predominated in Italian New York after 1900, and as families regrouped in New York, the city's Italian population peaked" (47). The city, according to Gabaccia, frowned upon single male immigrants. Yet, the movement of women in Helen Barolini's *Umbertina* (1979) and Melania Mazzucco's *Vita* (2003) questions the "single nation" status of women (the authors themselves as well their characters) and explores the fluidity of identity between Italian and Italian American. As Mazzucco states late in her work, "We belong less to the place we come from than to the place where we want to go" (244), and still that destination ever-shifts. These women, in both America and Italy, are unsettled, more so—as we will see—than the men who accompany them. As Barolini writes, "every time Tina got used to a place, she had to leave: She got to Italy, hated it, loved it then had to leave for America, hated it, loved it, and so back to Italy" (*Umbertina* 291). Barolini's novel is one of the seminal works in Italian American literature and Mazzucco's more recent narrative, an extraordinary work, received the Premio Strega in 2003. Both are family sagas in which characters move back and forth between Italy and America; both works have interesting autobiographical elements.

The women in *Umbertina* and *Vita* are unsettled seekers rather than makers-of-the-home. In her 1920 essay on Italian immigrants, Lilian M. Skinner, special Episcopal diocesan worker with Italians in Rhode Island, writes, "The men go to work; they are getting what they came for. The children go to school; they are getting more than they ever dreamed of. The women came to make the home, and they are making it as well as they can, just as they always have" (97). But in these two autobiographically based novels about ancestors and the relation between identity and nation it is the men who stay at home and the women who move about. Barolini quite self-consciously wrote so that Italian American women could find themselves and could leave the invisibility of the home and enter the public world of literature. She writes in her introduction-as-manifesto to her anthology of Italian American women's writing *The Dream Book* (1985):

> Italian American women had long been denied the possibility of finding themselves in literature. How could they affirm an identity without becoming familiar with the models by which to perceive themselves? We are what we read, but, in the case of Italian American women writers, we could seldom read who we are. (28) Although thousands of copies of *Umbertina* were shredded when it was first published, the novel served as an important step toward visibility. For Mazzucco the invisibility differs: the invisible is a historical past that has been rendered absent rather than a women's voice that might recall that past or engage the present. As Stefania Lucamante has observed, *Vita* replies to "a problem-

atic lack of national memory" (294) regarding the emigration of millions. Mazzucco also had a more personal motivation for composing this work. As Lucamante has explained, Vita, the character, "functions as a liberating literary *doppelganger*: she frees the writer from the claustrophobia and agoraphobia that have long afflicted her" (308). (Curiously, in her notes, Lucamante makes connections to di Donato's *Christ in Concrete* and to Puzo's *The Fortuante Pilgrim* [304], but she makes no reference to Barolini's *Umbertina*.) In other words, writing this autobiographical fiction that freely moves from continent to continent gets its author out of the house!

"Where are the people?" Helen Barolini asked the village priest in Castagna when she visited this ancestral Calabrian town in 1969. "They've all gone elsewhere to work, he said" ("Journey and Return" 78). Barolini recalls that she immediately knew that her work "would be to fix in story the place and the people who [...] had themselves followed the sun west and come to the new world to become a new people, Italian Americans. That story," she adds, "became my novel *Umbertina*" ("Journey and Return" 78). *Umbertina* has three sections and a "Prologue." The latter concerns identity struggles that Marguerite undergoes. She visits her analyst, Dr. Verdile, and this section, famously now, ends with his suggestion: "'Start with your grandmother'" (19). The first section narrates the life of Umbertina, the grandmother; the second section returns to Marguerite; while the final part of this transnational saga ends with Marguerite's daughter, Tina, named for her great-grandmother Umbertina.

According to Baldassar and Gabaccia, "traditional models of stages of labor migration" postulate that "[o]nly through the nurturing provided by relocated women were immigrant families imagined to integrate and put down roots in new lands" (4), but Barolini complicates this theme and perhaps even counters it. Although the sign outside the family business reads S. Longobardi & Sons, both Umbertina and the reader know that she founds the business and enables it to succeed, which means the family has to move and not settle down upon arrival in the new nation. Umbertina devises their means of escape out of the New York City tenement and Umbertina realizes and then meets a need of the workers in the upstate town where they have moved. Of course, even her name, "Umber" / "Tina," may imply little shadow person, but at the section's end her husband Serafino has long been deceased and it is the matriarch, not a patriarch, around which the family gathers.

In Barolini's saga an ambivalence regarding place, not a settled calm, dominates. Umbertina will not look back, but her final thought before dying recalls the water from the Castagna spring, the same water that Tina, in part three, cannot drink. Tina during her visit to Calabria concludes that, "One had to get more out of life than the slot where one was born. Positioning meant moving" (399). In the tenement neighborhood "there was solidarity among the countrymen who stuck together" (70), but there was also continuous despair and trickery; any roots put down here might quickly turn to rot. Back in her village in Southern Italy the townspeople had said of Umbertina, "'She'll be the man of the family'" (23) and this alteration of gender expectations undermines the model of labor migration that has it that women put down roots and men cross all sorts of borders for employment.

Marguerite's husband and Tina's father, Alberto Morosini, in both parts two and three, seems much more concerned with the stability of home than are the ever-migrating women of the household. Marguerite realizes at an early age that "bettering oneself meant getting out of the Italian neighborhood" (156). Her paradoxical life finds her back in Italy, married to an Italian poet and diplomat. "The wife lives in the husband's country because his work is there and so her life becomes his," Barolini states (180). And yet they move back and forth from Italy to the United States and Alberto remains more perplexed and desirous of a single home than Marguerite. For Marguerite,

> Her irritation was the mark of her uncertainty. Why Florence? Why even Italy? Why anyplace? It would all be the same. She was part of the permanently dispossessed. She couldn't belong completely in the States anymore and had never completely belonged in Europe. (212)

And with Marguerite's daughter, Umbertina's great-granddaughter, Tina, this unsettledness becomes even more pronounced. (This is also true for Tina's sister, Weezy.) Again, my point here is that this problematizes or counters the notion that women establish not just the home but also identification with a new nation. "Only through the nurturing provided by relocated women were immigrant families imagined to integrate and put down roots in new lands and so develop new homes and communities with emotional attachments to receiving nations," Baldassar and Gabaccia write regarding the traditional conception of migration (4).

Tina refers to the transnational existence of her parents as "Two separate libraries, two separate worlds that had never merged" (305). Marguerite does not define for her family a national identity. Tina tells Jason, her friend and later her betrothed, that she is "two different people": "The Italian part, when I get back to Rome, likes civilized comforts" while in New York she dresses "in blankets and clogs" like "a hippie" (323). And later she tells Jason, "I have these two things in me that are beginning to be worked out, my work [a Dante scholar as is Barolini's actual daughter, Teodolinda] and my Italian-American identity" (359). The unsettledness of Tina, Marguerite, and Umbertina provides their purpose. On the other hand, Carla, Marguerite's mother, does establish a rooted home, but the roots here are not valorized. Barolini skips over this generation, describes them as shallow, and reports that theirs "was a home in which they never lit fires in the fireplaces ...Fires of understanding and affection never glowed in that household" (153).

When Tina visits Castagna, she realizes that "There was no return. Umbertina's message in fact was: Leave, take a direction, go forward, do not look back" (384). In other words, not only do these women go out into the world, leave the house, but they also postulate that *nostos* of any sort cannot be achieved and should not be sought. Again, Tina's father, Alberto, seems to express the socalled feminine values of a single secure home. He wants Tina to stay in Rome with him and pursue her Dante studies rather than do so in a room of her own in New York City. It is true that Tina refers to her Southern trip as "hapless," her mother's moves as "an erratic, blind dashing around, away from every center and certainty" (390), and therefore one may be tempted to read the novel as linear progression and Tina as perfect synthesis, yet Tina also believes, "Positioning meant moving" (399). And near the book's end during her stay at Jason's New England ancestral home she tells him, "'The Cape tells the truth: It is not permanent, as nothing is permanent. It is changing, as everything is changing'" (421). Tina, then, has not synthesized Rome and New York into a new stasis, a "rhythm to which her life would march already programmed" (33) as dictated by tradition and a traditional model of immigration, and also the life her great-grandmother had abandoned. Rather, like Umbertina, Tina would not only keep "it all together for the future" (408), but she would also be a "catalyst of change" (57), not an encourager of stasis.

Matthew Frye Jacobson in an oft-cited essay entitled "More 'Trans-,' Less 'National'," has said that historians and sociologists need to conduct "a closer analysis of the lands the migrants left behind, and not just before the period of great migration, but after as well" (83) and this is precisely what the novel *Vita*, by Melania Mazzucco, does so extraordinarily well. This work of fiction, autobiography, essay, and historical document may be the best immigration novel of our time. Whereas Barolini draws from the myth, if you will, of her grandmother, Mazzucco relies on her grandfather Diamante's past and on that of the somewhat obscure figure, Vita, to whom the author seeks to give a voice. Innovative in form, emotionally powerful in content, this retelling of Vita's life "cures," Lucamante says, not only "the amnesia of her father Roberto, but also, and perhaps more importantly, a more generic intellectual Italian amnesia that pervades Italian society at large" (300).

Years ago in her *MELUS* interview Barolini said, "It's always intrigued me that no Italian author has ever written of this great exodus that took place from their country. It's a wonderful subject. It's a magnificent one, and nobody has dealt with it" (105). This may be a bit of an exaggeration, but nonetheless true. The exceptions prove the rule: think of Cesare Pavese's 1950 *La luna e i falo* (*The Moon and the Bonfires*) or Elena Gianini Belotti's 2006 *Pane Amaro* (*The Bitter of Taste of Strangers' Bread*).[1] As Lucamante has said, Mazzucco's aim in *Vita* "is to fill an embarrassing vacuum in our literary histories, as well as the hollow void in the hearts and minds of many Italians [and Americans, I'd add] whose families were abruptly severed in two by this exodus to America" (297).

Certainly Diamante journeys all across America for work (and hence fits the traditional labor migration model) while Vita remains longer in the tenement community of New York City, and yet from the very start Vita challenges societal boundaries rather than simply playing house at 18 Prince Street. Vita instigates their plan to stay on deck one bitter night during their crossing. Vita "sells" English words to Diamante for the price of kisses. Vita tires of waiting for Diamante and runs off with Rocco. When Diamante returns to Italy for the First World War, Vita marries rather than waits for him. Like Umbertina, Vita achieves financial success through the food industry, a New York City restaurant. Vita names her son Diamante. This Diamante goes to Italy as a soldier during the Second World War. Later, he attempts to enter into a series of business ventures with Roberto, Melania's father. The elder Diamante, who stays in Italy, names his daughter Vita,

---

[1] Belotti's book received the Elsa Morante Award. Based in part on a notebook that belonged to her father who suffered terrible immigrant horrors in America and eventually returned to Italy, this linear and descriptive narrative does not have the passion and genre mixing of Mazzucco's book and yet Belotti's work with its patient unfolding of events also has a powerful message for the present about the past.

Melania's aunt. The Italian-American Vita visits the Mazzucco family, including the elder Diamante, in Italy years later. It is the woman who moves, the man who stays put. When Diamante as a young man travels for manual labor, he becomes in name, if not in fact, imprisoned:

> At the end of the season, Diamante is fiercely determined to quit the railway and take any job he can get in Cleveland. But he hadn't calculated correctly. Once expenses are subtracted...not only is there nothing left to send to his parents [in Italy] or put aside so he can go back to Vita or ask her to come out, but he finds himself indebted to the foreman who'd hired him. There's only one way to pay off the debt: work for him for another season. (267)

And another season stretches to another and another and Diamante realizes the railway is "a life sentence" (274).

On her very first day in New York City at the age of nine Vita thinks that "Maybe in the sun of this city, she, too, would grow up to be like them" (32), *le donne americane*. It is as if these two cousins, friends, fellow townspeople, star-crossed lovers, Vita and Diamante, are opposites that, as they say, attract. Vita seems all possibility and provides hope for Diamante through his years of drudgery just as he does for Vita. Mazzucco writes:

> Rocco notices that her eyes sparkle when she talks about Diamante, and he begins to understand how a girl like Vita could survive three endless years of reform school. Diamante gave her hope, somehow. The vision of what could be. And she gave it to him. (285)

And in the end they both long for some ambiguous notion of home. When Vita visits Rome, Roberto asks her, "And where is it you would like to go?" To which she replies, "Home" (244). And for Diamante, "It was as if the ship I was sailing on never arrived in port, as if I were still wandering on the ocean, suspended between two shores, without a destination, without a way to go home" (253). Whereas Diamante "lacked the ambition" (273) to forge ahead in America, Vita had learned "the great lesson of America: trust in a better tomorrow" (405) and so Vita believes, "All this keeping one's feet on the ground means human beings have lost their wings" (365). Diamante moves back to Italy so as not to move anymore, whereas Vita remains ever-in-flux, in flight with wings perhaps, like the objects she reportedly can move in space through the power of her mental concentration. Before returning to Italy, Diamante comes to the conclusion that "Without Vita he never would have come to America. None of this would ever have existed. She was the one who had brought him here" (396). "Men will move," we are told, while women are "ensconced within the family or household and thus within a single nation" (Baldassar and Gabaccia 6) and yet in *Vita* as well as in *Umbertina* women are depicted as transnational and men as deeply desirous of a single safe, womb-like home.

WORKS CITED

Baldassar, Loretta and Donna R. Gabaccia. "Home, Family, and the Italian Nation in a Mobile World: The Domestic and the National among Italy's Migrants." *Intimacy and Italian Migration: Gender and Domestic Lives in a Mobile World.* Loretta Baldassar and Donna R. Gabaccia, eds. NY: Fordham UP, 2011: 1-22.

Barolini, Helen. "A Calabrian Journey and Return." *Italian Americana* 20.1 (2002): 75-81.

_____. "Introduction." *The Dream Book*. 1985. Helen Barolini, ed. Syracuse: Syracuse UP, 2000: 3-55.

_____. *Umbertina*. 1979. NY: The Feminist P, 1999.

Belotti, Elena Gianini. *The Bitter Tastes of Strangers' Bread: An Italian Immigrant in America*. 2006. Translated by Martha King. NY: Bordighera P, 2012.

Gabaccia, Donna R. "Peopling 'Little Italy'." *The Italians of New York: Five Centuries of Struggle and Achievement*. Philip V. Cannistraro, editor. NY: The New-York Historical Society and The John D. Calandra Italian American Institute, 2000: 45-54.

Greenberg, Dorothee von Huene. "A *MELUS* Interview: Helen Barolini." *MELUS* 18.2 (1993): 91-108.
Jacobson, Matthew Frye. "More 'Trans–' Less 'National.'" *Journal of American Ethnic History* 25.4 (2006): 74-84.
Lucamante, Stefania. "The Privilege of Memory Goes to the Women: Melania Mazzucco and the Narrative of the Italian Migration." *MLN* 124 (2009): 293-315.
Mazzucco, Melania G. *Vita*. 2003. Translated by Virginia Jewiss. NY: Farrar, Straus and Giroux, 2006.
Parati, Graziella. *Migration Italy: The Art of Talking Back in a Destination Culture*. Toronto: U of Toronto P, 2005.
Pavese, Cesare. *The Moon and the Bonfires*. 1950. Translated by R. W. Flint. NY: NYRB Classics, 2002.
Skinner, Lilian M. "Our Italian Neighbors." *Neighbors: Studies in Immigration from the Standpoint of the Episcopal Church*. NY: Domestic and Foreign Missionary Society, 1920: 85-108.

WOMEN AT A CROSSROADS
RITES OF PASSAGE IN ITALIAN AMERICA

Camilla Dubini

For somebody who is familiar with the canon of Italian American female writers, the names of Diane di Prima and Marianna de Marco Torgovnick might seem a strange paring. Today, the former teaches meditative practice on the West Coast, whereas the latter is a scholar and literary critic working as a Professor of English at Duke University. Although these women now inhabit entirely different worlds, they hail from very similar places. They were both born and raised in Italian American sections of Brooklyn, and both left these communities in their early twenties. Both have retrospectively written memoirs of their Italian American childhood. *Recollections of My Life as a Woman* and *Crossing Ocean Parkway* are two autobiographical texts that capture the experience of abandoning Italian America with hindsight and self-awareness. These memoirs consider what is at stake for a third-generation Italian American woman, torn between heritage and assimilation, patriarchy and feminism, ethnic enclaves and multi-ethnic America. Because of their different handling of the same subject matter, these two texts lend themselves to comparative reading. This article analyzes *Crossing Ocean Parkway*, by Marianna de Marco Torgovnick, and *Recollections of My Life as a Woman*, by Diane di Prima, and their different, yet complementary ways into life-writing as a means to coming to terms with their Italian American upbringing.

These two texts are representative of a typical third-generation Italian American movement: immigrants abandoned their ethnic neighbourhoods and assimilated into wider America. Despite following different trajectories of emancipation from their authors' backgrounds, these life-stories articulate a dynamic both of distancing from the ethnic past and ultimate reconciling with it. The crossroads that chart the movement of these two women from the ethnic neighbourhood into wider America, is firstly geographical, but also social and literary. By means of thresholds, infrastructures and transitions, these memoirs establish an interaction between the ethnic neighbourhood departed from and the multi-ethnic environs led to, in the process of fashioning identities that, in Smith's words, "challenge earlier versions of ethnicity as fixed in place, history and culture […] and question the notion of inherent belonging and posit communities that are multiracial" (157). If, as it has been argued, autobiographical discourses work as "palpable means through which Americans know themselves to be American and non-American in all the complexities and contradictions of that identity," this article interrogates *Crossing Ocean Parkway* and *Recollections of My Life as a Woman* as arenas for negotiating existences at the crossroads between ethnic ghettoes and mainstream America (Smith 7).

The metaphor of crossroad as a rite of passage, if meaningful in itself, also foregrounds the spaces it connects and separates. The landscape of these memoirs sees the Italian American ghetto giving way to other, quintessentially American, territories: the road and suburbia. As traditional Italian American iconographies are waning, the ethnic identity of third and fourth-generation Italian Americans is reconfigured and reshaped by new communities with which they affiliate themselves. In the attempt to describe new dimensions of the Italian American female experience through the transitions that engendered them, a spatial approach proves particularly rewarding to the close reading of these memoirs. The correlation between place and ethnicity that emerges from these texts encourages exploring their geographical apparatus, inclusive of the routes these women travel, the houses they live in, and the material culture that surrounds them.

Apart from sharing same themes, *Crossing Ocean Parkway* and *Recollections of My Life as a Woman* belong to the same genre, which, taken together, form the premises of my comparison. These memoirs fit into an existing tradition of writings by Italian American women, but also take into account two intertwined and mutually fuelling cultural trends representative of multiculturalism: the ethnic stirrings and feminism. *Crossing Ocean Parkway* and *Recollections of My Life as a Woman* spring from the so-called "memoir boom," which, since the early 1990s has seen life-writing proliferating on the book market, growing increasingly multifarious in a wide-ranging spectrum of forms and formats, amongst which ethnic women's memoirs form a category in their own right (Smith 127). Even though this genre gained new currency in the 1990s, its popularity took root a few decades before, at the time of the so-called Ethnic Revival. In the 1970s a burgeoning version of "hyphenated" Americanism founded on Ellis Island as the national myth of origin and predicated upon stories of ethnic incorporation was replacing the melting pot paradigm. Life writings by European immigrants are only one strain within the eclectic "heritage industry," which, by recovering and marketing European ancestries, has cast ethnicity as a cornerstone of the nation's identity (Jacobson 78).

Despite the popularity of the word "root" and "heritage" in the 1970s, it took a few decades for Italian American women writers to be recognised as such. Italian Americans struggled more than other groups to find their place on the shelves of American bookstores. An article entitled "Where are the Italian-American Novelists?" which, at the late date of 1993, Gay Talese published on the *New York Times Book Review*, reveals the cultural blind spot that blights a flourishing tradition of writing. The fact that this question was raised by an Italian American, also an author and writer for *Esquire* and the *New York Times*, is indicative of the reach of this non-recognition even to some members of the community.

The stigmatization of Italian American writings often acquires a gender twist. If the male voices of Italian American literature have been deemed coarse and mainstream, its female voices have been ignored, with little attention given them by reviewers and quick exits from print. Though dating as far back as the Italian migration itself, the existence of this body of work remained largely unacknowledged until 1985, when Helen Barolini in her groundbreaking *Dream Book*, anthologized a number of important pieces, in the attempt to establish a maternal ancestry for future generations of Italian American women writers. This was an attempt to redress the notion that such writers were "literary Person(s) out of context," existing in a vacuum, "self-birthed, without models, without inner validation" (*Circular Journey* 183).

Thankfully, the contribution of a new generation of Italian American scholars has brought about the long-overdue acknowledgement of Italian-descended women authors. Since 1985 a fully-fledged framework for reading Italian American women literature has developed. Identifying gender as an important articulation of the Italian American identity, these critical enterprises have continued the work of canon foundation initiated by Barolini. Anthologies of Italian American writings bear witness to younger Italian American female voices whilst recovering older ones, and offer innovative critical angles for reading these texts. Transcending the boundaries imposed by identity politics and de-essentializing the significance of Italian American experience, these critical interventions operate at the intersection between race, gender, and sexuality. Italian American studies have explored the connections with other marginalised groups, concerning themselves with issues that reverberate beyond the boundaries of Italian America (Bona; Giunta; Vigilante Mannino; Romano). Other scholarly works have focused on specific areas of Italian American women's writings such as food, queer identities, and political radicalism, attesting to a broader and more inclusive version of Italian America (DeSalvo, Giunta; Cannistraro, Meyer; Tamburri).

Though written at the turn of the century, when the literature of Italian American women has been incorporated in the research agendas of ethnic and gender studies, an awareness of intellectual marginalization still speaks through Marianna de Marco Torgovnick and Diane di Prima's memoirs. This cultural prejudice merges with the discrimination suffered by these women within their male dominated households. A strong gender and ethnic consciousness gives voice to these tales of female emancipation and literary affirmation. The authors engage in "ethnically gendered explorations" of their place in American society, on the borderline between Little Italy and wider America, Old and New World, which Mary Ann Vigilante Mannino has identified as the hallmark of Italian American women writings (13).

Despite sharing a similar upbringing in what they describe as ethnically segregated enclaves, Marianna de Marco Torgovnick and Diane di Prima make their entry into American society through different doors. Marianna de Marco Torgovnick abandons Bensonhurst to marry a Jewish man and become a professor of English at Duke University, whereas at the age of nineteen di Prima departs from her Italian-American house in Brooklyn to embrace the life of 1960s counterculture in Greenwich Village, New York. If the former climbs the ladder of professional life to join a respectable institution, academia, the latter escapes her family life only to become part of another marginal group, though not one established on an ethnic basis—Beat Bohemia. Writing from the vantage point of their established positions of professor and creative writer, Marianna de Marco Torgovnick and Diane di Prima transcribe into their memoirs their coming-of-age as Italian American daughters in the American mainstream. These life-trajectories are reflected in the emotional temperatures and the generic definition of their life-writing: Marianna di Marco Torgovnick recalls her Italian American memories through the prism of cultural studies, engineering a balanced mixture of autobiography and critical theory, while Diane di Prima's *Recollections of my Life as a Woman* reads as a fluid stream of anecdotes, thoughts and dreams, collected by a passionate, lyrical voice.

The cultural trends that predominate within the communities these women join, Beatniks and 1980s Academia, filter the recollection of their Italian American past. It is through the spectrum of these cultural experiences that these women describe their ethnic selves. Marianna de Marco Torgovnick emerges of a mature phase of multiculturalism, when the post-civil rights American love affair with "minority" and "difference"—be they ethnic, sexual, or racial—has become a vivid object of academic inquiry. Marianna de Marco Torgovnick's self-fashioning as 'White, Female, and from Bensonhurst', articulates a highly conceptualised identity, determined by a sum of personality traits which are imprinted by multicultural thinking (3). Moreover, an anthropological angle that characterises her Italian American memoirs reflects the institutionalisation of the "Ethnic Revival" phenomenon in the academic field of cultural studies. On the other hand, Diane di Prima's sentimental embrace of her Italian American origin as an exotic and pan-European foreignness echoes the humanitarian and universalistic appeal that characterized the Beat Generation.

Marianna di Marco is a third generation Italian American who grew up in Bensonhurst. A racial killing that took place in Bensonhurst in 1989 by the hand of a local Italian American triggers her discussion about her community of origin. On August 23, 1989, a 16-year-old African American boy was walking in Bensonhurst with three friends. Mistaken for another Black man "accused" of dating a half-Hispanic girl in the neighborhood, Yusuf Hawkins was attacked by a gang of bat-wielding Italian American youths and was beaten and shot dead. The hate crime unleashed latent racial tensions, and galvanized the Civil Rights leader Al Sharpton to organize marches in New York protesting the crime and demanding justice. The third racially motivated killing in Brooklyn in the space of seven years, the death of Yusef Hawkins raised awareness of the aggravated status of racial relationship in the city and had a great impact on the upcoming mayoral election. Looming large in the national consciousness, the episode turned into a politically meaningful cause, a vehicle "for crystallizing debating and attempting to resolve contemporary social problems" (Chancer 5).

The discussion of Yusef Hawkins as the opening of *Crossing Ocean Parkway* demands attention. Though relevant to the history of the neighborhood, the analysis of this high-profile crime is an interesting choice in the context of a childhood memoir. When the author discusses a popular and controversial news story to introduce her Italian American upbringing, she is approaching her culture of origin as an outsider, though a knowledgeable and articulate one. Through the filter of the shocking murder that gave Bensonhurst an infamous name, the neighbourhood is evoked as a bubble of racial tension, ethnic pride, and monetary stagnancy. The author, with a sociological take on her own people, describes Bensonhurst's narrow-mindedness with eloquent objectivity:

> Italian Americans in Bensonhurst are notable for their cohesiveness and provinciality; the slightest pressure turns these qualities into prejudice and racism. Their cohesiveness is based on the stable economic and ethical level that links generation to generation, keeping Italian American in Bensonhurst and the Italian American community alive as the Jewish American community of my youth is no longer alive. [...] Their provinciality results from Italian Americans' devotion to jealous distinction and discrimination. (7)

Benshonurst's parochialism is reflected in the sedentary behaviour of its denizens, settled from generation to generation in the same neighbourhood:

> Bensonhurst's Italian Americans seem to have felt that one large move, over the ocean, was enough. Future moves could only be local: from the Lower East, say, to Brooklyn, or from one part of Brooklyn to another. Bensonhurst was for many of these people the *summa* of expectation. If their America were to be drawn as a *New Yorker* cover, Manhattan would be tiny in proportion to Bensonhurst itself, and to its satellites, Staten Island, New Jersey, Long Island. (4)

This imaginary, unreliable map of the misconception of US geography by Marianna de Marco Torgovnick's neighbours can be read as a metaphor for their misunderstanding of American culture at large. The author causally links the Italian American's unfamiliarity with American society to their geographical immobility. On the assumption that mobility fosters integration, the author suggests that Italian Americans' loyalty to Bensonhurst's confines, by contrast, breeds isolation and exacerbates their disconnection from the realities of their adoptive land. Because Bensonhurst's residents never travelled nor mastered the new territory, in their eyes America retains those mythical and unrealistic features of that 'promised land' they had imagined from Italy. In Marianna de Marco Torgovnick's account, Bensonhurst fosters Italian Americans' cohesion within its confines. Since the neighbourhood grants Italian Americans identification as a group, its residents are prone to remain there in order to perpetuate their sense of entitlement to the ethnic community. Against the backdrop of racial riots, ethnic tribalism, and turf defence, ethnicity is reduced to its territorial component.

The immobility of Italian Americans is also revealed by their relationship to housing. Not only did Italian Americans from Benshonhurst find it hard to abandon that neighbourhood over the course of generations, they even tended to stick with the same home. Marianna de Marco Torgovnick contextualises her parents' longevity in a single apartment as a generalized pattern, by which, in her own words, "many people live for decades in the same place or move within a ten block radius" (6). In light of these stationary tendencies, home-owning becomes a deeply craved source of security, and the *leitmotif* of Marianna de Marco Torgovnick's childhood. She recalls house-buying as "the tragedy of my parents' life" (20), an illusion courted—through viewings, negotiation with landlords, room allocations—but brutally frustrated by the fear of not being able to meet the mortgage payments.

Diane di Prima is also a third generation Italian American from Brooklyn. Similarly to *Crossing Ocean Parkway*, her Italian American memoirs are grounded in a specific ethnic milieu and convey a strong sense of space. Nonetheless, in *Recollections of My Life as a Woman* Italian American spaces are of a different kind, and their representation serves other purposes. In *Crossing Ocean Parkway* the public space predominates, and private houses are heavily called into question as assets, material goods fiercely desired but hard to obtain. By contrast, Diane di Prima's memoirs revolve around her grandparent's house, described as locus of her sentimental education. If the former identifies her ethnic past with a segregated district, the latter foregrounds a teeming living room. The zoom from neighbourhood to household signals a transition into the private sphere of family life. This move indoors also affects the quality of writing. A nostalgic register characterises Diane di Prima's home-centred evocation of her early years in Italian American Brooklyn, which opens on this family frame:

> My earliest sense of what it means to be a woman was learned from my grandmother, Antoinette Mallozzi, and at her knee. It was a house of dark and mellow light, almost as if there were fire kerosene lamps, but to my recollection there was electric light, the same as everywhere else. It is just that the rooms were so very dark, light filtering as it did through paper shades and lace curtains, and falling then on dark heavy furniture and onto floors and surfaces yellowed with layers of wax, layers of olive oil. The light fell as if on old painting, those glazes, that veneer. Sepia portraits: Dante, Emma Goldman. There was a subtle air of mystery. The light fell on my grandmother hands as she sat rocking, saying her rosary. She smelled of lemons and olive oil, garlic, waxes and mysterious herbs. I loved to touch her skin. (*Recollections of My Life as a Woman* 1)

This passage gives the domestic space a strong sentimental value, as it speaks to the child of her Italian family past and mediates her connection to her culture of origin. It is around the motherland's memory, forcefully transmitted by di Prima's grandparents, that the house is re-constructed, designed, and refurbished. Italy, ubiquitously homely and exotic, tinges every aspect of family-life: food, décor, music, flavours, spirituality, and language. The widespread phantom of the faraway country causes di Prima to fall into the emotional paradox of "grow[ing] up nostalgic for a land she had never seen" (7). The family home, the small-scale simulacrum of the homeland relocated to the New World, is the bridge linking the two separate spheres of the hyphenated writer. It is within the four walls of the Italianate Brooklyn flat, dedicated to reviving life overseas, that di Prima's ethnic identity develops and reposes.

The centrality of the house in di Prima's Italian American memoirs also reflects the family's withdrawn attitude towards the outside world. Diane di Prima tells a story of how her grandmother once left the house and did not come back home for hours, until her husband found her wandering around the neighbourhood. It turned out that a boot hanging from the door of a cobbler's, which her grandmother used as a visual cue to turn into her street, had been taken back inside. Without the boot, the wordless sign, the woman was lost, minutes from her own house. Apart from sheltering Diane di Prima's family, the house represents the only secure refuge in the unmapped landscape of the foreign land, whose culture is perceived as cryptic and unwelcoming. This example shows how the immigrant, lacking points of reference, can hardly "find his way" within the foreign culture.

This anecdote echoes the aforementioned example of the map drawn by Bensonhurst's residents in *Crossing Ocean Parkway*. Both the map's disproportions and the woman's loss of directions bespeak the immigrant's disorientation in the US. Both these episodes establish a strong connection between ethnic identity and its territories. In both cases, the characters' bewilderment with regard to geography is also broadly characterised as an existential status, which grounds their desperation for a house, a space of belonging. In fact, despite the diverging writing styles—Marianna de Marco Torgovnick's description of Bensonhurst is redolent of an anthropological commentary, whereas Diane di Prima engages with her past through intimacy and narration—these accounts both foreground family home as the core of their community of origin. In the two memoirs, home assumes the polysemic significance of source of stability, symbol of belonging, container of the Italian 'post-memory', which anchors third-generation immigrants to their root and heritage. If both the authors cast the home as the Italian American epicentre, once they have crossed the neighbourhood's borders, these women's lives will be differently configured in response to their family-centred, sedentary upbringing.

At the age of nineteen, Diane di Prima drops out of college and escapes Brooklyn, to join the artistic community gravitating around Greenwich Village. The transition from the space of ethnic subculture to the Beat counterculture across the Brooklyn Bridge marks the passage from a domestic everyday, to a migrant lifestyle. Reckoning that what she describes as "immigrant impasse" had tied her relatives to the enclosed perimeter of the neighbourhood whilst hindering their emancipation, Diane di Prima refuses to walk the world as her grandmother did (49). Alongside the Beats she experienced the anti-conformism of "life on the road," peregrinated across New York and explored the West. The one household dominating her Italian American reminiscences, the domestic fortress that protected, nurtured but also isolated her family, is replaced in her new life by a chain of bohemian pads transiently moved in and out of by di Prima and her group of friends. In turning the Beat section of her memoirs into sort of 'pad narrative', and staging herself as a countercultural matriarch, di Prima reinterprets the domestic culture that she inherited in the nomadic and maverick fashion of her generation. The ethnic sign has not dissolved, then, but merely mutated.

If *Recollections of My Life as Woman* is about di Prima's transition from the ethnic subculture to multi-ethnic counterculture, *Ocean Parkway* is a more typical tale of upward mobility, which the autobiographer articulates as "a two step process: first identifying with school and hence Jewish culture rather than the Italian American group into which I was born; then, moving into universities and middle and upper-middle-class America" (vii). Ocean Parkway, the three-lane avenue that divides Bensonhurst from the territories of Torgovnick's adulthood, is the gateway to this ascending path. The author describes Ocean Parkway as a monumental boulevard that on its western side aligns several ethnic districts "bristling with racial tension" while separating them from Manhattan, the skyline-shaped American Dream looming on the other side (vii). This borderline transforms into "a powerful state of mind," "ecumenical crossroads," "rite of passage," and a stage set for the bastions of elite American life." Once again, the topography underpinning the plot raises personal aspirations, collective psychology, and social patterns. Marianna de Marco Torgovnick's memoirs is punctuated by other people orbiting around her, who also blur boundaries of class, move house, advance professionally, to converge in what she describes as a choral "parable of our culture's mobility" (32). The social climb is marked by a succession of increasingly luxurious houses that lead them from Brooklyn into suburbia. Marianna de Marco Torgovnick's preoccupation with houses as social signifiers reminds of her parents' obsessions with home buying, though displaced in a more bourgeoisie environment. The ethnic signed, revisited and relocated, has not dissolved.

The path Marianna undertakes by way of crossing Ocean Parkway will eventually lead her to her modern house surrounded by acres of trees, where she lives in North Carolina. It is from this domestic achievement she feels entitled to pronounce on Bensonhurst's narrow-mindedness, whilst also confessing that:

> The precise stages differ for each group and person, but assimilation always has a double movement: first the desire to be like others; then the realisation that the likeness is never completed. To use a metaphor: I will always be crossing Ocean Parkway; I have crossed it; I will never cross it. (vii)

The idea of the crossroads that informs this paper originates in the in-between space, which these women, metaphorically speaking, inhabit, a condition that resonates with Said's definition of the intellectual as an exile who "cannot go back to some earlier and perhaps more stable condition of being at home; and alas, [you] can never fully arrive, be one with your new home or situation" (39). The state of homelessness prompts mobility, a fact built into these two memoirs. A meaningful geography of labyrinthine neighbourhoods, unreliable maps, thresholds, and road trips, charts the migrations of these women within the social landscapes of the adoptive country that their parents did not dare to travel. Self-removed from the ethnic neighbourhood of their youth, di Prima's picaresque migrations across tattered pads and Marianna's way up into suburbia allow these women to explore vistas of America much wider than the one they grew up into. Nonetheless, these diverging journeys take these two women to a shared destination, that is, back to their home-bound Italian American origin; and towards revealingly similar recognitions that in Marianna de Marco Torgovnick's words "You can take the girl out of Bensonhurst (that much is clear); but you might not be able to take Bensonhurst out of the girl" (*Crossing Ocean Parkway* 10), or, in di Prima's, "I had moved away from Brooklyn, at last, but Brooklyn has followed me" (*Recollections of My Life as a Woman* 104). It is from this very recognition that their life-writings gets underway and retraces the experience of distancing and reconciliation with Italian American origins on the written page, inscribing what Helen Barolini had coined as the 'Circular Journey' in her essays about the immigrant conditions.

The study of *Crossing Ocean Parkway* and *Recollections of my Life as a Woman* raises awareness of the role of life-writing for a generation of writers raised in Little Italies but moved elsewhere. The path mapped upon these memoirs accommodates new ways of being Italian American, mobile and untied from the neighbourhood, the incubators of Italian memories relocated overseas. As Italian America exits its urban fortresses, it becomes a territory of the imagination, couched in printed-paper. As Little Italies shrink, the space of literary memoirs expands to receive an experience that is gradually disappearing from reality. For Marianna de Marco Torgovnick and Diane di Prima, crossing the neighbourhood line provokes a rupture with the background and determines the entrance into a new space of belonging. Only fictionalising this break, with the ink bonding and assembling, can suture the edges of an identity split across two cultural spaces. It is only by writing memoirs that these women can accept the sacrificed Italian American past as integral to who they have become. Only as they write their memoirs can they reimagine the divisive border between Italian America and America, as a crossroad, a connective interface, liable to be crossed back.

Works Cited

Barolini, Helen. *The Dream Book: An Anthology of Writings by Italian American Women.* New York, Schocken Books, 1985.

———. *A Circular Journey*, New York, Fordham UP, 2006

Bona, Mary Jo. *Claiming a Tradition: Italian American Women Writers*, Carbondale, IL: SIU P, 1999.

Bona, Mary Jo, ed. *The Voices We Carry: Recent Italian American Women's Fiction*, Toronto, Guernica, 2007.

Cannistraro Philip V. and Gerald Meyer, eds. *The Lost World of Italian American Radicalism: Politics, Labor, and Culture.* Westport: Greenwood, 2003.

deSalvo, Louise, and Edvige Giunta, eds. *The Milk of Almonds: Italian American WomenWriters on Food and Culture.* New York: CUNY, 2003.

di Prima, Diane, *Recollections of My Life as a Woman*, New York: Penguin, 2001.

Chancer, Lynn S. *High-Profile Crimes: When Legal Cases Become Social Causes.* Chicago: U Chicago P, 2010.

Giunta, Edvige. *Writing With An Accent: Contemporary Italian American Women Authors*, New York: Palgrave, 2002.

Jacobson, Matthew Frye, *Roots Too: White Ethnic Revival in Post-Civil Rights America*, Harvard UP: 2006.

Vigilante-Mannino, Mary Ann, and Justin Vitiello. *Breaking Open: Reflections on Italian-American Writers.* West Lafayette, IN: Purdue UP, 2003.

Romano, Anne T. *Daughters of Italy: The Journey of Italian American Women Writers*, Xlibris Corporation, 2010.

Tamburri, Anthony Julian, ed. *Fuori: Essays by Italian/American Lesbians and Gays.* West Lafayette, IN: Bordighera Press, 1996.

Said, Edward W. *Representations of the Intellectual.* New York: Pantheon, 1994.

Smith, Sidonie. *Reading Autobiography.* Minneapolis: U Minnesota P, 2010 2nd.

Smith, Sidonie, and Julia Watson. *Getting a Life: Everyday Uses of Autobiography*, Minneapolis: U Minnesota P, 1996.

THE ITALIAN INFLUENCES OF FELLINI AND PIRANDELLO ON DON DELILLO

Rebecca Rey

In this paper I will focus my attention on two Italian masters who have influenced New York writer Don DeLillo's work: the director Federico Fellini and the playwright Luigi Pirandello. These artists add two different but similarly antirealist flavors to DeLillo's work: Fellini in terms of playfulness, dream sequences, and the satirizing of celebrity, and Pirandello in terms of the theme of identity.

Born in the Bronx in 1936 to Italian immigrants, Don DeLillo spent his early years in the Italian-American neighborhood of Belmont. His cultural background means he cites his influences to be what he "consider[s] the great era of European films: Godard, Antonioni, Fellini, Bergman."[1] Federico Fellini and playwright Luigi Pirandello were to bring the Italian flavor into his novels and plays: Pirandello's identity and role-playing themes directly influenced *The Day Room* (1986) and *White Noise* (1985), and traces of Fellini's film *8 ½* can be found in the celebrity circus of *Valparaiso* (1999).

The young DeLillo exhibited an outsider's disposition from an early age. Regarding his childhood context as the middle of post-war America, he admits of his generation, "[W]e have roots elsewhere. We are looking in from the outside. To me, that seems to be perfectly natural."[2] Despite his Italian roots, his parents from Abruzzi

---

[1] Anthony DeCurtis, "'An Outsider in this Society': An Interview with Don DeLillo," in Thomas DePietro, ed. *Conversations With Don DeLillo* (Jackson: University Press of Mississippi, 2005) 67.

[2] Robert McCrum, "Don DeLillo: 'I'm not trying to manipulate reality—this is what I see and hear'," *The Observer* 8 Aug. 2010, 20 Aug. 2010 <http://www.guardian.co.uk/books/2010/aug/08/don-delillo-mccrum-interview>.

"wanted American kids," and the writer admits that "my sister and I had no motive in speaking Italian" (McCrum, n.p.). Having had a monolingual childhood spent among immigrants who deeply desired to assimilate into American culture places DeLillo in the advantageous position of spectator of both cultures, passing between both without fully belonging to either.

DeLillo and Fellini's Cinema

Cinema was a beloved pastime of the young DeLillo's. He said that "[b]eing a New Yorker, I always, even as a kid, was aware of theatre, but I never really became fervent about theatre the way I did about movies. And that, in fact, is still true".[3] In a 1988 interview with Anthony DeCurtis, he cites his influences to be what he "consider[s] the great era of European films: Godard, Antonioni, Fellini, Bergman" (DeCurtis, 67). These directors, he says, "seem to fracture reality. They find mystery in commonplace moments." From the very beginning, cinema influenced this writer in terms of narrative structure and the privileging of the image. Remnants of Fellini, in particular, can be seen in DeLillo's work.

As Tullio Kezich writes regarding Fellini's *La strada*, the director found his calling rather late:

> The awareness that he's somehow learned to control a language melds with his urgent need to communicate. At thirty-two, Fellini, with clarity and pride, finally knows what he wants to be when he grows up—and what he will be forever.[4]

Kezich also reveals that "[e]ver since he was a child, Fellini has liked to let his mind wander, to fantasize and float in a half-sleeping, half-waking state" (Kezich, 223). Fellini's tendency to dream and lose himself in his thoughts is paralleled by DeLillo's early adult-

---

[3] Jody McAuliffe, "Interview with Don DeLillo," *South Atlantic Quarterly* 99: 2/3 (Spring/Summer 2000), p. 610.
[4] Tullio Kezich, *Federico Fellini: His Life and Work* (London: I. B. Tauris & Co, 2002 [trans. 2006]) 143.

hood, wherein he had trouble fitting into the corporate world. DeLillo worked for a time as a copywriter for Ogilvy & Mather and as a park attendant, the latter of which allowed him time to read classic novels undisturbed on a park bench. This was the beginning of his literary career. He notes that "I had a personal golden age of reading, in my 20s and my early 30s, and then my writing began to take up so much time".[5] His first novel, *Americana*, was published in 1971 when DeLillo was 35 (compared to Fellini's first film at a close 32), marking a starting point in his new career as a novelist.

Fellini's influence on DeLillo is explicit in *Americana*. The first literal reference to the filmmaker alludes to Fellini's ability to present a variety of dreamlike characters in surrealist fashion:

> Then, alone, down to rusty dead Roma, German tourists saluting each other, everyone waiting for Fellini to come skipping along the Via Veneto in clownface and opera cape, trailed by virgins, camels, Nubians, publicity men.[6]

We can see here DeLillo's view of Fellini as Pan and Pied Piper, summoning a circus of fascinating characters reminiscent of *La dolce vita*. The cinema—people making, acting in, and watching films—is a recurrent theme in DeLillo's in his work. In *Americana*, for example, DeLillo's character Wendy privileges being on screen:

> People dream of money and love. It was Wendy's ambition to be hired as an extra in a big-budget Technicolor movie. She had no illusions of stardom. Fragmentation, the settling of a myth into the realism of its component parts...She would have been satisfied to get the back of her head in a movie... (145)

Wendy's attitude towards movies indicates a fondness for the symbolic, mythical aspect of film, where "the settling of a myth into

---

[5] Kevin Rabalais, "Dancing to the music of time". *The Australian*, March 06, 2010, Retrieved 04/08/2012.
[6] Don DeLillo, *Americana* (London: Penguin Books, 1990) 236.

the realism of its component parts" represents the myth of the American dream being displayed cohesively in a cinematic storyline; however, although cinema links both Fellini and DeLillo, we must remember that for Fellini, "the cinema is primarily a visual medium whose emotive power moves through light, not words."[7]

CIRCUSES OF CHARACTERS AND DREAM-LIKE SEQUENCES

Fellini's *La dolce vita* (1960) is an incisive portrayal of the young and hip in Rome, a "kingdom for the few carefree people who circulate between parties and cruises, scandals and follies" (Kezich, 203). Yet, as Kezich also notes, the film is a "tragic allegory of the desolation lurking behind the façade of a perpetual carnival" (203). Although Fellini has said that the title had "no moral or denigrating purpose," but was rather exhibiting life's "profound undeniable sweetness" (Bonadanella, 81). I maintain that there is indeed the potential to interpret it differently. The title, translated literally as "the sweet life," can be read both literally and ironically, much like the title of DeLillo's novel *White Noise* can be read as the impressive omnipresence of technology, or a vacuous, meaningless void of sound.

Fellini is a master of depicting circus-like collections of fascinating characters on screen; DeLillo does something similar on the page. One example of this occurs in *La Dolce Vita*, when Marcello breaks into Riccardo's beach house with his friends and the party descends into gaudy, confused chaos. Marcello throws feathers around from a torn pillow, covering a woman and riding around another woman as if she were an animal. As Peter Bondanella writes,

> *La dolce vita* is the last film Fellini made with obvious mimetic intention: It provides a panoramic view of a society gone wild with press conferences, image-makers, paparazzi and celebrities, and in spite of its ability to create stirring images of an unfor-

---

[7] Peter Bondanella, *The Films of Federico Fellini* (Cambridge: Cambridge University Press, 2002) 100.

gettable character...its subject matter remains steadfastly connected to the society within which Fellini lived. (93)

In *8 ½* also, to an even greater extent, mismatched characters comprising a kind of cross-section of past and present society parade through the film, as Guido Anselmi battles with his director's block. These Fellinian parades of varied characters are present in similar fashion in DeLillo's writing, often when he classifies New Yorkers walking the streets. One instance of this is in *Mao II*, when Scott tells Karen about the time he lived at the Y. He stood by the windows, watching

> the march of faces and pathologies, people going by in trance states and dancing manias, the crosstown stream of race and shape and ruin, and in these hard streets even the healthy and well-dressed looked afflicted.[8]

This example—and others—of DeLilloan crowds comprised of collections of comical, absurd, or commonplace people could have its roots in the troupes present in Fellini's films.

THE BLURRING OF REALITY AND FANTASY

The second time Fellini is explicitly mentioned in DeLillo's *Americana* it is to highlight his fantastical tendencies. His dualism between the real and imaginative is highlighted in the oft-quoted line: "Fellini says the right eye is for reality and the left eye is the fantasy eye" (*Americana*, 293). Though metaphorical, the idea that there is a dualism between reality and imagination, and that these realms intertwine to create a kind of magical realism, is something that is present in both Fellini's cinema and DeLillo's work. Bondanella explains that in *La dolce vita*, Fellini changed the

> representation of reality in his film in much the same way as the cubist artist Picasso has smashed the traditional painter's obses-

---

[8] Don DeLillo, *Mao II* (London: Vintage, 1992) 59.

sion with vanishing points and mimesis by deconstructing the reality of material objects into their potential surfaces. (27)

Fellini's *avant-garde*, fantasy-filled *8 ½*, for instance, is an "exploration of the Jungian anima and animus."[9] The entire plot hinges on a melding of the reality of Guido's director's block and memories and daydreams that inhabit his mind. The film is about the creative process itself, and unites these fantastical elements with reality, with no real cues regarding the end of the reality and the start of fantasy.

In *White Noise*, an oft-quoted scene is protagonist Jack Gladney's short but potent conversation with his daughter Steffie. Here he asks her about on the subject of SIMUVAC, a simulated evacuation practice she was to attend:

> "How did the evacuation go?"
> "A lot of people never showed up. We waited around, moaning."
> "They show up for the real ones," I said.
> "Then it's too late."[10]

In this example, DeLillo is satirizing the contemporary importance of the false simulation over the terrifying real. Again, Jack Gladney ponders the prominence of false over real:

> But there is no substitute for a planned simulation. If reality intrudes in the form of a car crash or a victim falling off a stretcher, it is important to remember that we are not here to mend broken bones or put out real fires. We are here to simulate. Interruptions can cost lives in a real emergency. (*White Noise*, 206)

In addition to SIMUVAC, his "most photographed barn in America" also emphasises the modern phenomenon of image surpassing reality. Jack Gladney and Murray Jay Siskind, his university col-

---

[9] Loc. cit.
[10] Don DeLillo, *White Noise* (Picador: New York, 2002) 212.

league, drive to the barn. The photographing of the building metaphorically eliminates the authentic version. Murray says, "No one sees the barn," because "[e]very photograph reinforces the aura" (*White Noise* 12).

In the filming of *La dolce* vita the synthetic nature of film surpassed reality in Rome. Kezich describes how a very real and dangerous fire is mistaken for a movie scene at the time of filming:

> The idea that *La dolce vita* is somehow a realistic movie about life on via Veneto has become so widespread that, when there's a fire at the Ambasciatori Hotel on June 21 and four coatroom attendants trapped in the flames are forced to jump out a window onto via Liguria, some newspapers report that Fellini has added the scene to his movie. (201)

The effect of Fellini's film on authentic life is directly parallel to DeLillo's satire of simulation and photography as re-enactments and reproductions of reality. As we will see later, in a further link between Fellini, Pirandello and DeLillo, Pirandello's antirealism played out in reality too, with spectators wondering where the play ended and real life began.

THE SATIRIZING OF CELEBRITY

In addition to the blurring the distinction between reality and fantasy, Fellini masterfully satirizes celebrity culture in *La dolce vita*. The word 'paparazzo' was first coined in this movie—named after the buzzing of a mosquito—and in the film, paparazzi fall over themselves in the quest to take the best photograph of movie stars, royalty, and other newsworthy figures. As Kezich writes, "[P]hotographers morph from witnesses of reality to participants and creators of it" (23), shifting from recorders to provokers and catalysts of news. Celebrity in *La Dolce Vita* is the ultimate, the pinnacle of belonging to a collective society, and is still presented as elusive to anyone other than the most beautiful and most talented. With Fellini, modern celebrity comes into being, as a "whole new strategy of provocation blossoms: Making important people lose their temper leads to more interesting photos, which then earn higher fees from the gossip rags" (195). Marcello Mastroianni, the actor playing the handsome protagonist, is somewhat spiritually empty and seems perhaps undeserving of the attention lavished on him by the lurking photographers. "Marcello," describes Kezich, "has no real roots; he doesn't have anything to prevent him from falling into perdition at any time. But he's sensitive enough for epiphany" (204). Jack Gladney in DeLillo's *White Noise* is similarly empty, admitting that he is "the false character that follows the name around" (*White Noise*, 17). Fellini's portrayal of the carefree young, rich and famous in 1920s Rome is one of the most memorable depictions of celebrity culture in European film. Hence, we can assume that DeLillo, a self-confessed enjoyer of European film, and of Fellini's in particular, could have continued Fellini's portrayal of celebrity culture in his own work. Before I explore DeLillo's portrayals of celebrity, we should note that there are, of course, significant differences between DeLillo's celebrity culture and Fellini's, largely as a result of the differing time periods and modes of technology present in each. Additionally, the products of celebrity in the twenty-first century are more quickly disseminated than they were in the twentieth.

The theme of pervasive technology and its effects on mediated human experience is one for which DeLillo is well known. Most of his works depict worlds in which experience is mediated in some way, most noticeably present in the novels *Americana* (1971), *White Noise* (1985), *Mao II* (1991) and *Cosmopolis* (2003), as well as in the plays "The Rapture of the Athlete Assumed Into Heaven" (1990) and *Valparaiso* (2004). His play *Valparaiso* (2004) is a dissection of the process of fame and its potential catastrophic results. The Fellinian elements cannot be denied: swooping, demanding reporters, family complications, and a pensive male protagonist searching for firm ground on which to found his identity. Michael Majeski is, to some extent, a contemporary Marcello: Both characters engage with the media seeking their stories. After Michael takes a plane to the wrong city, repetition is the key to the media frenzy: He must answer question after question in the same manner. Instead of approach this task as a chore, Michael revels in it. Whereas in *La dolce vita*, Sylvia runs from the paparazzi, as does Steiner's wife, Marcello enjoys their company, and Michael, in *Valparaiso*, laps up the attention. We could say that Fellini, in 1960, was satirizing the cheekiness of the media, while DeLillo, in 1999, was satirizing the emptiness of the celebrity. DeLillo has shifted the attention from the reporters and their antics to their antics' consequences on the celebrity. Through DeLillo's contemporary lens, Fellini's circus shrinks to a spotlight shining directly on the protagonist.

Jungian Dream Sequences

In 1928 Jung published *The Self and the Unconscious*, wherein he analyses the relationship between the individual and the collective subconscious. Fellini was greatly influenced by Jungian philosophy of the collective unconscious. He preferred Jung to Freud, because whereas Freud considered dreams to be a symptom of a neurosis needing to be cured, Jung believed our dreams connected us to each other. Fellini kept dream notebooks and took inspiration from their contents, especially in *8 ½*, *Juliet of the Spirits*, and *The City of Women*. According to Jung, dreams contain archetypal images—like the Hero, the Sage, the Devil, the Child—that unite humanity, rather than separate it. Jungian archetypes exist in Fellini's work; they are mentioned explicitly in *La Dolce Vita*, in one of the most famous lines in film history: "You are the first woman on the first day of creation. You are mother, sister, lover, friend, angel, devil, earth, home." Marcello's words to the beautiful young actress Sylvia summarize her facets and those that connect all women.

Fellini then blends reality with memories and fantasies in a Jungian manner. Bondanella describes Fellini's rich imagery and style as "baroque," adding that the director "tells stories with images, not with words. And these images, when successful, connect to our subconscious in a way that transcends barriers of culture or language."[11] DeLillo imitates Fellinian strangeness in passages where he presents New York life's moments of extravagance and caricature. These passages are dream-like and saturated with symbolic content, exhibiting a richness, both of imagination and of possibility. For instance, in *Cosmopolis* (2003) protestors dressed as rats storm the diner in which protagonist Eric Packer and his wife Elise Shifrin are having lunch:

> Something was happening behind them...Eric swung around on his stool and saw two men in gray spandex standing in the narrow aisle between the counter and the tables. They stood motionless back to back, right arms raised, each man holding a rat by the tail. They began to shout something he could not make out. The rats were alive, forelegs pedaling...[12]

The banal context of the diner makes the appearance of pseudo-rats carrying rats seem like a dream sequence too absurd to be true, but the difference is that DeLillo works in the real. Fellini, on the other hand, uses flash forwards or backwards into dreams or memories, such as in *8 ½*, where the "mass of images Fellini creates is held together in almost a miraculous state of grace by the use of dream and fantasy sequences" (Bondanella, 98). Whereas Fellini takes fantasy and presents it as lucidly as reality, DeLillo works the opposite way, taking reality and caricaturing it into fantastical images.

Despite both artists exposing and satirizing their societies, neither Fellini nor DeLillo uses his authorial power to sermonize. As Bondanella writes, "In *8 ½*, Fellini makes no pronouncements, presents no theories about art, and avoids the heavy intellectualizing about the nature of the cinema that characterizes so much academic discussion in recent years" (Bondanella, 99). DeLillo also avoids self-analysis of his work by not participating in book tours, and

---

[11] Loc. cit.
[12] Don DeLillo, *Cosmopolis* (Scribner: New York, 2003) 85.

even refusing an honorary doctorate from his *alma mater*, Fordham University.

DELILLO'S AND PIRANDELLO'S THEATER

I turn now to DeLillo's second influence explored in this paper: the playwright Luigi Pirandello. Born in Sicily in 1867, Pirandello began studying philosophy at the University of Palermo, then philology in Rome and postgraduate studies at the University of Bonn. His context of Fascist Italy under Mussolini—with whom Pirandello held political sympathies—and, in particular, his origin from Sicily, formed the foundations for his anti-realist concerns, self-analytical characters, and cerebral themes. "In Pirandello's Sicily", Glauco Cambon writes, "every man is…compelled to acknowledge the incommensurability between one's own inner reality and public reality. Who is to say what truth is?"[13] Umberto Mariani situates Pirandello's work in the late-nineteenth-century collapse of the Italian intellectual bourgeoisie. "Pirandellian characters," he writes, "proclaim the loss of their own form, of their unity, of the certainty of their knowledge and understanding of their own truth, and of its communicability; this is the condition at the root of the drama they bring with them on to the stage."[14]

As we will see, Pirandello and DeLillo share similar thematic concerns, and are further linked to Fellini through the supporting of antirealism and its creative effects. Roger W. Oliver sums up Pirandello's:

> Pirandello's plays do explore such complex issues as the multiplicity of the human personality, the relativity of truth, and the difficulty if not impossibility of establishing the dividing line between reality and its illusions. The focus, however, is usually on

---

[13] 'Introduction' by Glaudo Cambon, in his edited *Pirandello: A Collection of Critical Essays* (Englewood Cliffs, NJ, Prentice-Hall) 4.
[14] Umberto Mariani, *Living Masks: The Achievement of Pirandello* (Toronto: University of Toronto Press, 2008) 4, 5.

the interaction of these concepts with the characters who must deal with the effects such ideas have on their lives.[15]

DeLillo similarly shows deep interest in the relativity of truth and the creation of reality, but primarily through the power of language. Klaus Benesch writes that DeLillo "conceives of language not just as a tool to reproduce or imitate reality as fiction but rather as generically involved in creating that very reality itself; put another way, DeLillo is convinced that language is a determining factor in the construction of subjectivity."[16] As we will see, DeLillo has explicitly admitted to director Robert Brustein that he was influenced by the Italian master Pirandello.

PLAYING OUT ANTI-REALISM IN A TIME OF REALISM

Both Pirandello and DeLillo believe in the illusion of reality: Pirandello noticed our need to constantly "deceive ourselves by creating a reality (different for each individual and never the same for all) which is unmasked now and again as vain and illusory."[17] DeLillo also struggles against the expectation of realism and the stability of reality, citing, for example, the rewarding aspect of his 1979 play "The Engineer of Moonlight" as being "deeply rooted in real people and real things," although theater, for him, is "not about the force of reality so much as the mysteries of identity and existence."[18]

---

[15] Roger W. Oliver, *Dreams of Passion: The Theater of Luigi Pirandello* (New York: New York University Press, 1979) x.

[16] Klaus Benesch, "Myth, Media, and the Obsolescence of Postmodern Drama: Don DeLillo's Tragicomedy *Valparaiso*," *Global Challenges and Regional Responses in Contemporary Drama in English*. Ed. Jochen Achilles, Ina Bergmann, and Birgit Däwes (Trier: Wissenschaftlicher Verlag Trier, 2003) n.p.

[17] Robert David Macdonald, preface to *Enrico Four*, by Luigi Pirandello (London: Oberon Books, 1990) 9.

[18] Jody McAuliffe, "Interview with Don DeLillo." *South Atlantic Quarterly* 99 2/3 (Spring/Summer 2000): 615.

Pirandello's famous groundbreaking antirealist play *Six Characters in Search of an Author* premiered at the Teatro Valle in Rome in 1921. As Donato Santeramo writes, *Six Characters* "can be seen both as the breaking point within Pirandello's dramatic production, and as his first attempt to explore the narrow boundaries between fiction and reality in general and on the stage in particular."[19] *Six Characters*, we will remember, showcases a play being rehearsed on stage by a group of actors, and interrupted by a group of "characters" searching for actors to play their roles and act out their story. As such, the anti-realist and meta-theatrical nature of *Six Characters* significantly influenced DeLillo's writing of *The Day Room*. There, a troupe of people inhabits a hospital and a motel room; they could be actors or patients.

Six Characters caused an enormous stir at the time of its debut production. In 1921, the meta-theatrical nature of the play on its opening night in Rome was met with violent hostility, showing the audience's disdain for anti-realism, and the playwright was forced to quickly escape the bourgeois audience's taunts and jeers by sneaking out of the theatre with his daughter. Interestingly, the scholar Ann Hallamore Caesar writes that in December 1927 when "peasants" attended a performance of *Sei Personaggi*, they

> stayed put in their seats, silent and still, at the end of the performance and when eventually the actors returned to the stage as 'themselves' to tell the audience that it was all over and they could go home, this too was taken to be part of the performance and nobody stirred. It was only very, very gradually, when they realized that nothing further was going to happen, that silently and cautiously they left the theatre.[20]

---

[19] Donato Santeramo, "Pirandello's Quest for Truth: *Sei personaggi in cerca d'autore*," in *Luigi Pirandello: Contemporary Perspectives*, Gian-Paolo Biasin and Manuela Gieri, eds. (Toronto: University of Toronto Press, 1999) 42.

[20] Ann Hallamore Caesar, *Characters and Authors in Luigi Pirandello* (Oxford: Oxford University Press, 1998) 183.

One might consider this reaction to be the result of a revolt against anti-realism and meta-theatricality, but, rather incredibly, something similar happened at a Perth performance in 2010. In Western Australia, during a performance of *Six Characters* as part of the 2010 Perth International Arts Festival, the evening's 600-strong audience took their seats and awaited the show, only to be told the night's performance was cancelled due to technical problems. The reactions were surprising:

> "Everyone was stunned," an audience member told PerthNow. "Until then, we were pretty unsure about what was going on. There was a TV set and a computer and the cast members were standing round on stage and the lighting was dim, but until the production person came out and made the announcement we thought it was all part of the show."

Such a strong reaction from even contemporary spectators well versed in anti-realist theatre is remarkable.[21]

Playing Roles and Discussing Playing Roles

The link between Pirandello's *Six Characters* and DeLillo's *The Day Room* is unmistakable in theme and content. In a letter, Robert Brustein, a Pirandello expert and the director of the American Repertory Theatre, highlighted the

> similarity between Pirandello and DeLillo's THE DAY ROOM. I don't know if he had SIX CHARACTERS in mind when he wrote that play, but he certainly was writing under the influence of Pirandello, particularly in the way the characters move in and out of their identities and roles. When I asked him

---

[21] Lisa Quartermain and Maria Noakes, "Festival 10 theatre-goers turned away as problems plague headline show," *PerthNow*, 9 February 2010, 12 February 2010

<http://www.perthnow.com.au/entertainment/perth-confidential/festival-10-theatre-goers-turned-away-as-problems-plague-headline-show/story-e6frg30l-1225828527260>.

about this myself, he did confess that Pirandello was his theatrical guide—but not limited to Pirandello.[22]

The Day Room is filled with examples moving in and out of multiple identities. For instance, the following exchange occurs between patients Grass and Wyatt in their hospital room:

Grass (to Wyatt): And you are Mr.—
Wyatt: Wyatt.
Grass: A promising idea for a name.
Wyatt: It's not an idea for a name. It is a name.
Grass: Could be improved with a little work.
Wyatt: I'm Wyatt. I like being Wyatt.
Grass: Who else have you tried?
Wyatt: I didn't know there was a choice.
Grass: There's always a choice. Do I buy my apartment or keep renting?[23]

Grass's insinuation that one can choose to try out others' names—and its being as easy a choice as considering real estate options—indicates that identity is presented in this play as malleable, dynamic, and easily changed.

The characters' exchanges in *The Day Room* directly reflect Pirandello's own thoughts of identity being comprised of various masks that one puts on and takes off: "[W]e play one character for some, another for others. If one were to remove all the masks, there would be nobody underneath."[24] Pirandello was concerned with the human need to play roles in everyday life, taking this very real need and translating it through the metaphor of acting upon a stage. In Robert David Macdonald's preface to Pirandello's *Enrico*

---

[22] Don DeLillo, letter dated February 9, 1989, Box 15, Folder 3: The Day Room: Handwritten notes in notebook. Found at the University of Texas at Austin, Harry Ransom Center, Don DeLillo Collection. Capitals in original.

[23] Don DeLillo, *The Day Room* (New York: Penguin, 1986) 11.

[24] Pirandello in a conversation with André Maurois, in the preface to Pirandello's *Enrico Four*, trans. Robert David Macdonald (London: Oberon Books, 1990) 14.

Four, André Maurois recalls a conversation in which Pirandello said the following:

> Since childhood, I have been obsessed with the idea that the unity of the personality is not a true picture of the person... Sometimes we find it painful to be with two friends at the same time; we cannot play two contradictory roles at once.[25]

Pirandello's *Six Characters* consists of characters who do not belong, and whose "place of origin," Santeramo says, is *"otherness"* (44). We see this most clearly played out in his play *Enrico Four* (or *Henry IV*).

Enrico Four employs meta-theatricality by having characters explicitly discuss the roles they play and their falsehoods. One of the actors, Bertoldo, admits to his colleagues his confusion about the time period in which they are supposed to be acting, and Arialdo and Landolfo then admit their own identity confusion:

> Arialdo: Trouble is, we don't know who are you are either.
> Landolfo: If it's any comfort, we don't know who we are either. He's called Arialdo, he's Ordulfo, I'm Landolfo.... We're used to it by now. But who we really are? (*Enrico Four*, 24)

Compare the above Pirandello excerpt with the following exchange between Nurse Walker and Dr. Phelps in DeLillo's *The Day Room*:

> Nurse Walker: What I wonder about is the narrow scope of the roles we have to play. Can't we stop being doctor and nurse for just a minute? Can't we give you a glimpse of the people behind the uniforms? People with their own doubts, fears—
> Dr. Phelps: What lies beneath? (21-22)

Later in *The Day Room*, when hospital patient Budge tells his roommate Wyatt that his doctor Dr. Bazelon is not really a doctor

---

[25] Loc. cit.

but actually an inmate in the mental ward upstairs, Wyatt cannot believe the extent of the identity deception, and then becomes paranoid and starts to question Budge's own role:

> Wyatt: If everything has been set up, all my life, and if its been running smoothly until today, when a defect suddenly appeared, then who are you, Mr. Budge, and what are you doing here? (45)

A short while later, Budge himself is carried off by a nurse, who in turn is carried off by orderlies. The identity circus continues like this relentlessly, sending spectators' expectations flying. The characters push against the roles assigned to them in a Pirandellian foregrounding of characters' wills, and the power they hold with respect to narrative construction and story verisimilitude.

THE CHARACTER-CENTERED RELATIONSHIP BETWEEN AUTHOR AND CHARACTERS

When preparing to write *Six Characters* and *The Day Room*, both Pirandello and DeLillo experienced similar authorial inspiration. Pirandello's account of his inspiration is a moving description of the personal relationship between the writer and his characters:

> These creatures of my brain were not living *my* life any longer: they were already living a life of their own, and it was now beyond my power to deny them a life which was no longer in my control.[26]

We can compare the above imaginative visualization with DeLillo's, who also says that, upon imagining a character, "he is usu-

---

[26] Luigi Pirandello, "Pirandello Confesses...," *The Virginia Quarterly Review*, Spring 1925, 18 Feb. 2010 <http://www.vqronline.org/articles/1925/spring/pirandello-confesses/>.

ally somewhere, and it's usually pretty specific. I think visually."[27] DeLillo's impetus to write his first play 'The Engineer of Moonlight' (1979) was also a similar imagining of characters in physical space, as he admits to Jody McAuliffe in an interview: "I'm not quite sure how to explain what brought it about. I think I saw people on a stage, actually, and began to follow them and to listen to them" (McAuliffe, 609). Likewise, DeLillo's impetus to write *The Day Room* can be gauged from an interview with Dominic Maxwell:

> 'I'm not sure how it all began,' he says in a gentle New York cadence, 'except that it was roughly 20 years ago when I had an idea that seemed to demand a limited space. This was a play called *The Day Room*. What I saw was characters in an artificial setting, a hospital that is not necessarily a hospital: it wasn't the kind of reality a novelist imagined. And I knew at once that this could not be anything but a play. And of course it's happened only several times in my life as a writer. But in each case there seemed to be no doubt that I was headed toward the stage rather than toward the printed page.'[28]

DeLillo saw characters in a physical reality, then wrote *The Day Room*. Likewise, for Pirandello, "[i]t is not the drama that makes the characters, but the characters who make the drama,"[29] so rather than a realistic narrative where an author carries his characters through a story, the characters are presented as weaving their own stories according to their own personalities and needs. In essence,

---

[27] Letter to Ms Wallace from Lino Belleggia, who forwarded Don's reply, May 15, 2002. Found at the University of Texas, Austin, Harry Ransom Center, Don DeLillo Collection.

[28] Dominic Maxwell, "Novelist Don DeLillo Stumbled Into Writing for the Stage." *The Times* 24 April 2006, 2 May 2008. <http://entertainment.timesonline.co.uk/tol/arts_and_entertainment/article708118.ece>.

[29] "L'azione parlata," *Marzocco* (7 May 1899), *Spsv* 1016. In Ann Hallamore Ceasar, *Characters and Authors in Luigi Pirandello* (Oxford: Oxford University Press, 1998) 13.

both *The Day Room* and *Six Characters* not only rely on the artificiality of their characters' roles, but they also express their *awareness* of this reliance, and this is what most distinguishes them from the realm of theatrical realism. Both writers have consciously made it seem as if they have handed over control to their characters, to do with the plot what they will. Consequently, their characters seem to assert their freedom to question the truth of their identities and of the story.

Unresolved Endings

A further antirealist technique used by both Pirandello and DeLillo is unresolved narrative endings. Judith Laurence Pastore flags the "similarity of [*The Day Room*'s] themes to the philosophical issues which preoccupy Pirandello: the existential nature of modern existence; the tenuousness of personal identity; the deceptions of role-playing; the illusory nature of time, space, and memory; and the open-endedness of what we perceive as reality and our ongoing desire for closure."[30] Both Pirandello's *Six Characters* and his *That's The Way Things Are* end without resolution or certainty. This realism more than likely influenced DeLillo's own penchant for unfinished narratives. Peter Straus, former British Editor-in-Chief of Picador, defends DeLillo's characteristic (ir)resolutions:

> It's not really fair to say he's bad at endings. He's not prescriptive as a writer, so therefore the end will sometimes be inconclusive. Everybody expects a resolution, just like everybody expects to be happy. He's pointing up the chimeras that contemporary society has highlighted. The penultimate sentence in [*Cosmopolis*] is "this is not the end."[31]

---

[30] Judith Laurence Pastore, "Pirandello's Influence on American Writers: Don DeLillo's *The Day Room*," *Italian Culture* 8 (1990): 431.
[31] Emma Brockes, "View from the Bridge," *Guardian Unlimited*, 24 May 2003, 10 April 2008 <http://books.guardian.co.uk/departments/generalfiction/story/0,,962337,00.html>.

Toby Silverman Zinman also suggests "it is no accident that DeLillo leaves all [of *White Noise*'s] plots and sub-plots unfinished."[32] Robert Brustein places Pirandello "among the rebels who subverted classical conventions from which he himself grew,"[33] and likewise, Mark Osteen notes that in the novels "*End Zone, Players*, and *The Names*, DeLillo interrogates the value of plot, and scrutinizes his and our participation in the games of novel reading and film watching. He does so by withholding satisfaction."[34] Both DeLillo and Pirandello, then, revolt against their readers' and audiences' realist expectations of rounded endings.

CONCLUSION

I have developed two main ideas above: DeLillo's exposure to Fellinian themes of fantasy, Jungian symbolism, and celebrity culture, has influenced his works *White Noise, Americana* and *Valparaiso*; and the influence of Pirandello's concerns with identity and his role-playing are evident particularly in the meta-theatrical play *The Day Room*.

DeLillo takes from Fellini and Pirandello not only antirealist intellectual themes, but, perhaps more important, the drive to be unique and to push the boundaries of what can be imagined and created. Being placed as an outsider looking in has its benefits; he developed his role of novelist politically by situating himself within the broader global context of novelists as commentators on society. He noted in a letter to Jonathan Franzen that a writer "ought to be skeptical about the values of society and ready to write in opposi-

---

[32] Toby Silverman Zinman, "Gone Fission: The Holocaustic Wit of Don DeLillo," *Modern Drama* 34/1 (1991): 77.

[33] "Introduction," Glauco Cambon, ed, *Pirandello: A Collection of Critical Essays* (Englewood Cliffs, NJ: Prentice-Hall, 1966) 8.

[34] Mark Osteen, *American Magic and Dread: Don DeLillo's Dialogue with Culture* (Philadelphia: University of Pennsylvania Press, 2000) 117.

tion to them."[35] And to Ioanna Kleftoyianni he wrote, "This is why we need the writer in opposition, the novelist who writes against power, who writes against the corporation or the state or the whole apparatus of assimilation."[36] Such a view is founded upon and further enhanced by his status as an outsider. Although his writing techniques and subject matter are influenced by Pirandello and Fellini, perhaps the biggest impetus that he shares with these artists is belonging to a society whose realist expectations leave much to be desired.

---

[35] Letter from DeLillo to Jonathan Franzen, August 18, year unknown. Found at the University of Texas, Austin, Harry Ransom Center, Don DeLillo Collection.

[36] Letter to Ioanna Kleftoyianni, August 30, 2002. Found at the University of Texas, Austin, Harry Ransom Center, Don DeLillo Collection.

NEW YORK CITY AS PLACE IN DON DELILLO'S FICTION

Alan J. Gravano

In *New York and the Literary Imagination*, Edward Margolies remarks that many fin de siècle artists such as Stephen Crane, O. Henry, Theodore Dreiser, and Eugene O'Neill thought of New York as "undiscovered country" (114). This characterization highlights a unique relationship between the immigrant and the city, because New York was like a vast and complex country in itself, a geopolitical synecdoche of the American nation to which the immigrants had come. In the novels of Don DeLillo, New York participates in the evolution of an Italian American identity. More than a mere background or a conventional setting, the city serves as a key actor, playing a leading role in the novelist's strategies and the characters' lives. More precisely, New York appears to play several different roles, and the characters and the city depend upon one another for their development.

To begin with, New York provides much of DeLillo's fiction with a fundamental referential background and therefore with the necessary verisimilitude. This is the reason that DeLillo includes real place names, street names, rivers, museums, and hotels. From this point of view, readers follow the characters' movements as on a city map—one thinks of *Cosmopolis*—and from novel to novel they receive an accurate sense of the atmosphere in the metropolis before, during, and after 9/11, which serves as a chronological center in DeLillo's world.

As has often been shown, DeLillo resorts to a subtle use of irony to depict the damaging effects of postmodernism on his contemporaries. In novels such as *Underworld* (1997), *Cosmopolis* (2003), and *Falling Man* (2007) not only does he describe the fragmentation characteristic of the modern urban life, he also denounces its damaging impact on the individual and the community alike. In so doing, he sheds light on the artificiality of city life, since commodities, consumerism, and the illusion of control reign absolute, while moral and spiritual values have greatly diminished. While DeLillo proves to be fully aware of the dangers of technological progress, like many contemporary writers he appears to be fascinated by its power—hence the key role always played by technology in his works (Russo 219-20). As with most postmodern works, however, these novels are both "a celebration of a technological age and a condemnation of it," with images of the city suggesting both "new possibility and ... unreal fragmentation" (Bradbury and McFarlane 46, 49). What is striking about DeLillo's narrative approach is that the negative features of the urban world are turned to aesthetic advantage such as the significant role of waste in *Underworld*. In this respect New York is appropriated, even transfigured, to serve his purpose.

The examples that follow represent a modest overview of New York in DeLillo's fifteen novels and sixteen short stories published to date (2011). In *Americana*, his first novel, David Bell, the protagonist, is a New York television executive "who attempts through his self-produced film to respond creatively and cinematically to his sister's running off with a mobster" (Giaimo 118). *Great Jones Street* derives its title from an actual street in Manhattan's Noho Historic District. In *Ratner's Star*, Billy Twillig's father is a third rail inspector in the New York subway system (4); his parents live in the Bronx. In *Players*, a Wall Street couple runs off with terrorists. The search for the secret Hitler pornographic film in *Running Dog* takes place partially in Manhattan with descriptions of Canal Street (3) and a "high rise in the East Fifties" (4). Jack Gladney's colleagues in *White Noise* are "New York émigrés" (9), one named Alfonse Stompanato, after an alleged gangster. Part I of *Libra* is entitled "In the Bronx" and *Mao II*'s first section is called "At Yankee Stadium." In *Libra* DeLillo creates the character of Carmine

Latta, while in *The Names* there is the Italian American filmmaker, Frank Volterra. In *Underworld*, Nick Costanza Shay grew up in the Arthur Avenue Little Italy of the Bronx, and his mother still lives there in the 1990s. *Cosmopolis* follows the peregrinations of Eric Packer, a billionaire asset manager, who travels cross-town in Manhattan to get a haircut. In *Falling Man* Keith Neudecker emerges from the smoke and ash of one of the towers on September 11th. In *Point Omega* published in 2010, DeLillo bookends the story of the protagonist, Richard Elster, with the description of an art exhibit at the Museum of Modern Art. Through the unfolding of events the reader realizes that the woman viewing the *24 Hour Psycho* exhibit in "Anonymity 2, September 4" is Elster's daughter, Jessie. New York City operates on the historical level in these examples and constitutes the essential identity of DeLillo's various characters, many of whom struggle with the meaning of the city and their own identity outside of it. Many characters never escape it.

The short stories that pre-date DeLillo's first novel, *Americana* (1971), are almost exclusively set in New York. In "The River Jordan," the Psychic Church of the Crucified Christ is located on Ninth Avenue. The protagonist, Cavallo, in "Take the 'A' Train," lives in the Bronx, while Santullo of "Spaghetti and Meatballs" is thrown out of his Bronx apartment. "Coming Sun. Mon. Tues." focuses on Greenwich Village and the West Side, while Baghdad Towers West on 72nd Street, also the title of the short story, provides the setting for its action. "In the Men's Room of the Sixteenth Century," a male police officer dresses in women's clothing on the streets of Times Square.

An iconic image of New York is its cityscape, especially the skyscrapers—Céline famously said that it is the only city in the world that stands up to greet you. In *Cosmopolis*, DeLillo's first post-9/11 novel, this emphasis on the cityscape brings into focus the cultural expectations of New York. Besides the Empire State and Chrysler buildings, tourists visit the New York Stock Exchange, which ties into DeLillo's critique of global capitalism through asset manager, Eric Packer. The site of the World Trade

Center Towers is still empty eight years after. Non-New Yorkers, besides touring the Empire State building, make the journey to Ground Zero as an additional tourist destination.

In contrast, Eric Packer of *Cosmopolis*, looking at the building where he once lived, thinks that "they shared an edge or boundary, skyscraper and man" (8). He then takes "out his hand organizer and" pokes a brief note to himself about the "anachronistic quality of the word skyscraper. No recent structure ought to bear this word. It belonged to the olden soul of awe, to the arrowed towers that were a narrative long before he was born" (9). Those towers, which are the Empire State Building and the Chrysler Building, speak to the construction of the 1920s and 1930s versus the square-topped World Trade Center Towers constructed in the 1970s. He realizes that "the tower gave him strength and depth ... in the soaring noise of the street and [he] studied the mass and scale of the tower. The one virtue of its surface was to skim and bend the river light.... He scanned its length and felt connected to it" (9). Randy Laist acknowledges that Eric's reflections "recall similar descriptions of the World Trade Center articulated by Pammy Wynant in *Players*, Bill Gray in *Mao II*, and Klara Sax in *Underworld*, and his sense of existential continuity between himself and his ultra-modern high rise looks forward to Keith Neudecker's intuition on the morning of September 11, 2001" (258). The skyscraper reappears in DeLillo's work as a symbol of American society itself, not only in terms of economic achievement but as monuments of the sublime. Whether man-made such as Fresh Kills Landfill in *Underworld* or structures such as the World Trade Center, they are perhaps his most essential landmarks in the geography of New York.

The staccato happenings from the world outside Eric's limo engulf him. The limo runs "into stalled traffic before it reache[s] Second Avenue" (13); he hears "stray words in French and Somali seeping through ambient noise" and he thinks "that was the disposition of this end of 47th Street" (17). On route to get his haircut, Packer makes frequent stops. He meets his currency analyst Michael Chin (21) where the limo drifts "into gridlock on Third Avenue" (21). After his tryst with his mistress, Didi Fancher (27), Packer returns to his white stretch limo, looks up, and observes how "[t]he bank towers loomed just beyond the avenue. They were covert structures for all their size, hard to see, so common and monotonic, tall, sheer, abstract, with standard setbacks, and block-long, and interchangeable, and he had to concentrate to see them" (36). Packer understands the topography of the city. His limo, his actions participate in a symbiotic exchange with these "towers." Yet Packer's fascination with the exterior of these buildings turns inward: the towers "looked empty from here. He liked that idea. They were made to be the last tall things, made empty, designed to hasten the future. They were the end of the outside world. They weren't here, exactly" (36). Breakdown occurs because the tallest point represents where the towers meet the sky; the point where the structures end and the sky begins. According to Laist "the tall building represents neither a monument to human industry and intellect capable of building spires to abrade God's firmament, nor a cathedral of corporate supremacy," but "a cenotaph: a monument to the disappearance of the human through the surpassing of the present" (263). Technology and in this case skyscrapers may act as a tomb of postmodern New York itself; however, they also remain destinations—the Empire State, the Chrysler, and the World Trade Center—populated by tourists.

This melding of the "outside world" and the "inside" occurs in chapter 2. Eric stands "in the poetry alcove at the Gotham Book Mart, leafing through chapbooks" (66). DeLillo places one of the most well known independent book stores in *Cosmopolis*; the historical significance of the Gotham Book Mart blends into the fiction. Readers familiar with the geography of Manhattan will notice that Packer travels through iconic streets such as "Times Square with the billboards ghost-lighted now and the tire barricades nearly cleared dead ahead, leaving 47th Street open to the west" (106). From Times Square the limo crosses Eighth Avenue, "out of the theater district, out of the row of supper clubs and lounges…and into the local, the mixed, the mostly unnoticed blocks of dry cleaner and schoolyard, just an inkling here of the old brawl, the old seethe and heat of Hell's Kitchen, the rake of fire escapes on old brick buildings" (129). The limo drives past Tenth Avenue and "the first small grocery and then the truck lot lying empty. The barbershop was on the north side of the street and faced a row of old brick tenements" (158-9). The "small grocery," "barbershop," and "old brick tenements" are perhaps remnants of a Little Italy.

DeLillo returns to New York's skyline and the Bronx Little Italy in *Underworld* for the first time since "Take the 'A' Train" (1962) and "Spaghetti and Meatballs" (1965) (Hendin qtd. in Olster 99). In Chapter 1 of the novel's first section, Klara Sachs gazes at "the World Trade Center...under construction, already towering, twin-towering, with cranes tilted at the summits and work elevators sliding up the flanks. She saw it almost everywhere she went...there it was, bulked up at the funneled end of the island" (372). DeLillo captures the essence of New York's cityscape through his use of language, with the phrases "twin-towering" and "funneled end of the island," even the repetition of "towering." The skyscrapers such as the World Trade Center reach up into the heavens. Klara's comments about the structures recall Eric Packer's thoughts about how "the bank towers loomed just beyond the avenue" (36). Eerily, in a post-9/11 New York, new towers will rise up out of the ashes.

In this section of *Underworld*, Klara stresses the importance of the architecture of New York City. She acknowledges that "she loved the biplane sculpture on a roof downtown, an old mail plane maybe, full-scale, with a landing strip and lights. And the stepped pyramid atop a building on Wall Street and the machined-steel spire of the Chrysler Building and the south face of the Hotel Pierre like some scansion of rooftop Paris, only elongated many times, shot versingly skyward" (379). Klara and Eric share an interest in architecture of the city. Although Packer's feelings about "skyscrapers" are the opposite of Sachs, both characters spend ample time pondering the skyline of the city. The cityscape connects

New York and its architecture with the characters, each with their own zone: Manhattan for Klara Sachs and the Bronx for Nick Shay, Matt Shay, Rosemary Shay, and Albert Bronzini. New York becomes a part of each of these characters. Staten Island's Fresh Kills Landfill for Nick and New York City's architecture for Klara shape their lives. Rosemary and Bronzini never leave the city, while Klara, Matt, and Nick move westward; however, the characters never escape the lure of the Manhattan.

Although Nick and Klara move westward, the family and the community of the Bronx persist as a central metaphor in their lives. Margolies states that "a few go West in a kind of mock reversal of history" (122). DeLillo's exploration of the characters' lives occurs back in the East where the reader learns about the formative years of Nick and Klara, which happen in the Bronx including their affair, Nick's killing of George Manza, and Klara's divorce from Albert Bronzini. Nick in his 50s moves to Phoenix to work as a waste executive, while Klara in her 70s works on the B-52 bomber art installation in the desert of New Mexico. The history of the characters, their childhood, adolescence, and maturation, happens mostly in New York.

The reverse chronological order of *Underworld*, which starts in New York with the 1951 pennant game between the New York Giants and the Brooklyn Dodgers and ends in Phoenix during the 1990s in cyberspace, disjoints the reader. DeLillo introduces Nick and Klara in their advanced age in the West. The B-52 bombers installation early in the novel foreshadows the "biplane" and "mail plane" buildings of New York and Klara's interest in found objects, which earns her the nickname "Bag Lady" (392). Nick, on the other hand, remains attached to the Bronx because of his personal memories and his relations to individuals such as Klara, Albert, and his mother, Rosemary Shay, to places such as the Bronx and the Polo Grounds or objects such as Bobby Thompson's homerun ball. He distances himself from people, places, and objects from his upbringing, but he never escapes it.

In Chapter 3 of "The Cloud of Unknowing," DeLillo shifts through the meaning of the phrase "back east":

> I've heard that term a lot since coming to this part of the country. But I never think of the term as a marker of geography. It's a reference to time, a statement about time, about all the densities of being and experience, it's time disguised, it's light-up time, shifting smoky time tricked out as some locus of stable arrangement. When people use that term they're talking about the way things used to be before they moved out here, the way the world used to be, not just New Jersey or South Philly, or before their parents moved, or grandparents, and about the way things still exist in some private relativity theory, some smoky shifting mind dimension, or before the other men and women came this way, the ones in Conestoga wagons, a term we learned in grade school, a back-east term, stemming from the place where wagons were made. (333)

Nick's decision to mention "New Jersey" and "South Philly" reveals the importance of the Italian American community to him because his mother, Rosemary, is Irish Catholic and Nick's Catholic education occurred in New York as well as Minnesota. Nick explains that the phrase "back-east" is a time-marker, rather than a place-marker, if New York City or the Bronx is the starting point, then "New Jersey" and "South Philly" do not represent a significant journey westward.

Nick's move West coincides with a break from his family and their traditions. Nick Costanza/Shay is not first generation—he is second-generation Italian American. In *The Madonna of 115th StreetI*, Robert Orsi comments that "the first generation...wanted to introduce its children to Italian culture" such as "traditional patterns of respect, familial obligations, and social behavior" (20-1). Besides the importance of Manhattan to Nick, the Bronx remains the home to Nick's mother, Rosemary Shay, and his high school science teacher, Albert Bronzini. In Chapter 5 of "Elegy for Left Hand Alone," Matt and Nick Shay argue about their mother. Nick wants to bring her to Phoenix to live with him and his wife. Matt attempts to explain to Nick why their mother does not want to leave: "you have to understand this woman is not afraid. She lives a free life. People know her. They respect her. The neighborhood's still a living thing" (202). Her run-down neighborhood is "a living thing," as opposed to the dead suburbs around Phoenix where Nick lives. Although the neighborhood in the Bronx has changed ethnically over forty years, Matt understands his mother's vital connection to it. Nick only sees the serious decay of his childhood neighborhood, most readily in the trash in the hallway of her building. His concern for the trash represents his larger view, the "trash" outside—the blacks and Hispanics. The community is no longer the idealized Italian America.

Albert Bronzini lives in the same neighborhood as Rosemary, and like her, he has refused to leave. Matt visits his old chess teacher, Albert, who discusses "the old streets" not in terms of "mourning" but of "choice" (214). Bronzini states that he and Rosemary "made our choice. We complain but we don't mourn, we don't grieve" (214). Rosemary and Albert do not mourn because their neighborhood is not dead; it is "a living thing." Like Rosemary's ruminations on her upbringing, Bronzini recounts a trip to "the pork store the other day" to show Rosemary "the ceiling. Hundreds of hanging salamis, such bounty and fullness, the place teeming with smells and textures, the place teeming with smells and textures, the ceiling covered completely. I said, Rosemary, look. A gothic cathedral of pork" (214). Albert transforms the Italian delicatessen into a "cathedral"; it has become another remnant of community for residents like Rosemary and Albert; and it preserves a remnant of the sacred, thereby illustrating the immanent southern Italian Catholicism.

New York City and the Bronx influence each character's development, and this community defines them. Whether it is the architectural cityscape of Manhattan for Klara or the people, places, and objects of the Bronx for Nick, this geographic space remains a sacred place to them both. The older generation represented by

Rosemary and Albert refuse to leave the Bronx; they have their monuments in the form of cathedrals of pork.

Unlike the private/public binary of *Underworld*, in *Falling Man*, the reader encounters two New York's, pre-9/11 and post-9/11. The protagonist, Keith Neudecker, emerges from "the roar" that "was still in the air, the buckling rumble of the fall. This was the world now" (3). Neudecker (a play on new deck of cards) and the other characters represent "the falling man." Keith and his wife have been separated for some time before the September 11th attacks. The audience witnesses DeLillo develop these characters in a post-9/11 world. Everything is different.

After Keith and his estranged wife, Lianne, have sex, and she takes "an early-morning run," they talk:

> "You're one of those madwomen running in the streets. Run around the reservoir."
> "You think we look crazier than men."
> "Only in the streets."
> "I like the streets. This time of morning, there's something about the city, down by the river, streets nearly empty, cars blasting by on the Drive."
> "Breathe deeply."
> "I like running alongside the cars on the Drive."
> "Take deep breaths," he said. "Let the fumes swirl into your lungs."
> "I like the fumes. I like the breeze from the river."
> "Run naked," he said.
> "You do it, I'll do it." (70-1)

In this post-9/11 New York, Keith is "naked," the quintessential "falling man." Lianne cannot name what it is "about the city" but "there's something." For Lianne, it is ephemeral such as "breaths," "fumes," and "breezes." Like *Underworld*, with the recurrent scene of the trash ritual, the last descriptions of Lianne and Keith are about ritual and religion. As Keith looks "into" the glass he recites "fragments from the instruction sheet. Hold to a count of five. Repeat ten times. He did the full program every time, hand raised, forearm flat, hand down, forearms sideways, slowing the pace just slightly, day to night and then again the following day, drawing it out, making it last. He counted the seconds, he counted the repetitions" (236). The litany of the mental exercises gives Keith and his life meaning in a post-9/11 New York. The iconic images around their apartment such as Central Park and the Hudson River remain amid the absence of the World Trade Center. Lianne's physical exercise (ritualistic running) through the streets reflects their mutual renewed intimacy and connection with their home.

Lianne's cardio ritual connects with her renewed interest in God; she "obsesses over the *New York Times*'s long-running feature, 'Portraits of Grief'—capsule obituaries of 9/11's victims" (Kauffman 371). She goes to mass and thinks "that the hovering presence of God [is] the thing that created loneliness and doubt in the soul and she also thought that God [is] the thing, the entity existing outside space and time that resolve[s] this doubt in the tonal power of a word, a voice. God is the voice that says, 'I am not here'" (236). Lianne's feeling of "I'm not here" connects with Packer's word choice "empty," while looking up at the skyscrapers of Manhattan in *Cosmopolis*. Although Eric is a billionaire living in a penthouse in Manhattan, chauffeured around in a white, stretch limousine, he is "empty" like the skyscrapers among other cars, indeed, his limo is like a horizontal skyscraper in traffic. He even states that "they weren't here, exactly" (36). Continuing with the development of that theme in *Falling Man*, DeLillo's character, Lianne, in a post-9/11 New York, turns to religion to combat a feeling of "I am not here," finding "the strength to go on alone in a return to the forms of her long-forgotten Catholic faith" (Duvall qtd. in Olster 152). Unfortunately for Keith, Lianne, and Eric, they do not comprehend that God is found within; he is what is within the skyscrapers, cathedrals, and individual characters.

In the most powerful section of *Falling Man*, DeLillo recreates the moment of impact and fall of the World Trade Center. After

Keith has exited the tower, he walks down the street among the fire trucks and bystanders. He then looks up and "saw a shirt come down out of the sky. He walked and saw it fall, arms waving like nothing in this life" (246). By the end, Keith realizes that he himself is that "falling man" without knowing if he has a bungee cord attached. The characters grapple with the trauma of living through and witnessing the 9/11 attacks. Neudecker as his name suggests receives a new deck, a new life.

Whether Keith or Lianne in *Falling Man*, Klara or Nick in *Underworld*, or Eric in *Cosmopolis*, New York represents not only the referential setting of these novels but also the site of spiritual transformation for these characters. New York as character participates in the lives of these figures altering them in unknown ways until revealed at the completion of each novel. Whether we are New Yorkers or not, the city seduces us, takes hold of us, and changes us. Ultimately, the Fall of Man is the prelude to redemption and reconnection.

WORKS CITED

Bradbury, Malcolm and James Walter McFarlane. Eds. *Modernism: 1890-1930*. New York: Penguin, 1976.

Chandler, Aaron. "'An Unsettling, Alternative Self': Benno Levin, Emmanuel Levinas, and Don DeLillo's *Cosmopolis*." *Critique: Studies in Contemporary Fiction* 50.3 (2009): 241-60.

DeLillo, Don. *Americana*. New York: Penguin, 1971.

——. "Baghdad Towers West." *Epoch* 17 (1968): 195-217.

——. "Coming Sun. Mon. Tues." *Kenyon Review* 28 (1966): 391-4.

——. *Cosmopolis*. New York: Scribner, 2003.

——. *Falling Man*. New York: Scribner, 2007.

——. "In the Men's Room of the Sixteenth Century." *Esquire* (1971): 174-77, 243, 246.

——. *Point Omega*. New York: Scribner, 2009.

——. "The River Jordan." *Epoch* 10.2 (1960): 105-20.

——. "Spaghetti and Meatballs." *Epoch* 14:3 (1965): 244-50.

——. "Take the 'A' Train." *Epoch* 12.1 (1962): 9-25.

——. *Underworld*. New York: Scribner, 1997.

Giaimo, Paul. *Appreciating Don DeLillo: The Moral Force of a Writer's Work.* Santa Barbara: Praeger, 2011.

Izzo, Donatella. *Point Omega* Book Review. *Italian Americana* 29.1 (2011): 111-13.

Kauffman, Linda S. "The Wake of Terror: Don DeLillo's 'In the Ruins of the Future,' 'Baader-Meinhof,' and *Falling Man*." *MFS: Modern Fiction Studies* 54.2 (2008): 353-77.

Laist, Randy. "The Concept of Disappearance in Don DeLillo's *Cosmopolis*." *Critique: Studies in Contemporary Fiction* 51.3 (2010): 257-75.

Margolies, Edward. *New York and the Literary Imagination.* Jefferson: McFarland & Co., 2008.

Olster, Stacey, Ed. *Don DeLillo: Mao II, Underworld, Falling Man.* New York: Continuum, 2011.

Orsi, Robert. *The Madonna of 115th Street.* New Haven: Yale UP, 1985.

John Paul Russo. *The Future without a Past: The Humanities in a Technological Society.* Columbia: U. of Missouri P, 2005.

INDEX

Acheson, Dean 242
Alba, Richard 104, 156, 159-160, 172
Alda, Alan 296-297, 301
Aldrich, John 203
Ali, Mohammed 315
Alioto, Joseph 91
Alito, Samuel 260
Allen, Henry 296, 301
Amore, B. 112, 122, 124-125
Andriano, Sylvester 86, 91
Angelone, Sgt. Anthony A. 70
Anger, Kenneth 286
Antonini, Luigi 210-212
Antonioni, Michelangelo 357-358
Antonucci, Giovanni 143
Arcade, Penny 281
Arnold, Chuck 276
Auleta, Vincent H. 206-207
Avildsen, John 312

Baccari, Alessandro 91
Baldassar, Loretta 333, 335, 337, 341
Banes, Sally 329
Barolini, Helen 114-115, 118, 120-121, 333-339, 346, 355
Barrett, William 231
Basile, Carmine A. 63
Basile, Salvatore 63
Battisti, Danielle 241
Baumgardner, Jennifer 267
Bean, Carl 289

Bencivenni, Marcela 249
Benesch, Klaus 378
Berg, Michael 279
Bergman, Ingmar 357-358
Beyoncé 280
Biaggio, Laura 328-329
Bioni, Sgt. Ernest 65
Blow, Isabella 271
Bogart, John N. 47
Bona, Mary Jo 149
Bondanella, Peter 293, 312-314, 324, 360-361, 365
Bordo, Susan 293, 295
Brasacchio, Sgt. Anthony 65
Brickell, William and Mary 35-36, 39
Browder, Earl 212
Brustein, Robert 368, 370
Bucci, Sam 40
Butler, Smedley D. 12

Caesar, Ann Hallamore 369
Calderone, Joe 272
Calhoun, Craig 84
Califano, Joseph 260
Camilli, Edoardo 40
Candeloro, Domenic 161
Cannistraro, Philip
Canzoneri, Tony 317
Carbo, Frankie 314
Carter, Rubin 322
Caruso, Frank 62
Celebre, John 62
Celebrezze, Anthony 259-260

Céline, Louis-Ferdinand 380
Chalfin, Paul 41-42, 48-50
Chamlin, Mitchell 156,
Ciccimarro, Cpr. Joseph I. 67
Clemente, Gary 231
Clooney, Rosemary 275
Cohen, Andy 278
Cohen, Selma 332
Cohn, Nik 292-293, 304
Collins, John 39, 42
Conforti, Joseph 172
Coppola, Francis Ford 125
Cordasco, Francesco 30, 43, 48
Corsi, Edward 210, 215, 220
Costa, Enrico 234
Crane, Stephen 378
Crespi, Cesare 96
Cruikshank, John 41
Cuomo, Andrew 245-246, 261
Curcio, Joseph 72-73
Cyrus, Miley 276

Dahl, Robert A. 203
Dahl, Steve 290
Daniels, Roger 244
de Carlo, Frank 40
De Clementi, Andreina 222
De Curtis, Antonio 125
De Gasperi, Alcide 225, 227, 232, 234-235, 237, 241-243
De Liberty, Fr. Anthony 60, 62, 66, 69-70, 74, 76
de Marco Torgovnick, Marianna 343, 346-347, 350, 355
De Martino, Ernesto 228
De Sabata, Victor 234
De Simone, Roberto 331

DeCurtis, Anthony 358
Deering, James 31, 39-42, 48-54
Degenenes, Ellen 274
Del Casino, Anthony 66
Del Casino, Vincent 66
DeLaura, Fr. Anthony 60, 67-68
DeLillo, Don 357-368, 373-376, 378-380, 382-385, 387-388
Desiato, Joseph 189
Desiato, Salvatore 189
Di Bartolo, Francis E. 3-18, 20-29
di Leonardo, Michaela 303
Diggins, John 16, 83
DiPietropaolo, Celest 328, 330
Di Donato, Pietro 116-117, 128, 335
di Prima, Diane 343, 347, 350-353, 355
Di Salvo Family 112-118, 120, 122-129
DiFabio, Pasquale 31
Dreiser, Theodore 378
DuBois, W. E. B. 18
Dyer, Richard 288-290, 295, 297-298

Eliot, Charles W. 134, 140
Ertola, Charles 92

Faludi, Susan 279-280
Famiglietti, Joseph 65
Fante, John 116-117, 128
Farizzi, Pvt. Al 68
Farrell, Warren 296

Fawcett, Farah 300
Fellini, Federico 357-361, 363, 365-367, 376, 377
Ferraro, Thomas 159
Ferri, Joseph 51
Ferri, Tito 48-49, 51-52
Figone, John 91
Fiore, Anthony 88
Fisher, Carl 39, 42
Fisher, Ham 316-317
Flagler, Henry 36-38, 42, 44-45, 47-48
Foppiano, Vivian 65
Ford, Sgt. Thomas 65
Fosdick, Charles 142-143
Fosdick, Frederick 139, 142
Franchini, Amadeo 189
Francis, Connie (Franconero, Concetta Rosa Maria) 268-270, 272, 275, 278-281
Franco, Francisco 21
Frank, Gillian 290
Frank, Henry 206
Franzen, Jonathan 376
Frazier, Joe 315
Frere-Jones, Sasha 273
Freud, Sigmund 365
Friedan, Betty 296

Gabaccia, Donna 34, 333, 335, 337, 341
Gallardi, Sgt. Joseph I. 65
Gambino, Richard 157, 161, 303
Gans, Herbert 159-160, 172-173,
Gardaphè, Fred 156, 159, 174, 312

Garland, Judy 274
Germanotta, Cynthia 279
Giammarino, Pvt. Anthony 70
Giannini, Alberto 8
Giannini, Amadeo P. 97
Giardello, Joey 322
Gibson, Hugh S. 233
Gilder, Richard W. 134
Glazer, Nathan 217
Godard, Jean Luc 357-358
Godfrey, Arthur 268
Gordon, Milton 104
Gorshin, Frank 269
Grant, Madison 140
Graziano, Rocky 312, 315, 319, 321-325
Guarini, Robert 73
Guglielmo, Thomas 13

Halberstam, Judith Jack 271, 280
Haller, Herman W. 126-128
Handlin, Oscar 62-63
Hansen, Marcus Lee 173
Haraway, Donna 267
Haring, Keith 279
Harley, David E. 47
Hart, Delores 269
Hawkins, Yusuf 348
Hitler, Adolph 20, 24, 379
Hobsbawm, Eric 332
Hodson, William
Hough, Charles M. 47-48
Huff, Frank A. 47

Impelliteri, Vincent 220
Imperiale, Marie 65
Intondi, Urban Barney 69

Iorizzo, Luciano 168
Iovine, Jimmy 271

Jacobson, Matthew Frye 338
Johnson, Lyndon B. 259-260
Jung, Karl 365
Kael, Pauline 286, 295, 300

Kashatas, William C. 318
Kennedy, John F. 259
Kezich, Tullio 358, 363-364
Kinder, Marsha 304
Klinger, Barbara 306
Knetsch, Joe 45, 47-48
Kleftoyianni, Ioanna 377
Krase, Jerry 158
Kraut, Alan 150, 154

La Guardia, Fiorello H. 204-210, 214, 218
Lady Gaga (Germanotta, Stefani Joanne Angelina) 267-268, 271-281
LaGumina, Salvatore J. 203
La Morte, Joe 40
La Motta, Jake 312, 315, 319, 321, 325
Lanzetta, James 204, 207-211, 213, 215-216, 218-219
Lawrence, Tim 288
Lee, Bruce 295, 300
Levine, Martin 299
Levy, Shawn 323-324
Locke, James W. 44
Lord, Eliot 150
Lovato, Demi 276
Luconi, Stefano 7, 18, 256, 259

Macdonald, Robert David 271

Madonna (Ciccone, Madonna Louise) 268-269, 276, 279-280
Magano, Tony 291
Malpezzi, Giuseppe 137
Manago, Anthony 73-74
Mancuso, Edward 92-93
Mancuso, James 322
Mannino, Mary Ann Vigilante 347
Marcantonio, Vito 204, 208-221
Marchisio, Juvenal 248
Marciano, Rocky 321, 325
Marshman Rose, Philip 156
Martini, Dirty 281
Mastrarrigo, Maria 189
Mastroianni, Marcello 364
Mateotti, Giacomo 7
Maurois, André
Maxwell, Dominic 374
Mazzini, Giuseppe 250
Mazzucco, Melania 333-335, 338, 340
McAuliffe, Jody 374
McCarren, Sen. Pat 237
McCarthy, Cpr. Joseph 65
McQueen, Alexander 271
Mercury, Freddy 271
Merrick, George Edgar 39
Messina, Elizabeth G. 278
Messner, Michael A. 302
Michael, Vaughn Cordasco 30, 43, 48
Michaud, Marie-Christine 159-160
Miller, D. A. 298
Mimieux, Yvette 269

Minaj, Nicki 273
Minelli, Liza 268, 274-275
Minelli, Vincenzo 274
Molinari, John 91
Molinari, Susan 245
Molloy, Bishop Thomas E. 76-78
Monti, Daniel 160
Moore, Sarah Wool 133, 135-138, 142, 144-145
Moretto, Giovanni 143
Mormino, Gary 34
Moroni, Gerolamo 43
Moynihan, Daniel Patrick 217
Mucciolo, A. Charles 219
Mulvey, Laura 294-295
Musumeci, John 36
Mussolini, Benito 3-4, 6-9, 11-12, 14-16, 18, 20, 23-27, 81-82, 212-213, 216-217, 234, 246-248, 250, 367

Neale, Steve 294-295
Nenni, Pietro 226
Newman, Paul 322-325
Nixon, Richard 260
Norma Jean 290
Novello, Pvt. Frank 67
Nystrom, Derek 287, 300

Obama, Barack 245
O'Dwyer, William 74
Olin, Laurie 39-40, 49-50
Oliver, Roger W. 367
O'Neill, Eugene 378
Orsi, Robert 385
Osteen, Mark 376

Pacino, Al 298, 304, 306

Paglia, Camille 271
Pagnotta, Joseph C. 62
Paist, Phineas 40
Paladino, Carl 246
Palermo, Blinky 314
Palumbo, V. 37
Pampalone, Antonella 119
Papetti, Viola 272
Pasqualicchio, Leonard 231
Pastore, Judith Laurence 375
Patrizi, Ettore 86, 91, 96
Pavone, Claudio 96
Pecora, Ferdinand 220
Pellegatta, Ettore 40
Pelosi, Nancy 245, 261
Perri, Peter 75-76
Pirandello, Luigi 367, 363, 367-368, 370-377
Pitrè, Giuseppe 153
Pozzetta, George 34, 42
Pope, Anthony 235-236
Pope, Fortune 235-236
Pope, Generoso 235-236, 248

Quardri, Victor 40

Renzetti, Giuseppe 88
Richards, Amy 267
Richards, Kyle 278
Roberts, Peter 139
Rolle, Andrew 204
Ronchi, Ottorino 96
Roosevelt, Franklin D. 207, 209, 211, 213-215, 217, 218, 256, 259
Rossi, Angelo 97
Rossi, Elena Aga 247
Rossi, Ernest 158

Rybczynsky, Witold 39-40, 49-50

Sabbia, Francesco 45, 47
Salvemini, Gaetano 8, 87, 247
Salvetti, Patrizia 83
Santangelo, Alfred 221
Santeramo, Donato 369, 372
Savoca, Nancy 112, 269
Schaffer, Alan 211
Scherini, Rose 84, 87
Schiaffino, Cpt. Francesco 187-188
Serpico, Frank 298
Sforza, Carlo 236
Shapiro, Peter 290
Sinatra, Frank 125
Skinner, Lillian M. 334
Smith, Al 258
Sontag, Susan 267
Spagnola, Pfc. Joseph 66
Spano, Rocco 10-14, 16, 18-25, 27-29
Spera, Enzo 120, 122
Speranza, Gino 133-136, 138, 144
Spellman, Archbishop Francis 66
Stella, Dr. Antonio 150
Strangis, Pvt. Pat C. 66
Straus, Peter 375
Sudano, Pvt. Don 65

Taibi, Angelo 16
Tamburri, Anthony Julian 159, 176, 245, 263, 346, 356
Tancredo, Tom 245
Tarchiani, Alberto 225-226

Thompson, Bobby 384
Tinarelli, Roger 51
Travolta, John 286, 304-306
Triay, E. J. 45-47
Truman, Harry S. 225, 232, 234-237, 239, 241-243
Tupper, George William 139-142
Turco, Renzo 86
Turner, Victor 261,
Tuttle, Julia 35-36

Varalle, John
Varallo, Johnnie 36
Vecoli, Rudolph J. 31-32, 160, 245-246
Versace, Donatella 277
Vetere, Cpt. Louis 66
Vetro, Fr. William 61
Viscomi, Sgt. Frank 65
Viscusi, Robert 116-117, 119-121, 125
Volpe, John 260

Walter, Sen. Francis E. 237
Waters, Mary 160
Waters, T. Wayne 317
Williams, Phyllis 152
Wise, Robert 322-325
Wolfe, Tom 291

Zavarella, Andrew 31
Zinman, Toby Silverman 376

www.ingramcontent.com/pod-product-compliance
Lightning Source LLC
Chambersburg PA
CBHW031844220426
43663CB00006B/497